Advance praise for *The Myth of Male Power*

"I have never read a manuscript more likely to be a bestseller. It will change forever the way men view their position in society. I wish I were its publisher."
—JEREMY P. TARCHER, Publisher

"Intellectual dynamite! By asking new questions, proposing new paradigms, and giving us a deeper insight into the forces that have shaped us, Dr. Farrell continues to open genuine communications between the sexes.
—ANTHONY ROBBINS, author of *Unlimited Power* and *Awaken the Giant Within*

"The single most important book I've ever read on male-female relationships. It is compelling, powerful, and seminal."
—WARREN BENNIS, Ph.D., Distinguished Professor of Business Administration at the University of Southern California; author of *On Becoming a Leader*

"More riveting than most novels, *The Myth of Male Power* is brilliant, insightful, and devastating. If you thought Robert Bly and Camille Paglia shook up gender discourse . . . prepare for a major earthquake! Farrell's truths explode like bombshells. No one who reads this book with an open mind will ever look at men—or women—in the same way. It is a quantum leap into a more humane future."
—EUGENE R. AUGUST, Ph.D., Professor of Literature, University of Dayton; author of *Men's Studies: A Bibliography*

"If you can imagine Sherlock Holmes investigating men and women and presenting his arguments with the clarity of a Perry Mason, the political irreverence of a Camille Paglia, and the compassion of a therapist, you have an image of *The Myth of Male Power*. There is no more brilliant and original book ever written on men, or on how we can move from gender war to gender love."
—BOB BERKOWITZ, former Men's reporter, "Today" show; host, CNBC's "Real Personal"; author of *What Men Won't Tell You But Women Need to Know*

THE
MYTH
OF MALE
POWER

WHY MEN ARE
THE DISPOSABLE SEX

Warren Farrell, Ph.D.

SIMON & SCHUSTER
NEW YORK LONDON TORONTO SYDNEY TOKYO SINGAPORE

SIMON & SCHUSTER
Simon & Schuster Building
Rockefeller Center
1230 Avenue of the Americas
New York, New York 10020

Designed by Irving Perkins Associates
Manufactured in the United States of America

10   9   8   7   6   5   4   3   2   1

Library of Congress Cataloging-in-Publication Data

Farrell, Warren.
   The myth of male power : why men are the disposable sex / Warren Farrell.
      p.   cm.
      Includes bibliographical references and index.
      1. Men—United States.   2. Men—United States—Psychology.   3. Sex
   role—United States.   4. Women—United States—Psychology.
   I. Title.
   HQ1090.3.F36   1993
   305.32—dc20   93-18894
                                                                      CIP

ISBN 0-671-79349-7

Grateful acknowledgment is given to the following for permission to reproduce
art and quote from previously published material:

"Do You Love Me" from *Fiddler on the Roof* by Joseph Stein (New York:
Crown, 1964); music by Jerry Bock, lyrics by Sheldon Harnick.

Illustration "The Evolution of Power." Oatmeal Studios, Box 138, Rochester,
VT 05767.

Illustration "The Buckets." Reprinted by permission: Tribune Media Services.

"OSHA Safety Inspector." By permission of Mike Luckovich and Creators
Syndicate.

Photographs "Girl playing with doll; Boy holding rifle" AP/WIDE WORLD
PHOTOS.

To Dad, Mom, Lee,
Gail, and Wayne

Contents

Acknowledgments

My father (Tom), "new" mother (of twenty-four years, Lee), and sister, Gail, offer a base of love and stability from which all my writing flows. Watching my father traverse his eighties with skis and tennis racquets offers me hope; seeing him support my mother through bouts of cancer teaches me love; feeling us grow closer as we grow older brings me peace. Watching my mother go from a hospital bed to a church organ strengthens my own faith and courage; experiencing the way she listens has modeled for me the glue that unites a family while allowing each member to feel heard. Knowing that my sister has patience and compassion for the children whose lives she touches through teaching lightens my worry for our future.

Joyce McHugh has managed my in-home offices, computers, and speaking engagements, and served as a closet editor—weaving precision, clarity, and flow through every page of this book during its dozen or so drafts over the past four years. Marilyn Abraham, my editor, has the soul of an earth mother and the editorial axe of a warrior, and seems to know exactly when to use each. Her faith in this book remained steadfast even as it became its own child.

Every chapter of this book has haunted me as I saw how my observations conflicted with what is considered politically correct (PC). The support of three people—Nathaniel Branden, Jeremy Tarcher, and Elizabeth Brookins—helped me past the political cowardice that is PC. Nathaniel's intellectual strength, Jeremy's creative social consciousness, and the balanced insight and love of Liz combined to remind me that although I beat a different drum, it brings balance to the orchestra.

The letters from hundreds of men who wrote that *Why Men Are the Way They Are* put their feelings into words assured me that the direction I was taking was helping men open up; and letters from hundreds of women who wrote that *Why Men Are . . .* allowed them to feel closer to men reassured me that I was deepening love rather than dividing families.

Lisa Broidy and Dayna Miller searched thousands of publications and double-checked the accuracy of the more than 1,000 sources in this book. When in the future *I* read *their* writings, I will trust what I read. Thanks also go to Marla Robb and Mary Colette Plum for their research assistance, as well as to Julianna Badagliacca, Monika Chandler, Melissa Rosenstock, Karen Wilson, and to Richard Doyle for his careful legal research in his publication *The Liberator*.

Special thanks are due Steve (Goss) Asher for his daily supply of clippings; to Steve Collins for thoughtful commentary and tireless double-checking of data; to Eugene August for his balanced commentary to most every chapter; to Donna Morgan and Spring Whitbeck for bringing their gifts of gentle peace to office management; and to Keith Polan for introducing me to the computer.

This book was greatly enhanced by the insights of thirty additional readers, including the in-depth commentary of Suzanne Frayser, Ron Henry, Natasha Josefowitz, Aaron Kipnis, Judy Kuriansky, and Sari Locker, as well as to the chapter reviews of Rob Becker, Randy Burns, Tom Chadbourne, Ferrel Christensen, Deborah Corley, Greg Dennis, Sam Downing, David Gilmore, Herb Goldberg, Bruce Hubbard, Rikki Klieman, Ziva Kwitney, Alex Landon, John Macchietto, Roman Mathiowetz, R. L. McNeely, Becky and Tony Robbins, Chris Ruff, Jim Sniechowski, and Bill Stephens.

Consultants such as Devors Branden, Helen Fisher, Maurice Friedman, Fred Hayward, John Hoover, Joseph Kinney, Michael Mills, Marilyn Milos, Jim Novak, Joe Pleck, Jon Ryan, Murray Straus, Ivan Strauss, Robert Wade, and Richard Woods have all added to both my knowledge and the book.

Finally, in addition to Marilyn Abraham, I wish to acknowledge the dedicated efforts of these other "Simon & Schuster Women": Dawn Marie Daniels, Joann DiGennaro, Marie Florio, Eve Metz, Victoria Meyer, Carolyn Reidy, Isolde C. Sauer, and Jennifer Weidman.

Introduction

In the quarter century that I have worked on women's and men's issues, there has never been a moment when I have seen men feeling more gagged, and more ready to remove their gags, than now. I see men searching for ways to explore the only space men have been unwilling to explore—their inner space. The next quarter century will provide an opportunity for thousands of men and women to be pioneers in this exploration. The discoveries will assist men out of isolation—and, therefore, out of the drugs, divorce, depression, suicide, and the early deaths that are isolation's legacy.

Male anguish is not the concern of men alone. A man's suicide affects his wife, children, parents, colleagues, friends. So does his early death, his alcoholism, his addiction to beautiful young women. . . . Each affects corporate profits and national productivity. When men are victims, we are all victims.

The Myth of Male Power is not a return to the 1950s man; it is a leap forward to the 2050s man. And the 2050s woman. It is about why male-female roles that were functional for the species for millions of years have become dysfunctional in an evolutionary instant.

WHAT DOES IT TAKE TO SPEAK UP FOR MEN?

For three years I served on the board of directors of the National Organization for Women in New York City. As I explained women's perspectives to men, I often noticed a woman "elbow" the man she was with, as if to say, "See, even an expert says what a jerk you are." I slowly became good at saying what women wanted to hear. I enjoyed the standing ovations that followed.

The fact that my audiences were about 90 percent women and 10 percent men (most of whom had been dragged there by the women) only reinforced my assumption that women were enlightened and men were "Neanderthals"; that women were, after all, Smart Women stuck with Foolish Choices. I secretly loved this perspective—it allowed me to see myself as one of America's Sensitive New Age Men. A New Top Gun. Feminists who asked me, "How can we clone you?" or "What in your background made you so secure?" reinforced that secret pride. And the three or four invitations for new engagements following each speech allowed for some financial security.

Years passed. As most of the women who were my strongest supporters got divorced, I could only assume the problem was their husbands. The women agreed. But I observed something my feminist womenfriends had in common: an increasing anger toward men, a restlessness in their eyes that did not reflect a deeper inner peace.

Then one day (in one of those rare moments of internal security) I asked myself whether whatever impact I might have had was a positive one; I wondered if the reason so many more women than men listened to me was because I had been listening to women but not listening to men. I reviewed some of the tapes from among the hundreds of women's and men's groups I had started. I heard myself. When women criticized men, I called it "insight," "assertiveness," "women's liberation," "independence," or "high self-esteem." When men criticized women, I called it "sexism," "male chauvinism," "defensiveness," "rationalizing," and "backlash." I did it politely—but the men got the point. Soon the men were no longer expressing their feelings. Then I criticized the men for not expressing their feelings!

I decided to experiment with ways of getting men to express feelings. I noticed men were often most open about their feelings on the first date. On the first date, the woman often used what I came to call "awe training"—those looks of "Wow, that's fascinating" in her eyes (if not in her words). The men felt secure and opened up.

So when men in my men's groups spoke, I exercised some awe training. It worked. I heard things I had never heard before— things that forced me to reexamine my own life and motives. The combination created a new dilemma. . . .

Now when women asked, "Why are men afraid of commitment?" or feminists said, "Men have the power," my answers incorporated both sexes' perspectives. Almost overnight my standing ovations disintegrated. After each speaking engagement, I was no longer receiving three or four new requests to speak. My financial security was drying up.

I would not be honest if I denied that this tempted me to return to being a spokesperson only for women's perspectives. I liked writing, speaking, and doing television shows. Now it seemed that all three were in jeopardy. I quickly discovered **it took far more internal security to speak on behalf of men than to speak on behalf of women.** Or, more accurately, to speak on behalf of both sexes rather than on behalf of only women.

Fortunately there is another side. Although it was women's standing ovations that had tapered off, it was also mostly women who wrote me that these new perspectives were helping them feel much more loving toward their husbands or fathers, their sons, or a man at work. And it was mostly women who said it would help them if these new perspectives were in writing.

How to Cherish Feminism's Baby, but Not Its Bathwater

I will be saddened if this book is misused to attack the legitimate issues of the women's movement—issues for which I spent a decade of my life fighting. The challenge is both to go beyond feminism and to cherish its contributions. And feminism's contributions are many.

Without feminism, fewer companies would have experimented with part-time workers, flexible schedules, child-care options, and improved safety standards. Without women in police work, few police forces would have discovered that 95 percent of conflicts are *not* resolved by physical strength; without women doctors, few hospitals would be cutting back ninety-hour work weeks for doctors; without women therapists, short-term counseling and couple counseling would be much less available. . . . The feminist movement has allowed thousands of workplace assumptions to be reexamined; feminism brought into the workplace not only females but female energy.

When I see girls playing baseball, my eyes well up with tears of happiness for what I know they are learning about teamwork, and tears of sadness for what the girls I grew up with missed. Without the feminist movement, those girls would be on the sidelines. Without the feminist movement, millions of girls would see only one dimension of their mothers and, therefore, of themselves. They would have to marry more for money than for love. They would be even more fearful of aging.

I am often asked what made me so empathetic with the early feminist movement. It was often assumed my mother or former wife must have been an active feminist, but neither was. That is, my mother wasn't a "movement feminist," but I can recall coming home after being elected seventh-grade class president, proudly announcing it to my mother, and saying, "Our class meetings are on Fridays. . . . I was wondering if maybe I could have an ironed shirt just on Fridays when I have to preside in front of the class." She said "sure" and without missing a beat, took out the ironing board and showed me how to iron my shirts.

At the time, my mother's response seemed consistent only with her oft-repeated statement, "I'm your mother, not your slave." But as I get older I reframed those experiences both as preparation for my comfort with feminism in its initial egalitarian form and as one of my mother's ways of expressing love—not by doing *for* me but by teaching me to do for myself. Predictably, I have grown up seeing that my way of expressing love is to endorse that part of the feminist movement that empowers women to support themselves and to withdraw from that part that blames and plays victim.

The Myth of Male Power is not designed to create popularity. Unlike most self-improvement books, it is not a female self-assurance book; *it loves women in a different way*.

WHY DO WE NEED TO STUDY MEN—ISN'T HISTORY ONE BIG STUDY OF MEN?

The most common justification for studying women without studying men is that "history is men's studies . . . women's studies is just an attempt to give women something equivalent to what men already have." True? No. Women's studies questions the female role; nothing questions the male role. History books *sell* to boys the *traditional* male role of hero and performer. Each history book is 500 pages of advertisements for the performer role. Each lesson tells him, "If you perform, you will get love and respect; if you fail, you will be a nothing." To a boy, history is pressure to perform, not relief from that pressure. Feminism is relief from the pressure to be confined to only the traditional female role. To a boy, then, history is not the equivalent of women's studies; it is the *opposite* of women's studies.

Women's studies does more than question the female role—it tells women they have rights to what was the traditional male role. Nothing tells men they have rights to what was the traditional female role—rights to stay home full-time or part-time with the children while his wife supports him. . . .

Just as, from a girl's perspective, history books are filled with men, from a boy's perspective, school itself is filled with women. It is women teaching him how to be a boy by conforming to what women tell him to do after he's been trained to conform to what his mother tells him to do. On the one hand, history books show him that his role is to be a hero who takes risks and, on the other, his female teacher is telling him not to take risks—to not roughhouse, not shout out an answer spontaneously, not use swear words, not refer to sex, not get his hair mussed, his clothes dirty. . . . Just as women's studies helped women see they have a right to female teachers in business school, so men's studies will help men see they have a right to male teachers in grade school.

WHY FEMINISM HAS INTENSIFIED THE NEED FOR STUDYING MEN

Feminism suggested that God might be a "She" but not that the devil might also be a "she." Feminism articulated the shadow side of men and the light side of women. It neglected the shadow side of women and the light side of men. And neglected to acknowledge that each sex has both sides *within* each individual. When the issue of sexual harassment surfaced, then, we were told "men don't 'get it' " when, in fact, *neither* sex "gets" it. Men don't get women's fears of harassment that stem from the passive role; women don't get men's fears of sexual rejection that stem from the initiating role. Each sex is so preoccupied with its own vulnerability that neither sex "gets" the other's vulnerability.

The difference? Feminism has taught women to sue men for sexual harassment or date rape when men initiate with the wrong person or with the wrong timing; no one has taught men to sue women for sexual trauma for saying "yes," then "no," then "yes," then "no." Feminism left women with three sexual options—their old role, the "male" role, and the "victim" role. Men were left with less than one option—they were still expected to initiate, but now, if they did it badly, they could go to jail. For an adolescent boy who barely knows what sex is, this is a scary half-option.

Feminism justified female "victim power" by convincing the world that we lived in a sexist, male-dominated, and patriarchal world. *The Myth of Male Power* explains why the world was *bi*-sexist, both male- *and* female-dominated, both patriarchal and matriarchal—each in different ways. It explains why "patriarchy" and "male dominance" doubled as code words for male disposability.

By the 1980s and '90s, feminism's ability to articulate women's light side and men's shadow side led to women's magazines, talk shows, "self-improvement" books, and TV specials all equating "progressive" with women as victims and men as victimizers but rarely with men as victims (of false accusations, emotional abuse, visitation deprivation . . .) and women as victimizers. It was soon considered progressive to critique "male legislators" for making war but not to credit them for making democracy. We saw TV specials titled *Does the Man Next Door Molest Girls?* but not *Does the Man Next Door Save Girls?* In our everyday lives we might see six firefighters saving women, but no TV special titled *Men as Saviors* points out that all six were men—or that firemen who save women's lives are far more ubiquitous than men who jeopardize women's lives.

To acknowledge the full truth was no longer considered progressive, but regressive. Women bought the books and the publishers pandered to women the way politicians pander to interest groups. Women became *Women Who Love . . .* and men became *Men Who Hate . . .* (women's light side, men's dark side). The pandering transformed a female strength—understanding relationships— into a female weakness: misunderstanding men.

In the past quarter century, feminism has been to the daily news what bacteria is to water—we consumed it without knowing it, both the good and the bad. From the male point of view, feminism turned the Battle of the Sexes into a "War in Which Only One Side Showed Up."[1]

Men have not been perfect listeners during the last quarter century as women articulated what they wanted, but men did listen enough to absorb dozens of new concepts ("sex object," "glass ceiling," palimony, the "Battered Woman Syndrome," "deadbeat dads," the "feminization of poverty"), heard dozens of slogans focused on female concerns ("a woman's right to choose," "equal pay for equal work," "our bodies, our business"), and to see their sexuality blamed for most everything (sexual harassment, sexual molestation, pornography, incest, rape, date rape).

Men not only listened but accepted as truth dozens of assumptions of discrimination against women (women are the victims of most violence; women's health is neglected more than men's; women are paid less for the same work; husbands batter wives more; men have more power; we've lived in a patriarchal, sexist, male-dominated world). Many men condemned these "discriminations against women" even as they accepted the "necessity" for discrimination against men (affirmative action for women; government-subsidized women's commissions in almost every state and county; women's studies; women-only clubs; government programs for women, infants, and children [WIC] . . .).

THE COURAGE TO CONFRONT: WOMEN CANNOT HEAR WHAT MEN DO NOT SAY

Have we been misled by feminists? Yes. Is it feminists' fault? No. Why not? Men have not spoken up. Simply stated, women cannot hear what men do not say. Now men must take responsibility to say what they want—to turn a "War in Which Only One Side Shows Up" into a "Dialogue in Which Both Sexes Speak Up."

I am often astonished at how men collude in turning relationship issues into women's issues. When a book like *The Myth of Male Power* arrives in a newsroom, male journalists often reflexively say, "This is for Mary over at the Family Page—*she* specializes in 'women's' issues." It is time for men to take responsibility to end the "Era of Relationship-Issues-as-Women's-Issues."

Looking at relationships as if women were the center is like looking at the solar system as if Earth were in the center. But as

Galileo discovered, only half the job is in the discovery; the other half is in the courage to present the findings. Most men are still invested in getting women's love by protecting women. And many women are still invested in receiving the special protection we accord the victim.

Adjusting our relationship assumptions almost always rubs like sandpaper on our psyches. But just as the key to real estate is "location, location, location," the key to relationships is "listen, listen, listen." How well we listen to men will determine whether the result is a civil dialogue or a civil war.

If women listen in the future better than men did in the past, men will not need to speak for a quarter of a century; if women withdraw emotionally, interrupt with "yes, buts," respond with personal accusations ("You must hate women"), or tell men, "I'm receptive, you just chose the wrong *time* to speak," men will clam up and it will take more than a quarter of a century for them to gain an equal hearing. It never feels like the right time to listen to what we might be afraid to hear (it *always* feels like sandpaper on our psyches).

Women have contributed a tone. Men must contribute theirs before we are ready for a synthesis.

Is *THE MYTH OF MALE POWER* THE FLIP SIDE OF FEMINISM?

It will be tempting to see *The Myth of Male Power* as the flip side of feminism. It is not. Feminism says, "The world is patriarchal and male-dominated." The flip side is, "The world is matriarchal and female-dominated." I explain why it is *both* patriarchal and matriarchal, *both* male- and female-dominated. The book explains male disposability without denying female disposability (e.g., when a man turns in his wife of forty for two twenties). That is an integrated approach.

How has feminism gotten us to see a one-sided approach as integrated? By telling us not that "*women see* the world as patriarchal, sexist, and male-dominated" but rather that "the world *is* patriarchal, sexist, and male-dominated." *Whenever* feminism portrays itself as the whole picture, it is a form of sexism—in the same way a "masculist" approach would be sexist if it portrayed itself as the whole picture.

AM I A MEN'S LIBERATIONIST? A FEMINIST? BOTH? OR NEITHER?

Like everyone else, I prefer to be listened to rather than labeled. But labels do give us a foothold in a complex world. And any movement that has impact develops an identity—or label—in the public mind. So . . .

I am a men's liberationist (or "masculist") when men's liberation is defined as equal opportunity and equal responsibility for *both* sexes. I am a feminist when feminism favors equal opportunities and responsibilities for both sexes. I oppose both movements when either says our sex is *the* oppressed sex, therefore, *"we deserve rights."* That's not gender liberation but gender entitlement.

Ultimately I am in favor of neither a women's movement nor a men's movement but a gender transition movement. However, I oppose skipping past a men's movement until men have equally articulated their perspective. *Then* we will be ready for a synthesis.

A MESSAGE TO MEN . . . MOSTLY

It will be tempting to discuss this book with a feminist because that's probably the person you know who's most interested in sex roles. But this is like a man bringing a book that questions the Bible to a born-again Christian because that's the person you know who's most interested in religion. The person who studies their bible daily is the *least* likely to question their bible fairly.

If your "family" has many feminists, you will have to confront yourself about the degree to which you need their approval. This book will put you in touch with a lot of new feelings. You will have to be secure enough to handle the possibility that perhaps it wasn't your *feelings* that were desired but rather your *agreement*.

Start a support group of other men with whom you can explore these feelings.* As men, we tend to place all our emotional eggs in the basket of the woman we love and then become fearful of saying anything that might crack those eggs. A group allows an alternate source of emotional support. And a place to sort out feelings worth discussing before you say what you later wish you hadn't.

---

* See Part III of my *The Liberated Man* (New York: Berkley, 1993 edition).

Exactly what do men discover when they share their feelings with other men? Here's an example. In the past few years, I have asked more than 10,000 American and Canadian men from all walks of life if they would *prefer* to take off work for six months to a year after each child was born to be involved with the child *full* time. *More than 80 percent of the men said that full-time involvement with their children would be their preference*—but only if their wives approved and they weren't hurting their families economically. (About 17 percent of the men prefer part-time involvement; about 3 percent prefer to remain working full time.)

But notice that the men I surveyed had to have this question asked of them. And even then, many felt inhibited about raising their hands. As men express feelings with other men, they begin to ask questions like this of themselves. They are shocked to discover that so many of them want something for which they have never asked. Which stimulates them to wonder why they never asked.

Why? Unconsciously, men feel it is a waste to be in touch with feelings because, well, "If I tell my wife I want to take off from work to care for the children while she pays the bills, it would just create an argument, I'll lose, and she'll withdraw; so what's the use?" Why was the "courageous sex" so afraid of their wives' withdrawal? Exactly because all their emotional eggs were invested in one basket—a problem a support group helps solve.

This book will create growth. But growth is a personal challenge. It can be in conflict with love—a relationship challenge. Your next challenge is getting the women you love to feel receptive to your genuine feelings. The trick is in learning to grow without turning those who love us into the enemy. Start by reading to her excerpts from this book that reflect the values you both share. (Don't introduce *The Myth of Male Power* to a woman by saying, "You need to read this.") Be sure your tone reflects your understanding that almost everything in this book will ultimately empower her and deepen your love.

A MESSAGE TO WOMEN . . . MOSTLY

The challenge to women will be to be as open to the man's experience of powerlessness as you would to the woman's—to care as much about a man who joins the army for money as about a woman who has sex for money. Men will compound that challenge because they have not had a lifetime of practice in knowing how or when to express those feelings to you. So when they read a book that makes them start wanting to create changes, they might express themselves in an angry tone of voice or choose the wrong time. The trick is in knowing that even if the anger is directed partly at you, if it is heard and acknowledged (rather than argued with and discounted with "yes, buts") he will quickly see you as his ally rather than his enemy. When he knows he has a safe environment for his feelings, his anger toward you will be short-lived and his love for you will be deepened.

Women tell me these new perspectives on men help them soften their attitudes toward men *if* they keep reminding themselves, "This is *his* perspective—not necessarily mine. . . . I have to think of myself as reading about a foreign culture." Almost everything in this book has passed the "rings true" test with men; despite the statistics, the book reflects men's feelings. The data are there only to help you know he's not crazy.

The professional woman—or a powerful woman—often has the most difficulty understanding male powerlessness. Why? The powerful woman tends to connect with a powerful man. (The less powerful man—like the garbage man—is invisible to her.) And what she sees of the powerful man is deceptive: the powerful man is best at repressing his fears.

The professional woman is more likely to know the name of her secretary than of her garbage man. And therefore more likely to know how her secretary experiences men than how her garbage man experiences women. Because a less powerful woman tends to work in the office and a less powerful man tends to work outside the office (e.g., in hazardous jobs), she is more conscious of the dilemmas of the less powerful woman around whom she works.

The powerful woman doesn't feel the effect of her secretary's miniskirt power, cleavage power, and flirtation power. Men do. The powerful woman tends to use these forms of power much more cautiously in the workplace because she has other forms of power.

Taken together, all of this blinds the professional woman to the powerlessness of the great majority of men—who are not at the tip of the pyramid but at its base. And without the sexual power of many of the females at its base.

Some women, when they get a glimpse of the degree to which

they have misjudged men, feel a bit overwhelmed, as in "What can I do?" Fortunately, most of the solution is fairly simple. Most men want little more than to feel appreciated and understood—from the male perspective (not the *Cosmopolitan* or *Glamour* version of the male perspective). So just allow time for him to reveal his version of himself by providing a safe environment (not withdrawing) even when those feelings involve criticism of you. **I have never had a man come up to me and say, "I want a divorce; my partner understands me."**

I have repeatedly heard from women that when they are, for example, at a party and they share these perspectives with men, they soon find themselves surrounded by men who are pouring out their feelings to them! Thus they begin to see men in a new way. It is at that point the woman begins really loving men. Prior to that, she was loving an image of men. (Or maybe *not* loving men.) It was not her fault she loved only that image—that was all he showed; it was not his fault he showed that image—that was what he thought she would love.

The more a man is deprived of expressing feelings, the more he feels loved when he finally does feel heard. The woman who experiences this new view of men becomes special, in part, exactly because so few women do.

To Both Sexes . . .

The Myth of Male Power violates both sexes' biologically inherited instinct to protect the female. Protecting the female implied listening to her needs and repressing his own—even to the point of dying. It will therefore literally be *natural* to find flaws as a defense against hearing the male world view. There are flaws enough to find, but *I will ask you not to make your ability to hear men dependent on my perfection.*

When a statistic seems unbelievable, check out the endnote. I have eliminated more than a hundred statistics from my initial drafts that illustrated my point but did not prove reliable under scrutiny. However, if I missed something, don't let my oversights allow you to miss the deeper understanding.

. . .

Men can be thought of as in search of their inner *perestroika*. Just as it happened for Soviet citizens when they were watching the world around them become freer, it began happening for men as they watched the women around them become freer. In the same way Soviet citizens began to question whether their perception of themselves as a "powerful nation" was really a distraction from facing their powerlessness, so men are on the verge of questioning whether their perception of themselves as the "powerful sex" is really a distraction from confronting their powerlessness. Men are appropriately beginning to see themselves for what they've become—a Third World sex. Or so I am asserting . . . but I haven't yet backed up that assertion. Is male power really a myth? Let's look. And as we're looking, share your own insights with me so I can grow from you and return that growth in my next book.

Warren Farrell, Ph.D.
103 North Highway 101
Box 220
Encinitas (San Diego), CA 92024

PART I

THE MYTH OF MALE POWER

CHAPTER 1

Is Male Power Really a Myth?
A First Glance

The weakness of men is the facade of strength; the strength of women is the facade of weakness.[1]

There are many ways in which a woman experiences a greater sense of powerlessness than her male counterpart: the fears of pregnancy, aging, rape, date rape, and being physically overpowered; less socialization to take a career that pays enough to support a husband and children; less exposure to team sports and its blend of competitiveness and cooperation that is so helpful to career preparation; greater parental pressure to marry and interrupt career for children without regard for her own wishes; not being part of an "old boys" network; having less freedom to walk into a bar without being bothered. . . .

Fortunately, almost all industrialized nations have acknowledged these female experiences. Unfortunately, they have acknowledged only the female experiences—and concluded that women *have* the problem, men *are* the problem. Men, though, have a different experience. A man who has seen his marriage become alimony payments, his home become his wife's home, and his children become child-support payments for those who have been turned against him psychologically feels he is spending his life working for people who hate him. He feels desperate for someone to love but fears that another marriage might ultimately leave him with another mortgage payment, another set of children turned against him, and a deeper desperation. When he is called "commitment-phobic" he doesn't feel understood.

When a man tries to keep up with payments by working overtime and is told he is insensitive, or tries to handle the stress by drinking and is told he is a drunkard, he doesn't feel powerful, but powerless. When he fears a cry for help will be met with "stop whining," or that a plea to be heard will be met with "yes, buts," he skips past *attempting* suicide as a cry for help, and just *commits* suicide. Thus men have remained the silent sex and increasingly become the suicide sex.

Since this chapter is only an overview, it will generate more of those "yes, buts" than any other. The rest of the book is about answering those "yes, buts." So this chapter is offered with the trust that you will go beyond it. This chapter *is* a case of "a little knowledge is a dangerous thing." But staying with the book until the end will leave us more balanced in our view of the sexes—*not because this book is balanced, but because the book balances what we now know.* Here goes. . . .

A MAN'S GOTTA DO WHAT A MAN'S GOTTA DO

ITEM. Imagine: Music is playing on your car radio. An announcer's voice interrupts: "We have a special bulletin from the president." (For some reason, you decide not to switch stations.) The president announces, "Since 1.2 million American men have been killed in war, as part of my new program for equality, we will draft only women until 1.2 million American women have been killed in war."

In post offices throughout the United States, Selective Service posters remind men that only they must register for the draft. If the post office had a poster saying "A Jew's Gotta Do What a Jew's Gotta Do" . . . Or if "A Woman's Gotta Do . . ." were written across the body of a pregnant woman . . .

The question is this: How is it that if any other group were singled out to register for the draft based merely on its characteristics at birth—be that group blacks, Jews, women, or gays—we would immediately recognize it as genocide, but when men are singled out based on their sex at birth, men call it power?

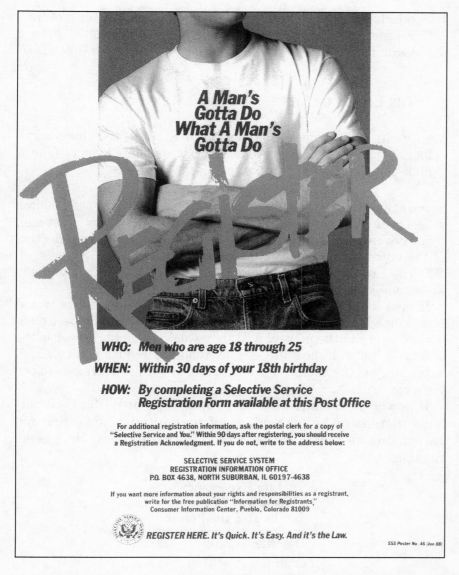

The single biggest barrier to getting men to look within is that what any other group would call powerlessness, men have been taught to call power. We don't call "male-killing" sexism; we call it "glory." We don't call the one *million* men who were killed or maimed *in one battle* in World War I (the Battle of the Somme[2]) a holocaust, we call it "serving the country." We don't call those who selected only men to die "murderers." We call them "voters."

Our slogan for women is "A Woman's Body, A Woman's Choice"; our slogan for men is "A Man's Gotta Do What a Man's Gotta Do."

THE POWER OF LIFE

ITEM. In 1920 women in the United States lived *one* year longer than men.[3] Today women live *seven* years longer.[4] The male-female life-span gap increased 600 percent.

· We acknowledge that blacks dying six years sooner than whites reflects the powerlessness of blacks in American society.[5] Yet men dying seven years sooner than women is rarely seen as a reflection of the powerlessness of men in American society.

Is the seven-year gap biological? If it is, it wouldn't have been just a one-year gap in 1920.

If men lived seven years *longer* than women, feminists would have helped us understand that life expectancy was the best measure of who had the power. And they would be right. Power is the ability to control one's life. Death tends to reduce control. Life expectancy is the bottom line—the ratio of our life's stresses to our life's rewards.

If power means having control over one's own life, then perhaps there is no better ranking of the impact of sex roles and racism on power over our lives than life expectancy. Here is the ranking:

Life Expectancy[6]
As a Way of Seeing
Who Has the Power

Females (white)	79
Females (black)	74
Males (white)	72
Males (black)	65

The white female outlives the black male by almost fourteen years. Imagine the support for affirmative action if a 49-year-old woman were expected to die sooner than a 62-year-old man.

SUICIDE AS POWERLESSNESS

Just as life expectancy is one of the best indicators of power, suicide is one of the best indicators of powerlessness.

ITEM. Until boys and girls are 9, their suicide rates are identical;
—from 10 to 14, the boys' rate is twice as high as the girls';
—from 15 to 19, four times as high; and
—from 20 to 24, six times as high.[7]

ITEM. As boys experience the pressures of the male role, their suicide rate increases 25,000 percent.[8]

ITEM. The suicide rate for men over 85 is 1,350 percent higher than for women of the same age group.

Here is the breakdown:

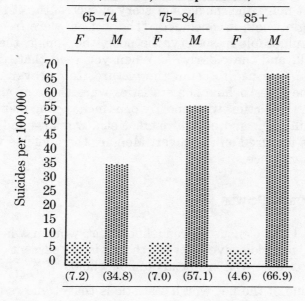

Suicide Rates: Men vs. Women
(Per 100,000 Population)

	65–74		75–84		85+	
	F	M	F	M	F	M
	(7.2)	(34.8)	(7.0)	(57.1)	(4.6)	(66.9)

Suicides per 100,000

SOURCE: National Center for Health Statistics[9]

THE INVISIBLE VICTIMS OF VIOLENCE

ITEM. When Rodney King was beaten by police, we called it violence against blacks, not violence against men. Had *Regina* King been beaten, would no one have mentioned violence against women?

Myth. Elderly women are the most susceptible to violent crime.

Fact. Elderly women are the *least* susceptible to violent crime. The U.S. Department of Justice finds that a woman over 65 is less likely to be a victim of violent crime than anyone else in any other category. And she is less than half as vulnerable as a man her own age.[10]

Myth. Women are more likely than men to be victims of violence.

Fact. Men are almost twice as likely as women to be victims of violent crimes (even when rape is *included*).[11] Men are three times more likely to be victims of murder.[12]

When *Time* magazine ran a cover story of each of the 464 people shot in a single week, it concluded: "The victims were frequently those most vulnerable in society: the poor, the young, the abandoned, the ill, and the elderly."[13] When you read that, did you think of men? One had to count the pictures to discover that 84 percent of the faces behind the statistics were those of men and boys. In fact, the victims were mostly poor men, young men, abandoned men, ill men, and elderly men. Yet a woman—and only a woman—was featured on the cover. Men are the invisible victims of America's violence.

NET WORTH POWER

ITEM. The U.S. Census Bureau finds that women who are heads of households have a net worth that is 141 percent of the net worth of men who are heads of households.[14]

(The value of the net worth statistic is that it allows us to see what he and she have left when their different liabilities are subtracted from the different assets. The women's average net worth is $13,885; the men's is $9,883. This is because although male heads of households have higher gross incomes and assets, they have much higher spending obligations. They are much more likely to support wives [or ex-wives] than wives are to support them and thus their income is divided among themselves, a wife, and children—not only for food and housing but for tuition, insurance, vacations. Divorces often mean the woman receives the home the man pays for and also gets custody of the children the man pays for. A woman's obligation to spend more time with the children leaves her earning less and the man earning more but paying out more.)

ITEM. Among the wealthiest 1.6 percent of the U.S. population (those with assets of $500,000 or more), women's net worth is *more* than men's.[15]

How can so many of the wealthiest people be women when women hold none of the top corporate jobs? In part, by selecting the men who do and outliving them. And in part by having greater spending power and lower spending power obligations. . . .

SPENDING POWER

A study of large shopping malls (including men's shops and sporting goods stores) found that seven times as much floor space is devoted to women's personal items as to men's.[16] *Both* sexes buy more for women. The key to wealth is not in what someone earns; it is in what is spent on ourselves, at our discretion—or in what is spent on us, at our hint.

Overall, women control consumer spending by a wide margin in virtually every consumer category.[17] With spending power comes other forms of power. Women's control over spending gives them control over TV programs because TV is dependent on sponsors. When this is combined with the fact that women watch more TV in every time slot,[18] shows can't afford to bite the hand that feeds them. Women are to TV what bosses are to employees. The result? Half of the 250 made-for-TV movies in 1991 depicted women as victims—subjected to "some form of physical or psychological mistreatment."[19]

THE "SPENDING OBLIGATION GAP"

In restaurants, men pay for women about ten times as frequently as women pay for men—the more expensive the restaurant, the more often the man pays.[20] Women often say, "Well, men earn more." But when two women go to a restaurant, they don't assume that the woman who earns more will pay the bill. The expectation on men to spend more on women creates the "Spending Obligation Gap."

I got a sense of this "Spending Obligation Gap" as soon as I thought about my first date. As a teenager, I loved baby-sitting. (I genuinely loved kids, but it was also the only way I could get paid for raiding a refrigerator!) But then I got to the dating age. Alas, baby-sitting paid only fifty cents an hour. Lawn mowing, though, paid two dollars an hour. I hated lawn mowing. (I lived in New Jersey, where bugs, humidity, and noonday sun made mowing a lawn less pleasant than raiding a refrigerator.) But as soon as I started dating, I started mowing lawns.

For boys, lawn mowing is a metaphor for the way we soon learn to take jobs we like less because they pay more. Around junior year of high school, boys begin to repress their interest in foreign languages, literature, art history, sociology, and anthropology because they know an art history major will make less than an engineer. Partially as a result of his different spending expectation (the possibility he might have to support a woman but cannot expect a woman to support him), more than 85 percent of students who take engineering as a college major are men; more than 80 percent of the art history majors are women.[21]

The difference in the earnings of the female art historian vs. the male engineer appears to be a measure of discrimination, when in fact both sexes knew ahead of time that engineering would pay more. In fact, the woman who enters engineering with the same lack of experience as the man averages $571 per year *more* than her male counterpart.[22]

In brief, the spending obligation that leads a man to choose a career he likes less that pays more is a sign of powerlessness, not power. But when he takes that job, women often assume he will pay because "after all, he earns more." Thus both sexes' expectations reinforce his powerlessness.

INFLUENCE POWER

The Catholic church is often quoted as acknowledging, "Give us a child the first five years and we will shape its life." We acknowledge the influence power of the church over its youth; we often ignore the influence power of a mother over her children—including her sons. But it is the mother who can make the child's bedtime earlier, take away desserts, or ground the child if it doesn't obey. It is the hand that rocks the cradle that creates the child's everyday heaven or hell.

Few men have a comparable amount of influence. While theoretically the man was "the master of the house," most men felt they were visitors in their wives' castle in the same way a woman would have felt like a visitor had she entered her husband's place of work. From a woman's perspective, a man's home is his castle; from a man's perspective, a woman's home is his mortgage.

Almost every woman had a primary role in the "female-dominated" family structure; only a small percentage of men had a primary role in the "male-dominated" governmental and religious structures. Many mothers were, in a sense, the chair of the board of a small company—their family. Even in Japan, women are in charge of the family finances—a fact that was revealed to the average American only after the Japanese stock market crashed in 1992 and thousands of women lost billions of dollars that their husbands never knew they had invested.[23] Conversely, most men were on their company's assembly line—either its physical assembly line or its psychological assembly line.

CONTROL-OVER-LIFE POWER

Influence power, though, is not real power. If we told mothers, "The more children you have, the more power you will have," they would laugh. If we then said, "The more children you have, the more everyone will love you and respect you," the mother would feel pressured, not empowered. But when we tell men, "The more people you supervise, the more power you will have," they buy it. Real power does not come from caving in to pressure to expand obligations, it comes from controlling our own life.

Historically, a husband spent the bulk of his day under the eye of his boss—his source of income; a wife did not spend the bulk of her day under the eye of her husband—her source of income. She had more control over her work life than he had over his.

SECURITY POWER

The prohibition against divorce gave a woman security in her workplace. Nothing gave a man security in his workplace. His source of income could fire him; her source of income could not fire her. Even today, if he quits his job, he doesn't get severance pay; if she initiates divorce, she takes half the "corporate stock."

"MY BODY, MY CHOICE" POWER

In the 1990s, if a woman and man make love and she says she is using birth control but is not, she has the right to raise the child without his knowing he even has a child, and then to sue him for retroactive child support even ten to twenty years later (depending on the state). This forces him to take a job with more pay and more stress and therefore earlier death. Although it's his body, he has no choice. He has the option of being a slave (working for another without pay or choice) or being a criminal. *Roe* v. *Wade* gave women the vote over their bodies. Men still don't have the vote over theirs—whether in love or war.

THE POWER OF APPRECIATION

ITEM. The Mike Tyson trial. The hotel in which the jury is sequestered goes ablaze. Two firefighters die saving its occupants.

The trial of Mike Tyson made us increasingly aware of men-as-rapists. The firefighters' deaths did not make us increasingly aware of men-as-saviors. We were more aware of one man doing harm than of two men saving; of one man threatening one woman who is still physically alive than of dozens of men saving hundreds of people and two of those men being dead. In the United States, almost one million municipal firefighters *volunteer* to risk their lives to save strangers. Ninety-nine percent of them are men.[24] In exchange they ask only for appreciation. In exchange they are ignored.

THE "WORK OBLIGATION GAP"

The media popularizes studies reporting women's greater amount of time spent on housework and child care, concluding, "Women work two jobs; men work one." But this is misleading. Women do work more hours inside the home, but men work more hours outside the home. And the average man commutes farther and spends more time doing yardwork, repairs, painting. . . . What happens when all of these are combined? The University of Michigan's study (reported in the *Journal of Economic Literature* in 1991) found the average man worked sixty-one hours per week, the average woman fifty-six.[25]

Is this just a recent change in men? No. In 1975, the largest nationwide probability sampling of households found that when all child care, all housework, all work outside the home, commuting, and gardening were added together, husbands did 53 percent of the total work, wives 47 percent.[26]

THE UNPAID BODYGUARD

ITEM. Steve Petrix was a journalist who lived near me in San Diego. Every day he returned home to have lunch with his wife. Recently, as he got near his door, he heard his wife screaming. She was being attacked with a knife. Steve fought the assailant off his wife. His wife ran to call the police. The intruder killed Steve. Steve was 31.[27]

A friend of mine put it this way: "What would you pay someone who agreed that, if he was ever with you when you were attacked, he would intervene and try to get himself killed slowly enough to give you time to escape? What is the hourly wage for a bodyguard? You know that is your job as a man—every time you are with a woman . . . any woman, not just your wife."[28]

What do men as women's personal bodyguards and men as volunteer firefighters have in common besides being men? They are both unpaid. Men have not yet begun to investigate their unpaid roles. . . .

MAN AS "NIGGER"?

In the early years of the women's movement, an article in *Psychology Today* called "Women as Nigger" quickly led to feminist activists (myself included) making parallels between the oppression of women and blacks.[29] Men were characterized as the oppressors, the "master," the "slaveholders." Black congresswoman Shirley Chisholm's statement that she faced far more discrimination as a woman than as a black was widely quoted.

The parallel allowed the hard-earned rights of the civil rights movement to be applied to women. The parallels themselves had more than a germ of truth. But what none of us realized was how each sex was the other's slave in different ways and therefore *neither* sex was the other's "nigger" ("nigger" implies a *one-sided* oppressiveness).

If "masculists" had made such a comparison, they would have had every bit as strong a case as feminists. The comparison is useful because it is not until we understand how men were *also* women's servants that we get a clear picture of the sexual *division* of labor and therefore the fallacy of comparing either sex to "nigger." For starters . . .

Blacks were forced, via slavery, to risk their lives in cotton fields so that whites might benefit economically while blacks died prematurely. Men were forced, via the draft, to risk their lives on battlefields so that everyone else might benefit economically while men died prematurely. The disproportionate numbers of blacks and males in war increases both blacks' and males' likelihood of experiencing posttraumatic stress, of becoming killers in postwar civilian life as well, and of dying earlier. Both slaves and men died to make the world safe for freedom—someone else's.

Slaves had their own children involuntarily taken away from them; men have their own children involuntarily taken away from them. We tell women they have the right to children and tell men they have to fight for children.

Blacks were forced, via slavery, into society's most hazardous jobs; men are forced, via socialization, into society's most hazardous jobs. Both slaves and men constituted almost 100 percent of the "death professions." Men still do.

When slaves gave up their seats for whites, we called it subservience; when men give up their seats for women, we call it politeness. Similarly, we called it a symbol of subservience when slaves stood up as their master entered a room; but a symbol of politeness when men stand up as a woman enters the room. Slaves bowed before their masters; in traditional cultures, men still bow before women.[30] The slave helped the master put on his coat; the man helped the woman put on her coat. He still does. These symbols of deference and subservience are common with slaves to masters and with men to women.

Blacks are more likely than whites to be homeless; men are more likely than women to be homeless. Blacks are more likely than whites to be in prison; men are about twenty times more likely than women to be in prison. Blacks die earlier than whites; men die earlier than women. Blacks are less likely than whites to attend college or graduate from college. Men are less likely than women to attend college (46 percent versus 54 percent) and less likely to graduate from college (45 percent versus 55 percent).[31]

Apartheid forced blacks to mine diamonds for whites; socialization expected men to work in different mines to pay for diamonds for women. Nowhere in history has there been a ruling class working to afford diamonds they could give to the oppressed in hopes the oppressed would love them more.

Blacks are more likely than whites to volunteer for war in the hopes of earning money and gaining skills; men are more likely than women to volunteer for war for the same reasons. Blacks are more likely than whites to subject themselves to the child abuse of boxing and football in the hopes of earning money, respect, and love; men are more likely than women to subject themselves to the child abuse of boxing and football, with the same hopes.

Women are the only "oppressed" group to systematically grow up having their own private member of an "oppressor" class (called fathers) in the field, working for them. Traditionally, the ruling class had people in the field, working for them—called slaves.

Among slaves, the field slave was considered the second-class slave; the house slave, the first-class slave. The male role (out in the field) is akin to the field slave—or the second-class slave; the traditional female role (homemaker) is akin to the house slave—the first-class slave.

Blacks who are heads of households have a net worth much lower than heads of households who are white; men who are heads of households have a net worth much lower than heads of households who are women.[32] No oppressed group has ever had a net worth higher than the oppressor.

It would be hard to find a single example in history in which a group that cast more than 50 percent of the vote got away with calling itself the victim. Or an example of an oppressed group which chooses to vote for their "oppressors" more than it chooses to have its own members take responsibility for running. Women are the only minority group that is a majority, the only group that calls itself "oppressed" that is able to control who is elected to every office in virtually every community in the country. Power is not in who holds the office, power is in who chooses who holds the office. Blacks, Irish, and Jews never had more than 50 percent of America's vote.

Women are the only "oppressed" group to share the same parents as the "oppressor"; to be born into the middle class and upper class as frequently as the "oppressor"; to own more of the culture's luxury items than the "oppressor"; the only "oppressed" group whose "unpaid labor" enables them to buy most of the fifty billion dollars' worth of cosmetics sold each year; the only "oppressed" group that spends more on high fashion, brand-name clothing than their "oppressors"; the only "oppressed" group that watches more TV during every time category than their "oppressors."[33]

Feminists often compare marriage to slavery—with the female as slave. It seems like an insult to women's intelligence to suggest that marriage is female slavery when we know it is 25 million American females[34] who read an average of *twenty* romance novels per *month*,[35] often with the fantasy of marriage. Are feminists suggesting that 25 million American women have "enslavement" fantasies because they fantasize marriage? Is this the reason Danielle Steele is the best-selling author in the world?

Never has there been a slave class that has spent a lot of time dreaming about being a slave and purchasing books and magazines that told them "How to Get a Slavemaster to Commit." Either marriage is something different from slavery for women or feminists are suggesting that women are not very intelligent.

The difference between slaves and males is that African-American blacks rarely thought of their slavery as "power," but men were taught to think of their slavery as "power." If men were, in fact, slavemasters, and women slaves, then why did men spend a lifetime supporting the "slaves" and the "slaves' " children? Why weren't the women supporting the men instead, the way kings were supported by their subjects? Our understanding of blacks' powerlessness has allowed us to call what we did to blacks "immoral," yet we still call what we do to males "patriotism" and "heroism" when they kill on our behalf, but "violence," "murder," and "greed" when they kill the wrong people the wrong way at the wrong time.

By understanding that what we did to blacks was immoral, we were willing to assuage our guilt via affirmative action programs and welfare. By thinking of men as the dominant oppressors who do what they do for power and greed, we feel little guilt when they die early in the process. By believing that women were an oppressed slavelike class, we extended privileges and advantages to women that had originally been designed to compensate for our immorality to blacks. For women—and only women—to take advantage of this slavery compensation was its own brand of immorality. For men to cooperate was its own brand of ignorance.

Did men do all this because they were more altruistic, loving, and less power hungry than women? No. *Both* sexes made themselves "slaves" to the other sex in different ways. Let's look at why both sexes did that; at why *neither* sex can accurately be called oppressed; at why we should be celebrating rather than blaming; and at why institutions that don't understand their new opportunities are adapting divisively because they don't understand how to adapt lovingly.

CHAPTER 2

Stage I to Stage II: How Successful Men Freed Women (But Forgot to Free Themselves)

FROM ROLE MATE TO SOUL MATE

For thousands of years, most marriages were in Stage I—survival-focused. After World War II, marriages increasingly flirted with Stage II—a self-fulfillment focus. In Stage I, most couples were role mates: the woman raised the children and the man raised the money. In Stage II, couples increasingly desired to be soul mates. Why? As couples met their survival needs, they "upped the ante" and redefined love.

In Stage I, a woman called it "love" if she found a man who was a good provider and protector; he called it "love" if she was beautiful and could take care of a home and children. Love meant a *division* of labor which led to a division of female and male interests. In Stage II, love meant *common* interests and common values. Love's definition is in transition.

Even before World War II, some parents began to redefine love. But they could usually afford to do that only after their last child was "married off," as with Tevye and Golde of *Fiddler on the Roof*.[1]

TEVYE: Golde. . . . Do you love me?
GOLDE: Do I love you?
    For twenty-five years I've washed your clothes,
    Cooked your meals, cleaned your house,

Given you children, milked the cow.
After twenty-five years, why talk about
Love right now? . . .
TEVYE: But my father and my mother
Said we'd learn to love each other. . . .
Do you love me?
GOLDE: For twenty-five years I've lived with him
Fought with him, starved with him
Twenty-five years my bed is his.
If that's not love, what is?

The people with the most freedom to redefine love were women who had married the most successful men. These women began asking Stage II questions, such as "Why should I be married to a man who can show me his wallet but not show me his love?"; "Why am I called Mrs. *John* Doe—who am *I*?"; "Why am *I* always serving *him*, deferring to *his* opinions?"; "When the children are grown, will my life have meaning?" She feared her own husband didn't really respect her; then she chastised herself for being so preoccupied with what he thought, anyway. She expressed her concerns aloud. Her concerns were institutionalized: the women's liberation movement.

His concerns were repressed. He kept to himself his hurt that his wife seemed more interested in the children, in shopping, and in herself than in him. That he felt criticized for working late rather than appreciated for working late. To him, his wife seemed to define communication as her expressing her negative feelings but not him expressing his. She seemed to avoid sex more than enjoy it. He felt hurt that soon after marriage his wife paid less attention to keeping weight off and started dressing sloppily unless she was meeting other people.

Turned off and unappreciated, he rumbled internally, "What am *I* getting from this marriage? Restaurants cook food better and give me a whole menu to choose from; housekeepers don't ask for half of my income; and my secretary is more attractive, has more respect for me, and is more in tune with my work. And besides, selling Product X is hardly what *I* call 'identity.' " Unlike her, though, he failed to express his concerns. His concerns became ulcers, heart attacks, cancer, and alcoholism.

When he did express his concerns, they were dismissed as his "male midlife crisis." **Essentially, though, women's liberation and the male midlife crisis were the same search**—for personal fulfillment, common values, mutual respect, love. But while women's liberation was thought of as promoting identity, the male midlife crisis was thought of as an identity crisis. Similarly, women's liberation was called insight, self-discovery, and self-improvement—akin to maturity; the male midlife crisis was called "playboy time" and selfishness—akin to immaturity. His crisis got the bad rap.

WAS STAGE II LOVE UNCONDITIONAL OR MORE CONDITIONAL?

My mom used to say, "When the money stops coming in the door, the love starts going out the window."

—BRIAN, 41, discussing the
unwritten rule of Stage I love

It is tempting to think of Stage II love as unconditional love. In practice, it is *more* conditional. Couples now *expect* communication skills, joint parenting, shared housework, sexual fulfillment, joint decision-making, a spiritual connection, mutual attraction, and mutual respect. They want both stability and change; both interdependence and a partner who is independent. They want time to grow and time to discover each other's growth. In Stage I, these pursuits would have taken time away from raising the children, raising the crops, and raising the money. "Discovering each other" was Stage I's Trivial Pursuit. It threatened survival.

WHY DIVORCE WAS THE TRADE-OFF TO RELATIONSHIP PROGRESS

Couples who pursued Stage II values created a new set of problems: The very qualities that made a "perfect couple" in a Stage I marriage made them "perfect for divorce" in a Stage II marriage—she was seen as "preoccupied with the home and b-o-r-i-n-g . . ."; he was seen as "preoccupied with work—and afraid of intimacy." The contrast between Stage I roles and Stage II goals and the resultant setup for divorce becomes apparent in this table:

Stage I Roles	Stage II Goals*
MARRIAGE	MARRIAGE (OR LONG-TERM RELATIONSHIP)
Survival	Fulfillment
Role mates: women and men married to create a "whole"	Soul mates: "whole" persons married to create synergy
Division of roles	Commonality of roles
Woman raises children; man raises money	Both sexes raise children; both sexes raise money
Children obligatory	Children a choice
Women expected to risk life in childbirth; men expected to risk life in war	Childbirth *ideally* risk-free; war *ideally* eliminated
Till Death Do Us Part	Till Unhappiness Do We Stay Together
Neither party can end contract	Either party can end contract
Women-as-property; men-as-less-than-property (expected to die before property was lost)	Sexes equally responsible for self and other
Both sexes subservient to needs of family	Both sexes balance needs of family with needs of self
Love emanates from mutual dependence	Love emanates from choice
Love less conditional	Love more conditional (no verbal or physical abuse; expectations of mutual respect, common values . . .)
CHOICE OF PARTNERS	CHOICE OF PARTNERS
Parental influence is primary	Parental influence is secondary
Women expected to marry their source of income ("marry up")	Neither sex expected to provide more than half the income

Stage I Roles	*Stage II Goals**
PREMARITAL CONDITIONS	PREMARITAL CONDITIONS
Men deprived of female sex and beauty until they supply security	Neither sex deprived more than the other

*Stage II goals are the ideal; most of these goals are not yet reality for most couples.

Many marriages consummated in Stage I, then, were suddenly held up to Stage II standards. They failed. Marriages failed not only because the standards were higher, but because the standards were also contradictory. For a Stage I woman, a lawyer was an ideal candidate for husband. For a Stage II woman, the lawyer, often trained to argue more than to listen, was an ideal candidate for divorce. The very qualities that led to success at work often led to failure at home. **Sex role training had always been divorce training, but without the option to divorce.** Stage II brought with it the option. *Thus the divorces of the 1960s–'90s.*

HOW DIVORCES LED WOMEN TO REDEFINE DISCRIMINATION AND EQUALITY

Practically speaking, when more than 90 percent of women got married and divorce was rare, discrimination in favor of men at work meant discrimination in favor of their wives at home.

When workplace discrimination worked in favor of women at home, no one called it sexism. Why? It was working for women. Only when discrimination switched from working *for* women to working *against* women (because more women were working) did it get called sexism. For example:

During the years I was on the board of directors of the National Organization for Women in New York City, the most resistant audiences I ever faced in the process of doing corporate workshops on equality in the workplace were not male executives—they were the *wives* of male executives. As long as her income came from her husband, she was not feeling generous when affirmative action let another woman have a head start vying for her husband's (her) income. To her, *that* seemed like sexism. To her, my seminars on "Equal Opportunity for Women at Work" read "*Un*equal Opportu-

Reprinted with special permission of King Features Syndicate.

nity for Wives at Home." And, to the executive's wife, they still do.

Why still? Almost 70 percent of the wives of male executives (vice-presidents and above) do not hold paid jobs outside the home—not even part time.[2] They *still* get their incomes completely from their husbands. An executive's wife often opposes a woman at work having an advantage over her husband, not only because it hurts her income but also because it discounts her contribution: she usually works hard to support her husband to support the company—that's her job. She feels her efforts—her job—have been discounted.

As soon as discrimination began to work against women, it led to measures to protect women. Immediately—in 1963—the Federal Equal Pay Act was passed.[3] Interestingly, the Equal Pay Act *preceded* the women's movement. The U.S. Census Bureau found that as early as 1960, never married women over 45 earned *more* in the workplace than never married men over 45.[4] Data like these—which implied a much different view from "woman as victim"—never reached the public's awareness because only women's groups organized.

Taking what had worked for most women and seeing it as a plot against them led us to see men as "owing" women. This created Stage II Entitlement: women being entitled to compensation for past oppression. Which prevented us from seeing the need to make a transition from Stage I to Stage II *together*: the need not for a women's movement or a men's movement, but for a gender transition movement.

In this book, **I define power as having control over one's own life**. The male *obligation* to earn more money than a woman before she would love him was not control over his life; in Stage I, neither sex had control over her or his life. And, as we saw in the opening chapter, both sexes had what was the traditional definition of power (influence over others and access to scarce resources) via different means.

Sexism? Or Bisexism?

Am I suggesting that sexism was a two-way street? Yes. We think of sexism as having kept women less powerful than men for centuries. In fact, for centuries neither sex had power. Each had roles. Her role: create a family. His role: protect a family. Her role: gather the food. His role: hunt the food. If *both* sexes were restricted to roles, it is not accurate to call it sexism, but sex roles. We have lived not in a sexist world, but a bisexist world.

HOW SUCCESSFUL MEN FREED WOMEN BUT FORGOT TO FREE THEMSELVES

Abigail, a typical 1890s woman, had eight children. She almost died twice in childbirth. By the time her last child left the house, she was dead.

Cindy, a typical 1990s woman, was single until she was 25. After she married, she bore two children. When her last child left the house, she had another quarter century to live.

Abigail never heard of a freezer. Cindy could pull a whole meal out of one. It took Abigail all day to shop and cook for her family of ten. Cindy often picked up gourmet food, put it in the micro-wave, and was eating twenty minutes later. (She often joked, "I don't cook dinner, I heat it.") On other evenings, she and her husband, Jeremy, took the kids to McDonald's, or had pizza deliv-ered, or Jeremy barbecued, or "made Cindy's favorite thing for dinner—a reservation." Both Cindy and Jeremy, though, did face expectations Abigail never faced (e.g., to play chauffeur, to pro-vide a college education).

Abigail shopped by horse and buggy or by foot. Cindy *or* Jeremy shopped by car or by phone. Abigail got groceries between nine and five—what she forgot she never got. Cindy *or* Jeremy got groceries round-the-clock.

Abigail had to wash dishes after every meal. Cindy gave the dishes to a dishwasher. (Sometimes she didn't touch the dishes at all—Jeremy or her older son did.) Abigail washed clothing by pumping water, building a fire to heat the water, and then using her own hands to scrub every inch. If it was raining or snowing, she hung the clothes around the house a clothespin at a time in corners she could find. Cindy set the right wash and dry cycles. (Sometimes she didn't touch the wash at all—Jeremy or her older son did.)

Abigail sewed by calloused hand in a cold house by candlelight. Cindy and Jeremy picked up wrinkle-free blends from discount clothing stores. It took Abigail two days to sew a shirt for one child, times a family of ten. It took Cindy *or* Jeremy twenty min-utes at the discount clothing store to pick up shirts for both chil-dren.

Abigail had eight children's needs focused on her. Cindy had two children's needs focused partially on a TV. And Cindy had one other thing: a husband who knew how to nurture as well as disci-pline.

In 1990, Cindy could still *choose* to bake bread in the oven or sew a shirt by hand—but now it was by option, not obligation; now it was occasionally, not daily; now it was for part of her adult life, not 100 percent of her adult life.

Did Cindy face pressures that Abigail never had? Absolutely. But those new pressures were rarely additions, but *substitutes* for her old burden. Had they been additions, women's life span would not have increased by almost 50 percent since 1920.[5]

Why, then, did men's life expectancy go from one year less than women's in 1920 to seven years less today? Because men's performances—inventing, manufacturing, selling, and distributing—saved women, but no one saved men from the pressure to perform. **She went from being a baby machine, cooking machine, and cleaning machine to having time for love. He went from being a performing machine near the home to being a performing machine away from home.** And having less time for love.

Men did a better job creating better homes and gardens for their wives than they did creating safer coal mines and construction sites for themselves. Few cared that only men died by thousands clearing paths through mountains to lay roads for cars and tracks for trains that allowed the rest of civilization to be served in a dining car.

The location of a man's work disconnected him from the people he loved, thus depriving his life of meaning . . . creating little deaths every day. And if he succeeded in all this, he became a male machine; if he failed, he suffered humiliation. Either way, the more he saved her, the sooner he died compared to her, leaving what he made to her and the children to spend. In these ways, successful men freed women but forgot to free themselves.

Despite this, feminists labeled "male technology"—and especially "male medical technology"—as a tool of the patriarchy designed to oppress women.[6] So our entrance into Stage II was marked by criticizing men for the destruction to the environment created by a dam, but not acknowledging men for the electricity created by the dam, or asking women to take responsibility for the female consumption that also led to the demand for electricity that required more dams.

As for male medical technology, it was probably the single factor most responsible for women's life expectancy increasing by almost 50 percent. It prevented women from dying in childbirth and developed vaccines for almost all the contagious diseases (polio, diphtheria, typhoid fever, measles, chickenpox, bubonic plague, smallpox, tuberculosis).

During wartime, experimental drugs were often tried on men. If a drug failed, the man died. But if a drug succeeded, it was used to save both women and men, but without women dying to develop it. Men were similarly used as guinea pigs in the development of emergency procedures, microwave ovens (a man was inadvertently "cooked" during the testing process[7]), and other advances that served both sexes. Later it was labeled sexism that physicians studied men more than women. No one labeled it sexism because men were used as guinea pigs more than women.

Feminists felt patriarchy and male technology conspired to restrict women's reproductive freedom—women's "right to choose." But male technology *created* women's "right to choose"—it created birth control. And it created safe abortions. The male technology of birth control did more than any other single thing to reduce women's work load; to move women from a one-option sex to the only multi-option sex. Overall, **technology led to the male role saving women more than the female role saved men.** Ironically, some of the feminists who complained of male technology would have died in childbirth or via abortions without it. (They literally owed their lives to what they complained controlled their lives.)

Male technology did not create for men the equivalent right to choose. Thus, each time a man had sex with a woman who said she was using birth control, he had to trust that she was, in fact, using it. If she wasn't, he could be responsible for supporting a child for eighteen years. If a man used a condom but the woman later said she had nevertheless conceived, the Stage II unmarried woman now had the right to inform the man or not to inform him; to abort the fetus unilaterally or secretly put the child up for adoption; to raise it herself and make him pay the bills; or even raise it for ten years by herself without telling him it was his child and then sue him for child support retroactively. All this is legal.

Every woman knows that if there was only male birth control, she would not feel in control, she would feel out of control. "Trust me" from a man is laughable; "trust me" from a woman is the law. Birth control created the right of women to choose and the expectation of men to trust. Today, every man who puts a penis in a woman's body also puts his life in a woman's hands.

In brief, **male technology and male laws freed women from female biology as female destiny and created *female* biology as *male* destiny.**

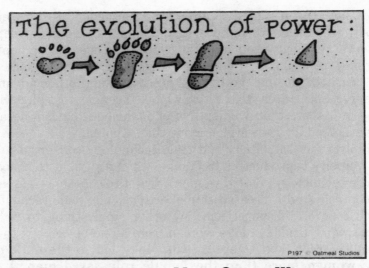

The evolution of power:

P197 © Oatmeal Studios

THE EMERGENCE OF THE MULTI-OPTION WOMAN AND THE NO-OPTION MAN

Today, when the successful single woman meets the successful single man, they appear to be equals. But should they marry and consider children, she almost invariably considers three options:

Option #1: Work full time
Option #2: Mother full time
Option #3: Some combination of working and mothering

He considers three "slightly different" options:

Option #1: Work full time
Option #2: Work full time
Option #3: Work full time

Mothers are still forty-three times more likely than fathers to leave the workplace for six months or longer for family reasons.[8] In most cases, this leaves him not just working full time but working overtime or working two jobs.

Ironically, then, it is his success that makes her more than equal to him—that gives her three options while he has none. Of course, a woman's choice to mother may hurt her career, but she can *choose* maternal opportunity or career continuity. In contrast, men who chose paternal opportunity—to be "pioneer househusbands"—soon learned that many reporters wanted them for an interview but few women wanted them for a marriage.

Women did even more than speak up for new options. They articulated the problems the new options created. So we heard about her "juggling act." Fathers did not articulate their pressure to intensify their commitment to the workplace when children arrived. We didn't hear about his "intensifying act." Nor did men discuss how hurt they felt being left out of their families.

The first time I asked a group of men whether they would choose to parent full time for six months to a year if they could (as mentioned above) and more than 80 percent said that being full time with their newborn child would be their preference if they were not hurting the family economically and their wife approved, I assumed I was either dealing with a group of liars or a self-selected sample. When I received only a slightly smaller percentage from an association of construction subcontractors,[9] I began to understand the degree to which men had not even thought about their options.

We often say, "In today's economy, women *need* to work outside the home—it's not an option." **We forget that women who work outside the home are usually exercising the option of paying for the technology that reduced women's burden inside the home.**

Most Multi-Option Women had one thing in common: a successful husband. But divorces eliminated many women's successful husbands—leaving us with six basic classes of women. . . .

THE SIX CLASSES OF WOMEN

1. *The Stage I Married Woman.* She never gave herself permission to work, or she felt "My husband won't let me." Psychologically, she was a No-Option woman.
2. *The Three-Options Woman with a Poor Marriage.* She remained married, but unhappily, often to avoid having to work.
3. *The Single Mother Married to the Government.* The government played substitute husband, providing her with three options but only if she remained at a subsistence level.
4. *The Stage I Single Working Woman.* This woman worked to

prevent herself or her family from *starving*. If she had children from a previous marriage, she usually did *not* receive child support.

5. *The Stage II Single Working Woman*. She was neither supported by a man nor supporting a man. If she had children from a previous marriage, she was likely to be in Stage II only if she received child support.

6. *The Have-It-All Woman*. This woman was married to a man who provided an economic safety net (a financial womb) from which she could choose among her three options. The Have-It-All woman was *happily* married. This created a class of people who had never before existed. In a sense, the Have-It-All woman was the "New Royalty." Virtually no man was in the equivalent position.

The political genius of the feminist movement was its intuitive sense that it could appeal to all six classes only by emphasizing expansion of rights and avoiding expansion of responsibilities. Had the National Organization for Women (NOW) fought to register 18-year-old girls for the draft, it might have lost a few members. Had feminism emphasized women's responsibilities for risking sexual rejection, or paying for men's dinners, or choosing careers they like less to support the family more, or marrying down, *its impact would have been more egalitarian but less politically successful.*

WHAT MADE WOMEN SO ANGRY AT MEN?

Women became angry at men in part because they compared themselves to the *successful* heterosexual white man—not to the plight of the black and native American man, or to the ostracism of the gay man, or the invisibility of the poor man. But this was only part of it. . . .

Women as the Disposable Sex

Divorces threw millions of women out of the Have-It-All class. But the woman who got divorced, more often 40 than 20, was tossed into the marketplace of men more addicted to two 20s than to one 40. Understandably she became angry.

HERMAN®

**"You're the one who wanted to get married.
You're the one who wanted kids. You wanted
the house and the furniture and now YOU
want to be LIBERATED!"**

In Stage I, reinforcing men's addiction to the 20-year-old woman
worked for her—the addiction made him agree to support her for
a lifetime; the taboo on divorce made him stick to his agreement.
When the taboo on divorce weakened and she was 40, his addiction
to two 20s worked against her. She felt disposable. Divorce had
altered the psychological relationship between men and women.

The more beautiful the woman was when she was younger, the
more she had been treated like a celebrity—what I call a genetic
celebrity—and therefore the more she felt like a has-been. It's

harder to lose something you've had than never to have it to begin with. As she became increasingly invisible, she felt increasingly disposable and increasingly angry.

Simultaneously, women who had never made it into the Have-It-All class—the New Royalty—also felt like failures. In different ways, both groups of women felt rejected—by men. And therefore angry—at men.

The divorced woman with children felt doubly disposable. She was not just a woman, she was a package deal: a woman-with-children. I recall a male friend of mine coming back ecstatic from his date with Carol. A week later, he went to Carol's home and she introduced him to her three children. When they all went on a ski weekend, he spent over $1,000 *on the children*. He knew he didn't *have* to, but, "I didn't want to be stingy so I paid for their ski-lift tickets, rooms for them separate from us, some of their meals, treats. . . ."

My friend was already supporting his former wife and two children. He feared becoming both a father of two families and a financial womb for two families. *He feared becoming a man with four jobs.* More precisely he feared doing each job inadequately. He soon backed off from the relationship. Carol felt hurt and never really spoke with him again. He felt disposable as a friend just because he couldn't commit to being a wallet; she felt disposable as a marriage partner. In fact they were both victims of the post-divorce phenomenon I call "woman-as-a-package-deal" (she was not just a woman but a woman-and-three-children). Had they understood how they were both victims of a setup, they could more easily have remained friends.

Divorce forced the middle-class woman who used to be able to take a job she liked more that paid less to have to take a job she liked less that paid more. When feminism explained that women were segregated into the lower-paying and meaningless jobs, she felt devalued. Feminism was so powerful it blinded her to the men around her who were also segregated into *different types* of lower-paying, meaningless jobs: the short-order cook and dishwasher in her local coffee shop; the migrant workers who picked the vegetables for her table; the custodians and carwashers, the busboys and gas station attendants. . . . By being blinded to the whole picture—that when *either* sex had minimal skills they commanded minimal wages in *different types* of meaningless jobs—women became increasingly angry.

Women interpreted men's tendency to earn more for different work as an outcome of male dominance rather than male subservience: they did not see it as an outcome of male obligation—obligation to go where the money was, not where fulfillment was. For him, following money was primary; following fulfillment, secondary. For him, divorce also created a change: he still followed money to support a family economically but without a family to support him emotionally.

Simultaneously, feminists focused on the fact that women as a whole earned less without focusing on any of the thirteen major reasons *why* women earned less (e.g., full-time working men work nine hours per week more [in the workplace] than full-time working women[10]; men are more willing to relocate to undesirable locations, to work the less desirable hours,[11] etc.). By calling the difference in pay "discrimination" and not explaining the reasons for the difference, women were left angry rather than empowered (had they known the reasons for the difference, they would have been empowered to make up the difference).

As female hurt and anger created an atmosphere that made it less safe for men to express their feelings, men became more passive-aggressive. Men increasingly felt that their only form of relationship power was not getting into one. Women labeled this a fear of commitment, accused men of a fear of intimacy, and began making masculinity virtually synonymous with evil: "Father Knows Best" became "Fathers Molest." Women became "women who loved too much"; men became "men who harassed too much." Women were labeled superwomen and men were labeled superspoiled.

The Politics of Housework

It soon appeared to most women that women had two jobs and men had one—that only her labor was increasing. In reality, she had less obligation inside the home, more obligation outside the home: we were really dealing with **a division of the locations of her labor.** A nationwide study made this clear.

In 1991, the *Journal of Economic Literature* reported that while

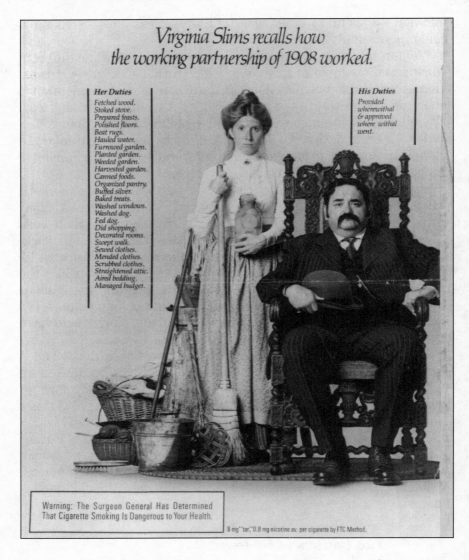

Virginia Slims recalls how
the working partnership of 1908 worked.

Her Duties
Fetched wood.
Stoked stove.
Prepared feasts.
Polished floors.
Beat rugs.
Hauled water.
Furrowed garden.
Planted garden.
Weeded garden.
Harvested garden.
Canned foods.
Organized pantry.
Buffed silver.
Baked treats.
Washed windows.
Washed dog.
Fed dog.
Did shopping.
Decorated rooms.
Swept walk.
Sewed clothes.
Mended clothes.
Scrubbed clothes.
Straightened attic.
Aired bedding.
Managed budget.

His Duties
Provided
wherewithal
& approved
where withal
went.

Warning: The Surgeon General Has Determined
That Cigarette Smoking Is Dangerous to Your Health.

9 mg''tar;''0.8 mg nicotine av. per cigarette by FTC Method.

women still do about seventeen more hours of work *inside* the
home per week, men do about twenty-two more hours of work
outside the home per week (including commuting time).[12] What
happens when we compare the hours of the average woman to the
hours of the average man *both* inside and outside the home? Hers
amount to fifty-six hours; his amount to sixty-one hours. By the
same measure. Why? The average woman works twenty-six hours

per week outside the home, the average man forty-eight hours.[13]

Studies of working wives that say that wives do two jobs while their husbands do just one and slough off on the second tell but half the truth. They are so misleading as to be a form of lying: they are women-as-victim studies. More importantly, they make women angry and increase the divorce rate, which deepens the anger, which . . .

Women's anger was intensified by the sense that women were changing and men were not. It was assumed this was because of male complacency. It was not. . . .

WHY DIDN'T MEN CHANGE?

Divorces also led to women changing because divorces changed women's source of income. Divorces did not change the pressure on men to focus on income in order to receive women's love. Millions of divorced men took on five payments rarely assessed to women:

- Child support
- Mortgage payments on a home no longer lived in
- Apartment rental
- Alimony
- Dating

Men faced more of the same old pressure to earn—just intensified. So instead of changing, they found themselves becoming more of the same. Unfortunately, the one feminist study that found men benefiting and women hurting after divorce completely ignored most of the five male payments and ignored much of female income, therefore not only ignoring men's burden but leaving men unappreciated (it was the only study with those findings and the only one to receive media attention).[14]

HOW THE GOVERNMENT PLAYED SUBSTITUTE HUSBAND WHILE NO ONE PLAYED SUBSTITUTE WIFE

When divorces occurred, women's greatest fear was of economic deprivation. Men's was of emotional deprivation. **Stage II divorce laws helped Alice make a transition from economic dependence**

to economic independence. No Stage II laws helped Jack make a transition from emotional dependence to emotional independence. (Which is why Alice rushed to a court for economic support and Jack rushed to a woman for emotional support.)

When divorces meant that husbands no longer guaranteed women economic security, the government became the substitute husband. It guaranteed women equality in pay and an advantage in hiring (affirmative action). It gave women Aid to Families with Dependent Children (AFDC); it provided special programs for Women, Infants, and Children (WIC); it gave women the preference for keeping children and then garnisheed men's wages if child support was not paid; it gave special opportunities for women in college, women in the armed services, women artists, women in small businesses; it severed him from future services from her.

Alice used to have only one option for economic security and Jack only one option for emotional security. Now Alice has multiple options for economic security (income via career, husband, or government) while Jack has fewer than one: income via career *minus* child support, minus alimony, and minus higher taxes to pay for the government-as-substitute husband. All of this kept him a prisoner of money, barred from exploring his inner self.

WHY STAGE I INSTITUTIONS WERE OPPRESSIVE AND HOW STAGE II INSTITUTIONS CAN BE FREEING

Part of women's anger at men comes from the belief that men made the rules, and made them to oppress women and benefit men. Since most institutions are headed by men, when these institutions don't meet our needs, we tend to blame men. The challenge is twofold: first, to recognize that these institutions helped women get to Stage II even before men; second, to understand how institutions that were functional in Stage I can now make a transition to become functional in Stage II.

How the Functional Family Became the Dysfunctional Family

Just as we held up Stage I marriages to Stage II standards and labeled them a failure, we currently hold up Stage I families to Stage II standards and label them dysfunctional. As many as 97 percent of our families of origin are said to be dysfunctional. So while in Stage I, "spare the rod, spoil the child" implied if you did *not* use the rod, you've abused the child, in Stage II, if you *do* use the rod, you've abused the child. Why?

In Stage I, using the rod was considered *functional*—it taught children that not obeying would create pain. Which was true— rules were designed to prevent starvation. But in Stage II, goals of self-fulfillment required being in touch with one's feelings. Us- ing the rod disconnects children from their feelings and is there- fore more likely to be dysfunctional.

In Stage I, mutual *dependence* was the cement in a family's foundation. So there could hardly be too much of it. Codependence was Stage I Functional. But when divorces forced us to prepare ourselves for independence, *then* codependence often became over- dependence and therefore dysfunctional. So the functional Stage I family became the dysfunctional Stage II family.

I would like to see us stop describing our families of origin as dysfunctional and begin describing them as *Stage I Functional*. This gives them credit for the contribution they made to taking care of our survival needs so that we have the freedom to decide what is functional in Stage II. It also allows them to rejoice in the opportunity to pursue that freedom themselves rather than feel blamed and guilty for screwing up.

Marriage

Feminists assume that marital traditions such as the father giving the bride away were a reflection of patriarchy. But the father "gave away" the bride because it was the father giving away *his* responsibility to protect. (No one gave the man away because no one would protect a man. The job of the parents was to turn the son into a protector, not give him away *to* a protector.)

Our parents were often criticized for discouraging a son from "doing his own thing." But because a Vincent van Gogh could barely support himself (much less a family of ten), it was the job of parents to make sure their son didn't become an artist, and to teach their daughter that being courted by such a man was court- ing disaster. Children often heard those instructions as parents exercising power. In fact, it was not parental power, it was *post- ponement* of parental power—the postponement of Tevye's and

Golde's ability to seek self-fulfillment and search for a deeper love. Thus Tevye was able to ask Golde Stage II questions only *after* their daughter was about to be "married off."

Because happiness was secondary, drinking, frustration, and abuse were rampant. But in Stage I, it was not functional to permit divorce: with eight children at home and no ability to support two homes, walking out was not an option. So we tolerated drinking and abuse rather than divorce and starvation.

In brief, the generations will learn to love each other more quickly if we see their socialization as Stage I Functional rather than labeling them dysfunctional; if we acknowledge that the children best able to pursue Stage II values today often can do so exactly because their parents had Stage I values. Discussions of family values without distinctions between Stage I and Stage II families are thus setups for deprecation rather than appreciation.

Religion in Transition

In Stage I, the church provided rigid rules and rituals designed to get people to make sacrifices for the next generation without questioning. In Stage II, questioning is needed to deal with life's options, and rigidity is poor training for life's ambiguities.

Stage I religions had to restrict premarital sex because premarital sex led to children without a guarantee for the children's and woman's protection. In Stage II, birth control allowed sex to become more associated with fulfillment, communication, and spiritual connection—goals of the Stage II relationship. So Stage II religions can focus less on restricting the sexes from access to each other's bodies and more on assisting the sexes to have access to each other's souls.

Stage II churches are now freer to teach how sexual inhibition often becomes spiritual inhibition. For example, teaching women to keep sex artificially repressed teaches men to tell women what they think women want to hear rather than what they are really feeling. Dishonesty inhibits spirituality. Women then begin to use their sexuality to get told what they want to hear rather than learn to enjoy their sexuality. They often contrast sexuality with spirituality rather than see how a sexual bond contributes to a spiritual bond. Women's sexual repression is an effective way of giving women control over men, but it keeps men less than genuine.

Many women are beginning to prefer men who are genuine to men whom they can control. In brief, Stage I religion's emphasis on rigid rules prepared a couple to be enduring role mates. Stage II religion's emphasis on communication prepares a couple to be soul mates.

Stage *I* churches will continue to seek *men* to lead as a symbol of men's responsibility to be a problem solver and savior. These churches will attract mostly Stage I female followers and Stage I male leaders. Stage II churches will seek both sexes to lead, not by blaming men for leading in the past but by helping both sexes make a transition into a different future.

Stage I Vs. Stage II Sexual Politics

Worldwide, politicians trained in Stage I sexual ethics were suddenly being judged by Stage II ethics. John Kennedy's affairs were kept secret but Ted Kennedy and Bill Clinton were seen as womanizers. Stage I Japanese prime ministers had geishas but Stage II prime minister Uno was toppled as soon as it was discovered he had had a geisha. British war minister John Profumo went from being the leading candidate for prime minister to being forced out of politics in disgrace when his having a mistress was judged by Stage II sexual ethics.

Why this change? **In Stage I, divorces were not allowed, so men's affairs did not put women's economic security in jeopardy; in Stage II, affairs could lead to divorce, so men's affairs did place women's economic security in jeopardy.** We did not want political leaders who would be role models for behavior that would put women's economic security in jeopardy.

Doesn't our supposed concern about women conflict with the sexual double standard that seems to have served only men? No. There were two double standards: (1) a man could have affairs, a woman couldn't; and (2) a married woman could force her husband to support the children from her affairs; a married man could not force his wife to support the children from his affairs. (Rather, *he* was ostracized if he refused to take care of a child that resulted from his affairs.[15]) It is the second double standard that we never hear about.

Both double standards, though, protected women. How? Had married men felt their wives were having affairs to create children they had to support, few men would commit to marriage and few women and children would receive protection.

Nevertheless, Stage I societies had a dilemma: marriage guaranteed women economic security for a lifetime but failed to guarantee men sexual gratification for a lifetime. So Stage I societies created a marital deal: what I call the "Marital Triangle."

The Marital Triangle was the husband, wife, and mistress (or, depending on the culture, the geisha, prostitute, second wife, or a harem). The deal was this: "Husband, your first obligation is to take care of your wife's and children's needs economically. If you're still doing this but you're not getting the sex, youth, beauty, attention, and passion that made you agree to do this for a lifetime to begin with, *then* you can take care of some of your needs, too, but under two conditions: you must continue to provide for your family (no divorce is allowed even if your needs aren't met); and you must also provide for some of the economic needs of this younger, attractive woman (geisha, mistress, prostitute) whose need for money otherwise might not be met."

In Stage I, no one group got their intimacy needs met—not husband, wife, mistress, or children. Of course, some individuals did, but that wasn't the primary worry of a Stage I marriage: it was stability, and the Marital Triangle was the "Great Stability Compromise."

By Stage II standards, politicians who declared they were moral but were having affairs were clearly hypocrites. But that missed the underlying spirit of morality that was bred into Stage I culture: morality meant taking care of your family. For most men, affairs would undermine that goal. But the man who could do both discreetly was not ostracized because on some level it was understood he was providing an incentive for a man to be successful and a better protector. All this changed when affairs signaled divorces and dumped millions of women into the workplace without workplace skills. Then politicians who had affairs soon also had no workplace.

By calling these changed standards a higher morality, women again appeared to have the higher morality. Women, though, did not have a higher morality. Why not? Every affair involved *both* sexes.

The difference? In the 1980s and '90s, Gary Hart's Donna Rice got commercial and TV roles, Bill Clinton's Gennifer Flowers got paid an estimated $100,000 to reveal her story . . . both sexes participated, but men were seen as perpetrators and women as victims even though the men's careers were being hurt while women's careers were being jump-started.

Stage II Politics

When we think of political bosses, bribes, and patronage, we tend to think of male power, male corruption, the "good ol' boys" network, male chauvinism, and male dominance. The unraveling of this process is associated with the unraveling of these symbols of male dominance. However, in Stage I, political bosses, bribes, and patronage were acceptable not because they served men but because they served families—including women and children. The boss remained in power only as long as he created jobs to feed those families. He built his "machine" from the economic underclass, so these jobs fed the poor. The fact that they were jobs, not welfare, allowed the families respect.

When a man became the boss it was often the first symbol of an economic underclass—Irish or Italians or Jews or blacks—breaking into the economic mainstream. One could call it Stage I welfare or corruption or job training, depending on one's point of view, but it benefited families, not just men. In its extreme forms (e.g., the Mafia), it not only provided for families but it disposed of men much more often than women.

CREATING GENDER TRANSITION

In brief, our genetic heritage is in conflict with our genetic future. **For the first time in human history, the qualities it takes to survive as a species are compatible with the qualities it takes to love.** To love the other sex, to love our children—by a Stage II definition of love. The challenge for a woman is to create enough economic independence that she doesn't compromise love for an economic safety net. The challenge for a man is understanding how preparation for Stage I protection is really preparation for disconnection—from children, wife, and life. The Stage I man had a role that was more disconnected from intimacy than the Stage I female role of nurturer. Which is why the challenge for men to enter Stage II is even greater than the challenge for women.

· · ·

To conclude that men did not have the power, though, we must be more secure that the male role in the past has not, after all, been just a way of keeping women in their place. We must deal with denying women the vote; treating women as property and second-class citizens; objectifying them as concubines, harems, and prostitutes; stoning them as witches; not writing them into constitutions; denying them access to roles of leadership, jobs outside the home, and so on. We must see if "power," "patriarchy," "dominance," and "sexism" were code words for male privilege or male disposability.

Are "Power," "Patriarchy," "Dominance," and "Sexism" Actually Code Words for Male Disposability?

> Patriarchy is "the universal political structure which privileges men at the expense of women."
>
> —*Encyclopedia of Feminism*[1]

I. A SLAVE BY ANY OTHER NAME . . . IS STILL A SLAVE

If power is defined as having control over one's life, then myths, legends, and Bible stories were often ways of getting both sexes to *forfeit* power. . . .

THE HERO AS SLAVE

Once upon a time, a mother who wanted to see the beautiful statue of Hera had no horses or oxen to carry her there. But she did have two sons. And the sons wanted more than anything to make their mother's wish come true. They volunteered to yoke themselves to a cart and take her over the mountains in the scorching heat to the faraway village of Argos, the home of the statue of Hera.[2]

Upon their arrival in Argos, the sons were cheered and statues (that can be found to this day) were built in their honor.[3] Their mother prayed that Hera give her sons the best gift in her power. Hera did that. The boys died.

The traditional interpretation? The best thing that can happen to a man is to die at the height of his glory and power. Yet had this been a myth of two daughters who had substituted themselves for oxen to carry their father somewhere, would we have interpreted the daughters' deaths as proof that the best thing that can happen to a woman is to die at the height of her glory and power?

The statues and cheers can be seen as bribes for the sons to value their lives less than their mother's request to view a statue. The fact that the statue was of Hera, the queen of the Olympian gods and the protector of married women,[4] is symbolic. The sons' sacrifice symbolized the mandate for men to become strong enough to serve the needs of mothers and marriage, and to be willing to call it glory if they died in the process. Which is why the name Hercules means "for the glory of Hera."[5]

Was a hero a servant? Yes. The very word "hero" comes from the Greek *ser-ow*, from which comes our word "servant," as well as "slave" and "protector."[6] *A hero was basically a slave whose purpose was to serve and protect.* To protect the community in general, women and children in particular. In exchange, heroes received the respect and love of those they protected. Just as the appreciation we gave our mother's cooking kept her cooking and gave her an "ego bribe" to be a slave to her role in the kitchen, so statues and tales of glory are ego bribes for males to be slaves to their roles as heroes. Appreciation keeps the slave a slave.

None of this denies the female contribution to protection. The female who protected in her way was Hera; the male who protected in his way was a hero.

WERE MEN LESS THAN PROPERTY?

Men were not "thought of" as property or animals, they were just used that way. The fifteenth-century Incas did not have horses to speed messages over the long distances up and down mountain paths. The men were given coca leaves (cocaine), which allowed them to run farther and faster . . . until they burned out.[7] The good died young. Unlike women-as-property, men were not to be protected—they were to be used and be disposable.

During the bubonic plagues in Europe (fourteenth century), men who carried the corpses were subject to catching the plague. Poor peasant men (*gavoti*) volunteered to do this, though, for the money it gave them. Many died. But their families were supported.[8]

On the surface, it would appear that the *gavoti* corpse carriers "had money" and that the Inca runners had physical strength and "power." But both knew they would be dying so their families could live. If these were rules made by men, what does it say about men that they made rules to sacrifice themselves for their families?

WHY WERE MEN SO FOCUSED ON WINNING?

When I was a boy and went to a museum I can remember seeing a head cut off from its body and being told by the curator that it was thought to be the head of the captain of the *winning* team in a Mayan ball court game (roughly a Mayan and Aztec equivalent of football). Other times, the losing team's captain—or the entire team—was killed.[9] Why? It depended on who the society felt would best protect them: the able-bodied winners, in which case the losers were sacrificed; or the gods, who might be more pleased by a sacrifice of the winners.

If winning per se were important, the winner would never have been sacrificed. The sacrifice of the winners taught the society that both men's lives and winning were secondary to society's protection. Men's focus on winning was, historically, a focus on protection—even at the expense of themselves.

THE CIVIL WAR: MEN AS SECOND-CLASS CITIZENS

During the Civil War in the United States, two groups were able to avoid the draft: females and upper-class males. *Any* female was the equivalent of an upper-class male in this respect. Except that even the upper-class men had to buy their way out of death. They did this by paying three hundred dollars[10] (roughly \$5,400 today[11]) to a poor man. This allowed the poor man's family to survive while he risked death. The poor man's self-concept—that he was worth nothing if he remained poor—was literal. Being cannon fodder at least made him worth something to someone.

Why could the upper-class male buy his way out of the Civil War? Because he had the ability to save the community in other ways—producing munitions or food supplies in factories, producing harvests via the property and slaves he owned (which might go unproductive were he to go off to war; and which might never again be productive if he was killed). The upper-class male did not have the privilege to avoid the savior role—only the privilege to play that role in various ways. He still inherited the obligation to save, not the option to be free from saving. Nor did he inherit the option to have a woman save him.

During the Civil War, *the government passed a Conscription Act*[12] *allowing, in essence, for an all-male slave trade.* More than a half million men (623,026) were killed in the Civil War[13]—the equivalent of eleven Vietnam Wars. Try to imagine eleven Vietnam Wars in a row in which only females were drafted, in which 620,000 female soldiers—your sister, your mother, your daughter—arrived home in body bags.

Was this war stuff, though, "men's thing"? Hardly. Women "hissed and groaned" at men who didn't fight.[14] In the South, men rarely ran ads for substitutes because, as the award-winning PBS series on the Civil War explained, "women wouldn't permit it."[15] Few women wanted to marry a man who was "afraid" to fight.

There is yet another lesson here. If men loved war so much, why did men riot, protesting the draft of men in the 1860s? Why did many *Northern* men risk ostracism by running ads in newspapers for substitutes so they could buy their way out? Today men still get hissed and booed when they succeed at avoiding war. Ask Dan Quayle, Bill Clinton. . . .

Some boys, of course, willingly go into war. If girls from disadvantaged backgrounds willingly had their limbs torn off so their families could have an extra $5,000 a year, we would call these girls saints. We call the boys "macho."

In the Civil War, as in most wars, *both* sexes believed in the principles for which their side was fighting. One of those principles was freeing black slaves. In essence, white male slaves fought to free black slaves. We have long acknowledged the slavery of blacks. We have yet to acknowledge the slavery of males.

In these respects, no man was equal to a woman: no man, of any class, could expect a woman to save him from attack. Or from starvation. And in Stage I, starvation and attack were the primary fears. In these ways, men were the second-class citizens. Boys died before the age of consent—before they had the right to vote.

If girls willingly risked their lives in the Civil War in exchange for a few medals, we would immediately recognize low self-esteem as a woman's issue. Yet boys do this and a best-selling feminist book in the 1990s, Gloria Steinem's *Revolution from Within*, claims that low self-esteem is a woman's issue.[16] Low self-esteem is also a man's issue—an issue deriving from the male version of being a second-class citizen. Our ability to address it is a Stage II privilege; our addressing it for only one sex is Stage II sexism.

When feminist historians call this slave class a warrior class and an elite class,[17] they miss this perspective: warriors were not so much an elite class as a dead class.

THE HAZARDS OF HEROISM

Heroism had its hazards: teaching a boy to kill and then expecting him to kill only to protect; instructing him to kill males, but not females or children. The tragedy of the warrior is that the more he fights the enemy, the more he begins to be like the enemy; the more he kills beasts, the more he becomes like a beast. (The myth of the Centaur—half man and half beast—symbolizes the resultant male schizophrenia.)

A parable from the Cherokee describes these hazards beautifully.[18]

Chief of the Pond

Once upon a time there was a gentle pond abundant with God's creatures: fish, snakes, and frogs. All day these creatures did as they pleased. In the pond was a log. The creatures thought of the log as their shelter, a podium for food, almost a Chief of the Pond. One day, though, an elegant heron with long legs poised its graceful body upon the pond's edge. All the creatures took its arrival as a sign that they were meant to be led to greater things. They held a powwow. They agreed that the log did nothing but sleep all day. So, they proudly elected the elegant heron their chief. Within a week or two, the heron had eaten all the fish, all the snakes, and all the frogs.

When females ask males to protect them with their strength, the risk is having the very strength that protects them in one instance be used against them in another. Thus the athletes for whom females cheer are also involved in one third of campus sexual assaults.[19] On a broader level, when people allow kings "divine rights," the upside is the potential for greater protection; the downside, the potential for greater misuse. **When individuals empower their drugs, religions, kings, or males, they risk being disempowered.** The log, by doing nothing, forced the creatures to take responsibility. The temptation in choosing a hero is to relinquish responsibility—to blame the hero, the patriarchy, the politician. But ultimately it was the creatures who had the power. *They* rejected the log—or self-responsibility—and *they* opted for the hero . . . for the heron. Just as genius walks a thin line with destructiveness, so heroism walks a thin line with both the destruction of others and self-destruction.

Don't leaders often manipulate their way into power? Yes. *And* people manipulate their leaders by choosing leaders who tell them what they want to hear. The Aryans were willing to make someone chancellor in exchange for being told they weren't doing as well as the Jews because the Jews were oppressing them. A young man named Adolf spoke to the Aryan fear of taking personal responsibility. He was soon rewarded. If the pay is good enough, the prostitute will appear.

II. SOCIALIZATION FOR SLAVERY

SCARS AS MALE ELIGIBILITY

Women's scars and rituals involved beauty (piercing ears and noses, binding feet, and wearing corsets); men's involved protecting women. In cultures in which physical strength is still the best way to protect women, as among the Dodos in Uganda, each time a man kills *a man*, he is awarded a ritual scar; *the more scars, the more he is considered eligible.*[20] In the Old South, the more duels a man won, the more he was considered eligible. The single ladies spoke of a single man's victories just as the single men spoke of the single woman's beauty.[21]

During the seventeenth and eighteenth centuries in many European countries, to be called a "gentleman," a man had to don a sword. A *gentle*man would use his sword to defend a woman's honor, to prove himself worthy of a woman, or to defend his own reputation. "Gentleman" was a term of the highest honor.

Why was a man with a sword called a gentleman? Because the sword was to be used only against men . . . to women he was to be gentle.

Think of the implications: calling a man "gentle" if he wore something with which to kill. Imagine requiring a woman to wear a sword before we called her a lady. Imagine expecting her to kill any woman who insulted a man. How many women would we have left?

This tradition—of men killing a man who insults a woman—is still with us in places like Sicily, and the verbal remnants of it are with us in men's hesitancy to talk behind women's backs, even in an era when calling men jerks behind their backs is virtually institutionalized.*

Scars, men's teeth being knocked out, and circumcisions were all "symbolic wounds"—symbols of the necessity for a boy to endure pain in subordination to his male role as warrior and protector.[22] In societies in which circumcision is commonplace, it is usually a prerequisite to marriage. (The prayer at the end of the *bris*, the Jewish circumcision ceremony which takes place on the eighth day of a boy's life, goes, "As he has been initiated into the covenant, so may he enter into matrimony. . . ."[23])

Today, scars that reflect a risking of life in sports still bring a man love when he is young, but when he is older, only if they translate into money. Thus, a high school dropout like Mike Tyson could find "love" with a beautiful Sarah Lawrence graduate like Robin Givens *only if* his scars translated into money.

Engagement Rings as Scars

An engagement ring is one modern equivalent of a ritual scar: *The scar symbolized the physical risk taken only by the man to bring physical security to the woman; the engagement ring symbolizes the financial risk taken only by the man to bring fiscal security to the woman.* Both symbolize the man's willingness to protect a woman. The bigger the diamond, like the bigger the scar, the greater the protection.

The Officer and the Gentleman: Modern Versions of the Duel

Today, when a man makes money killing and protecting, we still call him, well . . . *An Officer and a Gentleman.* The officer was,

---

* Men's hesitancy is documented in *Why Men Are the Way They Are*, in the section called "The Worst Infidelity." Male-bashing is in the chapter called "The New Sexism."

after all, a trained killer, but, as Richard Gere swept Deborah Winger off her feet, he became a gentleman. And in the theater in which I saw the film, the women burst into applause. We still call the trained killer a gentleman if he uses his money from killing to protect a woman.

DYING FOR GOD

The Christian Soldier

> As He died to make men holy,
> Let us die to make men free. . . .
>
> —*"Battle Hymn of the Republic"*

A man who died to save was said to be loved. For the Christian male, Jesus was love. Jesus saves. But Jesus also saved others by dying himself. *The military was the secular form of Jesus.* Jesus in uniform. For many boys, the bribe of military rank, the faith in God's support, and the power of music felt, in combination, like a personal call to put his life on the line: "Onward, Christian Soldiers."

Pressure on a man to become a savior or protector is part of every religion. Hindu men see the male images of Vishnu, Shiva, Krishna; Buddhist men see Guatama Buddha; Christians see the male Christ; Moslems see Allah. . . . Priests, rabbis, and ministers are mostly men . . . always protectors.

The message of religion for boys is that there really is no choice but to save. In the Garden of Gethsemane, Jesus begged God to take from him the cup that represented his role as savior. The Lord Jesus was so distraught he sweated blood. God would not grant him permission to forfeit the cup—God said nothing. When, ultimately, Christ was to die, he felt betrayed ("My God, my God, why hast thou forsaken me?").

Theologians have debated whether or not Christ had a choice in playing his savior role: could he really have refused? Theoretically, of course, he could have; but God's approval symbolizes the approval of everything that is meaningful and, when everything that is meaningful is saying, "You have a role: to save," sure, you can turn it down, but . . .

Today, men are returning to their Gardens of Gethsemane, asking an old question, seeking the courage to find an answer for our times.

Gladiators and Their Virgins

During Roman times, the highlight of the religious holidays was the gladiatorial combats. Essentially these were slaughters of men—ranging from slaves (who hoped to be freed) to knights and nobles (who hoped to be heroes).[24] The slaughters were presided over by female deities: the Great Mother, Ceres, and Flora.[25] Solemn religious processions kicked off the games as our national anthem might introduce a football game. While males were the ones subject to death, the Vestal Virgins (who, you might guess, were not males) occupied seats of honor at the games.[26] The Vestal Virgins were to the gladiator what the cheerleader is to the football player: female support for male violence. *Both* were socialized to play their roles before what we would call the "age of consent."

Why did female deities bless violence against men? Because **the deeper purpose of violence against men was to prevent violence against women.** Both sexes wanted the protection that came when potential invaders, upon seeing the strength of their potential victims, chose another village to pillage.

ARE WE STILL PREPARING MEN TO BE DISPOSABLE?

Today, violence against women is rightly abhorred. But we call violence against men entertainment. Think of football, boxing, wrestling; or ice hockey, rodeos, and auto racing. All are games used to sugarcoat violence against men, originally in need of sugarcoating so "our team"—or "our society"—could bribe its best protectors to sacrifice themselves. Yet even today the violence against men in sports is still financed by our public education system; and by public subsidies of the stadiums in which sports teams play. Violence against men is not just called entertainment, it is also called education. We all support it. Every day.

The celebration of that violence can be seen in our naming of school teams after violent societies (Vikings, Aztecs, Trojans) or fierce animals (Tigers, Bears, Panthers). Even our cars are called Jaguar, Cherokee, Cougar, Fury, and Stealth. Imagine your daughter being picked up by a guy driving a Ford Fairy, a Dodge Daisy, or a Plymouth Pansy. . . . Or (if you're getting into this), imagine a grown man rooting for a team named not the Giants but the Munchkins; not the Atlanta Braves but the Atlanta Sensitives.

It is not coincidental that a professional football team is named after the Vikings. The Vikings used to enter competitions to see who could best split their male victim's body from head to groin. In cheering for the Vikings, we honor the process that educates men to sacrifice one anothers' bodies for appreciation. We keep the slave a slave.

Imagine how we would feel if I began this section saying, "Today, violence against women is rightly *applauded*." We would know I favored the death of women; when we applaud for violence against men, we favor the death of men. We do it because we have learned that the more effectively we prepare men to sacrifice themselves, the more we are protected. The unconscious translation of "our team winning" is "our society protected." We applaud violence against men and abhor violence against women because part of the purpose of violence against men is to protect women.

III. WHY WERE MEN SO VIOLENT AND WOMEN SO LOVING?

ARE MEN INHERENTLY VIOLENT?

Men often become *non*violent in societies that (1) have adequate amounts of food, (2) have adequate amounts of water, and (3) perceive themselves as isolated from attack. For example, the Tahitian men, the Minoan men on Crete, and the Central Malaysian Semai were nonviolent during the period in their history when all three of these conditions prevailed.[27]

When men were not needed to kill, women were less likely to select men who killed and men were less likely to kill. (Choosing men who killed was no more women's fault than killing was men's fault—both were necessary to survive.)

The beautiful princess rarely married the conscientious objector. Why? Few societies could afford to give their highest reward to a man who wouldn't kill. If men were *inherently* violent, there would be no need to create a social structure bribing men to be violent.

The ability to kill always required the vulnerability of being exposed to *being* killed. Male eligibility was created by vulnerability masked as invulnerability. Men have been both violent and vulnerable, but they are neither inherently violent nor inherently vulnerable. For the first time in human history a "family man" no longer has to be a "killer man."

WERE MATRIARCHIES MORE PEACEFUL?

Some historians are now suggesting that matriarchal societies were superior because men and women worked more in partnership and that the society tended to be more peaceful.[28] But that missed the point: the reason partnership models were developed in societies like Tahiti was not because the societies were patriarchal or matriarchal, but because they were unthreatened and self-sufficient.

Some historians are labeling these societies matriarchal because, for example, female gods were primary, not male gods. But **male gods were the primary gods when protection was the primary need** (the gods that protected were male, not female, because protection via killing was the male role). The sad part of this matriarchal labeling is that it makes male sacrifice look like male dominance and makes peace and partnership look like the responsibility of women rather than the outcome of adequate food and water and a good defense.

ARE WOMEN INHERENTLY LESS WARLIKE THAN MEN?

Throughout history, women in power have used a rationale similar to men's to send men to death with similar frequency and in similar numbers. For example, the drink Bloody Mary was named after Mary Tudor (Queen Mary I), who burned 300 Protestants at the stake; when Henry VIII's daughter, Elizabeth I, ascended to the throne, she mercilessly raped, burned, and pillaged Ireland at a time when Ireland was called the Isle of Saints and Scholars. When a Roman king died, his widow sent 80,000 men to their deaths.[29] If Columbus was an exploiter, we must remember that Queen Isabella helped to send him.

In recent years, the so-called Iron Ladies—Indira Gandhi, Golda Meir, and Margaret Thatcher—have all sent men to their deaths at rates not dissimilar to those of the average male leader, and in wars as wasteful to male life as Thatcher's involvement in the Falkland Islands War.

What has remained consistent throughout history is that whether or not the leaders were female or male, almost 100 percent of the troops they sacrificed in battle were male.* When women led, it was still men left dead. Equality was at the top—not at the bottom.

WHY DID MEN CREATE EMPIRES?

Empires are often considered the quintessential example of men's desire for power and conquest. It is ironic that *we blame men for creating empires while we all live in the empires men create.* But *why* did men create empires?

Empires were to countries what insurance policies are to individuals: a source of security. For example, as European countries saw themselves as vulnerable to attack, empires became buffer zones—a good offense became the best defense. Similarly, if famine hit their country food could be obtained from the empire more easily than from the enemy.

Why did people invade countries that weren't a threat to them? Think of why Europeans invaded the native American Indians—who were never a threat to the Europeans. When a group within a country felt oppressed, it frequently fled, found another territory, and killed those gentler people who dared resist. The people who did the killing—and the people who were killed—were men, but the people who benefited were men and women.

The accumulated wars that eventually led to the United States are another example of men being less important than property. Men *died* for property; women *lived* on the property that was often their husband's grave.

Put another way, **major powers have become major powers via the deaths of boys.** Because boys died, empires can be seen as a

---

* Even in Israel, the combat role for women is optional, but obligatory for males; and the woman who volunteers for combat is, in practice, rare. See chapter 5, "War Hero or War Slave?"

male form of subservience; because others lived, empires can also be seen as the male contribution to survival.

How Long Does It Take Male Violence to Change?

How long does it take a firmly embedded male killer mentality to change? The Vikings (the head-through-groin choppers) are considered as ruthless as any. But after the Vikings conquered England, Englishwomen found the men who killed with axes attractive; soon wedding bells were ringing. Within two generations, instead of razing villages, they were raising children; instead of destroying the property of foreigners, they were planting on their own property. Within two generations, the Vikings had turned swords into plowshares.

More recently, Japan has taken less than two generations to turn swords into stock shares. The males are still performers, but not via violence. Why not? Both cultures reinterpreted what it would take to survive—and the males adapted accordingly. What is consistent among men is not violence but men's willingness to protect. When they can protect by killing enemies, they kill enemies; when men can protect by "making a killing" on Wall Street, they do that. Men's underlying motivator is neither swords nor plowshares . . . it's adapting to love and adapting to approval.

Are Women Nature's Civilizing Balance?

It is often said that women are a civilizing balance to the innately warlike male. **By taking care of the killing for women it could be said that men civilized women.** When survival was the issue, men killing to protect what women bore was the male form of nurturance.[30] It was men's contribution to the civilizing balance. (Later, as money was required for survival, the raising of money was the male "financial womb." Whether killing in war or making a killing on Wall Street, "making a killing" was men protecting what women bore.)

When a woman says she wants male sensitivity and then falls in love with the football player, surgeon, or rock star, she gives the male the message that he'll get the most love when he is most *un*balanced—most focused on his work, most focused on becoming a hero. Had she fallen in love with a sensitive nurse, an altruistic artist, or an empathetic cabdriver, she would have provided a real vote for civilizing men. She would have put her love where her mouth is.

Societies in which the man who "makes a killing" is most lovable create the male tragedy: they disconnect men from love to earn love. . . .

IV. DISCONNECTING FROM LOVE TO EARN LOVE: THE MALE TRAGEDY

SELF-ESTEEM AND MASCULINITY

In Sparta, boys were moved into barracks at the age of seven.[31] They would be forced to play "games" like "steal the cheese from the altar." To get the cheese, they had to run through a gauntlet and endure flogging so fierce that some died shortly afterward from concussions and blood gushing out of open wounds.[32]

This stealing of cheese was a perfect metaphor: the constant plagues and famines forced the military to defend what little food citizens had and to steal what it did not have. Stealing required the courage to risk death.

Why were the boys removed from home at age 7? **The less a boy valued intimacy, life, and loving, the more he would allow himself to be disposable.** We bribed him to do this by offering him respect—actually, *conditional* respect that we called "love" when he met the conditions. The catch-22 was that the process it took to get love disconnected him from love.

Disposability training started at birth. With the penis. Studies of male circumcision find that the more a society needed hunters and warriors in order to survive, the harsher were its procedures for circumcision of boy babies.[33]

The problem for the women these men married was that death training rarely included courses on "Intimacy in Marriage."

And the problem for fathers? . . .

DID FATHERS WHO DISCONNECTED FROM THEIR SONS REALLY LOVE THEIR SONS?: THE STORY OF THESEUS

When King Aegeus of Athens was about to become a father, he said he did not want to see his son until Theseus was stronger than all others.[34] Why? King Aegeus feared that a pampered prince could not protect his people. So Aegeus deprived himself of seeing Theseus until Theseus could lift a massive boulder that no one else could lift and then risk his life by slaying the Minotaur that threatened to destroy the people of his kingdom.

What was the importance of Theseus's having to risk his life—as in slaying dragons? **It demonstrated the purpose of power—the subservience of the life of the king to the life of those served by the king.** A good father was expected to prepare his son to be disposable.

A good Stage I dad was to prepare his son not to feel loved until his son could protect and save. He demonstrated this by not showing his son his own love until he had adequately trained the son to replace him as a savior.

Is it possible that all my words are just rationalizations for King Aegeus being a truly uncaring dad? Well, after Theseus had slain the Minotaur, he forgot to put up a white flag as a signal that he was still alive. Aegeus thought that his son had perished. His grief was so deep that he killed himself.[35]

"When You Comin' Home, Dad?"

To experience the male tragedy in its present form, listen to Harry Chapin's song "Cat's in the Cradle." The son asks, "When you comin' home, Dad?" The dad responds, "I don't know when." Yet the father's yearning for his son is so deep that the *moment* the dad was no longer preoccupied with providing for his son, he reached out for his son's companionship. Unfortunately, the pressure on the dad is relieved only when the son has a job of his own. So the son responds, "My new job's a hassle and the kids have the flu."

Historically, **the obligations of dads deprive dads of love while the obligations of moms provide moms with love.** Deprived of genuine love, dads are deprived of genuine power. Ironically, the son had ached for connection with his dad so intensely that he vowed, "Some day I'm gonna be like him. . . ."

Dead Poets Society

Not understanding the Stage I father's obligation to prepare his son to replace him (to "kill" him) creates a deep father-son wound.

If we review a video of the film *Dead Poets Society*, we can see how the son hated his Stage I dad and loved his Stage II teacher (Robin Williams) because he did not understand three things: first, how his dad's sacrifices had created the freedom for him to explore Stage II values; second, how the discipline his dad instilled was part of what the son would need to have the strength and security from which to pursue a Stage II life; third, that his dad's discipline was not only his dad's way of loving him but also his dad's way of preparing him to find a woman's love in the best way his dad knew how.

The father, of course, did not understand that he was discouraging his son from pursuing the very freedom he had created for his son. But the son can never be at peace with his father—and therefore himself—until he understands that his dad's best intent was to teach his son how to give and receive love.

The male tragedy, then, is that showing our love by providing takes us away from showing our love by connecting. Thus, loving our sons has taken us away from loving our sons.

V. MALE SUBSERVIENCE TO FEMALE BEAUTY

> The woman is life, and the man is the servant of life. . . .
>
> —JOSEPH CAMPBELL, explaining why women are in the center of a tribal dance, why they control the dance, and why men dance around the women.[36]

BEAUTY POWER: THE BIBLICAL STORY OF RACHEL AND JACOB*

Jacob lived with his uncle Laban. Uncle Laban had two daughters: Leah, who was homely, and Rachel, who was beautiful. Jacob fell in love with—guess who? But when Jacob asked for his beautiful cousin Rachel's hand in marriage, his uncle required that he work seven years for him to earn Rachel as his wife.

---

* The biblical quotes are all from Genesis. See endnotes.

When Jacob completed the seven years, the wedding took place. But when Jacob's bride removed her veil, Jacob realized his uncle had tricked him by substituting his homely cousin, Leah. Jacob was told he must work yet another seven years to earn the beautiful Rachel. Must he remain married to the homely Leah? Yes. And she will remain his first, the most-honored, wife. So it cost Jacob fourteen years of working for Uncle Laban to earn the right to continue supporting both Rachel and Leah.

Rachel, however, could not have sons, so she told Jacob to have sex with her maidservant so she could have sons whom Rachel would raise as her own.[37] Leah then got Jacob to create two more sons with *her* maidservant. When the process ended, Jacob was supporting four women, twelve sons, and a daughter.[38]

Why is God blessing bigamy, sex with maidservants, and first-cousin incest? Because, in each case, **what God blessed created offspring who were protected. Morality was not the issue. Immortality was.** As a result of the first-cousin incest, for example, instead of Uncle Laban's family line dying out, twelve sons were born, from whom came the twelve tribes of the Jewish people.[39]

How did God get Jacob to support four women and thirteen children? The answer tells us a lot about the purposes of female beauty. **Rachel's beauty served as a magnet to get Jacob to create offspring with three women who might otherwise be left out of the process of passing on their genes**: one woman who was homely, and two of lower-class status. By having sex with a *reliable* man of a higher class, the maidservants were creating offspring who were likely to be protected.

God did not bless Rachel and Jacob with sons right away because that would have given Jacob little incentive to have children with the maidservants, thus Rachel's beauty would have stopped short of getting many different women involved in the process of raising children with a man who was hardworking and successful enough to support all of them.

Beauty was God's gift—or the gift of the species—to Rachel; it was meant to be used by Rachel to serve God—or serve the species. When a person served God, then, he or she was serving humans. When God gave a blessing, that was God's way (or society's way) of instructing humans as to how to continue surviving: by having children. This is why the first of 613 commandments (*mitzvoth*) in the Torah is "Be fruitful and multiply."[40] What I began to see as I researched this chapter was how biology and the Bible shared the same first commandment: "Be fruitful and multiply."[41]

Beauty and the Beast *as the Modern-Day Version of Rachel and Jacob*

Beauty and the Beast is to fable what Rachel and Jacob are to the Bible. Both Rachel's beauty and Beauty's beauty are used to attract a man who will save her family from starvation. The man who does this might be a beast to the world, but to the woman, he becomes a prince.

Before Jacob could become a husband or a beast could become a prince, they had to be willing to give the fruits of their labor to the beautiful woman's family with no guarantee the beautiful woman would marry them, or that they would get along, or that she would still be beautiful when they had completed the process.

Are there modern-day remnants of this? Yes. The man buying the woman dinners, drinks, movie tickets, flowers, and an engagement ring which the woman is not required to return if they do not get married. Both historically and currently, the woman learned to ask for guarantees, the man learned to take risks.

This was not the woman's fault. In Stage I, she needed guarantees—guarantees were functional for her children to survive. But in Stage II, she needs preparation for risk-taking to survive. **In Stage I, the beast became a prince by offering the beautiful woman guarantees; the Stage II prince is the man who does not seduce the woman with guarantees.** He is secure enough to be the prince within; she is free to find a man who is a prince inside exactly because he did not become a prince of bribes.

WHY WAS A BEAUTIFUL YOUNG WOMAN SUCH A BIG DEAL?

Beauty was a sign of health and reproductive capability; thus, a beautiful woman historically had wide hips (for childbearing), body symmetry (indicating no deformities), hair and teeth that weren't falling out (indicating health). And she was young—at the beginning of her fertile years.

Society needed to reinforce men's biological dependency on female beauty for the same reasons it needed to make women dependent on male income: dependency created an incentive to marry. A man who was addicted to a woman's beauty, youth, and sex would temporarily "lose his mind"—he would make the irrational decision to support her for the rest of his life. Female beauty, then, can be thought of as nature's marketing tool: the way of marketing a woman for the survival of her genes.[42] Which is why female beauty is the world's most potent drug.

The ideal beauty varied . . . but there was always an ideal of beauty. Throughout history, the only constant about female beauty and female sex was that they were more valued than male beauty and male sex. Especially in Stage I cultures. **We have selected for women who consciously or unconsciously learned that their beauty and their sex were worth a man's labor, money, life. No, many men's lives.** Beauty power and sex power are parts of the female collective unconscious. Not every woman wants to give up these powers.

VI. IMMORALITY . . . OR . . . IMMORTALITY?

Were sexual freedom and premarital sex condemned because they sacrificed morality or sacrificed immortality? The Bible contains some astonishing answers. . . .

WAS RELIGION CONCERNED WITH IMMORALITY . . . OR . . . IMMORTALITY?

DAUGHTERS RAPE

DRUNK   DAD,

SAY GOD APPROVES

Why would the above "headline" make William Randolph Hearst and Rupert Murdoch blush and yet lead to Lot and his daughters receiving God's blessing? The Bible explains, "One day the older daughter said to the younger, 'Our father is old, and there is no man around who will lie with us. . . . Let's get our father to drink wine and then lie with him and preserve our family line through our father."[43] So, on two consecutive nights, both daughters got their father drunk, waited until he fell asleep, and had sex with him *without his being aware of it* ("He was not aware of it when she lay down or when she got up"[44]). They each became pregnant.

Were Lot and his daughters punished for incest or rape? (If a father had sex with his daughter while she was asleep, we'd call it rape.) No. They were blessed. By God. So blessed that both their sons became leaders of a people. Rather than feeling ashamed about the incest, not only was the first of the sons, Moab, named *after* the incest (Moab comes from the Hebrew meaning "from father"[45]), but so were the peoples of which he was the father: the Moabites. Why? The drunkenness, rape, and father-daughter incest led to the preservation of a family line.*

WHY PREMARITAL SEX, SEXUAL FREEDOM, AND HOMOSEXUALITY WERE CONDEMNED

Premarital sex and sexual freedom were condemned because the children they led to had no way of being protected. Masturbation, homosexuality, and sodomy (as in anal sex, oral sex, or sex with animals) were also condemned because none of them even led to children.

In contrast, affairs, polygyny, sex with maidservants, and even incest could be sanctioned—*if* they led to protected offspring; if they did not, they were also condemned. **Principles of immortality were clothed in the garb of immorality.** This might be called the "Immortality Rule."

Giving permission to homosexuality in Stage I involved the same problem as giving permission to masturbation: it was permission for sexual pleasure without a price. Think about it. A homosexual experience might mean two hours of sexual pleasure. The consequences?—two hours of sexual pleasure. A heterosexual experi-

---

* Scholars who contend the daughters were hopeless sinners do so on the argument that the daughters could have found other men with whom to continue the family line. Even these scholars seem willing to ignore the "immorality" if the immortality of the family line is guaranteed. See *The Pentateuch and Haftorahs*, Second Edition (London: Soncino Press, 1979), edited by Dr. J. H. Hertz, C.H., Late Chief Rabbi of the British Empire, p. 69, note 31.

ence might also mean two hours of sexual pleasure. But the consequences?—eighteen years of responsibility. In brief, *hetero-sexuality* was a bad deal!

Homophobia was a Stage I society's way of not allowing men to even *think* about having sex with anyone other than a woman. **Homophobia reflected an unconscious societal fear that homo-sexuality was a better deal than heterosexuality for the indi-vidual. Homophobia was like OPEC calling nations wimps if they bought oil from a more reasonably priced source.** It was the society's way of giving men no option but to pay full price for sex.

Homosexual *relationships* promised more than sex-for-free; they promised relationships for free, companionship for free, love for free. All free of the cost of feeding offspring. Since homosex-uality was the greatest temptation to avoid reproduction and, therefore, threaten survival, it was the primary candidate for the death penalty. (When death wasn't exacted literally, it was often exacted via ostracism.) So the Old Testament demanded the death penalty for male homosexuals. As did many Roman emperors, Spanish inquisitors, English monarchs, and some American colo-nists. Thus, homophobia.

The fear that homosexuality would tempt people away from het-erosexuality seems to have left us with a more intense fear of homosexuality today than of other forms of sex without offspring. For example, if we discover someone has masturbated, we don't say, as soon as their back is turned, "He's a masturbator." But when a man has sex with another man, we say, "He's a homosex-ual." The taboo against homosexuality tends to make the person secondary to his or her sexual expression, just as racism makes the person secondary to his or her race.

All of these fears might have been functional for survival in Stage I, but they are dysfunctional for love in Stage II. And ho-mophobia is also dysfunctional for Stage II survival—it teaches the objectification of a human, a prerequisite for killing humans, which, with nuclear technology, threatens survival. One trademark of a Stage II society, then, is the degree to which it frees itself from the Stage I fear of homosexuality, from the discrimination against homosexuals that is its consequence, and from the fear of loving our neighbor as ourself.

WASN'T POLYGNY AN EXAMPLE OF WOMEN AS MEN'S PROPERTY?

In no country at no period of time, were women safe from . . . the insistence that their bodies existed only in relation to man, for his pleasure and progeny.

—The Women's History of the World[46]

Academic feminism often equates mistresses, concubines, and polygyny* (a man having more than one wife) with male dominance. Once we understand the Immortality Rule, though, we can move to a deeper understanding of why God blessed the many wives and concubines of David—as in David and Goliath. As a king, David had enough wealth and power to support more than one woman—so why should other women miss out? Polygyny did *not* mean *any* man could have many wives—it meant a poor man would be deprived of a wife so a woman could have a rich man. No one took pity on the man who was poor for being deprived of love.

Polygyny, then, was a system by which the rich man, by having more than one wife, prevented a woman from being stuck with a poor man. Polygyny was a form of socialism for the poor woman: the rich man was taxed to help the poor woman. **Polygyny was to some Mormon women what the government is to some modern women—a substitute husband.**

Polygyny was man-made religious rules saving poor women at the expense of poor men. But polygyny was not a conspiracy against men. It was an outgrowth of Stage I survival needs. It was not designed to help anyone get their intimacy needs met.

POLYGYNY AND CHRISTIANITY: CHRIST AND HIS NUNS

The Christian sanctioning of polygyny takes the form of nuns actually "marrying" Christ—down to the taking of vows and the wearing of a wedding ring to symbolize the union. The polygynous marriage between Christ and nuns is ideal from the nuns' perspec-

---

* Poly*gamy* is often inaccurately used to mean a man having more than one wife, but it actually means *either* sex having more than one spouse; only poly*gyny* means a man having more than one wife.

tive because, while Christ assumes the protection of millions of women, the nuns take vows of celibacy. **Christ's wives would not have been celibate if polygyny's primary purpose was the satisfaction of male sexual desires. Polygyny's primary purpose was female protection by the best male saviors.**

Christ, then, is the superhuman male role model: protection, but no sexual demands; the ability to be a breadwinner—or bread multiplier—should that be needed in times of famine; a willingness to die to save us from our transgressions. Priests were the human manifestation—protection without sexual demands, listening without needing to burden the woman with his problems. The problem for the everyday man was that if he listened to women all day he would have left his family starving and, if he offered celibacy, the species would not have survived. The everyday man's sexual energy was stimulated from everywhere before marriage, and then channeled into monogamy after marriage.

The church "patriarchy," then, did what patriarchies did best—protect women and help men protect women. Which is one reason more women than men *attend* church. And why the more traditional the church, the more it expects men to play its savior roles. In these senses, "patriarchy" served women more than men.

WHY WAS DIVORCE CONSIDERED IMMORAL AND ILLEGAL?

As a rule, when women had enough food, water, and shelter so that they could live independently of men without starving, divorce was made legal and considered moral.[47] And therefore it was common. This was the case among middle-class Americans since the 1960s, the !Kung Bushmen of southern Africa's Kalahari Desert, the Yoruba of West Africa, the Hadza of Tanzania, and the Tamang of Nepal. Even in societies that married off every woman possible and prevented divorces for the masses, women who had economic security often ignored marriage—from Cleopatra to the empress Wa of the Wei dynasty of China to Elizabeth I in the sixteenth century or Catherine of Russia in the eighteenth century.[48]

The laws and religious rules, both made by men, almost always gave women the primary protection even when a man might have wanted a divorce. Calling the taboo against divorce "God's will" ("What God has joined together, let no man put asunder") was society's way of making that guarantee iron-clad for women. **Marriage-as-sacrament was the female's "divine right."** At least for as long as women needed it to prevent starvation.

The lesson? If men and women want the freedom to divorce, the socialization process must require women to take care of themselves from as early an age as it requires that of its men.

WHY WAS SEX SO FREE IN TAHITI, SO REPRESSED IN THE MIDDLE EAST, AND SO MIXED UP IN AMERICA?

Sex in Free Supply, Tahiti Style

What happened to sex when there was plenty of food and water and no invaders—so women didn't need to keep sex in short supply until they found a protector? The Tahitians possessed these conditions of abundance from the moment humans settled there. Tahitian parents actually taught their children sex at an early age, as did other elders.[49] When they became teenagers, the parents encouraged the children to enjoy sex with anyone they happened to meet and be attracted to. Even group sex was fine. The more lovers the children had, the more the parents were pleased.[50] Because children were easily cared for, pregnancy before a marriage was celebrated as a sign of fertility. Tahitian religion had no rules suggesting sex was sinful. Sex was considered a combination of pleasure, skill, and sport.

Within a century of Cook's discovery of these islands, though, Westerners imposed their concepts of morality, repressing sexuality. The Westerners, by not understanding *why* they considered sex immoral, sapped the spirit of the Tahitians. As Ian Campbell wrote in *Lost Paradise*, "Those who have nothing to live for, die. Within three generations, the population of Tahiti plummeted from more than 140,000 to less than 5,000."[51]

Sex in Short Supply, OPEC Style

We often think of countries that require women to wear a veil as keeping women powerless. In Muslim countries, the purdah keeps female beauty hidden, only to be shown to the selected few—who were invariably good providers. This prevented the average man from even *looking* at the average woman until he promised to protect and provide for her and her children for life (i.e., marriage). And until the man does this, he is deprived of her (and she of him) while traveling, eating, worshiping, etc. Her love, her nurturance, her affection, her cheers, *even her smile*, were made conditional—until he demonstrated willingness to provide, protect, and risk death for her. This got almost *all* women, not just the beautiful ones, protected by someone.

In the Middle East, female sex and beauty are to Middle Eastern men what oil and gas are to Americans: the shorter the supply, the higher the price. The more women "gave" sex away for free, or for a small payment, the more the value of every woman's prize would be undermined . . . which is why anger toward prostitution, purdah violation (removing the veil), and pornography runs so deep, especially among women. It is also why parents told daughters, "Don't be cheap." "Cheap" sex floods the market.

Think of this in reverse form: If women had to promise to provide for a man for a lifetime before he removed his veil and showed her his smile, would we think of this as a system of female privilege?

To this day, when we talk about someone giving sexual favors, we never speak of the man's sexual favor; therefore only women expect something *in return*. Billions of dollars are spent by men every year to uncover women's bodies, while men who expose theirs are put in prison. We call her exposure a centerfold, his is exhibitionism; we give her money, him a prison sentence. Her sexual power meant sexual payments. He learned to earn more to pay more; so he was surprised when he was told his need to earn more was a reflection of his *greater* power.

Sex in Alternating Supply, American Style

In the United States, when feminists in the late 1960s believed women's economic freedom would lead to women's economic abundance, they advocated sexual freedom. When it was discovered that divorces led to economic obligation, feminists, fundamentalists, and women's magazines all moved toward closing off sexual freedom. Headlines in *Cosmopolitan* read "Sex: Make Him *Earn* It"[52] even *before* the herpes scare. A careful analysis of the sexual revolution's decline helps us see why, if it hadn't been herpes and AIDS, it would have been something else.[53]

This need for economic security preceding female sexual open-
ness is probably unconsciously reinforced by our tradition of a man
taking a woman out for dinner and drinks *first*. The more traditional the woman, the more dinners, the more drinks, and the less
she feels sexually open until she receives a commitment—in essence, a commitment from him providing for life.

VII. DID MEN OPPRESS WOMEN?

DID MEN TREAT WOMEN AS PROPERTY?

It is only the understanding that men's lives were subservient to
property that allows us to reconcile women's combined status as
equal to property and "on a pedestal." When we hear that men
treated women as property, we rarely hear that men were expected to die before their property got hurt—that men's lives
were, in essence, subservient to property. Even in nineteenth-
century America, federal law required that if a wife committed a
crime, the *husband* would be tried for *her* crime and *he* would be
put in prison if *she* was found guilty.[54] Similarly, if the family went
in debt, only he went to debtor's prison.

Throughout history, both sexes were property in various ways.
Mayan boys indentured themselves to their fathers-in-law; in biblical times, Jacob indentured himself to Uncle Laban; in America,
Johnny indentured himself to Uncle Sam. . . . In almost every
society that had to defend its land, boys died defending it and,
before they were old enough to know better, were socialized to be
proud to die.

In America, tens of thousands of immigrants earned passage
as indentured servants. More than 90 percent of the indentured
servants were men. The men initially assumed slavelike status
for a seven-year period.[55] Some were single men who hoped to
earn enough money to become eligible for marriage. Others had
wives still in Europe. Think about this. What could be a greater
demonstration of love than a man enslaving himself for a woman
without any of the benefits of her cooking, cleaning, or companionship? Many of these men didn't do this just on Mother's Day—
they did it every day for between seven years and life. Only

men—the "unromantic sex"—did this unilaterally for women. But . . .

Many indentured men eventually extended their indenture to fourteen years or a lifetime to bring their families over. These men became, in essence, male slaves.

In Europe, between the time of the Roman Empire and the Middle Ages, it was common for men to need financial protection—so they sold themselves to lords. A ceremony developed involving the vassal taking vows, the count asking if the vassal wished to be "his man," and both kissing to seal their vows. The vassal, though, was *required* to do one thing for the owner that women rarely do for their husbands: consider it an honor to die to protect him.[56]

If men didn't have the power, why was property often passed down through men? Because men were responsible to provide property. Property was one of men's contributions to eligibility just as fertility and children were among women's contributions to eligibility. Men had property rights to take care of property responsibilities. Social pressure got most men to provide a wife with as much property as he himself had; and the taboo on divorce prevented a woman from losing the property before her husband did.

Women, then, were both equal to property and more than equal to men—and, therefore, "on a pedestal."

IF FEMALES WERE SO VALUED, WHY DID MOTHERS KILL BABY GIRLS AND NOT BABY BOYS?

Parents—and especially single *mothers*—sometimes killed female infants but not males. Why not? When starvation threatened, families had more need for boys to plow fields and produce food than for girls to produce more children who would consume more food. If boys were needed for war, the society sometimes disposed of the girls as infants and disposed of the boys in war. Why dispose of the girls at all? If the war wiped out women's economic support system of men, sometimes girl infants were "aborted" until women could get supported.

The issue was not female versus male. It was whether the female or male role was more needed at a given time. The solution? Socializing both sexes to play both roles.

DIDN'T MEN OPPRESS WOMEN BY DEVELOPING MALE-ONLY CLUBS?

Both sexes had single-sex clubs in the area of that sex's responsibility.

Female-Only Clubs

All known societies are ruled by men, who control and profit by women's reproductive capabilities.

—ENCYCLOPEDIA OF FEMINISM[57]

In most cultures the birthing process was a female-only club. Men were completely excluded.[58] Even women who were strangers were included while the husband who was the dad was excluded.

Both sexes, then, had single-sex clubs—each in their area of dominance. Or their area of responsibility. Each sex's area of responsibility was its area of business: women had women-only business clubs; men had men-only business clubs. The difference? We said male-only clubs were "proof" of male bonding, male dominance, and male chauvinism. And the female-only clubs? We said they were proof of women's nurturing instinct and men's failure to be involved with their children.

The First Men Admitted to the Female-Only Clubs Were . . .

The first men admitted to the female-only birthing clubs were not the dads, but the doctors. The male doctors were admitted only in the nineteenth century after they had developed anesthesia to reduce women's pain and breech-birth techniques to save women's lives. Husbands, who could offer only love and support to their wives, were still excluded. The choice to include the doctor and exclude the husband was a powerful message to men as to the female desire for a savior over the female desire for her husband's love and psychological support. The practice of including even female *strangers* before the husband deepens our understanding of the discounting of men-as-loved-ones, of men-as-dads.

If husbands had the power, how could they be excluded at all? If women were men's property, why were men not allowed even to be near their "property"? If male institutions offered male privilege, why did hospitals ("male institutions") exclude husbands from delivery rooms until the 1970s? If patriarchy were a male conspiracy to control women's reproductive processes, female-only birthing clubs that excluded men were an odd way of orchestrating a male conspiracy.

Did men *want* to be admitted? Well, on the one hand, once women said, "Men, get involved," millions of fathers immediately joined, many discovering the happiest moments of their lives. On the other hand, if men had really wanted to be admitted before that they could have made it an issue—and they didn't. Why not? The division of labor led to a division of roles and a division of interests. Which is why all this male-only club, female-only club stuff is not a result of a conspiracy by either sex, but a result of the division of roles.

Both sexes were resistant to change when their traditional area of responsibility—or dominance—was threatened (even when the help might save their lives).

Today women are often credited with being the creators of life, men labeled as being destroyers of life. I believe it is more accurate and compassionate to understand that both sexes were working to *promote* life—women risked death to *create* life; men risked death to *protect* life.

WASN'T WITCH BURNING PROOF THAT WE CARED LESS ABOUT WOMEN THAN ABOUT MEN?

When we think of burning witches at the stake, we often think of the Salem witch trials and men burning women. In fact, the Salem witch trials were a direct result of two *girls* who experienced epileptic convulsions and blamed their convulsions on the "witchcraft" of several women in Salem.[59] The Salem witch trials were a result of the community believing the girls without question and trying to save the girls.

When a community condemned a woman as a witch, they did not believe they were condemning a woman: they believed this woman was a nonwoman—that she was *supernatural*. The very purpose of the trial was to discover whether she was "in fact" a nonwoman. She increased her chances of becoming a nonwoman if she did not play the contribute-to-survival game: if she had never been married, was a midwife who had attended bad births or given birth herself to deformed children, was a heretic, or practiced forms of healing that led to deaths.[60] She multiplied her chances if she became an outspoken advocate of any of these practices.

Ten to 20 percent of witches were men[61] (often called warlocks[62]). Men who were Quakers—who refused to sacrifice themselves in war—were burned at the stake. As were homosexual men.[63] A "faggot" was literally a bunch of sticks that people tossed into the fire; it was less literally a heretic that people burned at the stake.[64] Often that "heretic" was a homosexual.[65] Witches (females who wouldn't reproduce) and homosexuals (males who wouldn't reproduce) were both burned.

Why were artists and writers often condemned? In part, because writing and art got people to question all this. But more importantly, **artists, sculptors, and writers were also condemned because they often gained this freedom to create by not supporting a family.** And because many homosexuals did not have to support a family to begin with, they could become writers and artists—thus putting homosexuals in double jeopardy.

Being an artist or being gay *was not in itself* the problem. When a gay man added to an institution's ability to protect its citizens— for example, by becoming a priest, minister, or rabbi, or otherwise adding to the grandeur of religion as Michelangelo did by painting the Sistine Chapel[66]—he could hope to be accepted. Similarly, in the old Soviet Union, the artist had to add to the grandeur of the state. Even shamans, witch doctors, or oracles were permitted as long as they were perceived as adding an additional layer to the community's protection.

VIII. SO, WAS IT A MALE-DOMINATED, PATRIARCHAL, AND SEXIST WORLD?

I govern the Athenians, my wife governs me.

—THEMISTOCLES, 528 TO 462 B.C.[67]

PATRIARCHY VS. MATRIARCHY: GOVERNMENT STRUCTURE VS. FAMILY STRUCTURE

You can cut off a man's head if a man be a bachelor, sir; but if he be a married man, no; for a married man is a woman's; for to cut off a married man's head is to cut off a woman's head, and I cannot cut off a woman's head.

—SHAKESPEARE IN *MEASURE FOR MEASURE*

When we say we lived in a patriarchy, we think of living under a male-dominated government or power structure. We forget that the family had at least as much power as the government in people's everyday life, and that the family was female dominated. We forget that it too was a power structure. As we have seen, though, almost every woman had a primary role in the female-dominated family structure; only a small percentage of men had a primary role in the male-dominated governmental and religious structures.

Although a man's home was more likely to be his mortgage than his castle, it has always been a characteristic of men that they give lip service to their dominance even as another part of them is aware of their subservience. . . .

If taking on a wife for life in an institution called marriage were a sign of male privilege, why did "husband" derive from the Germanic "house" and the Old Norse for "bound" or "bondage"?[68] Why did it also come from words meaning "a male kept for breeding," "one who tills the soil," and "the male of the pair of lower animals."[69] Conversely, if marriage were as awful for women as many feminists claim, why is it the centerpiece of female fantasies in myths and legends of the past, or romance novels and soap operas of the present?

Spartan boys who were deprived of their families were deprived, not privileged. Boys deprived of women's love until they risked their lives at work or war were also deprived—or dead. Training boys to kill boys was considered moral when it led to survival, immoral only when it threatened survival. In these respects, "patriarchy" created male deprivation and male death, not male privilege.

In any way that is meaningful, though, we have never lived solely in a patriarchy or a matriarchy but in a combined patriarchy *and* matriarchy within each society. There was not male dominance but male *and* female dominance—a division of dominance that reflected the division of roles—each sex "dominant" in the area in which they had responsibilities and risked death—dominant where they were also subservient.

Like male privileges, female privileges (e.g., to be protected without killing or being killed) were the rewards of a role well followed. Both sexes were rewarded with "identity" when they followed well, punished with invisibility when they failed, death if they protested. The paradox of masculinity was that the men who followed best were called leaders. In fact, they were not really leaders, but followers—of a program called leadership.

All of this can no more be called only patriarchy or male dominance than matriarchy or female dominance. In fact, it was neither. And both.

HOW CAN PATRIARCHY AND MATRIARCHY BE DEFINED?

How, then, can patriarchy be defined? Perhaps it can best be defined as the male area of dominance, responsibility, and subservience in a culture, reinforced by both sexes for the purpose of serving both sexes' survival needs.

How can matriarchy be defined? As the female area of dominance, responsibility, and subservience in a culture, reinforced by both sexes for the purpose of serving both sexes' survival needs.

But patriarchy is now too associated with defining men as evil to ever be used without that connotation. My suggestion: eliminate its use. When describing a society explain the roles both sexes played to keep its members alive. Then we uncover diversity rather than impose a conspiracy.

A flaw of feminism is the assumption that dominance and sexism was a one-way street. Feminism, in this sense, was a very traditional movement: it retained the underlying belief that men were responsible, knew what was going on, women were not. Which, aside from being untrue, implies women are inherently inferior or stupid. An ironic position for the feminist movement. Perhaps as important, though, the belief that men were responsible for women's bondage was the flip side of the belief that her prince would come to rescue her. In fact, both sexes were bound to do that which kept the next generation alive.

IX. OUR GENETIC HERITAGE VS. OUR GENETIC FUTURE

"Genetics be damned for the curse which remains, and praised for the fact that we, as human beings, also remain."[70]

Our genetic heritage is in conflict with our genetic future. **In the past, choosing the killer male could be said to have led to the "survival of the fittest." In the future, with nuclear technology, choosing the killer male leads to the potential destruction of everyone.** In the past, survival, marriage, and the family *all* required the killer male. In the future, survival, marriage, and the family will require the communicative male. For the first time in human history, what it takes to survive as a species is compatible with what it takes to love.

However, is it wise to violate what has been natural for millions of years? If it is wise, is it possible? And if it is possible, how do we do it?

THE IMPORTANT QUESTION IS NOT "IS IT NATURAL?" BUT "IS IT FUNCTIONAL?"

We tend to consider it helpful to reinforce what is natural. However, if a baby is born with a handicap, it might not be helpful to say, "Your handicap is natural, so we'll teach you how to increase it!" Yet, that's what we do with men's aggressiveness and women's passivity. We teach both sexes how to increase their handicaps.

If it is biologically proven that women are born with more passivity than are men, then the only relevant question is, "Will that be functional for the type of future we desire?" **If it is not functional, then the greater the biological propensity, the greater the need for change.** If female passivity is proven innate, then that increases the need for female assertiveness training. If male aggressiveness is ingrained, that increases our need for male assertiveness training (not aggressiveness training).

Biology is only the best hint as to what was functional in the past but not necessarily about what will be in the future. The most empowering question we can ask about the future is *not* "What is the future and how do we adapt?" but "How do we want our future to be and how do we adapt?"

IS THERE HOPE?

If even chimpanzees—with genes almost identical to humans'—have more aggressive males than females, is there hope for humans changing ourselves before we kill ourselves? Yes. Our hope lies in the instinct to adapt.

Within all of us, males and females, is the potential for killer-protector and the potential for nurturer-connector.[71] When Vikings got approval for being nurturer-connectors rather than killer-protectors, they soon adapted and became nurturer-connectors. The change was not impossible because killing-to-protect was just their method of adapting to what gave them approval.

Conversely, within each female is the potential for aggressiveness: females competing to see a rock star are more aggressive than males competing to see a rock star. What runs deeper than our propensity for aggressiveness or passivity is our ability to adapt to what makes us survive: to live in Beverly Hills or a concentration camp . . . to be an ambassador one day or a hostage the next. . . .

HOW DO WE ADAPT?

When we select certain types of men and women to have children with, each child becomes a vote for the type of man and woman we want. The type of man or woman we select is the most important vote any human casts. It is a vote that begins with the type of men and women we cheer for and ogle . . . continues with the type we marry . . . ends with the type with whom we create children. (Next to that, all our parenting skills are secondary.)

How do we get males to develop the nurturer-connector within them? When cheerleaders cheer for the men who listen rather than the men who play "smashface" . . . when men protest being selected for their ability to win more than their ability to nurture.

Women will continue choosing the updated version of the killer male—men who "make a killing" in their profession—until men protest. Men will not protest until they see the connection between that obligation and their earlier deaths from heart attacks, cancer, suicide, and all fifteen leading causes of death. In brief, men will not protest until they see how continuing to play their Stage I role is making them the disposable sex. Here's how. . . .

PART II

THE "GLASS CELLARS" OF THE DISPOSABLE SEX

CHAPTER 4

The Death Professions: "My Body, *Not* My Choice"

"Men are not human beings, they are human doings."[1]

We frequently hear that women are segregated into low-paying, dead-end jobs in poor work environments such as factories. But when *The Jobs Related Almanac*[2] ranked 250 jobs from best to worst based on a *combination* of salary, stress, work environment, outlook, security, and physical demands, they found that twenty-four of the twenty-five worst jobs were almost-all-male jobs.* Some examples: truck driver, sheet-metal worker, roofer, boiler-maker, lumberjack, carpenter, construction worker or foreman, construction machinery operator, football player, welder, mill-wright, ironworker. All of these "worst jobs" have one thing in common: 95 to 100 percent men.[3]

Every day, almost as many men are killed at work as were killed during the average day in Vietnam.[4] For men, there are, in essence, three male-only drafts: the draft of men to all the wars; the draft of Everyman to unpaid bodyguard; the draft of men to all the hazardous jobs—or "death professions." When men are not legally drafted, they feel psychologically drafted.

---

* The twenty-fifth job, the one job with about half women, was professional dancing, which, like professional football, doubtless earned low ranking due to the combination of poor job security, poor long-term outlook, high injury rate, and high stress level.

Just as women provide a womb to create the children, men often provide a financial womb to support the children. Many men are motivated to enter the death professions to provide this financial womb. The unspoken motto of the death professions is My Body, *Not* My Choice.

THE DEATH PROFESSIONS: MEN'S BIGGEST "GLASS CELLAR"

ITEM. 94 percent of occupational deaths occur to men.[5]

ITEM. The United States has a worker death rate three to four times higher than Japan's.[6] If the U.S. had the same rate, we would save the lives of approximately 6,000 men and 400 women each year.[7]

ITEM. The United States has only *one* job safety inspector for every *six* fish and game inspectors.[8]

ITEM. Work safety is yet to become a course requirement for even one MBA program in the United States.[9]

ITEM. Every workday *hour*, one construction worker in the United States loses his life.[10]

ITEM. The more hazardous the job, the greater the percentage of men. Some examples:[11]

Hazardous Occupations	
Fire fighting	99% male
Logging	98% male
Trucking (heavy)	98% male
Construction	98% male
Coal Mining	97% male
Safe Occupations	
Secretary	99% female
Receptionist	97% female

One reason the jobs men hold pay more is because they are more hazardous. The additional pay might be called the "Death Profession Bonus." And within a given death profession, the more dangerous the assignment, the more likely it is to be assigned to a man.[12]

Both sexes contribute to the invisible barriers that both sexes experience. Just as the "glass ceiling" describes the invisible barrier that keeps women out of jobs with the most pay, the "glass cellar" describes the invisible barrier that keeps men in jobs with the most hazards.

Members of the glass cellar are all around us. But because they are our second-choice men, we make them invisible. (We hear women say, "I met this doctor . . .," not "I met this garbageman. . . .")

THE MEN ALL AROUND US: THE SECOND-CHOICE MAN

Let me tell you a little story.

I had just completed the research for this chapter and wanted to clear my mind. I thought an "errands morning" might do the trick.

Well, if you've read the first few chapters you're suspicious. You know there are no little stories without little morals. Chalk it up to Farrell's Fables, but you're right, all around me the men I had been researching I now began to see.

As I prepared to leave the house, I heard the roar of the garbage truck. Usually that just triggers an "Oh yeah, it's Monday." This time it also triggered my memory . . . that the garbageman was two and half times more likely to be killed than a police officer. And that 70 percent of the collection crew for the City of San Diego (where I live) suffered job-related injuries in the last year alone.[13] Now, as I saw the garbageman pull up to my garbage, I connected the 70 percent figure to this man; to his disproportionate chances of back injuries, hernias, rectal cancer, cirrhosis of the liver, or just being hit by a passing automobile. I saw some things I hadn't seen before . . . first, just the lumbar support belt one of the men was wearing; then, eye contact; then, a name I had never bothered to ask. Ride with me for a moment on one of these men's trucks.

On Terry Hennesey's route (real person, true story) is a dental office.[14] When he recently compacted the trash, several plastic bags of human blood burst and splattered into his face. Just a few weeks later, he found a World War II hand grenade with the pin still in it* and about two dozen 9-millimeter, hollow-point bullets. Some months later he picked up a load of low-level radioactive waste. His colleagues tell stories of battery acid splattering on their clothes and faces; of the compacting process forcing chlorine to shoot out of a container, hitting a man in the back and setting him afire; of hot fireplace ashes being dumped in the trash and igniting the back of the truck; of a container of liquid cyanide. . . .

Why was I so unaware of these dangers? In part, because these men never speak up—instead they turn each other's misfortunes into humor, calling each other the "Cyanide Man," the "Radioactive Man," and so on. And in part, we are more conscious of the injuries of the football players, for example, because the absence of the football players has an impact on our egos: it makes "our team" lose. If our garbageman dies, he is replaced, like any part on the garbage truck.

I was more likely to think of it as sexism to call garbage collectors garbagemen than to understand that the real sexism is the pressure felt by uneducated, unskilled *men* to take more than 96 percent of the garbage collector jobs so they can get paid $9 to $15 an hour to support their families.[15] Or that the real sexism was in hiding something dangerous in our garbage.

Once I saw the garbagemen in a different light, I registered how differently I looked at a garbageman as opposed to, say, a pregnant woman. When I see a pregnant woman, I automatically smile a smile that expresses appreciation for her joy, her adventure, her contribution. But I had never supported the garbageman with a smile that expressed appreciation for his contribution (although he supports what the pregnant woman creates and carries a different load). Nor had I felt empathy for his lack of joy . . . I never expected him to be joyful. For all practical purposes he had been invisible. As were so many men in the death professions.

As with any new opening, new information flies in that would previously have flown by—like this letter to Ann Landers:

---

* Of course, it's hard to find a hand grenade without the pin in it!

Dear Ann,
I'm fed up with people using the garbage collector as an example of an easy job for morons. I'm married to a garbageman and this is what life is like:
He leaves for work at 4:30 A.M., six days a week. . . . One day it was 50 below zero. My husband was out in that miserable weather for 10 hours. . . . His route consists of 2,500 homes. . . . If he spent just a few extra minutes at each stop, he would be out there an additional two to three hours a day. . . . He works on commission, 17.5 cents per house.[16]

Of course, it's his *wife* who's writing. The garbageman remains silent. . . .

•   •   •

On my way to the Lucky supermarket in Encinitas, I picked up some cash from an ATM. At about the same time, an armed courier picked up cash from another ATM. He was the second armed courier to be fatally shot in the head that week.[17] Every time I cash a check, an armed courier helps. Such couriers transport virtually every cent of cash that flows through the American economy. One of these couriers, a veteran of three combat tours in Vietnam and whose delivery area in south-central Los Angeles is gang-infested, says, "As soon as you open the door, you're 'meat on the table.' "[18] So why do they do it? Well, as David Troy Nelson puts it, "I am a single parent with two preschool children." He is willing to be "meat on the table" so his two children might have meat on their table.

Which brings me to the meat and vegetables. Sorting through chicken breasts, I used to be more aware of the crimes committed against chickens than those committed against the workers preparing the chicken. Of 2,000 workers at the Morrell meat packing plant, 800 had become disabled *in one year.*[19] Some of these workers were chopping and carving at a rate of 1,000 movements per hour. With 40 percent per year being disabled, each worker's hands were essentially a time bomb. Almost 90 percent of the workers in the fifty-seven highest-risk jobs at Morrell were men.[20] Dozens who had to undergo surgery requiring one to two months to heal were instead required to return to work immediately after the surgery.

As I picked out the best-looking vegetables, I took for granted that I would be washing off parathion and other poisons that allowed the best-looking vegetables to get that way. Now I found myself thinking of the men who spent their lives inhaling the parathion as it blew back into their faces from the planes and tractors from which they did their job of spraying.

I had always thought of farming as a reasonably safe profession in which men and women worked "side by side." I was wrong. With the exception of mining, the agricultural industry has the highest death rate of any industry.[21] Young men are *twenty-four* times as likely to be killed in farm labor as are young women.[22] They are also a lot more likely to suffer the amputation of an arm, leg, or finger. In reality, men and women do not work "side by side." Men work where there's greater potential for death; women, where there is greater potential for safety. As I picked up a microwave dinner, I felt thankful for the many men who prepared that dinner—who plowed, lifted, sprayed, and risked amputations so I could heat and eat a meal.

As I exited from Lucky's down Encinitas Boulevard, I counted about thirty migrant workers in fewer than six blocks, each looking soulfully into the eyes of every passerby, each hoping to be picked to do a day's work in someone's fields. I saw a driver go by, look over the men, choose two, and leave the others behind. In the ten years I have lived in the town of Encinitas near San Diego, I have seen perhaps a thousand of these migrant workers waiting on these street corners. *All* of them have been men. Being rejected all day didn't mean returning to a warm home at night; it meant sleeping in the cold hills. In San Diego, these men are everywhere:

The field labor leaves the men permanently stooped over (after seven to ten years' work) and rips up their hands. The pesticides sprayed on the fields two or three times daily gradually soak into the men's skin, especially through open cuts on their hands. The poisons eventually deplete the men's brains or cause cancers. Those who make it back into the United States year after year to work in the fields thus face brain damage or early death (typically by age 40).

Most of these men are sending their wages back to their wives and children in Mexico, whom they see only once or twice a year before once again risking imprisonment by illegally crossing the

Highway Camp, © 1989, by DON BARTLETTI.

U.S. border. This might be thought of as the migrant worker draft. Another all-male draft.

This "sacrifice-to-feed" is the male form of nuturance. In every class, men with families provide their own womb, the family's financial womb. They provide their bodies. But the psychology of disposability leaves them without placards reading My Body, My Choice. No movement calls these men oppressed for providing money for women from whom they are receiving neither cooking nor cleaning; for providing their wives with homes while they sleep on the ground. When a field worker is radicalized, he is taught to see the classism but remains blind to the sexism. Yet we call Mexican men patriarchs—as if the rules of their society served them at the *expense of women.*

As I stopped by a Von's supermarket for some grapefruit juice, I waited for a huge truck to back into a narrow delivery space. It was a familiar scene, but it was only as I had become aware of how truckers' scheduling demands sometimes led to their falling asleep at the wheel (making their death rate among the highest of any profession[23]) that I registered the cup of coffee he was slugging down. In the process I saw more than a truck blocking my entrance into the parking lot, I saw a man in the truck. I visualized a trucker on his eighth cup of coffee at 4 A.M., stretching his limits so I can eat to my limit without paying to my limit.

I thought how I had been more likely to associate trucking with "teamsters" and the deaths caused *by* a truck accident rather than the deaths caused *to* the truckers. The difference in my feeling toward him turned a moment's wait into a moment's appreciation. I smiled at him with a warmth that must have been different because he returned the smile as if he felt the appreciation.

The impact was with me months later. As I saw *Thelma and Louise* and felt the audience's thunderous applause as they set a trucker's truck afire, I didn't miss what the audience felt, but I felt sad at what the audience was missing.

Before I returned home, I couldn't resist stopping by my fantasy house. It was being built on the bluffs over the ocean. As I watched the men putting nails through the lumber, I imagined the truckers navigating their semis through city traffic and the loggers navigating logs through half-frozen rivers (making logging one of the most dangerous of the death professions). I thought of logging lingo like "deadman" and "widowmaker" that referred to the various ways trees and branches could kill a man and make a widow. I realized my fantasy house would result not just from the risks taken by the construction workers but also by the truckers and loggers.

As some colder winds made me ready to leave, I saw one worker on the second story almost miss the beam he grabbed to keep himself from joining the ocean. Until that second I had forgotten about a friend of mine who had been hit by a crane boom almost a decade ago. Although he has recovered some, he will never be the same again—nor will the life of his wife. I wondered why almost no state hired enough safety investigators to do anything but investigate an accident site *after* a death.

The trip was taking longer than I expected, so I stepped on the gas a bit. A second later, I heard a siren. My heart skipped a few beats until my rearview mirror calmed me with the sight of a fire truck. As soon as I saw it wasn't heading toward my house (my real one!), I was free to recall the MGM Grand Hotel fire in Las Vegas—how it had left seventy-six people lying dead in almost sterile rooms, untouched by fire, unclouded by smoke.[24] It was my first awareness that fire fighters now face more danger from toxic emissions in fumes than from fire or smoke—not always immediately, but cumulatively. Why?

Plastics. Since World War II, plastics such as polyvinylchloride (PVC) have increasingly become part of our telephones, furniture, carpets, wallpaper, waste baskets, plumbing, and televisions. When they burn, they produce deadly chemical by-products such as chlorine, hydrogen chloride, and phosgene gas (deadly enough to have been used in World War I as a weapon for chemical warfare). When a fire fighter enters a home, he might see neither smoke nor flames, but the invisible fumes contain a literal bomb of poisonous gas. Toxic emissions become toxic munitions. The result?

Death from cancer has increased 400 percent *more* for fire fighters than for the population at large.[25] The average age for cancer deaths among fire fighters is 52.[26] Line-of-duty injuries such as back injuries, and occupational diseases such as heart attacks, force *one out of every three* fire fighters into early retirement.[27] One out of every twenty-one fire fighters is exposed to communicable diseases (a quarter of these to AIDS).[28]

While volunteerism has often been labeled a women's issue, 80 percent of all municipal fire fighters, almost one million, are volunteers—99 percent *male* volunteers.[29] I know of no equivalent numbers of women voluntarily exposing themselves to death to save the lives of strangers while virtually guaranteeing an earlier death for themselves.

Why don't more fire fighters use breathing equipment more often? Breathing equipment adds about 35 pounds to the 100 to 150 pounds fire fighters already carry in ladders, axes, hoses, and turnout coats. Handling a fire requires an organized attack with good communication; wearing masks prevents the fire fighters from talking.

The fire fighters know that every time they protect themselves, others might die. A flame might be moving as fast as eighteen feet per second, as was true in the 1980 fire that roared through the MGM Grand Hotel in Las Vegas. In a matter of minutes, eighty-five people were killed. The oxygen tanks take about a minute to put on. In that minute, a flame could move more than a thousand feet. In brief, many fire fighters choose to forfeit their own lives to save others'.

Why do volunteer firemen risk their lives? In part, to be appreciated. Some fireman feel a little unappreciated, though, when homeowners seem to resent the firemen's boots muddying their carpets.

As I pulled into my driveway, I spotted a moving van in front of a new home in the neighborhood. I was in time to see the movers slip their bodies under a large couch, angle the couch through the doorway, and juggle/balance it up a curving stairway. I could hear the father warn the son, "Watch the way you lift or you'll end up with a lower back like mine."

I looked around my home with a different appreciation for how the refrigerator and file cabinets were moved . . . appreciating the men who make my life convenient while they remain invisible.

When I showed a first draft of this chapter to a friend in the coal industry he said, "You've left out the most dangerous of all industries—mining." I responded that I guess I didn't see the evidence of that around me every day. He corrected me, "It's the miner you don't see around you, but you see the evidence of mining all around you."[30] I was intrigued.

"First," he said, "mining isn't just coal mining, but metal mining and oil and gas extraction as well. Now look in the shaving mirror and check out your teeth—the fillings contain gold, silver, mercury, and composite [petroleum]. Your eyeglasses contain not only metal but plastic, which is made with both petroleum and coal. And you doubtless have the light on, which is shining through glass bulbs containing tungsten, mercury, and phosphorus. The electricity to produce the light comes through copper and aluminum wires from generators also made of copper, spun by tungsten turbines, powered by steam produced from uranium, coal, or oil." I was impressed.

"Then, assuming you get dressed," he said, laughing, "your clothes usually contain iron, made from iron ore, limestone, coal. And as for your computers, they are made of plastic, glass, phosphorus, and dozens of metals that have to be mined. The chapters of the manuscript you sent me are currently bound together by binder clips made of steel [iron ore, limestone, coal]. By the time your readers get the book, they'll be reading these words on paper manufactured with sulfuric acid, a by-product of refining petroleum and sulfide metal ores. If the paper is acid free, it probably incorporates calcium carbonate [limestone] to neutralize the acid. Even the adhesives that hold the book together are made, in part, with petroleum. If the dust jacket turns out to be shiny, it will be that way by adding clay to the paper."

What makes mining so dangerous? Each week, rocks falling from mine ceilings cause concussions or deaths among miners; dangling electrical wires electrocute them, and moving equipment maims them. If an office had ceilings falling and killing secretaries, or electrical wires dangling from the walls onto desks and electrocuting them, or moving equipment crushing them, how many women would agree to work there (for any price)? How long would the employer remain free of a lawsuit?

That was enough thinking for the night. I turned on the TV to relax. Despite myself, I chose the news over a sitcom. It featured the War on Drugs; and, of course, the next morning, I couldn't help but do a little checking.

From 1921 until 1992, *every Drug Enforcement Administration (DEA) agent killed has been a man.*[31] The War on Drugs, then, is a war with a sex-segregated army: the women are in the safe positions; the men, in the combat zone.

Agents of the DEA used to go from induction to retirement without ever firing their weapons.[32] Now, says the training director at a DEA academy, "the DEA agent who graduates today probably will have to draw his gun within the first week."[33] Today the DEA has the highest assault rate of any federal law enforcement agency.[34]

I had never thought of the War on Drugs as another virtually all-male war.

THE SAVING PROFESSIONS

Complete these sentences with your first, gut-level thought:

- Shortly after they heard the alarm, a crew of _____ rescued some women from a blazing apartment.
- Two_____attacked a woman jogger in Central Park.

Most people think of the woman as being saved by "firemen" or "fire fighters." It is now considered sexist for TV announcers to use "fireman" rather than "fire fighter." But when a woman is attacked, the TV announcer says, "Two *men* attacked a woman."

When men *save* a woman, we emphasize their function (*fire* fighters, doctors). When men *hurt* women, we think primarily of their sex (men), not some men's behavior (violence). Which creates in our subconscious an anger toward men that, in turn, allows us to feel more comfortable with their disposability.

We call women who are nurses "helping professionals"; we call men who are police officers "cops" (or "pigs"), not "saving professionals." Thus we associate men's physical strength with how men use it to hurt women, but not how they use it to save women—not only as police officers and fire fighters but as women's personal bodyguards, ready to die before a woman they love is raped, robbed, or murdered.

The male propensity to save can be found even in places that we normally associate with the male propensity to destroy. When the white-hot core of the Chernobyl reactor had been about to drop into a pool of radioactive water, which would have set off steam explosions, spreading radioactive contamination and leaving hundreds of other families exposed to early deaths via cancer, three men voluntarily dove into the radioactive water to open valves to drain the water, thus preventing a steam explosion. Although the plant supervisor had given the workers permission not to enter the contaminated water, one of the men responded, "How could I refuse when I was the only person on the shift who knew where the valves were located?"

Chernobyl reflects, then, not only men's propensity for destruction but men's propensity to save.

THE DEATH PROFESSIONS' DOUBLE STANDARD

When mining, construction, and other death professions are discussed in feminist publications, they are portrayed as examples of the male power system, as "male-only clubs." However, when *Ms.* magazine profiled female miners, the emphasis was on how the woman was "forced" to take a job in the mines because it paid the best, and how taking such a job was the only way she could support her family.[35]

Ms. could never acknowledge that the male-only clubs of hazardous occupations paid best because of their hazards and had been male-only exactly because *men* risked their lives for the extra pay to support *their* loved ones. They could not acknowledge that almost no woman worked in a mine to support a husband. Or that, if the woman they were profiling had a husband, *he* would have gone to the mines—not her. This double standard—of the death professions being a privilege when men did them and an oppression when women did them—has made two generations of men feel a bit unappreciated.

WOMEN ARE SEGREGATED INTO THE WORST JOBS, AREN'T THEY?

While we have seen that twenty-four out of the twenty-five *worst* jobs are male jobs[36] and that many men also have low-pay jobs (busboy, doorman, dishwasher, gas station attendant, etc.), many of the lowest-paid jobs *are* predominantly occupied by women. Why the distinction between the "worst" and "low-paid" jobs? Because many of the low-paid jobs are low-paid because they are safer, have higher fulfillment, more flexible hours, and other desirable characteristics that make them more in demand and therefore lower in pay. When *either* sex chooses jobs with these desirable characteristics, they can expect low pay. Women are much more likely to choose jobs with seven of these eight characteristics—what might be called the "Female Occupations Formula."

The "Female Occupations Formula"

Women now constitute 15–30 percent of a few of the high-pressure, highly skilled, and highly paid professions such as law and medicine. But occupations which employ more than 90 percent women almost always have in common at least seven of the following eight characteristics. The combination of all seven characteristics makes the job high in desirability—so high that an employer has more than enough qualified applicants and, therefore, does not need to pay as much.

- *Ability to Psychologically "Check Out"* at end of day (department store clerk vs. lawyer)
- *Physical Safety* (receptionist vs. fire fighter)
- *Indoors* (secretary vs. garbage collector)
- *Low Risk* (file clerk vs. venture capitalist)
- *Desirable or Flexible Hours* (nurse vs. medical doctor)

- *No Demands to Move* out of town "or else"—to "move it or lose it" (corporate secretary vs. corporate executive)
- *High Fulfillment* relative to training (child-care professional vs. coal miner)
- *Contact with People* in a pleasant environment (restaurant hostess vs. long-distance trucker)

Note how this female occupations formula applies to the more than 90 percent female professions of receptionist, secretary, child-care professional, nurse, and department-store clerk or salesperson.

The "Exposure Professions"

After exposure to death, exposure to the elements is the most common hazard of male jobs. The hole in the ozone layer makes daily exposure to sun the equivalent of exposure to cancer. Just as the fire fighter's newest hazard is invisible, so the construction worker's newest hazard is invisible. And as for the road worker or garbage collector, well, not only does he take in ultraviolet rays through his skin but car fumes through his nose. All of which add the exposure professions to our list of death professions.

The more a worker's beat requires exposure to the sleet and the heat, the more likely is the worker to be a man: ditch digging, previously the work of chain gangs of prisoners, was protested as exploitive of prisoners.[37] It is not protested as exploitive of men. The gas station attendant who pumps gas in the rain is most likely male (whereas the one collecting money indoors can be of either sex). Be it roofing or welding, if it is an exposure profession, it is a male profession.

The willingness to expose oneself to death at work belies a deeper male-female difference in attitude toward work. In a death profession, the feeling of not being entitled to protection is a metaphor. Harassment is called hazing, and hazing weeds out those who desire protection and selects for a team of protectors. Issues like hazing and harassment pale in comparison to the need to prevent death.

This doesn't mean that hazing and harassment are good for the individual. To the contrary: the very attitude that protects others is a disaster for protecting self—thus more New York City police commit suicide than are killed on duty.[38]

Each man, whether in a coal mine near home or in a trench "over there," *expects* his body to be used. Male prostitution is a given; freedom from it, a luxury. Which is why the unspoken motto of the death professions is My Body, *Not* My Choice.

• • •

In brief, then, it is a myth that women are segregated into the worst jobs. Jobs that require few skills and few hazards pay less and jobs that have high fulfillment pay less—to *either* sex. The worst jobs are almost all "male jobs," which men take more because they have, on average, more mouths to feed.

WHAT IS OUR INVESTMENT IN MAKING MEN "THE DISPOSABLE SEX"?

Letting men die is a money-saving device. Safety costs money. When contractors bid low to get a job, they need to pressure men to complete work lest they go bankrupt. As one safety official put it, "When everything is hurry, hurry, hurry, when you start pressuring people and taking shortcuts, things can go wrong. And then people die."[39] No. And then *men* die. How many of us work in an office building in which a man's life or limbs were lost?

The solution? Strict *enforcement* of safety standards. Why the emphasis on enforcement? The safety standards are good; it is the enforcement that is bad. It is only when government enforces safety standards that the companies which incur safety costs do not saddle themselves with a burden that undermines their ability to compete. The alternative is what we are doing now: "selecting for" the survival of those companies that take shortcuts with men's lives.

THE GOVERNMENT: SUBSTITUTE HUSBAND IN THE WORKPLACE

I just read an article about protecting the owls in the Northwest. I wonder how many Senate staff people devoted how many years to that? There's *nobody* on the U.S. Senate staff who works full-time on worker safety year-round. I'd be perfectly happy to go back home to Kansas and box up all the goddamn owls they want and send them out to Washington and Oregon.

—JOSEPH KINNEY, National Safe
Workplace Institute[40]

No sooner had the government documented the much greater risk of death in the workplace for men than it cut back the programs to protect men and expanded the programs to protect women.

The government cut back the Occupational Safety and Health Administration[41] (OSHA), which enforces safety standards for both sexes equally and therefore would have helped more men,

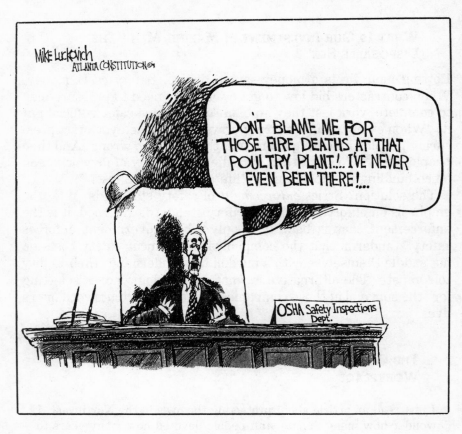

and created special programs to protect only working women. It passed the Federal Pregnancy Discrimination Act,[42] making pregnancy eligible for as much compensation as a disability resulting from an on-the-job hazard, even though pregnancy was an off-the-job choice. But that wasn't all. . . .

When some women claimed that exposure to video display terminals created their spontaneous abortions, the government immediately responded by funding a study of more than four thousand women—only to find that women using the terminals had *fewer* spontaneous abortions than those not using the terminals.[43] When other women complained they were being sexually harassed, the government radically expanded its protection of women by expanding its prosecution of men. Simultaneously, construction sites with shaky scaffolding and coal mines with shaky ceilings were left uninspected—and the men left unprotected. In brief, men were left unprotected from premature death while women were protected from premature flirtation.

How Both the Neglect of Men and the Overprotection of Women Leads to Discrimination Against Women

Women do not enter a profession in significant numbers until it is physically safe. So until we care enough about men's safety to turn the death professions into safe professions, we in effect discriminate against women. But when we overprotect women—and only women—it also leads to discrimination against women.

The more laws overprotect women, the more I hear employers whisper of their fears of hiring women. If they employ for a large company for which quotas prevent discrimination, they find themselves increasingly hiring free-lancers rather than taking on a woman and therefore a possible sexual harassment lawsuit and the possibility that anyone who criticizes her or fires her will be the victim of that lawsuit.

When the employer adds the fear of having the company's name dragged through the mud; of hiring lawyers; of awarding the woman $100,000 and having her leave the company because she no longer needs to work; of having the woman sue for exposure to video display terminals; of losing the woman to pregnancy and paying disability insurance; of having his male executives fear being critical of women on the one hand and fear joking with the women on the other; of having . . . *Then* the employer begins unconsciously to discriminate against the sex that will create these burdens; or begins to cut back staff and hire free-lancers; or retires early; or files for bankruptcy.

The American employer who is mandated to give the sexes equal pay but unequal protection faces the new American dilemma. Paying a *competitive* wage is in the employer's self-interest, but paying an equal wage to a woman who is a few hundred times more likely than a man to sue for harassments and hazards is not to an employer's advantage. **The overprotection of women and the underprotection of men, then, soon leads to discrimination against hiring women.**

This overprotection of women and underprotection of men is part of how we psychologically prepare men for a lifetime of protecting others. It creates the atmosphere for male disposability and the link to men's three Ws: women, work, and war. . . .

CHAPTER 5

War Hero or War Slave?: The Armed Prostitute

Every society rests on the death of men.

—OLIVER WENDELL HOLMES

ITEM. Almost one out of three American men is a veteran.[1]

ITEM. In one World War I battle alone (the Battle of the Somme), more than one *million* men were killed or maimed.[2]

Understanding men requires understanding men's relationship to the three Ws: women, work, and war. Only 18-year-old boys are legally required to register for future wars. Both sexes have the option of joining the armed services in peacetime, but only men in the services are required to be available for combat in wartime. Should a major war break out, it is only our sons who will be notified within forty-eight hours to report to boot camp. Before men can vote, they have the obligation to protect that right; women receive the right to vote without the obligation to protect that right.

I. THE PSYCHOLOGY AND POLITICS OF THE DOUBLE STANDARD

THE PSYCHOLOGICAL DRAFT

The psychological draft of boys begins before, and continues after, the legal draft of boys. It begins with unconsciously teaching infant boys to endure pain when we cut an infant boy's penis without

anesthesia but not an infant girl's clitoris; with taking longer to pick up our boy children than our girl children when they cry[3] (thus signaling to only our sons that complaining won't solve their problem); with violent sports for boys but not girls . . . Combined, these might be called the psychological draft. It starts with boyhood and continues throughout adulthood.

The Double Standard of Electability

When Margaret Thatcher's belief in a strong defense was coupled with her sending hundreds of men—but not one woman—to their deaths in the Falkland Islands War, she experienced such a huge surge in popularity from both sexes that polls which had just predicted her a sure loser in the upcoming election were soon predicting her a sure winner. *No headline stated "Woman Remains in Office by Killing Men."* Or, "Thatcher Called Hypocrite for Belief in Strong Defense While Using Her Gender as Excuse to Escape Fighting." When Thatcher used men to kill for her, she was not called a wimp, she was called stronger; she did not become less eligible to serve her country, she became more eligible.

In contrast, even though Dan Quayle did serve his country in the National Guard, just not in Vietnam, he became a laughing stock; and when Clinton objected to the Vietnam War and pursued legal means not to participate, he experienced an initial 20 percent drop in the polls that would have knocked any other candidate out of the primaries. We can say it was because of the way Quayle or Clinton *handled* the situation, but why did no one even ask Geraldine Ferraro for her war record—and then criticize the way she *handled* evading the draft? How did she evade the draft? Via the sexism of exploiting female privilege.

When a man who served in the ROTC and followed his conscience is identified more as a draft evader than as a Rhodes scholar while a woman who took advantage of traditional sexism is seen more as a pioneer than as a sexist, we have some rethinking to do. Specifically, why do we blame our male politicians for causing war, then blame them for not wanting to participate in war?

Throughout the world, our basic message is: **If you are born male, then a willingness to *serve* your country (e.g., as vice president or president) is not good enough. Only men must be willing to die before they may serve in another way.**

As mentioned above, Indira Gandhi, Golda Meir, and Margaret Thatcher all sent men to their deaths at rates not dissimilar to those of the average male leader; that when women led, it was still men left dead; that equality was at the top—not at the bottom.

Wars will not end via female leaders. Wars will end when any country that has significantly more men dying in combat than women is held in violation of international law as it would if it drafted only black men, only Jews, only women, or only gays.

War will end when, worldwide, men's lives are no more disposable than women's.

Combat for the Disposable Sex versus Combat for the Protected Sex

. . . I think women are too valuable to be in combat.

—Caspar Weinberger, U.S. Secretary of Defense (under Reagan)[4]

It is not appropriate for women to engage in combat . . . to be captured or to be shot, as opposed to pushing a button someplace in a missile silo.

—Sandra Day O'Connor, Supreme Court Justice[5]

Men get killed in wars all the time. But she's my daughter.

—Frank Mitchell, Retired Chief Master Sergeant[6]

If there's a fire at sea and you have to slam down a hatch to save the ship, you might do it on a man. But on a woman . . .

—Larry K. Kenavan, Master Chief Petty Officer, U.S. Navy[7]

Combat positions in the armed services are now divided into dangerous versus less-dangerous combat positions.[8] In wartime, *only men* can be *forced* into the dangerous combat positions. Restricting women from even volunteering for the most dangerous combat positions is clearly discrimination against women. But it also discriminates against the men who must fill these dangerous positions.

The service is often called the college for the poor, yet these dangerous positions are poor preparation for civilian life. *The New York Times* has few "help wanted" ads for cannon artillery positions, armored tank specialists, and infantry positions in civilian life. Poor men hope to be trained in jobs such as computer specialties, office jobs, food preparation, teaching, nursing, social work, flight controller, or jet mechanic. When only men are forced to fill the dangerous combat jobs, only men lose the opportunities for these civilian preparation positions.

In addition, cannon artillery and infantry positions are also more likely to reinforce the killer mentality, create the most psychological disturbances and the most difficulty adjusting psychologically to civilian life. The "restriction on women," then, makes men more disposable in military life and more disposable in civilian life.

COMBAT: THE PRO-CHOICE WOMAN AND THE NO-CHOICE MAN

I predict that women will increasingly be allowed to volunteer for *any* combat situation. But, by giving women more *options* in combat while still *requiring* only men to go to combat should a war erupt, we will be increasingly reinforcing the era of the Pro-Choice Woman and the No-Choice Man. It will mean that during wartime:

The woman in the armed services will have the choice to:

1. Enter combat
2. Not enter combat

The man in the armed services will have two "slightly different" choices:

1. Enter combat
2. Enter combat

This increase in women's military combat options will be hailed as an advance in equality, but in fact it will not be. A true advance in equality would be to *require* women to enter combat *to the degree men are required* to enter combat. Equality involves equal options and equal obligations.

HOW TO ACHIEVE EQUALITY WITHOUT DAMAGING MILITARY STRENGTH

The fear of the services is that if women and men are held to equal standards in combat training that either the standards will have to be lowered or, conversely, the standards kept the same and about 80 percent of women won't be able to hack it. Fortunately, though, there *is* a way of making all combat an equal-opportunity option that still preserves combat readiness.

The Combat Incentive Plan: Supply and Demand

The plan? The military increases its pay for the jobs it finds the toughest to fill and lowers its pay for the jobs it is easiest to fill. For example, if few recruits want assignments like infantry combat, the pay and benefits are raised until they obtain all the qualified recruits they need; if everyone wants to be a pilot and plenty of recruits are qualified, the pay for pilots is lowered. The result is that women pursuing real equality—sharing the least-desired assignments—would get higher pay. Neither sex is discriminated against; no standards are lowered for any specialty. The psychological result is respect for women because they are earning it, rather than resentment toward women getting equal pay for the safest and most glamorous of the combat jobs (pilot).

DIDN'T WOMEN IN THE PERSIAN GULF SHARE EQUAL COMBAT RISKS WITHOUT EQUAL COMBAT PAY?

During the U.S. invasion of Panama, front-page headlines heralded the first woman leading soldiers into combat.[9] Although *The New York Times* made it clear the woman thought she was approaching an *un*guarded dog kennel,[10] Congresswoman Schroeder used this incident to develop three myths—myths that were reinforced during the war in the Persian Gulf:

1. Women and men share *equal risks*
2. Women were being denied combat positions in order to deny them *equal opportunity as officers*
3. Women were being denied combat positions in order to deny them *equal pay*

These myths were reinforced by the cover stories of our news weeklies:

But the facts give a different picture:

1. *Equal risks.* If women shared equal risks, Panama would not have resulted in the deaths of 23 men and 0 women (also 0 women injured)[11]; and the Persian Gulf practice operations and war would not have led to the deaths of 375 men versus 15 women.[12] For both

wars combined, 27 men died for each woman[13]; but since there are only 9 men in the armed services for each woman, then any given man's risk of dying was three times greater than any given woman's.

If *men* accounted for less than 4 percent of the total deaths and any given man had only one fourth the risk of dying, would Congresswoman Schroeder have said men equally shared the risks? Equality is not making women vulnerable by chance when men are made vulnerable by design.

Were women being denied combat positions in order to deny them equal opportunity as officers? Or to deny them equal pay?

2. *Equal opportunity as officers.* Women constitute 11.7 percent of the total military, but 12 percent of the officers.[14] *Women receive more-than-equal promotions in the services despite less-than-equal time in the services* (the first females graduated from West Point in 1980).

3. *Equal pay.* Both sexes in the Persian Gulf received $110 per month extra combat pay.[15] *The sexes received equal pay despite unequal risks.*

In brief, men get fewer promotions and, therefore, less pay for longer periods of service and a threefold greater risk of death, yet we read about discrimination against women, not discrimination against men. When men do 30 percent of the housework, we *criticize* men for *not* sharing the housework; when any given woman receiving 100 percent of male combat pay takes 25 percent of the combat risks of any given man, we call her a warrior and credit her with "*sharing* the danger."

MY BODY, MY BUSINESS?

ITEM. If a fetus has a "right to life," but eighteen years later has an "obligation to death," which sex is it?

Registering all our 18-year-old sons for the draft in the event the country needs more soldiers is as sexist as registering all our 18-year-old daughters for child-bearing in the event the country needs more children.

At this moment, fifteen million American boys are in the data bank of draft-eligible men.[16] How realistic is it that the boys will, in fact, be drafted? We know only that in twenty-four to seventy-two hours the first induction orders can be in the mail.[17] That's how fast your son's life could change. National Guard and Reserve units are prepared to fill boot camps with 100,000 boys in four weeks.[18] The units practice one weekend a month on the finer points of setting up and operating headquarters and field offices, and giving refresher courses to draft boards. If there's a war, there's a way.[19]

Ironically, Selective Service officials are proud of their "equal opportunity" system—no longer biased in favor of class, race, student status, or job status. It is a metaphor for our times that something can be called equal opportunity that registers only men for potential death.

The Selective Service does legally what the death professions do psychologically. For women, it's "our bodies, *our* business"; for men, it's "our bodies, *government* business." A woman has the "right to choose"; a draftee has the choice of being "mined, mortared, shot, grenaded, blown up . . . you could fly apart so that your pieces would never be gathered, you could take one neat round in the lung and go out hearing only the bubble of the last few breaths, you could die in the last stage of malaria with that faint tapping in your ears."[20]

G.I. still means "government issue"; someday G.I. will be M.I.—a men's issue.

HIS ARMY VERSUS HER ARMY

Combat training strips you of your self-image so you can be rebuilt to fit the Army mold.

—BRUCE GILKIN, Vietnam
Veteran[21]

When every man in the armed services is required to enter combat upon command and every woman either has the option of combat or is protected from combat, we produce two distinct mentalities. Combat training requires the men to *de*value their lives;

training for technical jobs that can be used in civilian life is compatible with *valuing* one's life. The result?

Harassment and hazing are preparation for devaluation—which is why men haze and harass one another: they are amputating each other's individuality because the war machine works best with standardized parts. Harassment and hazing are therefore a prerequisite to combat training in the "men's army"; but in the "women's army," harassment and hazing can be protested—they conflict with valuing one's life.

If the men's and women's armies were physically separate, these differences would be less of a problem. However, when the men are told that the women are equals but if they harass and haze the women as equals they'll have their careers ruined (and often family life destroyed), this only reinforces the men's belief that women want to "have their cake and eat it, too."

THE PREGNANT-NAVY SYNDROME

It isn't politically correct to even discuss this in the services, but . . . a large percentage of women soldiers are electively aborting their fetuses after they've served their purpose of enabling them to avoid their tour of duty in Operation Desert Storm. . . . It is wrong to use a fetus to shirk the responsibility for which you have signed up, and then to kill that fetus.

—NAME WITHHELD, Army
Physician, Kuwait[22]

The mentality of valuing self also produces the "Pregnant-Navy Syndrome": the phenomenon of a woman benefiting from the technical training and then, just prior to her ship's being deployed, becoming pregnant so as to qualify for shore leave and not being deployed; or becoming pregnant immediately after her ship is deployed, thus allowing her increasingly to shirk responsibilities, forcing her shipmates to pick up the slack. This is all compatible with valuing self, but in a military situation—when more than *40 percent* of the women on ships like the USS *Acadia* become pregnant during workup for deployment[23]—this bailing out puts men's lives in danger. Why?

The navy trains teams. Each person on the team is trained to interact with the others in situations where a split second can save or lose a life. When part of that team is suddenly missing, they cannot just be replaced because part of what made them valuable is the way they learned to interact with the particular personalities who are part of their team. In essence, when even one woman is lost, the entire *team* is lost. The consequences? Imagine if Lieutenant Conklin were a pregnant woman when the two Iraqi missiles tore a fifteen-foot hole in the side of the USS *Stark.* . . .

The missile attack caused a rapidly spreading fire that threatened to blow the ship and its 200 men to pieces.[24] Twenty-seven-year-old Lieutenant Conklin (real person, true story) was severely burned and wounded in both feet, both hands, and both arms. Yet he knew that crawling through the burning, mangled wreckage to the crew cabin to shut off the firemain valves might possibly save the ship from exploding.

The path to the crew cabin was pitch black and about 400 degrees (paper bursts into flame at about 451 degrees, hence *Fahrenheit 451*). Yet he entered, protecting himself only with a T-shirt doused in salt water, keeping his eyes closed so that his eyelids would burn away rather than his eyes. Feeling his way through the piping system, each time he touched a searing pipe the skin was stripped off his fingers and hands—he described it as like walking into a blazing pizza oven and putting his hands on the hot griddles. He persisted until he closed off the firemain valves, worked his way back out, and then, discovering the ship was now in danger of sinking and still in danger of exploding, he continued his acts of protection.

While Conklin was doing this, Seaman Mark Caouette, whose leg had been blasted off and was bleeding profusely, refused his shipmates' efforts to drag him to safety. He chose instead to shut off other firemain valves. His charred, dead body was later found over one of those valves. Simultaneously Electronics Technician Wayne Weaver pulled between six and twelve men to safety before his own body was found clutching the body of another man he was trying to rescue.

These men, ages 19 to 36, saved the lives of 163 men as 37 died. To them, being a team meant being able to count on each member's willingness to make her or his life secondary to others. It did not mean receiving the benefits of training and finding a way to get shore leave just before deployment.

In the past decade or two, we have viewed it as sexism against women when men like this reacted defensively to the idea of women being on board such a ship (or joining a crew of volunteer firemen). One serviceman explained it to me like this: "We don't wait until an emergency to discover who's gonna risk his life and who's gonna walk away. When a new recruit arrives, we set up hazing situations, making it appear that someone's life is at risk. We wanna see if the new guy's gonna save the guy in trouble or save his own skin. But when we do this to women, they shout 'Discrimination.' Not all women, of course. But if a woman's wearing nail polish, well, I've never seen a woman with nail polish who didn't want to be saved."

The Pregnant-Navy Syndrome is only the outward sign of a problem reflected in almost every armed forces study—from the U.S. Signal Corps[25] to the U.S. Army.[26] Each study found that the men felt the women received easier assignments or undeserved promotions, often by offering sexual "favors." They felt resentment when these women nevertheless drew equal pay.

Questions about the seriousness of women in the military were reinforced by studies finding that only 21 percent of the women were considering a military career, compared with 51 percent of the men.[27] The men felt this attitude was reflected by female soldiers using skin cream, putting up their hair, and wearing makeup—even under simulated combat conditions.[28]

The service academies have responded to differences such as women at West Point going on sick call four times as often as men[29] not by making women's standards equal to men's, but by making a double set of standards. For example, a marine boot camp had to excuse women altogether from the infantry field training and all the obstacle courses.[30] The result? In the Gulf War, men were often expected to pick up the slack when women couldn't change truck tires, push a vehicle out of the sand, move heavy fuel cans, move a wounded soldier.[31] More importantly, though, the men could severely hurt their careers by complaining about this discrimination.[32] Ironically, complaining about discrimination would make them vulnerable to charges of discrimination.

The larger picture is two different mentalities: the combat-if-necessary mentality of "his army" and the combat-if-desired mentality of "her army"; an army of men who *de*value their lives and an army of women who value their lives. It reinforces the feeling that women are bluffing in their demand for equality. It splits the armed services in two.

To Kill or Be Killed . . .

If your son refuses to register for the draft when he turns 18, he can be barred from all federal jobs—from the U.S. Post Office to the FBI.[33] He faces a fine of up to $250,000 and five years in prison.[34] Once in prison, your son's nubile, young body combined with his reputation for not fighting makes him a perfect candidate for homosexual rape and, therefore, AIDS. In brief, he is subject to being killed. Why? He was too sensitive to kill.

Do male-only draft registration and combat requirements amount, then, to the legalized rape of men? Yes. But we can't help the feeling of exaggeration when we compare the mass execution of men—as shown in the Civil War film *Glory*—to legalized rape. Why is that? Well, we're so used to calling the death of men "glory."

The Multi-Option Woman and the No-Option Man

In many states, an 18-year-old boy who has not registered for the draft cannot attend a state school.[35] He cannot receive even a loan for a private school.

Male-only draft registration leaves a woman who doesn't register for the draft able to:

1. Go to a state school
2. Go to a private school with federal aid or
3. Get married and work; be single and work; have children . . .

It leaves a man who doesn't register able to go to:

1. Jail

Our different standards for women frees a woman from moral dilemmas, allowing her to see herself and other women as more innocent and moral than men. This is reinforced in wartime, when women aren't even required to leave their normal jobs and manufacture armaments for two years.

In brief, the problem with the Selective Service is that it *is* selective.

WHAT ARE THE TWO MOST UNCONSTITUTIONAL LAWS IN AMERICA?

Why will male-only draft registration and combat requirements ultimately be recognized as the most unconstitutional laws in America? They are a breach of America's most inalienable right: the right to life.

Depriving our fathers and sons of their right to live because of their sex is the greatest possible violation of the Fourteenth Amendment's guarantee of equal protection under the law. That guarantee was the basis of almost all civil rights legislation.[36]

THE MORE MALE CHAUVINIST THE COUNTRY, THE MORE IT . . .

The more chauvinist the country, the more it protects women. And therefore the more it limits women. Italy and Spain protect women completely from military service by not permitting them to join. Denmark gives women more options (to join and to be in combat) but still protects women from the draft.[37] Like the United States, it gives women options without obligations. These countries are, therefore, still male chauvinist and female chauvinist, not emancipated. **The degree to which a country is emancipated is the degree to which it frees men from the obligation to protect women and socializes women to equally protect men. No country is very emancipated.**

Aren't Women Equal to Men in the Israeli and Soviet Armies?

ITEM. The Women's Corps of the Israeli Defense Forces is called CHEN, Hebrew for "charm."[38]

We often think of the Soviet and Israeli armies as having equality of obligation between women and men. Not true. Less than 1 percent of the Soviet armed forces is female. No females are sent into combat.[39] In Israel, both sexes are subject to the draft, but combat duty is required only of the men. For women, combat duty is an option that is nowadays almost never pursued.

Soviet and Israeli women, like American women, are able to choose jobs that create opportunities *after* military service (flight controller, cook, teacher, technician).[40] **Taxpayer dollars, then, train Soviet and Israeli women in jobs that are profitable to them in civilian life while Soviet and Israeli men are trained to kill and be killed**. The men who escape death return to civilian life with training to be destructive—not constructive. (And then we blame men for being destructive.)

Aren't Israeli men and women required, though, to serve an equal number of years? In theory, almost: Israeli men, three; Israeli women, two.[41] In practice, though, *the Israeli man serves an average of thirteen years* before his eligibility ends at age 54; the woman, fewer than two.[42] Why? First, because only 50 percent of the women are called to serve (versus 90 percent of the men).[43] Second, an Israeli mother cannot be forced to serve beyond her two years; Israeli fathers can.[44] Third, even in peacetime, the Israeli man—whether father or not—is still required to serve *two months per year* (*after* his three-year minimum) until he is 54.[45] The mother has no requirement, and women without children need only be on call.[46] Fourth, in wartime, only the man serves as much as he is needed.

II. THE ULTIMATE "GLASS CELLAR"

THE "ELITE CLASS" OR THE "DEAD CLASS": IS THE MILITARY AN OUTGROWTH OF MALE COMPETITION AND POWER?

My policy? Sir, I am a soldier. I do not have a policy.

—French general HENRI GIRAUD[47]

We think of top military brass as the bastion of male power. In the United States, as in France, the policy to create war is determined by the legislature, the policy of when to fight or negotiate is determined by the president, and both the president and the legislature are determined by the voters. The general is just the chauffeur. His job is to get us where we tell him to go.

The individual soldier is trained not in dominance but in subservience. Only after he proves his ability to take orders can he give orders. In fact, his training to give orders is *created* by his ability to take orders; his training in dominance is created by his subservience.

We think of the Japanese male as being the quintessential example of the dominant male. Yet Japanese males in World War II were trained in the Way of the Warrior. The Way of the Warrior was the way of subservience: the Japanese warrior was willing to die for the emperor and his ancestors; he was trained to believe there was no acceptable alternative to victory except death. The kamikaze fighter is but an outgrowth of the Way of the Warrior— the way of total slavery to "the Other."

We often open our mouths about men's competitiveness and close our eyes to men's altruism. But in the military, a man sacrifices himself to a state and to the freedom of people he doesn't know. Pretty altruistic. Yet the military is also competitive. Men compete to serve. Or compete to be altruistic. **In men's lives, competition is often the pathway to altruism.**

THE "KILL-A-BOY" FUND

In the recent Iran-Iraq War, Iran—and later Iraq—put "human waves" of boys as young as 6 in the front lines. The boys were throwing grenades and shooting, which ultimately forced the Iraqis to fire back and kill the young boys. However, many Iraqi soldiers reported that the moment they killed a 6- or 8-year-old boy they "could not let it go." They suffered nervous breakdowns, nightmares, cold sweats, and haunting memories for years.[48] The Iranian boys were, of course, used for exactly that purpose: to wear down the Iraqi morale.

The use of young boys was so widely supported in Iran that if a city was being attacked, families reportedly encouraged their young sons to go to war, believing it was better to be martyred in battle and assured of paradise than to die in an air raid, not fighting at all. With paradise as the bribe to die, the boys "volunteered." Before the age of consent. The result of this early childhood socialization is producing Saddam Husseins who are detested and women who are protected.

Boy from Shiite Muslim militia learns to kill to provide safe space so girl can love.

War is sold to boys not only by the bribe of paradise but by the ignorance of its hell. No one warned the Soviet soldier he would be left with the memory of separating a baby from its dead mother in Afghanistan and having the tiny body come apart in his hands. . . . Or, for another Soviet soldier, the memory of an Afghan rebel making an incision around his buddy's waist, then pulling the skin up over his head like an undershirt.[49]

As we come to care more about people dying, we give them warnings, not bribes. *We put warning labels on cigarette ads but not on recruitment ads.* But with boys, well, if we paid taxes in the late seventies, we helped pay for arms that were sold to Iran; we made our contribution to the human wave; we contributed to the "Kill-a-Boy" fund.

HOW ARE BOYS TRAINED TO FACE DANGER?

In the picture below, Chinese boys are piling bricks on their heads and being hit with a sledgehammer in order to learn to become less fearful of death. (Imagine *Time* magazine showing only girls being hit over the head with a sledgehammer and making no reference to the sexism?)

In reality, the pound-the-bricks-into-the-boy's-head exercise involves two tricks. First, the bricks absorb a fair amount of the

A DAY IN THE LIFE OF CHINA

TAKE THAT!

Marine recruits learning to
become impervious to pain.

hammer blow.[50] The second trick, therefore, becomes the real one: the men are seduced into believing that facing danger head on (so to speak) doesn't feel as bad as it looks. It is part of the way the armed services get men to discount their fears—in this case by "scientifically proving" to men that "even a sissy" can handle a sledgehammer.

III. THE PSYCHOLOGY OF MAKING MEN DISPOSABLE

ITEM. The Defense Department gave $2 million to Louisiana State University to study how to return brain-injured soldiers to battle (rather than help them adjust to civilian life). The Physicians' Committee for Responsible Medicine protested. But wait. . . . *The protest was not over the recycling of brain-injured men, it was over the subjection of cats to brain injury* to determine how the men could best be reused. Even the headlines read "Doctors Assail Project in Which Cats Are Shot."[51]

WHY DO WE CARE SO LITTLE ABOUT MEN'S LIVES?

We have seen that it was the *sacrifice* of men's lives that historically led to everyone's survival. So societies unconsciously taught themselves not to care too much about men's lives. Notice how this greater caring about a woman's survival is unconsciously highlighted in headlines:

The New York Times

6 Americans, Including Woman, Among 10 Released by Baghdad

MARCH 5, 1991

If we don't care about men's lives, why did married men with children receive draft deferments? Because we began to care about men's lives when men helped women and children survive.

INNOCENT WOMEN, GUILTY MEN

Both conservatives and liberals passively accept phrases like "innocent women and children." When foreign hostages are captured and only women and children are released, neither ideology protests the sexism:

Los Angeles Times

WEDNESDAY, AUGUST 29, 1990
COPYRIGHT 1990/THE TIMES MIRROR COMPANY/CC†/ 114 PAGES

DAILY 25¢
AN EDITION OF THE LOS ANGELES TIMES

Foreign Women and Children Can Leave Iraq, Hussein Says

Imagine a law requiring our daughters to enter a jungle and risk being shot through their heads. If you heard a news report lamenting that "innocent *men* and children" were being shot, would you want to shout, "Wait a minute, my daughter is innocent too!"? We would all know the news reports were "blaming the victim."

When a country goes to war, all the citizens of that country are equally innocent and equally guilty. When the United States attacked Iraq, 76 percent of women approved, as did 87 percent of men.[52]

Who is guilty? Who causes war? **War is caused by our primal fear of not surviving. This is a two-sex fear.** And because the fear is so primal, we are easily seduced into exaggerating the evil intent of anyone we become convinced might threaten our survival. Why? One mistake of *under*estimating a threat could leave everyone wiped out; many mistakes of *over*estimating would just leave men wiped out. Because our fear of not surviving was so primal, it led to the distortions of nationalism and our willingness to make men's humanity secondary to their disposability. It is time to stop blaming men for this two-sex fear.

When conservatives and liberals passively accept phrases like "innocent women and children," few understand how phrases like this actually keep women in their place: the more the woman accepts the innocent role, the more she requires a protector, thus reinforcing her innocence and justifying more protection. It's actually a powerful place, but it comes with a price tag: the more she needs protection, the more she seeks male chauvinists who protect her but don't respect her. Why?

WHY DO MEN LOVE WOMEN MORE THAN THEMSELVES, BUT RESPECT THEMSELVES MORE THAN WOMEN?

Remember how we protected our children *before* we respected their ability to protect themselves? The ability to protect generates respect. But the process of protecting comes by coping with the shadow side of the world. And with that coping comes a loss of innocence. When the man who has mastered protecting meets the innocent woman, he "falls in love" because her innocence allows a reunion with the self that got lost in the process of coping with complexity. Although he appears to have fallen in love with her, he really falls in love with his own lost innocence. **He loved that innocent self because his innocence allowed him to see his soul directly, the way we see mountains in a land without smog**.

The more innocent—or traditional—the woman, the more she seeks the man who can handle complexity. It is exactly his ability to handle complexity that *allows her to retain her innocence*. (The protector literally protects her innocence.) But in the process of dealing with the shadow side of life, he distances himself from his own spirituality, thus decreasing her love for him even as she increases her dependence on him.

Conversely he becomes spiritually dependent on her and loves her more even as he respects her less. He respects the part of himself that can master complexity but hates the part of himself that had to compromise.

When women are seen as the innocent ones, they become worshiped by men almost religiously. Which is not coincidental. The appeal of religion, as with the "innocent" woman, lies in part in how it allows us to be in touch with our simpler spirit—or spirituality. In how it gives us temporary relief from life's complexities.

But don't women fall in love with men they respect? We *call* it love. But she has not really "fallen in love," she has "fallen in respect." A man with an ounce of introspection is often uncertain whether it is love that his football or military uniform has generated, or respect. Thus the crisis in the film *An Officer and a Gentleman*, when the woman "in love" suddenly falls out of love when the pilot-to-be decides to be true to himself and not become a pilot. The film became a female fantasy because of the one *officer* who carried the woman away, not because of his friend who looked inside himself and decided not to become an officer. Audiences ignored the man who would value self and applauded the man who would sacrifice himself. The choice was a pension over introspection. Most men follow the applause. And they see few women applauding *A Dropout and a Gentleman.*

Men will not love themselves nor will women love men as long as the killer-protector role is disproportionately the role of the male.

The solution? Both sexes developing their own spiritual integration by integrating the need for protection with the need to be in touch with our innocence. The integration gives us inner peace. It doesn't make spirituality dependent upon denying reality.

AREN'T WAR STORIES EVIDENCE OF HOW MUCH MEN LOVE WAR?

Our association of war stories with bragging leaves us with the impression that men love war—that war is a male "toy." This *is* the dark side. The light side is the celebration of self that compensates for the tearing down of self that prepared him to be disposable.

War stories are the male way of processing feelings. **"War stories" are what men tell to reframe their fear.** When Bruce returned from 'Nam, he told this story.

> We shared our hooches with rats that weren't afraid to come at you while you were awake, much less asleep. I'll never forget the time a rat ran across my face. Its tail dragged for what seemed like a mile.
>
> —BRUCE GILKIN, Vietnam Veteran[53]

It is doubtful that Bruce enjoyed the rat running across his face. But telling his story was therapy. It is like being in a relationship and having a big fight that later becomes our favorite story. War stories are to war what the *War of the Roses* is to relationships. It is our way of reframing the horror—of turning a negative experience into a bonding experience. It doesn't mean we wanted to fight.

Soldiers returning from Vietnam and Afghanistan returned to countries which didn't want to hear their war stories. Deprived of war stories to reframe their fears and affirm themselves, they were, instead, overwhelmed by their fears and overwhelmed by self-doubt. The Soviet soldiers went into sanitariums,[54] the American soldiers went into drugs, prisons, and suicide.

War stories create two war-story dilemmas. The first is that war stories can be healthy for the storyteller to tell but might be unhealthy for the son to hear. It unconsciously teaches the son that he can get his attention the way dad gets his attention—by doing things that will put his life at risk. The second dilemma is that these stories tend to lull the storyteller into forgetting that he also needs help to release deeper, uglier fears.

The solution? Make counseling mandatory for anyone who has experienced combat or combat training. And educate the dad to help his son (or daughter) understand that he risked his life to free his child to do something other than fight; then ask the child what his or her interests are, thereby actually giving attention to the child for exploring alternatives to war.

IV. THE POLITICS OF MAKING MEN DISPOSABLE

ITEM. *Parade* magazine announces that 40 million Soviet men were killed between 1914 and 1945.[55] The magazine's headline reads "Short End of the Stick." Because men died? No. The women were seen as getting the short end of the stick because they were stuck with factory and street-cleaner positions the men weren't around to do.

After the world wars, our concern for veterans resulted in veterans' benefits. But during the 1970s and '80s, our lack of concern for veterans led to veterans' neglect. . . .

FORGET-ME-NOT?—THE LEGACY OF POSTTRAUMATIC STRESS DISORDER

I got killed in Vietnam. I just didn't know it at the time.

—PAUL REUTERSHAN, Agent Orange victim[56]

ITEM. More Vietnam veterans have committed suicide since the war ended than were killed in the Vietnam War itself.[57]

ITEM. It is conservatively estimated that 20 percent of all Vietnam veterans, and 60 percent of combat veterans, were psychiatric casualties.[58]

ITEM. A presidential review found over 400,000 Vietnam veterans to be either in prison, on parole, on probation, or awaiting trial.[59]

ITEM. In Los Angeles alone, an estimated 20,000 homeless veterans walk the streets. The Veterans Administration Center has fewer than 300 beds in service for them.[60]

If we are to understand the psychological responsibility of being born male, it might start with understanding the disease suffered by 60 percent of the combat veterans.[61] After the Civil War, the disease was called soldier's heart—heart palpitations, chest pains, dizziness. After World War I, shell shock.[62] After Vietnam, post-traumatic stress disorder (PTSD).

WHAT DOES POSTTRAUMATIC STRESS DISORDER FEEL LIKE?

To many men, here's what posttraumatic stress disorder actually felt like:

> The headaches started a couple of years after I came home from Vietnam. . . . Then one night not long afterwards, my wife, Loretta, found me in the hallway of our apartment, wearing army fatigues and holding my bayonet. . . . It took me another 12 years to find out that when I returned from Vietnam, not all of me came home.
> . . . sometimes even in broad daylight, faces of the dead come to life.
> A story like mine can be told by thousands of Vietnam veterans. The problem is, many vets just can't talk about what went wrong. Hell, I had to almost die before I found that the only way to live was to talk it out.[63]

What is a flashback like?

> I'd be driving down an open road and a commercial jet flying overhead would become an F-4 taking off from the air strip in 'Nam. . . .

A hill in front of me would turn into a hot spot about to be strafed. . . . The thoughts switched back and forth. . . . I'm home; I'm in 'Nam. . . . Don't look at broken white lines on the black road—they're tracer bullets in the dark night.

If you could read that last paragraph 100 times faster, with 1,000 times the intensity, you'd have an idea of what a flashback is like.[64]

A friend of mine wrote, "My ex-father-in-law, who strafed and bombed a trainful of Nazi troops, woke up in a cold sweat and in terror night after night for years after having to kill."[65] As one military historian put it, "The fear of killing rather than the fear of being killed was the most common cause of battle fatigue in World War II."[66]

Why is it we seem to hear more about disabled vets and stress disorder after Vietnam than after other wars? Does this signal increased sensitivity? Not quite. Vietnam produced totally disabled servicemen at three times the rate of World War II.[67] Why? Ironically, because medical evacuation procedures were more efficient—men whose legs were blown off were eventually saved. In World War II, these men would have died.

So the death rate in Vietnam tells us less about the real toll than in other wars. The physical and psychological aftermath—the 50,000 who are blind, the 60,000 who committed suicide (that are detectable), the abnormally large number "dying in car accidents," the 33,000 paralyzed—tells us more.[68]

On a theoretical level, we have recognized that the real trauma of Vietnam is lack of appreciation; on a practical level, we have not translated that appreciation into adequate help for Vietnam veterans facing homelessness, unemployment, recurrent substance abuse, Agent Orange poisoning, delayed stress syndrome, incarceration, homicide, suicide, amputations, and chemical poisoning.

When a study published by the *New England Journal of Medicine* revealed that wounded Vietnam combat veterans suffered more from PTSD than victims of rape and muggings,[69] it received little publicity. And little action was taken. For example, we have only four social service organizations in all of New York City dealing with veterans.[70] Compare this with more than fifty such agencies dealing with women's issues, almost all publicly funded—either directly (by the government) or indirectly (by tax-exempt status).

WHY HAS THE U.S. GOVERNMENT REFUSED TO RELEASE DOCUMENTS ON PRISONERS OF WAR?

ITEM. June 1992. America sees Boris Yeltsin acknowledge in a television interview that American POWs from the Vietnam War, World War II, and the Korean War had been transferred to Soviet labor camps and that some might still be alive.[71]

Within two days, the news media were explaining that Boris Yeltsin had probably just "misspoken." In fact, his acknowledgment had first been made in writing to the U.S. Senate's Select Committee on POW–MIA Affairs.[72] And the U.S. government had long been in possession of some 11,700 reports about the more than 2,000 American men still missing in action from the Vietnam War— including 1,400 firsthand live sightings.[73] In Korea, more than 8,000 men were missing in action and another 559 were unaccounted for as prisoners of war.[74] Secretary of State John Foster Dulles was aware of numerous reports of American prisoners of war from Korea in Soviet custody as early as 1954.[75]

Was there a cover-up? Was it just by the media? And if so, why? There does appear to be a cover-up, but not by the media alone. Just months before, army colonel Millard A. Peck, originally put in charge of investigating such findings after his stance that there was no cover-up,[76] came to the conclusion that there was. He found that officials in the National Security Council, State and Defense departments were taking each lead and, instead of pursuing it, "finding fault with the source. . . . The mind-set to debunk is alive and well."[77] He was so frustrated he resigned, protesting that his office was being used as a " 'toxic waste dump' to bury the whole mess out of sight and mind in a facility with limited access to public scrutiny."[78]

Colonel Peck knew the risk he was taking. He asked immediately for permission to retire from the army "so as to avoid the annoyance of being shipped off to some remote corner, out of sight and out of the way."[79]

Why this cover-up? "Closing the case" on POWs and MIAs helps Americans to return to peaceful lives after the war. After World War II, the Korean War, and the Vietnam War, the U.S. government declared all prisoners of war and men missing in action dead.

It refused to release documents on POWs and MIAs. We can understand the desire for this, but it reflects a greater willingness to make our own lives peaceful than to make sure that the men who preserved our freedom and peace are alive.

Now consider this: Had these MIAs and POWs been 10,000 of our mothers, daughters, and sisters would we not have intuitively known it would be impossible for the country to heal until every last lead was pursued? It would have been such a political issue in World War II that we would never have considered a cover-up following the Korean or Vietnam wars.

Our caring so little about men's lives always hurts more than men: children have grown up recalling their dads only from pictures on night tables in their mothers' bedrooms, and women have not known whether to bury their husbands psychologically or await the next phone call.

THE POLITICS OF AGENT ORANGE

The United States sprayed Vietnam with roughly 11 million gallons of Agent Orange, a chemical defoliant that contains dioxin. Laboratory tests on animals link dioxin to birth defects, cancer, infertility, and miscarriage as well as to damage to the liver and to the nervous and immune systems.[80]

Admiral Elmo Zumwalt was responsible for the decision to use Agent Orange. Perhaps no other decision of the war cut deeper scars on the nation's postwar nerves. Was it motivated by the insensitivity of male power? Let's look.

Zumwalt was *opposed* to the Vietnam War. He was nevertheless put in charge of the in-country naval forces in Vietnam. After sending off hundreds of boys who were ambushed by Vietnamese soldiers hiding in the intense jungle cover, and seeing only their forms return in body bags, he learned that Agent Orange could destroy the jungle cover and reduce deaths from ambushes.[81] At the time, the negative effects of Agent Orange were not revealed to him, but to this day, Zumwalt feels the decision saved more lives than it cost—despite what happened later.

Soon after Zumwalt's decision, his own son, Elmo, Jr., was exposed to the Agent Orange and contracted cancer. (A generation later, his grandson was born with multiple birth defects.) Elmo Jr.'s reaction? He bought insurance policies and struggled to stay alive for the three years it would take for the insurance benefits to kick in for his family.[82] He then arranged to have his wife's brother pull the plug once the three years were up. He wanted to give his wife his insurance benefits yet spare his wife the agony of pulling the plug. *So he arranged for another man to live with that agony.*

Did he blame his dad? No. He said, "Certainly thousands, including me, are alive today because of his decision to use Agent Orange."[83]

When we think of the top military brass, we think of power; we rarely consider the internal hell experienced by the Zumwalts of the world who find themselves making decisions that cripple their sons and grandsons for a cause they oppose.

Throughout history we have assigned men to live with the hell of making decisions that killed one man so two could live. Few men consider it a feeling of power to explain that to the parents of the dead boy. And yet, just as God asked Abraham to sacrifice his only son to prove his love for God, so Zumwalt experienced the powerlessness of sacrificing his son as he proved his love of country.

Isn't part of being a man having the courage to voice opposition? Part. Elmo did speak up. But having done so and lost, he, like all the military, knew his obligation was to serve others—not to have power. He could become a hero, but only within a framework—the framework of serving.[84]

Today, Admiral Zumwalt is the special advisor to the secretary for veterans affairs, specializing in the issue of Agent Orange. After reviewing every study done on Agent Orange, Zumwalt listed twenty-seven illnesses for which Vietnam vets should be compensated because of the likelihood they were caused by Agent Orange.[85] However, only three have received approval. Why?

Zumwalt explains that chemical companies are fearful of acknowledging dioxin as a cancer-producing agent in humans because it is present not only in Agent Orange but in many commercial products as well, and they are afraid of civilian lawsuits. There's astonishing evidence, though, that the resistance runs much deeper than chemical companies.

In 1987, when the Center for Disease Control was conducting a study of the link between Agent Orange and various diseases, the study was suddenly cancelled, reportedly as a result of the White

House strategy to deny federal liability. This was part of a decade-long struggle in which veterans groups claimed everyone was trying to deny the connection for fear of liability. The government and chemical companies denied that was the reason. Who's right? Here is a clue.

Almost overnight the decade of deadlock was broken. A bill was signed into law to compensate Vietnam veterans exposed to Agent Orange.[86] Stunningly, the vote in the House was 412 to 0.[87] Why? Saddam Hussein was threatening to use chemical or biological substances against U.S. troops. Suddenly the United States wanted to link Agent Orange to cancer and wanted to establish a precedent for guaranteed compensation because Saddam Hussein would be paying the bill. So the bill provided for new studies and guaranteed compensation.[88] This reasoning was not kept a secret.

In brief, when it appeared that American companies or the American government might have to pay the bill, everything was done to avoid the connection between Agent Orange and cancer and thus avoid payments. When it appeared that Saddam Hussein might pay the bill, everything was done to *make* the connection and establish a precedent for guaranteed payments. Perhaps there is a no more poignant statement about our attitude toward men's lives. (The turnabout was blatant enough to make a cynic blush.)

Who's to blame? In the final analysis, the U.S. is us. When women request to use a chemical and it does damage (as with Thalidomide), we create the political atmosphere to guarantee that women win their lawsuits. When men have no option but to be exposed to chemicals, we hesitate to compensate.

The women's movement has tagged the military as the "warrior elite."[89] The warrior elite, though, is less an elite class than a servant class; less an elite class than a dead class.

When Zumwalt wrote a book about his experience, he said, "There was one universal aspect of being a Vietnam veteran that I shared with all the others: our silence about serving in that war."[90]

My purpose in writing this book is, similarly, to bring men out of isolation—and, therefore, out of the drugs, divorce, depression, and suicide that are isolation's false alternatives. Talk about learned helplessness. To this day, the military elite has done little to help itself.

V. THE CONSEQUENCES OF CREATING A KILLER CLASS

WHY ARE MEN SO CRUEL? WHY DO THEY NEED TO "PROVE THEIR MANHOOD"?: THE CONSEQUENCES OF TRAINING OUR MEN TO FIGHT

When John Beverly returned from Vietnam with posttraumatic stress disorder, the men at work reinforced his suffering. They popped milk cartons, broke beer bottles, and even set off fireworks to see his reaction. He became so anxious he could no longer hold a job.[91]

Why do some men do this? **Men who taunt each other are instinctively training each other to become protectors.** How? No one wants a protector who could be scared away by taunting; so, over the centuries, young males went on search and destroy missions to discover each other's weaknesses. Once they found a weakness, they would try to "destroy" the boy by taunting him— picking at his weakness until the boy either sank or swam. If he sank, he had "failed to prove himself a man." **What does "fail to prove himself a man" really mean? It means he couldn't protect women and children because he'd be too worried about protecting his own weaknesses.** Women who sensed this wouldn't marry him.

Our desire for men to be our protectors has left us with "police brutality," the military mentality, and the Mafia—all associated with men. How can we wonder why men are not tender when we use them as tenderizer (that which makes something *else* lovable and tender)?

When men play the protector role in wartime, their wives usually become more balanced while the men usually become more out of balance. When World War II produced Rosie the Riveter, for example, "Rosie" symbolized the female energy, the "riveter" the male energy. The jobs women took gave many women the opportunity to *balance* their female and male sides. Their husbands, however, were forced to *intensify* the male side of themselves. For many women, then, war created a psychological balance while pushing men psychologically out of balance.

War itself might lead to a physically amputated leg, but many a vet would suffer that in a minute to recover the intimacy his psychological amputation has cost him with his wife and children. One reason we have books like *Men Who Hate Women and the Women Who Love Them* is because our taxes pay men to hate and men's income pays women to love. The piper plays the tune we pay the piper to play.

WARRIORS OF PEACE

Men are likely to be not only the warriors of war but also the warriors of peace. Almost all those who risk their lives, are put in jail, or are killed for peace are men. While some of the peace warriors—Nelson Mandela, Martin Luther King, Gandhi, Dag Hammarskjold—are remembered, most are forgotten. Remember Norm Morrison?

After years of protesting the Vietnam War, Norm doused himself with gasoline and set himself on fire on the steps of the Pentagon. The incident fueled the opposition to the war and focused energy on what protesters felt was our "enemy within": the Pentagon.[92] But Norm Morrison is forgotten. As is Brian Wilson, who repeatedly lay on railroad tracks to stop navy trains from supplying munitions to bomb the people in Central America. One train went right over him.

It's a legitimate debate whether Norm Morrisons preserve peace or undermine the military strength needed to preserve peace; whether the military preserves peace or creates a military mentality with a propensity to create war; whether Japan's recent methods of economic and family strength or Switzerland's historic method of staying neutral makes a nation happier than either war warriors or peace warriors. But we tend to accuse men of being warriors of war and forget that men are also warriors of peace. No one gives the Brian Wilsons or the Norm Morrisons Purple Hearts for peace.

THE CIVILIAN SOLDIER OF REPRESSION

On Veterans Day, there's one soldier who gets neglected: the civilian soldier. CIA, FBI, and DEA agents are America's civilian soldiers. These soldiers have legally signed away their freedom of expression in exchange for their ability to support a family.

The requirements not to discuss his worries, fears, or ethical dilemmas—even with his wife or best friend—turn every evening into one of repressed posttraumatic stress. Without the help of war stories to reframe his fears, his cover-up becomes cancer, and he a premature corpse in a casket, covered with honor.

Do repressed feelings really become cancer? The most responsible cancer research finds that cancer is six times more likely to occur among people repressing feelings than it is to occur among cigarette smokers.[93] For the civilian soldier of repression, it is not what he doesn't know that kills him; it is what he knows that kills him. What he cannot release from his brain can become the tumor in his brain. When William Casey, the former director of the CIA, was accused of a cover-up in the Iran-Contra affair, he kept his feelings to himself; he died of a massive brain tumor. At the same time, Bud McFarlane, similarly accused, at first tried to kill himself, but then, upon opening up and testifying, recovered.

The feelings the civilian soldier doesn't share with his wife provide the income the civilian soldier does share with his wife. His repression allows for her expression—often the expression of criticism for his repression. His penchant for repression becomes her pension to explore. The Stage I man produces the Stage II widow.

VI. THE DILEMMA OF THE SOLDIER IN TRANSITION

STAGE I SOLDIERS FREE WOMEN TO BE STAGE II WOMEN

Ninety-five percent of women's experiences are about being a victim. Or about being an underdog, or having to survive . . . women didn't go to Vietnam and blow things up. They are not Rambo.

—JODIE FOSTER, *The New York Times Magazine*[94]

Muhammad Ali's refusal to participate in what he felt was the criminal nature of the Vietnam War forced him into prison during the height of his career and deprived him of four years that could never be recovered. At the same time Jodie Foster was safe at home, becoming wealthy and famous and cashing in on her sex appeal. What would Jodie Foster have said if a sexist law kept her in prison when she was 24, 25, 26, and 27? Or if her body was valued so minimally that the only way she felt she could make millions was to subject herself to batterings that could eventually lead to brain damage and Parkinson's disease?

Just as first-generation college students had been freed by Stage I fathers to think of themselves as intellectually superior to their parents, so the Jodie Fosters were freed by Stage I men to think of themselves as morally superior to men who freed them from the dirty work of war.

To many men, it doesn't feel good to hear the Jodie Fosters ignore men's victimization, then blame the victim, then claim herself to be the victim—especially a Jodie Foster who grew up in an era in which women had the fantasy of "a room of my own" while their brothers had the reality of "a body bag of my own." It saddened men who watched women their age get a head start on their careers while they fought in a war that tore apart their souls, to return from that war to hear a woman call herself the only victim of sexism because she was being asked to make coffee at a job that no law required her to take.

By the 1970s, the American woman was being called "liberated" or "superwoman" while the American man was being called "baby killer" if he fought in Vietnam, "traitor" if he protested, or "apathetic" if he did neither. Even men who came home paraplegics were literally spit on.

This was happening not only in America. Soviet women living safely at home were called "liberated" and "overworked" while a million Soviet men, after facing death in Afghanistan, returned home not to be called "heroes" but "dupes." We heard about Soviet housewives standing in lines to shop; we heard little about Soviet husbands sweltering in Afghan deserts, suffering from the poisonous stings of scorpions or contracting malaria, jaundice, typhus, hepatitis, and dysentery.[95] When they returned home, the Soviet government would acknowledge only that they were *non*combatant *aides*. The denial and dishonor led to alcoholism, hospitalization, and suicide. But we heard only of the overworked Soviet women.

The adults of the 1990s are a generation of men criticized for what they were obligated to do by a generation of women privileged enough to escape the obligation; they are a generation of unacknowledged men coexisting with a generation of acknowledged women.

Reprinted with special permission of King Features Syndicate.

This "acknowledgment gap" was widened by another media phenomenon. . . .

Trading Places?

With the War in the Gulf came hundreds of newspaper stories about women leaving for war and of men "trading places" with the women. The stories almost always focused on how men discovered the difficulties of the woman's role.[96] However, women with children married to male soldiers rarely hold down full-time professional careers; men home with children married to female soldiers almost always had full-time professional careers.[97] For example, a chief petty officer who had been home only seventeen months of the past five years was now taking full responsibility for his four children: ages 2, 4, 6, and 13.

The result of the media acknowledging only her new role, though, was the chief petty officer feeling guilty: "I am scared about my wife getting hurt. She wouldn't be there if I made enough money to be able to live on one income."[98] He felt guilty about not being able to financially support six people, even though he had 100 percent responsibility for four children's care and all the housework.

THE SOLDIER IN TRANSITION

When the Chinese soldier in Tiananmen Square hesitated to kill people his own age who were offering him food, and when he set fire to his own tank yet remained in uniform, we can only imagine his internal conflict. We like to frame this as a conflict between immorality and morality, but to the soldier it was a conflict between two methods of being moral, or two methods of being immoral.

What made life torturous for soldiers from Afghanistan to Vietnam to Tiananmen was facing both the old expectation of external conflict and the new introspection that created internal conflict—and then returning home to face not appreciation but isolation. Caring about our sons means creating a support network for our veterans to deal with this extraordinary range of fears.

As our veterans returned to their mirrors at home and saw two faces, they wondered if they have been the hired murderers of innocent women, children, and men—and even, sometimes, the unwitting murderers of a buddy, à la Ron Kovic of *Born on the Fourth of July* fame. We have a responsibility to help them know their fears and know themselves. It is difficult for them to talk about their fears and nightmares when they are either seen as a traitor or never acknowledged as having been in combat. We must also do this for female veterans, but without forgetting that it is combat veterans who face the most severe posttraumatic stress.

VII. TOWARD SOLUTIONS

IS THERE A WAY OUT OF MAKING MEN INTO OUR WAR SLAVES?

From Rambo to Reality

To this day, his legs still Missing in Action.

—LEROY V. QUINTANA[99]

Political shifts often begin with actions that don't just raise consciousness but shock consciousness. For example, if a Rambo doll shows the ideal of violence, perhaps a "Reality doll" can show the realities of violence.

The Reality doll might feature a variety of models . . . a Paraplegic Model with a wheelchair and accessories like racially diverse arms and legs that are interchangeable and miniature prostheses; a Corpse Model with body bags, caskets, and urns—the quality level depending on the poverty level; a POW Model with a bamboo cage and extra stationery; an Agent Orange Model with deformed children; an MIA Model that gets lost in shipping . . .

The Posttraumatic Stress Models all come with straitjackets, pills, and a fifth of Jack Daniel's (made from caramel water). The Posttraumatic Tom Model features a built-in noise sensor. When a door is slammed, Tom experiences a flashback. He releases his rage on a Battered Barbie. The best-selling accessory for the battered Barbie model is a phone with an easy-access 911 for reporting posttraumatic Tom to the police.

The real consciousness shocker is that using dolls to *prevent* violence sounds more violent than using dolls to *promote* violence.

The "Males-Per-Gallon" War

World War II is often thought of as a war that brought America from depression to prosperity. The War in the Gulf would never have been fought if Kuwait were known for carrots, not oil. In the Gulf War men were still 96 percent of those killed; it was just the most recent exchange of men for money. It was the "Males-Per-Gallon" War. Until we protest, it won't end.

How Can We Employ Men in Peacetime Whom We Deployed in Wartime?

If war requires the willingness to sacrifice life, peace requires the skills to live life. Because wartime requires the sacrifice of individuality, boot camp became the lobotomy of individuality. Because peacetime requires the rebirth of individuality, reentry programs must help the veteran take his individuality out of hibernation.

In war, mistrust and paranoia are functional; at home, they are dysfunctional. Reentry programs must train to trust.

In war, a soldier's crying and asking for help is virtually prohibited because attending to self would slow down his unit; in peace, the veteran must learn how crying creates not weakness, but strength—it strengthens his immune system by cleansing impurities; it strengthens his children by giving them permission to strengthen their immune systems by crying; it strengthens his family by making them feel part of the team rather than dependent on one person. In peace, the veteran can be taught the compatibility between self-help and the strength of his new unit—the family unit.

In wartime, family therapy and marital counseling distract from a nation's survival; in peace, they're necessary to reunite that which war tore asunder. Exactly why? Some examples. . . .

One of the unrecognized problems of a soldier reentering his family is that a soldier has been learning he has no rights while his wife has been learning she has all the rights. That is, his wife created all her own orders and listened to her children only as she saw fit. Admiral Zumwalt was commanding in a war he opposed because even an admiral takes orders from superiors who take them from policymakers who themselves are supervised by voters' votes and opinion polls' updates. The soldier has been trapped in a constant fluctuation between the dichotomy of subservience and the *appearance* of dominance while his wife-as-mother, although she might have been called "just a housewife," was nevertheless her own commander in chief, her own policymaker, the only vote that counted, and the only opinion poll that had to be tended to.

At the same time, training that is functional for being a soldier is dysfunctional for being a parent. The soldier learns first to take orders without questioning, and then to give orders without being questioned while still taking orders without questioning. A father who trains his child to act without questioning trains the child well for wartime, but poorly for peacetime. In brief, family therapy and marital counseling are necessary to create family love instead of family war.

The job of the warrior is to sacrifice his own rights to preserve the rights of others; to sacrifice his own ability to question authority so he might preserve the right of others to question authority. It is tempting, when war ends, to keep this cadre of self-sacrificers on hand. The society that cares about men, though, rebirths the individuality within each veteran. When we don't, we are unconsciously caring more about our own security than a soldier's life.

We become more secure, though, by training veterans to uncork emotions rather than liquor bottles, to prepare them for a home life rather than a prison life, to create fathers in families rather than fatherless families. A nation that cares retrains its veterans to *dis*associate war from career advancement; it does this by retraining the veteran so he has a better future if there is peace than if there is war.

SHOULD WE GIVE HELP TO MEN WHO REFUSE TO BE KILLERS?

We can't end war by telling men that if they don't fight, we won't "respect them in the morning." (Then we wonder why men fight to gain respect.) If women are eventually drafted, I predict women who resist will be acknowledged, and the resistance will be seen as evidence of women's more peace-loving nature. In contrast, when a friend of mine refused to go to Vietnam and claimed conscientious objector status but without a religion, he spent the next four years in court, fighting the FBI, losing his job . . . in living hell. Those of us who saw his life being ruined, his hair falling out, the anger in his eyes, and ulcers in his stomach knew there was no true escape from the combat zone. Or from the posttraumatic stress.

There were no organizations to help my friend, nor the men who went to Canada rather than kill, nor the Bill Clintons—all torn between two definitions of conscience and courage. There are also no organizations that see the 18-year-old boy as a victim if he joins the army based on deceptive ads. By the time he sees reality, his choice is the army or prison and a label of AWOL that will follow him for a lifetime. (Try getting a meaningful job with a dishonorable discharge.)

We gave presidential pardons to women who were traitors—such as Tokyo Rose—but not to these men, without whose draft resistance the Vietnam War might have expanded and consumed the conscience of yet another generation of men. Maybe the wisest of draft resisters should receive Medals of Wisdom for seeing a different way of saving others' lives—and sacrificing career, health, and relationships to do it.

IS EQUALITY IN THE MILITARY REALLY A POLITICAL POSSIBILITY?

When civil rights leaders asked John Kennedy to prioritize civil rights, he answered, "Make it politically possible." Although no laws can be more unconstitutional than male-only draft registration and combat requirements, both are living proof that the unconstitutionality of a law is not enough to change it if the political climate does not support that change.

What is the forecast for tomorrow's political climate (for equality of responsibility)? Partly sunny, partly cloudy. The sunny part: 75 percent of men and 69 percent of women already favor drafting both sexes (if anyone has to be drafted).[100] The cloudy part: 57 percent of draft-age women said they would be unwilling to serve if drafted, versus only 24 percent of draft-age men.[101] And as for "requiring combat roles for women," only 12 percent of men and 9 percent of women are in favor.[102] In brief, neither sex is in favor of real equality; women are less in favor than men; about 7 million more women than men vote in each presidential election.[103]

None of this will change until we confront antimale sexism just as we confronted anti-Semitism. We call the annihilation of the Jews a "holocaust," but the annihilation of men a "battle." When Jews were slaughtered, we were horrified; when men are slaughtered, the battle is glorified. Hitler called Jewish death camps "work camps." We call male-only draft registration "male power." The Germans who smelled the flesh from the nearby ovens and chose to buy the explanation of "work camps" are now judged just as guilty as those who ran the ovens. Are the voters who support male-only draft registration and buy the explanation of "male power" just as guilty as those who make the laws to register only men? Yes. The voters elect the lawmakers.

In brief, attitudes create politics and politics precedes equality. The biggest hope comes with asking parents whether they want their sons to be more disposable than their daughters . . . with asking sons to value their own lives equally to their girlfriends' . . . with helping draft-age women understand the connection not only between responsibilities and rights but between responsibilities and respect . . . with helping draft-age women think of whether they want to bring up their own sons with the feeling that merely because they are boys they have to be prepared to kill . . . with helping everyone understand it is time now for an evolutionary shift that we all have an opportunity to pioneer.

Political shifts come from reframing the fundamentals: by demanding, for example, that whatever killing both sexes vote for, both sexes do; by explaining why we will never get rid of the "innocent woman/guilty man" if we keep women innocent and keep men killing; by understanding that men will continue to be perpetrators of violence as long as we give men unequal responsibility for violence.

What can each of us do while we are waiting for this paradigm shift to occur—while twenty-seven men are still being killed for each woman? We can express our appreciation. Kay Schwartz and her son chose something very simple.

On the tenth anniversary of the end of the war, my son made a banner on the computer, which we put across the front of the garage. The banner said "Vietnam—10 years—We Remember. To Those Who Died—Thank You. To Those Who Returned—Welcome Home." . . . I was sitting on the front porch having coffee and a young man came by delivering telephone books. He went up to the garage and read the banner. He came over to my porch and put the telephone books down, and stood there crying.

He said, "Lady, I love your sign."

I started crying and said, "I'm sorry it's ten years late."

We were both crying and then he said, "Lady, it is never too late."

—KAY SCHWARTZ, Addison, Illinois[104]

CHAPTER 6

The Suicide Sex: If Men Have the Power, Why Do They Commit Suicide More?

ITEM. A husband whose wife dies is about ten times more likely to commit suicide than a wife whose husband dies.[1]

ITEM. *Unemployed* men commit suicide at twice the rate of *employed* men. Among women, there is no difference in the rate of suicide based on whether or not the woman is employed.[2]

ITEM. In the middle of the Great Depression, men were 650 percent more likely to commit suicide than women.[3]

ITEM. The suicide rate of adolescent boys has recently increased three times as quickly as the girls'.[4]

ITEM. Just twenty years ago, young men (between 25 and 34) committed suicide at only twice the rate of young women; today, it is four times the rate. (Men's rate *increased* 26 percent; women's rate *decreased* 33 percent.)[5]

The Items stimulate a range of questions: *Why* has boys' suicide rate been increasing so much more than girls' more recently? Why is the loss of love so devastating for men? If unemployment among men leads to suicide, is it at all comparable to rape for a woman? Is female depression the equivalent of male suicide? Why do women attempt suicide more often while men succeed four times as often?[6] Why is the "Suicide Class" also the "Successful Class"? Is there any possibility that men commit suicide more because we care less—that the "Suicide Class" is the "Unloved Class"?

Let's start with adolescent boys. Why does boys' suicide rate, but not girls', increase 25,000 percent as their sex roles become apparent?[7]

WHY BOYS COMMIT MORE SUICIDE AS THEIR SEX ROLES BECOME APPARENT

ITEM. When a Trukese boy (in the western Pacific islands) has a troubled relationship, he is expected to respond by displaying *amwunumwun*, a kind of emotional withdrawal. Trukese males commit suicide 25 times more often than their American male counterparts.[8]

*Pre*adolescent boys and girls express emotions equally and commit suicide at about the same rate. It is adolescence that also pressures American boys (as it does the Trukese boys) to withdraw emotionally. And it is adolescence during which boys' suicide rate goes from slightly less than girls' to four times as great as girls'.[9]

For both sexes, adolescence sharpens sex-role anxiety like a pencil sharpener sharpens a pencil; the fear of rejection creates an emotional state as fragile as the sharpened pencil's point. Less attractive girls feel especially vulnerable . . . as vulnerable as they feel invisible. As for the more attractive girl, she eventually senses her dependency on a power that will fade, and as boys compete for her attention as if she were a celebrity, she becomes, in essence, a genetic celebrity—and genetic celebrities become entitlement dependent. As difficult as this is for girls, I believe that something is happening to boys during this time that makes suicide a greater probability.

By addicting boys more to girls' bodies than vice versa, we make boys feel less than equal to girls. This reinforces boys performing for girls, pursuing girls, and paying for girls to compensate for their inequality. When they perform and pursue inadequately—or feel they will never be able to earn enough to afford what they are addicted to—this creates anxiety which, in its extreme form, leads to suicide. Performing, pursuing, and paying—the "Three Ps"— are so anxiety provoking because the boy senses these are metaphors for adult versions of performing, pursuing, and paying. (So if he can't hack it when he's a kid . . .)

The adolescent boy notices that the boys who get the "love" of the genetic celebrity are best able to:

- *Perform*. Become a leader (jock, student-body president), have "potential," or have a car.
- *Pursue*. She has the option to pursue, he has the expectation. He is supposed to understand female cues when he doesn't even understand himself. To the degree the girl doesn't understand herself, his fear of misreading what can't be read becomes overwhelming. His hormones prepare him to reach out for sex but not for the rejection. He is supposed to initiate sex perfectly before he knows what sex is. He knows he wants to be sexual with girls; he's not sure if they want to be sexual with him (and the girls he's most interested in reject him the most). And nowadays if he misinterprets a cue, he could be in jail. Not true for her. This creates some anxiety.
- *Pay*. The greater her beauty, the more he will have to pay— and therefore earn.

These "Three Ps" are what boys learn they must do to earn their way to equality with girls' love. The teenage female has her own set of anxieties but has, *on average*, less demand to perform and more resources to attract love. Her body and mind are more genetic gifts. Thus, a popular girl is more a genetic celebrity, a popular boy more an earned celebrity. The more he is addicted to the genetic celebrity, the more he must become the earned celebrity.

The Demand to Perform without the Resources to Perform

What makes a teenage boy's anxiety so overwhelming is that **a teenage boy's socialization is the demand to perform without**

the resources to perform. As a result, not only are his risks many, but his failures many. And so apparent. Almost every boy feels like a silent member of the Frequent Failures Club.

Second, the biggest winners—the football players—are receiving love via self-abuse. **For some boys, receiving love via self-abuse creates anxiety. But losing love creates even more anxiety.** So he is caught between the anxiety of abuse by boys and the anxiety of rejection by girls.

The boy who performs mentally but not physically (the "nerd") is having his identity formed during years when the boys he least respects are getting the "love" of the girls he most desires. On the other hand, the boy who performs physically but not mentally often fears his hero days will end with the last day of high school.

Neither the short-term winners nor the short-term losers have the meaning of all this sorted out. Nor do you hear them talk about it. The anxiety tightens the stomach, is numbed by alcohol, and vented behind the wheel of a car. When a teenage male is fifteen times more likely than the average driver to unwittingly kill someone with his car,[10] male socialization has combined with technology to transform the protector as killer of the enemy into protector as random access killer. It is tantamount to the random release of killers. We defeated Michael Dukakis at the polls for releasing Willy Horton, but all of us create Willy Hortons. We even cheer for them. And then we marry Willy Lomans.

As a boy sees no alternative to performing, as each ritual highlights his inadequacy amid his search for identity, as he is without permission to speak with his peers of his fears, his isolation and self-doubt become his suicide. Thus boys' suicide rate goes from less than girls' to four times greater than girls'.[11]

WHY HAS BOYS' RATE OF SUICIDE BEEN INCREASING SO MUCH MORE QUICKLY THAN GIRLS' RECENTLY?

Girls are preparing for a world that increasingly allows them to be whatever they wish to be—homemakers, mothers, secretaries, executives. Girls can perform outside the home, nurture inside the home, or do some combination, depending on their personalities. Boys must still perform outside the home, no matter what their personalities. For some boys, life is still a round peg in a square hole, as it used to be for both sexes. This is especially true for gay boys, who still have little permission to be "feminine," versus gay girls, who now have much more permission to be "masculine." And perhaps as a result, gay teenage boys commit suicide three times more often than gay teenage girls.[12]

Previously, both sexes followed a narrow path of expectations to love—she: attract, resist; he: pursue, persist. Now she has the new option to pursue; he has the old expectation to pursue and no new options (if he expects to find love). In the past, both sexes were anxious about sex and pregnancy. Now the Pill minimizes her anxiety and condoms increase his. Now the pimple-faced boy must still risk rejection while also overcoming his own fear of herpes and AIDS and reassuring her there is nothing to fear. He must still do the sexual risk taking, but now he can be put in jail if he takes risks too quickly or be called a wimp if he doesn't take them quickly enough.

A girl now has the option to take the Pill or not; a boy's option does not include knowing if she is taking the Pill or not. Previously, pregnancy meant trouble to both the boy and the girl, but even more to the girl. Currently, pregnancy for a girl means the option of a quick abortion (no matter how the boy feels) or of suing the boy for eighteen years' worth of child support (no matter how the boy feels). In brief, today her feelings matter, his don't. Each time she has sex, she has an option; each time he has sex, he risks being the prisoner of her decision for the rest of his life.

Throughout the industrialized world, because boys have not found relief from performing, their adolescent games still prepare them for performing. Boys still dare each other to jump in front of moving trains, speeding cars, out of trees, or steal[13] in an almost ritual reenactment of their genetic heritage of proving their willingness to sacrifice their lives to protect.

The impact of this—making men's lives secondary to their ability to perform—is still with us. The following TV ad plays off of that reality:

ITEM. The girl signals. Two boys drive their cars toward a cliff. The boy who jumps out of his car first is "chicken." One boy's door jams; he and his car careen over the edge, splattering onto the rocks and into the ocean. Only a denim jacket and a pair of jeans surface. Across the TV screen we see "Union Bay—Fashion That Lasts."[14]

If a girl's body were splattered over rocks and into the ocean, no advertising executive would even think of exploiting that girl's death to sell a "fashion that lasts" . . . of using female disposability to celebrate fashion durability. It would be seen as the quintessential example of women being the disposable sex.

WHY IS "THE SEX WHO CAN'T LOVE" SO DEVASTATED WHEN THEY LOSE LOVE?

The most respected feminist therapists, such as Carol Gilligan and Jean Baker Miller, claim that a relationship loss is more pervasive for women than for men.[15] If it is, though, why do husbands whose wives die commit suicide ten times more often than wives whose husbands die?[16] A womanfriend of mine speculated that "it must be because widowers are mostly retired and they can't bury themselves in their jobs." So I checked. I discovered that **even a 30-year-old man whose wife dies is eleven times more likely to commit suicide than a 30-year-old man whose wife is living.**[17] At age 30, when men can bury themselves in their jobs and are physically and financially attractive to women, the loss of the one woman a man loves is so devastating it is often not softened even by the opportunity for many women. Men might bury themselves in their jobs, or even in another woman, but they don't bury the pain. In brief, **it is the loss of love that devastates men**.

The Military Man: The Roughest, Toughest Cream Puff

ITEM. In the 1980s, more men in the military committed suicide than were killed in Lebanon, Grenada, and Panama combined.[18] And for each suicide, there were an estimated eight attempts.[19]

We often think of the military man as being focused more on power and sex than on sensitivity and love; but the military man seems most likely to commit suicide *not* when he's lost a promotion or been rejected in sex but when he's been rejected in love.[20] The second biggest reason? Lack of friends.[21] Third? Lack of respect from family (e.g., a family still not respecting him after they've seen him on graduation day).[22] The common denominators? The absence of love and family respect.

Why is "the sex who can't love" so devastated when they lose love? *Why* are men such "rough, tough cream puffs"? Here's why.

Suppose you lost all your relationships in one fell swoop and couldn't discuss the loss with anyone for more than three minutes at a time? That's what divorce or the death of a wife can feel like to a man: his wife is often "all his relationships"—his total connection to intimacy. (He feels he has about a three-minute window of time to discuss a divorce with a colleague at work—often his "best friend.")

Feminist therapists telling the therapeutic community that women are more relationship focused and therefore hurt more from relationship loss is like saying a man is more financially focused and therefore should receive a better monetary settlement after divorce. This takes an advantage of female socialization and uses it as an excuse to get her another advantage—under the guise of "victim." The result? We care for grieving women and isolate grieving men, reinforcing the atmosphere for male suicide. As a womanfriend of mine put it, "When my grandfather died, grandma immediately joined the Greeley Widows' Society . . . I've never heard of a Greeley Widowers' Society." We don't even think of support systems for widowed men, let alone fund them.

DO WOMEN REFUSE TO COMMIT SUICIDE BECAUSE IT IS A SELFISH ACT?

ITEM. Jimmy Stewart's film character considers killing himself for his $5,000 insurance policy for his wife. The film is called *It's a Wonderful Life*. (Wonder what he would do if it were a horrible life!)

ITEM. When the farming crisis led to foreclosures and bankruptcies in the upper midwestern states in the early 1980s, the suicide rate among male farmers tripled.[23]

When I discuss the male suicide rate in workshops, a woman will often ask, "But isn't suicide a selfish act? It leaves behind people who need you and love you." That's correct—but much more correct for *women*. Here's why. When a woman is divorced, she has physical custody of the children 90 percent of the time. She feels an everyday connection to her loved ones, to her feeling of being needed. In my listening to thousands of women and men whose relatives or friends have committed suicide, I observed that **people who feel genuinely loved and needed rarely commit suicide**. Since the woman is more likely to be leaving behind people she knows need her and love her, she is less likely to commit suicide.

In contrast, men commit suicide more often when they are unemployed or lose their life savings in a depression because then **the man feels that by killing himself, he is "killing the burden." For him, then, committing suicide is not a selfish act, but an act of love**—relieving his loved ones of a burden. (At least that's the way he sees it at that moment.) However, if he thinks he'll be able to earn more money again—and *not* be a burden—he stays alive. Or if someone *really* convinces him he's not a burden even if he does remain unemployed, he'll live.

When a woman gets angry at a man for committing suicide, she is usually assuming selfishness on his part because that's what it would have been for her, given *her* situation. But it isn't usually his.

The single biggest solution to male suicide is making men feel needed as humans. Not just as wallets. When men feel needed primarily as wallets, they are more likely to commit suicide when their wallets are empty.

Why Do Women Attempt Suicide More Often Than Men?

Why is a woman three times more likely than a man to *attempt* suicide? We often hear it is because she wants attention, but that doesn't leave us with an understanding of what she wants the attention to accomplish: **She wants to become the priority of those she loves rather than always prioritizing them.** She is tired of love being defined as her being there for others rather than others being there for her. That is accomplished by an "attempted" suicide—which is really *not* an attempted suicide but a warning signal, just as an orange traffic light is not an attempted red light but a warning signal.

Many men have a deep need to send warning signals, but their belief that they have no right to ask others to rescue them from a disaster they feel they must have brought upon themselves keeps them from even letting themselves know they have that need.

They also know that the admission of some failure can in reality lead to more failure, because when colleagues and friends see some failure, the result is fewer referrals, fewer promotions, and therefore a greater likelihood of financial failure. This gives men but a tiny opening in which to experiment with asking others for help. So they tough it out in isolation. If they succeed, fine; if they don't, well, no one will love them, they're a nothing; no, they're worse than a nothing—they are a burden.

I believe men who commit suicide, then, do it when they feel *either* that (1) no one loves them or needs them (and therefore it is not selfish) *or*, worse, (2) that they are a burden on those they love.

WHY IS THE "SUICIDE CLASS" THE "SUCCESSFUL CLASS"?

The "Suicide Class" is 91 percent white,[24] usually well educated, and at least middle class. They are the "Success Class." Or at least they were—until they lost their job or their savings. But why suicide when I've been saying it's feeling not loved or needed that's the catalyst? Because **the men who are successful have become the most dependent on success to attract love. When this man loses his success, he often fears he will lose love.** Is this true? Well, it's usually about two parts fact, one part fear. It's usually a fact that his wife might not have considered him eligible had he been a supermarket checkout clerk, and it might be a fact that the success it took to attract love made him a specialist more in success than love; but he might also be underestimating his wife's or womanfriend's real love. Nevertheless, the fact and fear are both real for him, thus the connection between men, love, success, and suicide. Or, should we say, the disconnection between men and life.

IS UNEMPLOYMENT TO A MAN THE PSYCHOLOGICAL EQUIVALENT OF RAPE TO A WOMAN?

What do you call a Texas oilman? . . . Oh, waiter!

—JAY LENO, "Tonight" show

ITEM. Once upon a time a woman met a talking frog. The frog said it was under a wicked spell . . . it was really a Texas oilman.

"If you'll kiss me, you'll break the spell," the frog explained. "Then I'll love you and take care of you the rest of your life." But the woman did nothing.

"What's the matter?" asked the talking frog.

"You must be kidding!" the woman said, laughing. "You can get a whole lot more for a talking frog!"

ITEM. George Reeves, television's Superman, had gone a long period without being able to find other acting jobs. He was now 45. His fiancée watched him walk upstairs and heard him pull open a drawer. She announced to friends, "He's going to kill himself." A few seconds later a shot rang out. Superman was dead. Superman had been unemployed.[25]

Many women report that rape leaves them feeling humiliated, violated, helpless, angry, guilty, self-blaming, depressive, lower in self-esteem, and suicidal. Their vulnerability leaves them feeling powerless, as if the whole world were an elephant and they are an ant. Similarly, men who are fired or experience any of "the three unemployments—underemployment, unemployment, and the fear of unemployment"[26]—often feel humiliated, violated, helpless, angry, guilty, self-blaming, depressive, lower in self-esteem, and suicidal. Their vulnerability leaves them feeling powerless, as if the whole world were an elephant and they are an ant.

Unemployment deprives men of that which has given many men the respect and love of women; rape violates the body that has given many women the appreciation and love of men. Few men feel they chose unemployment, just as few women feel they chose to be raped.

Of course, unemployment affects women and rape also affects men. But the unemployed man is the subject of ridicule. The unemployed woman is not (no Texas oilwoman jokes abound). The attractive, unemployed woman with the potential for being a homemaker is sought after by many men; the attractive, unemployed man with the potential for being a homemaker is not sought after by many women.

Despite the similarity between the unemployment of men and the rape of women, no one would dare joke about the worthlessness of a raped woman. When men are valued according to net worth, men begin to confuse net worth with self-worth. No hope for work means no hope for love means no hope for life . . . means suicide. We will help men more when unemployment hotlines are as common as rape hotlines, when jokes about the unemployed man are as *un*common as jokes about the raped woman.

WHY FORCED EARLY RETIREMENT CAN LEAD MEN TO SUICIDE AND DEPRESSION

When a man is forced into early retirement, he is often being "given up for a younger man." **Being forced into early retirement can be to a man what being "given up for a younger woman" is for a woman.** When that is compounded by forced unemployment, feeling to men like rape feels to a woman, it becomes easy to understand why men who are retired or fired are soon expired.

Why do many men get more upset by retirement than women do from the "empty nest"—when their children leave home? **When females retire from children, they can try a career; when a man retires from a career, his children are gone.** Often they only grudgingly return (à la "Cat's in the Cradle"). We empathize with the new woman who has grown up and "forgotten to have children,"[27] but not with the man who has always (due to the responsibility of providing the family's financial womb), in essence, "forgotten to have children." But no men's movement explains a man's feelings of "powerlessness" for being his child's wallet while feeling deprived of his child's love.

WHEN IT COMES TO MALE SUICIDE, DO WE KNOW THE HALF OF IT?

When a teacher I know asked her class, "If you were going to commit suicide, how would you do it?" most of the girls said, "By overdosing on pills or drugs." But half the boys said they would get drunk and either drive off a cliff or into a telephone pole.

The method the girls chose—overdosing—becomes a statistic called "attempted suicide" or "suicide" (à la Marilyn Monroe). The method the boys chose gets recorded as a drunk-driving accident. Is it possible that we would have a more realistic picture of the numbers of male suicide *attempts* if we studied the frustrations of boys prior to drunk-driving accidents? If we did, perhaps we would be adding to the number of male suicides about half the number of deaths from drunk-driving "accidents," giving us a more accurate estimate of the number of actual male suicides.

The suicide rate of elderly men is also underreported. Just as elderly men commit suicide directly at a rate 14.5 times that of elderly women,[28] nurses note they seem to be more likely to just fail to take their medicine. But these deaths are not recorded as suicide.

When do men stop taking medicine? When there is no woman around. Because men can't live without being served? No. Because men can't live without being loved.

Perhaps the greatest cover-up of men's suicides emanates from the fact that if an insurance policy is less than two years old and a spouse commits suicide, the policy will not pay.[29] Therefore it is likely that thousands of suicides get covered up as accidents each year. Practically speaking, since elderly men are far more likely to commit suicide, when it comes to our fathers and grandfathers committing suicide, we might not know the half of it.

When a Man Commits Suicide, a Woman Is Wounded

When either sex is hurt, so are the ones they love. A friend of mine walked in on her dad hanging from a rope. There has hardly been a day of her life she has not had to deal with the consequences. Similarly, many women in my workshops have shared with me their fear that if they left their alcoholic husband, he might commit suicide. These fears are well founded, as recent studies prove.[30] That dilemma traps many women.

The solution? Until we do a better job of reaching out to men to be involved in men's groups and other support systems, hundreds of thousands of women will feel guilty leaving husbands. Were suicide a women's issue, would not special Women's Suicide Units in hospitals be federally funded? Would not every church and community group have Women's Suicide Support Groups? Would there not be corporate seminars that were federally financed to help women who were unemployed or fired? None of this will happen for men (and, therefore, for women) until we have the same compassion for men's powerlessness as we do for women's.

IS FEMALE DEPRESSION THE EQUIVALENT OF MALE SUICIDE?

Myth. Women experience more depression.

Fact. Women do not experience more depression, they *report* more depression. New studies find that clinicians fail to recognize depression in two thirds of men versus half of women. Women are also more likely than men to be diagnosed as suffering from depression even when it was later discovered they were not.[31] It is only when we actively solicit men and women that we discover that *equal numbers of men and women experience depression.*[32]

Myth. Female depression is the equivalent of male suicide.

Perspective. Female depression is not the equivalent of male suicide. Reporting depression empowers women; suicide does not empower men. Reporting depression allows the woman to get help; suicide leaves everyone helpless. Reporting depression is part of the solution. Suicide is the only symptom without a chance of solution.

Women report depression more because they seek out doctors more, have more of their problems identified (e.g., anorexia, bulimia, burnout, depression, spouse abuse), and have a support system making it safer to report depression. **The expression of depression is better than the repression of depression.** The expression of depression is the single best hope for preventing the "common cold" of depression from becoming the "pneumonia" of suicide. It is, therefore, part of the solution.

What makes if safe for women to report depression? Womanfriends listen, women's centers listen, and women's shelters both listen and protect. For example, women's crisis lines are there to listen to the 12 percent of American wives who suffer spousal abuse, or to stories of a daughter being sexually abused by Dad. (But who listens to the 12 percent of American husbands who suffer spousal abuse,[33] or to stories of a son being sexually abused by Mom?)

Her problems are given names by women's books and feminist psychologists, and then popularized in every women's magazine.

There are doctors for women's problems, but it is hard to name the male equivalent of an ob/gyn. In all these ways, when it comes to expressing problems, "when women speak, everyone listens."

Isn't Depression More a Woman's Issue Because It Is Associated with Women's Dependency on Men?

The *reporting* of depression *is* often associated with the dependency of women on men.[34] But it is dependency on men successful enough to allow a woman the time to think about more than survival. Which is why, when we think about women who report depression, we think of middle-class women, not working-class women. The working-class woman is too worried about survival to report depression. **Depression is a diagnosis that tends to increase among those with the luxury of worrying about something other than survival.** The more a person is in Stage II, the more that person can afford to focus on depression.

In contrast, the more successful the man is in the workplace, the more his depression must be repressed, not expressed. And what gets repressed in one place comes up in another—via alcoholism or suicide.

The solution? The woman who shares economic responsibilities feels more focused and challenged, less unfocused and depressed; her workplace gives her sources of approval besides her husband. She develops, in brief, the skills to control her own life: a major antidepressant.

If the Expression of Depression Is Part of the Solution, Who Is Helping Men Express Depression?

Are men taking responsibility to help themselves express their depression? Hardly. Men are still most likely to buy adventure books, financial journals, and sports magazines that teach men to solve problems, overcome barriers, or repress feelings. There are few men's shelters, "masculist" psychologists, men's crisis lines, or men's centers. The biggest "men's center" is San Quentin.

Are psychologists helping men? Once sought out, yes. But when the American Psychological Association first discovered that *peo-*

ple born in the last thirty years report depression more, most agreed it was due to young people being more *psychology* minded and more willing to report depression.[35] They saw the reporting of depression as a sign of people being empowered. However, when it was later found that *women* report depression more, a task force was formed to explore the problem, and the head of the task force immediately announced that women doubtless reported depression more because they were the greater *victims* of recent social change. The moment depression was associated more with women, the reporting of it went from being seen as evidence of progress to being seen as evidence of victimization.[36] And by the American *Psychological* Association!

Similarly, Dan Kiley (of *Peter Pan Syndrome* fame) estimates that between 10 and 20 million *women* live with a man and still feel alone.[37] Why only *women*? Here's his explanation: "The vast majority of these sufferers are females (males typically do not let lonely feelings manifest themselves)."

In fact, people who suffer but *cannot express it* are suffering more deeply. They need more help, not less.

Isn't it bad therapy to identify *only* the woman as a victim? Yes. But it's good politics. Why? Singling out the woman allows us to make her feel special. But special as what? Special as a victim.

The solution? Focus on the *couple*. Or on the *issue*—for *both* sexes. But this would require us to tell the woman equally as often, "Your husband is also feeling lonely with you, perhaps because *he* is *also* involved in a dysfunctional relationship." It is a sign of our respect for women when we are equally willing to ask a woman to look at the ways she might also be contributing to a dysfunctional relationship.

The woman-as-victim approach results in self-improvement books telling their female readers they take too much responsibility for the happiness and welfare of others. What is fairer is that both sexes do this in different ways. For example, when women cry, men take too much responsibility for trying to solve their problems.

The typical husband of this woman is characterized as "critical, demanding, and uncommunicative." But how can a man be critical and demanding if he's not communicating? Well, it is possible, but when his criticism is heard rather than labeled, it is often the first step to real communication.

We need to hear when men communicate rather than deny they are communicating because they do it imperfectly, and then deny they suffer because they don't communicate. Until we do, men will not report their depression to therapists—or to anyone. They will be rough, tough cream puffs: the suicide class.

CHAPTER 7

Why Do Women Live Longer?

Is It Biology?

ITEM. In Bangladesh today, *men* live *longer* than women. In Harlem today, women live longer than men. Correction. In Harlem, women live *much* longer than men.[1] If biology is the only variable, why these differences?

What Our Life Span Tells Us about Who Has the Power

When we learn that nonwhites have about 80 percent of the chance of whites to reach 85,[2] we know that it is because of the relative powerlessness of nonwhites. But. . .

ITEM. A boy infant is only half as likely as a girl infant to live to age 85.[3]

ITEM. When a man is about 25, his anxiety about "making it" is at its height. Here are the odds of a person living out that year:

Odds of Living Out This Year (25-Year-Olds)[4]	
Females (white)	1,754 to 1
Females (black)	943 to 1
Males (white)	561 to 1
Males (black)	311 to 1

In graph form, this looks like:

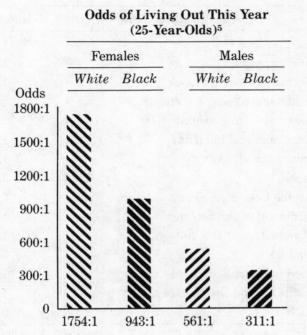

Odds of Living Out This Year
(25-Year-Olds)[5]

	Females		Males	
	White	*Black*	*White*	*Black*
	1754:1	943:1	561:1	311:1

ITEM. Blacks die earlier than whites from *twelve* of the fifteen leading causes of death. Men die earlier than women from all *fifteen* of the leading causes of death.[6]

THE INDUSTRIALIZATION FACTOR

ITEM. The more industrialized a society becomes, the more both sexes' life expectancies increase. But industrialization increases women's life expectancy roughly twice as much as men's.[7]

In preindustrialized societies (e.g., Italy and Ireland in the nineteenth century), a gap of only one to two years between the life spans of women and men was common.[8] When Robert Kennedy, Jr., examined his heritage, he found that rural Irishwomen around the turn of the century had a life expectancy that was actually

Male–Female Ratio of Age-Adjusted Death Rates for the 15 Leading Causes of Death[9]*

Rank**	Cause	Male to Female
1.	Heart disease	1.9 to 1
2.	Cancerous cysts	1.5 to 1
3.	Cerebrovascular diseases	1.2 to 1
4.	Accidents and adverse effects	2.7 to 1
5.	Obstructive lung disease	2.0 to 1
6.	Pneumonia and influenza	1.8 to 1
7.	Diabetes mellitus	1.1 to 1
8.	Suicide	3.9 to 1
9.	Chronic liver disease and cirrhosis	2.3 to 1
10.	Hardening of the arteries	1.3 to 1
11.	Inflammation of the kidneys	1.5 to 1
12.	Homicide	2.0 to 1
13.	Blood infections	1.4 to 1
14.	Deaths around the time of birth***	1.3 to 1
15.	AIDS	9.1 to 1

* The original chart with the technical names of the diseases is in the endnote.

** Rank based on number of deaths.

*** Inasmuch as deaths from this cause occur among infants, ratios are based on infant mortality rates rather than on age-adjusted death rates.

lower than men's.[10] Women who lived in the countryside died more than men from tuberculosis, diptheria, pneumonia, measles, heart disease, burns, and scalds.[11] When women moved to the cities, as they did in England in the early 1800s, their death rate declined by more than a third.[12] What happened?

When women and men have approximately equal life expectancies, it seems to be because women die not only in childbirth (fewer than thought) but about equally from contagious, parasitic diseases; poor sanitation and water; inadequate health care; and diseases of malnutrition. In industrialized societies, early deaths are caused more by diseases triggered by stress, which breaks down the immune system. **It is since stress has become the key factor that men have died so much sooner than women.**

Industrialization's Double Standard

Industrialization pulled men away from the farm and family and into the factory, alienating millions of men from their source of love. Industrialization allowed women to be connected with the family and, as we discussed above, increasingly surrounded with fewer children and more conveniences to handle those children, more control over whether or not to have children, less likelihood of dying in childbirth, and less likelihood of dying from almost all diseases. It was this combination that led to women living almost 50 percent longer in 1990 than in 1920.[13] **What we have come to call male power, then, actually produced female power.** It literally gave women life. It was an almost all-female club that took the first bus from the Industrial Revolution to the Fulfillment Revolution.

Men's new role—performing away from home—is enough to lead either sex to drugs, suicide, and accidents. The result is reflected in the song title "Only the Good Die Young." What two things do those who died young have in common? Think of Jim Morrison, Jim Croce, Jimi Hendrix, John Belushi, Janis Joplin, Buddy Holly, Charlie Parker, Patsy Cline, Elvis, Martin Luther King, and the Kennedys. They were all good *performers*; and they all spent most of their lives *away from home*—disconnected from their center, from their source of love. And in one way or another, it killed them.

Industrialization made performing away from home the male role. The fact that members of both sexes who performed away from home were vulnerable gives us a clue as to the impact of role over biology.

Don't women today perform away from home? Yes, but when the first child comes, *two thirds* of working women do not return to the workforce for at least a year.[14] Husbands suddenly support three people rather than one. Overall, women are forty-three times more likely than men to leave the workforce for six months or longer for family reasons.[15] **It is the options that allow a woman to tailor her role to her personality**, whereas the male mandate—to work full time—does not allow him flexibility to suit his personality. If he expects to provide well, he expects to wear a suit, not to wear what suits him.

Why has the gap between women's and men's life span been *reduced* slightly (from eight to seven years) between 1975 and 1990? In part because men's health habits are becoming more constructive, women's more destructive. Thus women are dying more from what the Chinese call "the disease of affluence"—breast cancer. But women are also working more away from home and suffering the stress-related diseases that go with the territory.

On the other hand, why has the gap not decreased even more? Because the husband of even the *full-time* working woman still works nine hours more per week *outside* the home and commutes yet another two hours more per week.[16] Her equal work burden still provides more balance between work and home. If her husband is reasonably successful, she can tailor this balance not only to her personality but also to her stage in life. Her greater options, greater balance, and greater connection to the family still keep her alive seven years longer.

Industrialization, then, has broadened women's options and deepened men's mold. Her juggling act allows her connection to everything; his intensifying act creates disconnection from love. Both are better off than they were, but her connection creates life, his disconnection creates death.

"Making a killing" on Wall Street thus became the updated version of the killer-protector: he still gets killed; she still gets protected. Or, more accurately, he protects both of them better, but protects her much better than he protects himself.

THE GENETIC FACTOR

If men had genetically superior immune systems, this would be our rationale for paying more attention to female health: "women are fragile; women need protection." However, women's double-X chromosomes give them a kind of genetic backup system.[17] That is, if a woman has a defective gene along one thread of her X chromosome, the odds are very high that the matching gene on the other X will be perfect.[18] Men don't have that backup system.

So while women have that initial advantage, it is not an all-encompassing advantage. In birds, butterflies, and moths, it is the males who have this genetic backup system and the males still die sooner.[19] And in humans, almost all premature deaths after the first year are related to stress-induced diseases and pressures related to men's role—from suicides to heart attacks, from cancer to murder.

More powerfully, the vulnerability of men because of their social role cannot be separated from their vulnerability because of their biology. For example, when men reflexively rescue women, they are not only more likely to get physically stabbed, shot, or punched but these rescuing behaviors generate "emergency hormones." For examples, testosterone is generated, but testosterone weakens his immune system;[20] adrenaline (or epinephrine) is generated, but adrenaline also causes his blood to be more likely to clot, making him more vulnerable to heart failure.

Just as countries build missiles "just in case" and then find the cost of those missiles has taxed their ability to strengthen themselves in other ways, men similarly pay a biological price for their external role as women's constantly available, unpaid bodyguards.

WHY THE MALE ROLE IS SO LIFE DEPLETING

When boys and girls are young (1 to 4), boys die only slightly more frequently than girls. Once adult sex roles are experienced—between ages 15 and 24—men die at a rate more than three times that of women.[21] The male role, then, might be thought of as being about three times as life depleting for men as is the female role for women.[22] We discussed above how the need of boys to perform, pay, and pursue to be equal to girls' love led boys to anxiety that sometimes resulted in suicide. It also leads to a series of coping mechanisms that prepare boys to die more quietly even as they are succeeding more overtly. Two examples:

Male Pattern Flaw Finding

If you've ever had an adolescent son (or been one), you know a boy's "best friend" is the one with whom he trades "wit-covered put-downs." Why is "the put-down trade" the commerce of male adolescence? And why is this "male pattern flaw finding" so damaging?

The put-down trade is our adolescent son's rehearsal for taking criticism as an adult. Taking criticism is a prerequisite to success. The upside is that it prepares men to handle criticism at work and in their personal relationships without taking it personally. The downside is the "hidden tax."

The hidden tax? The *New England Journal of Medicine* has recently reported that speaking about one's faults creates abnormalities in the pulsations of our heart. Tiny abnormalities? No. Abnormalities as great as those produced by riding a stationary bicycle to the point of either exhaustion or chest pain.[23] Perhaps the criticism, then, contributes to men being four times more likely than women to suffer heart disease before age fifty.[24] In essence, our sons might be practicing heart-disease training.

While men are bonding by giving each other criticism, women are bonding by giving each other support. The price men pay is the feeling of isolation and loneliness. Only now we are discovering that **loneliness is a strong predictor of heart disease**.[25] Heart disease, then, is the hidden tax of the put-down trade. Male pattern flaw finding becomes male pattern heart attacks.

Male Nurturance

In almost every men's group I have formed, men discuss problems they face at work—especially feelings of being unappreciated or criticized by bosses and colleagues. If we ask a man whether he has discussed this with his wife or womanfriend, he usually says he has, but only superficially. Why? He says he doesn't want to worry her.

Not worrying his wife about work fears is one of many male forms of nurturance—protecting the woman he loves from insecurity. So he puts on a facade of security that prevents him from asking for help through his deepest insecurities.

It is this male dilemma that creates the stress that silently damages men's immune systems. He might seek temporary satisfaction from a "substitute wife" (a second woman, second job, second drink, or second needle) . . . which is one reason he is three times more likely than a woman to have a drinking problem.[26] If he doesn't turn to an escape, an escape turns to him: cancer, a heart attack . . .

Killing Him Softly

These coping mechanisms—or defense mechanisms—kill men a lot more softly than in the past. Fewer men die in coal mines, more die inside when a lifetime of doing everything he could to support a family leads to his income becoming an incentive for his wife to leave him. When he sees his children walk out the door and be turned against him, his spirit burns out as quickly as the flame of brandy on a cherries jubilee.

When the demands to perform outpace the resources to perform, men become the disposable sex:

The Disposable Sex

	Men	*Women*	*Percentage of Men*
Homeless[27]	165,000–231,000	32,000–45,000	83
Deaths from AIDS[28]	69,929	7,421	90
Names on Vietnam Veterans Memorial in Washington, D.C.[29]	58,183	8	99.99
Americans Still Missing in Action in Southeast Asia[30]	2,267	0	100
People in Prison[31]	758,294	46,230	94

No group of men is more a victim of the demands to perform without the resources to perform than the black boy and his dad.

THE BLACK MALE: NOT-SO-BENIGN NEGLECT

The only group that can expect to live shorter lives in 1990 than in 1980 is black men.[32] Why? For starters, it is black men who experience the greatest gap between the Stage I expectation to survive by being a physical slave and the Stage II need to be a master of technology. Thus the black male now lives nine years fewer than the black female.[33] Nevertheless, we hear more about the double jeopardy of racism and sexism encountered by the black female.

More black males are in the prison system than are in the college system.[34] That is, an incredible one out of four black males is either in jail, prison, on probation, or on parole.[35] That's almost 50 percent greater than the number in college.[36] This does not even come close to being true of black women. If it were, imagine the number of job training, education, and rehabilitation programs we'd be sponsoring for black women. The black male does not face double jeopardy, he faces quadruple jeopardy: racism, sexism, antagonism, and neglect.

For different reasons, few whites or blacks are willing even to discuss how the use of the black male as a field slave required a greater dependency on physical strength for most black men than it did for most black women—and that it is physical strength that current technology makes increasingly irrelevant. Similarly, when white females or males worked hard, *their* families benefited. But when black females or males worked hard, someone *else* benefited. So for the white person, hard work meant survival; for the black slave, hard work meant the survival of someone else—at the expense of self. Our unwillingness to discuss this has prevented us from developing affirmative-action programs encouraging, for example black father–black son businesses (rather than giving the black mother money to keep the father *away* from the son).

The black man is sometimes called an endangered species but receives little of the protection an endangered species is normally accorded. In regions where the owl is endangered, we wouldn't think of depriving the male owl of its children or the owl's children of their dad. Yet the U.S. government has a huge program that creates exactly that outcome for the male human who is poor, and especially for the male human who is black and poor. It is called Aid to Families with Dependent Children; it deprives a family of aid if the dad is present, thus depriving the father of the two most important incentives for living: love and feeling needed.

DOESN'T MEDICAL RESEARCH NEGLECT WOMEN?

The belief that sexism has led to a focus on men's health at the expense of women's has led both the federal government and private industry to focus on women's health at the expense of men's. Thus the government has recently established an Office of Research on Women's Health but no Office of Research on Men's Health.[37] It has also established an Office of Minority Health that defines women as a minority,[38] but no Office of Minority Health that defines men as a minority (due to only men dying at a younger age from all fifteen of the major causes of death). The belief in women's neglect has led private hospitals and health-care companies to start women's health-care centers but almost no men's health-care centers.[39] So let's look at the myths versus the realities.

Overall Myth. **Less money and attention are given to female health than male health.**

Supporting Myth #1. "Less than 20 percent of the research budget of the National Institutes of Health [NIH] is spent on women's health."[40]

Fact. No governmental agency focusing on health spends as much on men's health as on women's health. The reason less than 20 percent of the research budget of the NIH is spent on women's health is because 85 percent of the research budget is spent on *non*gender-specific health issues (or basic science); 10 percent is spent on women's health; 5 percent is spent on men's health. (This is the analysis of the NIH's Office of Research on *Women's* Health.[41])

Supporting Myth #2. Sexism is the reason that more studies have been done on men in almost all areas of medical research.

Fact. In a search of more than three thousand medical journals listed in *Index Medicus, twenty-three* articles were written on women's health for each *one* written on men's.[42]

Fact/Perspective. With that larger picture in mind, it is true new products and potentially dangerous drugs were often tested on prisoners. But this is because we care less about prisoners; and they were often tried on men because we care less about men. Similarly, sulfa drugs, LSD, and other experimental research was often conducted by making guinea pigs of military men. Did the men in the military get anything in return? Yes. Time off from time which only men were required to serve. In brief, **we do more research on men in prison, men in the military, and men in general than we do on women for the same reason we do more research on rats than we do on humans.**

Supporting Myth #3. If diseases were killing men as fast as breast cancer is killing women, men would get the funding to solve the problem.

Fact. A woman is 14 percent more likely to die from breast cancer than a man is from prostate cancer,[43] yet funding for breast cancer research is 660 percent greater than funding for prostate cancer research.[44] The death-to-funding ratio is 47 to 1 in women's favor.

Fact. The death rate for prostate cancer has grown at almost *twice the rate* of breast cancer in the last five years.[45]

Fact. Black men in the United States have the highest incidence in the *world* of cancer of the prostate.[46]

Supporting Myth #4. Virtually all of women's health has been neglected—from ovarian cancer to menopause. The neglect comes in both research and treatment.

Fact. There is a neglect in research for women's health such as ovarian cancer and menopause that is now being remedied by the new Office of Research on Women's Health of the NIH; there is *also* a neglect in research in the following seventeen areas of men's health that is *not* being adequately remedied by anyone:

- A men's birth control pill
- Suicide
- Posttraumatic stress syndrome
- Circumcision as a possible trauma-producing experience
- The male midlife crisis
- Dyslexia
- The causes of male violence
- Criminal recidivism
- Homelessness
- Steroid abuse
- Color blindness
- Testicular cancer
- Prostate cancer
- Hearing loss over age 30
- Sexual impotence

- Nonspecific urethritis
- Epididymitis (a disease of the tubes that transmit sperm)
- Klinefelter's disease, ALD, and other male-only inherited diseases

Fact. Men are more likely to suffer from mental illness; women are almost twice as likely to be treated for mental illness.[47]

Yes, there is a need for more research on women's health—as there is a need for more basic research and more research on men's health. Yet all of these needs for specific research must not be dictated so much by gender politics that the basic research (DNA, cellular, transplant, etc.) gets neglected—research which can help both sexes live longer. So how can we do it all? We can start by funding medical researchers more than missile researchers.

Supporting Myth #5. Women are now as vulnerable as men to death from heart attacks, but sexism is why only men have been studied.

First, the vulnerability to death from heart attacks. . . .

Fact. Compared to other diseases, heart attacks have now become the number one killer of women. But men are still far more vulnerable to death from heart attacks than women: before the age of 65, men still die from heart attacks at a ratio of almost 3 to 1 vis-à-vis women.[48] Even after the age of 85, men's death rate is still slightly higher.[49]

Put another way, **almost three quarters of women who die of heart attacks are 75 or older.[50] By this time, the average man has been dead for three years.[51]**

Second, concerning the cause célèbre of medical sexism—that only men had been studied related to the effects of aspirin on heart attacks. . . .

Fact. Yes, there was a study on only male physicians on the effects of aspirin on heart attacks.[52] *And* there was a simultaneous study conducted only on female nurses (also on the effects of aspirin on heart attacks).[53] The press touted only the male study as sexism. Yet the women's study was longer in duration and there were four women studied for each man.[54]

Would more research on why men die of heart disease so much earlier serve any real purposes? Yes. For example, when men with heart attacks were randomly put into two groups, one group experiencing group therapy, the other group not, the men in therapy reversed coronary artery blockage; the men not in therapy experienced an increase.[55] If heart attacks are induced by stress and reduced by stress control, we need to know more about the types of stress that induce it and the types of therapy that reduce it. The answers will help both sexes.

Nevertheless, one-sex studies—whether with the intent of preventing heart attacks or preventing spouse abuse—should be rare. The rule of thumb for funding a one-sex study should be to require *proof* that the other sex doesn't need studying rather than accepting the *assumption* that the other sex doesn't need studying.

Supporting Myth #6. Sexism is the reason men with heart attack symptoms are more likely to receive the most advanced tests and most effective operations: coronary bypass and angioplasty.

Fact. Coronary bypass operations are more than twice as likely to lead to death for women than for men.[56] Why? In part, because women as a group have smaller coronary arteries which are more likely to close after the operation.[57] And in part because almost three quarters of women who have heart disease are over 75 and are also much more likely to have cancer of the breast or other complications that make the demands of surgery far more likely to lead to death.[58] As a result, a woman is more likely than a 60-year-old man to refuse a coronary bypass or angioplasty operation. Which is why she is also less likely to ask for a costly and somewhat demanding diagnostic test.

The policy of informed consent means the final decision is not the doctor's, but the patient's—and these are the circumstances the patient considers that lead to fewer tests and less surgery. To call the female patient's decision sexism is to call her stupid for saving her own life.

Fact. When age and other complicating factors (e.g., diabetes, hypertension, obesity) are controlled for, there is no difference between the treatment of men versus women with heart attacks.[59]

In brief, medical research has been perhaps the single biggest contributor to women's life span increasing almost 50 percent since 1920. Medical research was responsible for a female pill (but no male pill), fewer female deaths in childbirth, and research on the diseases women once died of in equal numbers to men (TB, diphtheria, polio). It is ironic that feminists are calling it sexism against women when it is women's lives that have gone from one year longer than men's to seven years longer than men's. What would feminists be calling the medical community if men lived longer? Or if women died at a younger age of every one of the fifteen major causes of death?

THE POLITICS OF THE BREAST VERSUS THE POLITICS OF THE PROSTATE

Why does breast cancer receive over 600 percent more funding than prostate cancer despite men being almost as likely to die from prostate cancer? Is it possible that we pretty much know what we need to know about prostate problems? Let's look.

ITEM. In the 1920s, a new operation for enlarged prostates replaced an old one. *For sixty years no one studied the records to determine whether the new operation was as beneficial as the old one.* When these studies were done, they found the new operation resulted in a 45 percent greater chance of dying in the five years after surgery. Finally, in 1989, seventy years later, the data were published in the *New England Journal of Medicine.*[60]

From prostate cancer research we know that a man with a vasectomy might be four times more likely to have prostate cancer than a man without a vasectomy.[61] A similar connection has been found in mice. Despite these findings, the shortage of research funds has not allowed scientists to explore whether prostate cancer is caused by vasectomies or by something correlated with the vasectomy (e.g., testosterone level).

Similarly, testicular cancer is one of the most common cancers in men 15 to 34. When detected early, it has an 87 percent survival rate.[62] But it is only women whom we educate to do early detection of their cancer:[63]

Mary Brodie won't feel the lump in her breast for another two years.

Like a lot of women, Mary Brodie understands the importance of regular breast self-examination. And because she's never felt a lump, she thinks everything is fine. It's the same conclusion a lot of women reach.

Unfortunately, it's wrong. The tiny tumor that's forming in her breast is too small to feel. But with mammography, it's not too small to see.

And tomorrow Mary is getting her first mammogram. Thanks, in part, to a new x-ray film created by DuPont that makes it safer for women to start mammography early.

And for Mary, early detection means a two year head start on the rest of her life.

At DuPont, we make the things that make a difference.

Better things for better living. DU PONT

If we educated men to go for routine rectal exams for prostate cancer prevention and to do routine testicular self-exams—the way we educate women to do routine breast self-exams—we would keep tens of thousands of men alive just as we are now keeping tens of thousands of women alive. Supreme Court Justices Blackmun and Stevens had their cancer of the prostate detected through just one of those routine exams.[64] They caught it in time to live.

WASN'T THE LACK OF RESEARCH ON THE PILL AN EXAMPLE OF NOT CARING ABOUT WOMEN?

When birth control pills were available in Europe but not in the United States, American women created an uproar about how the unwillingness to make the pill available showed a contempt for the lives of women who might die in childbirth or via abortions. But when the Food and Drug Administration (FDA) released birth control pills with dosages of hormones that were later found to be unnecessarily high, they were attacked for not caring about women enough to do the necessary tests to make the dosage level as low as possible.[65]

In brief, when women's lives were at stake we stumbled all over ourselves until we were caught between a rock and a hard place. When men's lives were at stake, even readily available data sat dormant for more than half a century without a single person studying it.

DON'T MALE DOCTORS TREAT MEN'S SYMPTOMS MORE SERIOUSLY?

The feeling that male doctors treat men more seriously seemed to have been respectably documented when the *Journal of the American Medical Association (JAMA)* reported on such a study conducted by Lawrence Schneiderman.[66] But when I spoke with Dr. Schneiderman, he explained that he had, in fact, done two studies: one found that men were treated slightly more seriously; the second found no difference. The first study not only made the prestigious *JAMA* but also received wide media attention.[67] The second was published in a small, nonprestigious journal and was ignored by the media.[68] In the first study, though, the female patients had visited the doctor 150 percent more often than the male patients; in the second study, the female and male patients had visited the doctor equally as often.

Is it necessarily sexism that a doctor will treat a man more seriously? Not if men are more likely to end up in the hospital,[69] more likely to die sooner of all fifteen major causes of death, and less likely to seek help until the symptoms have reached an advanced stage. Given that, the second study suggests that men get *equal* treatment for *worse* problems. Which is really sexism against men.

None of this denies that many doctors are more sensitive to efficiency than to their patients. Insensitivity is the shadow side of dealing daily with death. And there is no doubt that patients feel more condescension than attention. Condescension is the shadow side of protection. Do women get more condescension than men? Probably. Women get more protection than men. And condescension is the shadow side of protection. . . .

TOWARD SOLUTIONS

Although a government study found that men's health was much worse than women's health or the health of any minority group, headlines around the country read: "Minorities Face Large Health Care Gap."[70] They did *not* say: "*Men* Face Large Health Care Gap." Why? Because we associate the sacrifice of men's lives with the saving of the rest of us, and this association leads us to carry in our unconscious an incentive not to care about men living longer. When that changes, the government will be initiating searches for our POWs, not stonewalling searches. But nothing will really change until we effect a disassociation.

If we care enough to start an Office of Men's Health, will it really make any difference? Yes. An Office of Men's Health can introduce us to men's problems we haven't even heard of. Remember the boy in grammar school or high school with enlarged breasts and speech problems? In my school, the kids called a boy like this "Blubber" and "Baby Huey." But if he had Klinefelter's disease, he had a chromosomal condition (47 chromosomes instead of 46) that affects only boys (1 out of every 400) and that also made him sterile. If this boy had Klinefelter's, his parents probably didn't know it; neither did his teachers; neither did he. He needed those who loved him to know *how* to love him, not to tell him to eat less or speak more clearly. He needed a support group giving him love, not a peer group calling him "Blubber." I am sure he was left with a lifetime of psychological damage that each of us could have helped him avoid. An Office of Men's Health could have helped us help him.*

A good education program could keep more men from dying of prostate cancer each year than were killed each year in the Vietnam War.[71] And good research can help us know to what degree the vasectomies that are linked to prostate cancer in mice are also linked to prostate cancer in men.[72]

Although cancer of the testes is about ten times more likely to develop among men whose testes descended into the scrotum after age 6, I have yet to meet a man who knows at what age his testes had descended into his scrotum. Few men know that it is relevant to know. And few mothers or fathers know enough to let their sons know.** An Office of Men's Health could provide this type of education, but not without asking a few questions—such as, "Why do we show on TV a real woman's breasts and not even a pencil outline of a man's penis and testicles?"

An Office of Men's Health can pioneer suicide crisis hotlines nationwide, create support networks for elderly men who are 1,350 percent more likely to commit suicide than women their age, and education programs for high school guidance counselors on the connections between adolescent male stress and adolescent male suicide.

An Office of Men's Health could educate men about why men are seven times more likely than women to be arrested for drunk driving[73] while only three times more likely than women to be hospitalized for alcoholism.[74]

We often interpret women's increased drinking and smoking as reflections of women's increased stress level (which it often is) but rarely interpret the facts that men are three times more likely to be alcoholics and more likely to die of lung cancer as reflections of men's continuing higher stress level. In brief, we keep ourselves open to new ways of understanding (and helping) women, which is wonderful, but fail to use the same mind-set to better understand (and help) men.

We have a choice. We can continue socializing our sons to fight

---

* Until that time, contact Klinefelter Syndrome and Associates, Box 119, Roseville, CA 95661-0119.
** If you wish to pursue this, call 1-800-4-CANCER and ask for "Testicular Self-examinations," NIH Publication No. 87-2636.

our fires and be amazed when they fight their feelings. *Or* we can reach out to counter boys' socialization and the socialization of girls to love the boys who pay, perform, and pursue; to stop subsidizing male child abuse in the form of football and calling it education; to develop programs to prevent men from being 95 percent of the prisoners and 85 percent of the homeless; to do for men what we would be doing for women if women used to live one year less but now live seven years less, used to be equal victims of the fifteen major causes of death and were suddenly the first victims of every one of the fifteen major causes of death.

CHAPTER 8

The Insanity Track

A male said to me once after years of standing on the platform of the subway, "I die a little bit down there every day, but I know I am doing so for my family."

—BILL MOYERS, coauthor, *The Power of Myth*[1]

I've never done a single thing I've wanted to in my whole life.

—SINCLAIR LEWIS, *Babbitt*

What distinguishes the married male executive from the married female executive? The higher up the married male executive goes, the *less* likely is his wife to work outside the home. (Eighty-seven percent of wives of top executives [vice-president and above] work inside the home, not outside the home.[2]) Conversely, almost all the husbands of female executives work *full time* outside the home. So the married male executive has a wife who is a *financial* burden. A married female executive has a husband who is a financial *buffer*. The married male executive has more home support from his wife, but he pays for that by treating his profession more as an obligation; she has less home support, but she can treat her profession more as an opportunity.

A man in one of my workshops put it this way: "When I was fired, the mortgage payment became the mortgage nightmare. When my wife got sick and I hesitated—just for a moment—to find the best and most expensive doctor, I felt guilty. And when I saw my children say good-bye to their best friends because we had to move, it broke my heart. Just days after I had watched them cry saying good-bye, I got a heart attack."

When we hear a female executive say, "What I need is a wife," everyone says, "Yeah!"; no one says, "Take on the financial burden of a husband and you'll find a 'wife.' " Or, "Just ask a man to be a househusband and you'll find one." In my workshops, I have met thousands of men willing to parent, cook, manage the home, and arrange the social life in exchange for the income of an executive woman he loves. I meet few executive women volunteering to financially support these men. And I see few ads in the personals saying, "Successful woman wants handsome househusband."

It is exactly, then, the tendency of a family to mean "financial burden" to an executive man and "financial buffer" to an executive woman that leads to men being more likely to fall into the "lawyer trap," the "doctor-as-slave trap," and the "paper warrior" incinerator. . . .

The Lawyer Trap

ITEM. Forty-one percent of lawyers would enter another profession if they had to do it all over again.[3]

ITEM. The alcoholism rate among lawyers is almost twice as high as among the general population.[4]

Many lawyers enter law with the fantasy of becoming a Perry Mason. Instead they become a paper mason. They expect to work with people. They become isolated from people. They desire to be a legal pioneer. They become a legal prostitute.

Both male and female lawyers are much more likely to feel like prostitutes when they work for corporations. One woman who quit being a corporate lawyer to become a mountain trail guide put it like this: "Lawyers are trained to separate their feelings from the position the client wants them to take, which serves you well as a lawyer, but it is lousy for you as a human being."[5]

While both sexes are disillusioned by this pioneer ideal and prostitute feel and often face an $80,000 or so debt when they have completed law school, I've heard only the younger male lawyers say what a friend of mine said: "I've always wanted to enter public service law, but it pays so little; unless I go into corporate law, I'll never be able to get married and have kids."

It has been my men friends, then, who have been most likely to succumb to the bribe of big salaries and least likely to quit when they hated what they were doing. When corporate law did not fit their personalities, the men were more likely to change their personalities than to change their careers. This made them more vulnerable to the lawyer trap: To earn the big salary, he has to bill clients for sixty to eighty hours of work per week. But since many staff meetings and administrative tasks are not billable to clients, the attorney's real work week becomes seventy-five to ninety hours.[6] Thus, the lawyer trap.

The trap is also a setup for corruption. For example, when Anita Hill worked at a private firm, she was suspected of falsifying time sheets and billing clients for work she had not done. Why? A former colleague feels "she couldn't meet the demands placed on young associates at the firm."[7] She left to work for the government and then a university—she was not supporting a man and children.

In their search for pay and respect, many lawyers find instead chest pains, hypertension, arthritis, and insomnia—in their thirties. It is just this greater willingness by men to prostitute themselves for the pay-and-respect bribe that makes us think of a man when we hear a "lawyer joke."

Doctor as Slave

ITEM. First-year residents in pediatrics and obstetrics *averaged* 90 hours per week, with one in ten surgical residents exceeding 122 hours per week.[8]

ITEM. Medical residents in New York who are "on call" average 2.4 hours of sleep per night.[9]

When a young woman's death in a New York hospital was attributed to mistakes made by exhausted doctors, a state committee was appointed to determine whether doctors' long hours were jeopardizing *patients*.[10] The result after one female died? New York became the first state in the nation to recommend limits for doctors' hours: "no more than 24-hour shifts and 80-hour weeks."[11] In two lengthy *New York Times* articles on the committee's work, though, **there was not one mention of how the doctors' long hours damaged the doctors' lives, hurt their marriages, deprived them of time with their children, or turned them into slaves.**

A Central African legend illustrates the universality of the understanding that training to be a medical doctor is done at the risk of one's life. The legend goes . . .

> Once upon a time there was a half-man: one-legged, one-armed, so one-sided that, if viewed from the off-side, he was invisible. If he encountered you, he would challenge you to a fight. You did not have to accept. And if you did accept and lost, you would die. But if you accepted and won, he would show you how to use so many medicines that you could become a proficient doctor.[12]

When I taught at the School of Medicine at the University of California in San Diego a few years ago, I saw young, fresh, bright, first-year med students enter medical school "on top of the world." A few years later, most of the men were drained, distant, and preoccupied. They had become half-men. Most of the women, however, had become "three-quarter-women." Why the difference?

First, with a few exceptions, most of the women in my classes, usually first-year students, knew by the end of the first year that they would choose a field which (1) created the fewest demands at odd hours and (2) gave them more contact with human life than human death. Nationwide, this propensity leads female doctors to choose fields such as child psychiatry or adult psychiatry; to avoid all surgical specializations and all cardiovascular and pulmonary disease specializations.[13] In brief, the women avoided becoming half-women by avoiding the fields that would put them in constant contact with death or make them prisoners of other people's schedules. The men could learn from these women.

The male students were more likely to compete for the long-term, ideal position—one giving them control over their lives as doctors. Since the competition for the ideal positions was fierce, many men compromised, chose the contact-with-death specialties, and worked 100-hour weeks, earning money that only their families would have time to spend. In the process of gaining control of their lives as doctors, they lost control over their lives as people.

Unfortunately, the process of gaining money in his life usually meant alienating the wife in his life. Sometimes this leads to a legal divorce, but more often to a psychological divorce. Which is why a survey of doctors' wives reported in *Medical/Mrs* found the doctors' wives harboring hostility that was "stunning to behold."[14] Yet the wives remained married to the doctors. Why? More than anything else, the wives said, they wanted security from marriage. Apparently their husbands picked up their wives' desire for security more than their wives' hostility toward the persons who provided it. The men, then, were often prostitutes to an *illusion* of emotional security. At least their wives had the reality of economic security.

The "Paper Warrior"[15]

ITEM. The Japanese call it *karoshi*—death from overwork. In the past twenty years in Japan, sudden deaths among top executives have increased 1,400 percent.[16]

"*I was at my sister's today. They have two pots.*"

Drawing by Leo Cullum; © 1983 The New Yorker Magazine, Inc.

A survey by the Japanese government found that executives *average* seventy hours per week: twelve-hour workdays, six days per week.[17] It is not unusual for these executives to go without a single vacation day.[18]

When I was in Japan, I discovered that the workday was only part of the work assignment. The office-to-home commute usually exceeded an hour each way—adding another ten hours to the seventy-hour week. More than 95 percent of the people boarding commuter trains during rush hour and later were men. Dinner meetings with clients, while on one level pleasant, rarely proved to be stress free since a good impression could create a deal and a bad impression could break a deal.

How do Japanese executives prepare for this corporate subservience? A typical Japanese executive training program is called "hell camp."[19] The executives are asked to do things such as stand on their heads and shout a fifteen-page speech backward. The executive does not graduate from hell camp until he passes through a structure. "Passing" each step requires him to encounter a new set of humiliations.

Why does executive training look so much like subservience training? Is this really big men playing little boys' games? Does it have its equivalent in the United States?

First, the purpose. Rent a video of *Full Metal Jacket*—a portrayal of life in the U.S. Army, especially in boot camp. The sergeant humiliates the men, kicks them, puts their lives at risk. Why? "Your purpose is not to be individuals—but to be a machine." A killing machine. A prerequisite is the devaluation of self: the man who values himself will not risk death on the front line. Military boot camp is America's hell camp.

On a gut level, we have less trouble associating this subservience with army privates than with Japanese executives. Yet the similarity between hell camp and boot camp is that they both turn men into efficient "machines" by devaluing them as humans, thus making the male-as-individual subservient to either the corporate goal or the military goal.

What strikes us about the differences between the men in boot camp and the top male executives, though, are the perks, status, and income. These are really bribes for the individual to sacrifice individuality. The more the corporation or the army trusts an individual to serve its end consistently and intelligently, the more it gives that person perks, status, and income. Many men interpret this as standing out as an individual when, in fact, they stand out for their superior performance as a piece of the machinery.

The irony is that he is being honored as an individual for conformity to a group. The army uniform, the corporate uniform, the academic uniform, all represent his conformity. **Whether a promotion or a Purple Heart, each represents individual recognition for a superior level of conformity—a superior subservience to a larger machine.** Within this framework he might make effective decisions, take total responsibility, and lead well, but he leads well because he knows the rules for leadership, and those he leads know the rules to follow. But the rigidity of the framework is what makes his individuality more akin to subservience. And in the process, men who reach high levels are often "high-level mediocres."

Playing boys' games is preparation for making their lives secondary to their roles. Put-downs, hazing, and daring each other to take risks—even of life—are preparation for the devaluation of self necessary to make a boy regard his life as less important than his role. First, his role in sports (basketball and ice hockey players are injured even more than football players), then in an army, a company, an academic institution. . . . And gangs? Just poorly financed football teams. Male adolescence is a universal male boot camp.

Is it, then, men playing boys' games or . . . boys playing men's games?

SAVING THE "PAPER WARRIOR" FROM HIMSELF

The "paper warrior" is a prisoner of approval. He rarely changes until his marriage fails or his career fails. The moment his career fails, he is dumped back out into a job market which demands he work even harder to prove himself again (after all, he has just failed). The moment his marriage fails, he gets dumped back out into the meat market where he finds himself valued more if he's a top corporate lawyer than if he's a kindergarten teacher. His periods of self-determination are short-lived. He is vulnerable to hints to remain "driven."

And do we give those hints! Try to find a couch in a men's room. (Only once in my life have I seen so much as a chair in a men's room—even at exclusive hotels.) Try to find a national leader who admits he takes naps. Why? We ridiculed Ronald Reagan for taking naps rather than applauding him. Ironically, Nancy Reagan explained in her memoirs that he did not take naps and that it was a struggle just to get him to stretch out on a couch and rest even during long flights. She said, "I could never understand where this idea came from, because the press received a copy of his schedule every day, and knew he didn't come back for a nap."[20]

Didn't Reagan gain his reputation in part from "nodding off" in public meetings? Yes, in part. But Nancy Reagan explains, "It is true that Ronnie once nodded off during a public meeting with the Pope in 1982. . . . He got almost no sleep that night, and early the next morning we flew to Rome, where we drove straight to the Vatican for the meeting with the Pope."[21]

The point? **We don't subject housewives to national ridicule for taking naps during the day.** Why not *encourage* the "executive nap" and the "employee nap." The One-Minute Manager could use a Five-Minute Nap. Or a meditation room next to the exercise room. Some Japanese companies provide workers with glass-enclosed capsules that surround them with darkness and soothing music. "When time is up, the worker's face is blasted with cold air and he is sent back to work."[22] (The cold air I can do without, but the nap . . .)

Ultimately, though, only the paper warrior can save himself from the "insanity track." Women can help by altering their system of approval—by "marrying down" as often as they "marry up." But realistically few women will change if men are too weak to ask.

WHAT HAPPENS WHEN MEN "JUST SAY NO" TO PROVIDING A FINANCIAL WOMB?

ITEM. Black men, Indian men, and gay men have the toughest time among American males. **And they all have something in common: they do not provide an economic security blanket for women.**

The Men Who Couldn't *Protect Her: The Black and Indian Man*

Indian men could not adequately protect their food, water, and land from white invaders. Despite legends and myths that trained the Indian man to sacrifice himself, when legends, bows, and arrows could not keep up with technology, guns, and bullets, his family was confined to the reservations of their defeat. Unable to protect by killing buffalo or by "making a killing" on Wall Street, the Indian man became disposable. He received little love and, with little love, found much liquor.

Similarly, as those black men with a slave heritage entered an industrialized era without adequate training to protect their families, they were also rejected by women. Only the black male performers—usually physical performers such as the Wilt Chamberlains and Magic Johnsons—found thousands of women. Black men who could not perform were subject to ridicule in novels and films (e.g., *The Color Purple, The Women of Brewster Place*).

As a result of this inadequate preparation to protect, many African-American men often chose aberrant, quick fix, lottery-type attempts to "make it"—via drug dealing, gambling, or the lottery itself. When these methods failed to bring them the money to protect, they, as with Indian men, found themselves inadequate for women's love, gambling for a last hope of love, and, if they failed, drugging themselves to death.

The Men Who Wouldn't *Protect Her: The Gay Man*

The ostracism incurred for being a gay man runs deeper than it does for being black or Indian. Black men and Indian men who could not provide adequate protection for women at least *wanted* to protect women—they just didn't do it well enough. Gays, though, weren't even trying to take care of women. So we called their unwillingness to protect women "immorality." And we ostracized them—as in cutting them off from survival. Like witches, we called them heretics. The very word *faggot* means a bundle of sticks that were burned in the fire. When homosexuals were burned at the stake as heretics, they were called "faggots."[23]

Why? Well, think about it. Gay sex meant two hours of sexual pleasure in exchange for two hours of sexual pleasure. Heterosexual sex meant two hours of sexual pleasure in exchange for a lifetime of responsibility. Heterosexuality was a bad deal! The fear behind homophobia was that no one would be providing for the next generation. Everybody would be having fun. Thus "fun" became a sign of immaturity; "hedonism" in many forms became illegal. Most cultures, then, tolerated homosexuality only when they were no longer worried about survival (e.g., the United States middle class after World War II and the Greeks and Romans once they had the security of an empire).

Do we actually care less about the lives of men who are unwilling to reproduce and to protect? Our initial lack of attention to AIDS—until it became apparent that heterosexuals were also at risk—makes our attitude quite transparent.

The Men Who Fail to Protect Her: The Homeless Man

ITEM. Ninety-six percent of the adult homeless in San Francisco are men.[24] In other cities it is less—a median of 85 percent men.[25]

ITEM. There are three times as many homeless men living on the streets by themselves as there are homeless children, adolescents, and adult women *combined* who are living on the streets by themselves.[26]

Single Individual Homeless Living on the Streets by Themselves	
Children or adolescents (19 or younger)	6%
Adult women	20%
Adult men	74%

When we think of the homeless, we often think of a woman and her children. In fact, nationwide, only 16 percent of the homeless are in a family group of any type.[27] And even when family groupings are counted, there are still more single men among the homeless than there are children, single women, married women, or married men *combined*.[28]

We also tend to think of homeless *families* being the worst off, but studies of the homeless find that they are treated the best—the most likely to be sheltered, fed, and reemployed. By far the worst off are the single individual homeless.[29]

When I have delivered food and clothing to the homeless, I was struck by the degree to which the street homeless—the *un*sheltered homeless—were men and boys. I can still remember one of these men shivering and cuddling his four children on a filthy mattress. His one coat was used to cover his two youngest children. When I lived in New York, I can remember a man competing with a rat for garbage, his freezing hand sorting out wilted lettuce from baby diapers and tampons.

Almost every report on the homeless has a sentence like this one (from an official report on California's homeless): "While women are a small part of the homeless (estimated at 10 percent in California), they face special problems."[30] Which is fine. But there was no section on the problems men face.

Homeless men are not just without a home, they are without love and virtually without hope of finding love as long as they are homeless. Many once had homes, children, and a wife, but when they lost their ability to protect, they also lost everyone they loved. On the street, they joined an almost all-male club.

Why do we resist giving help to homeless men? In part because we don't understand how our pressure on men to support families often forces men to take transient jobs that are but a step away from homelessness (the death-of-a-salesman jobs, the migrant worker jobs, the merchant marine jobs, the trucker, the road and railroad builders . . .). And in part because we respond differently to men who fail. . . .

Do We React Differently When a Man and a Woman Fail to Protect?

Remember when almost all the homeless were men? We called them "bums." Then some women appeared. We called the women "bag *ladies*." When about 15 percent were women, we called them all "homeless" and we suddenly began to care. This distinction—between "bums" and "bag ladies"—is only a metaphor for the difference in our attitude toward men who fail versus women who fail.

ITEM. When a male captain failed to control his ship and the resultant oil spill destroyed wildlife, the names *Exxon Valdez* and Captain Joseph Hazelwood became infamous. Captain Hazelwood was put on trial, fined, and imprisoned. He became the pitiful butt of jokes by Johnny Carson and Jay Leno. His drinking was highlighted. The fact that a sudden schedule change had pushed an exhausted captain and crew back to sea and into a ruined career was ignored.

ITEM. When a female air traffic controller failed at her job and the resultant air crash killed thirty-four humans (not wildlife), her colleagues took her to a hotel to shield her from publicity. They spent days comforting her. Instead of being the butt of jokes, she received humor therapy, paid for by taxes.[31] Rather than sue her, the Federal Aviation Administration provided her with a counselor. Instead of publicizing her name, the National Transportation Safety Board cooperated in keeping her identity secret from the public.[32] To this day, her name remains virtually unknown.

Headlines in papers from the *Los Angeles Times* to *The New York Times* focused on *her* grief, not the grief of the families of those killed or the ruined lives of those injured.

Los Angeles Times

Controller Was Stricken by Grief, Tears After Crash

■ **Disaster:** Co-workers spent hours after the accident counseling her and hid her from publicity for days.

To this day, I have yet to see an article focusing on Captain Hazelwood's grief. I am a strong supporter of the humor therapy the government supplied the woman, but I can also imagine the public's response had the government trained Captain Hazelwood to laugh after *Exxon Valdez*. When a man fails to protect, we persecute the man; when a woman fails to protect, we protect the woman. We care, in brief, about female grief.

IF MEN EXPERIENCE BEING FIRED AS BEING RAPED, DO THEY EXPERIENCE THE BOSS WHO FIRES AS A RAPIST?

If being fired or involuntarily unemployed is the male version of rape,* then the boss who fires an employee is unconsciously experienced as a type of rapist. Because this boss is usually a man, millions of men who fire a few to save the jobs of many feel they are one part rapist and one part savior. Because few people understand the manager's internal conflict, the manager feels isolated, lonely, even alienated from parts of himself. A setup for alcoholism.

His drinking usually leads to others attacking him for his drunkenness. Friends often try to hear his problem but, because he can't articulate what he doesn't understand, both he and his friends feel helpless.

In most areas of life, we can turn to education to deepen understanding. But most executives discover the academic community also views the executive who fires as a type of rapist, although the academic's anger is disguised in ideas. Thus Marxist ideology— lamenting, in essence, the rape of the working class—might be the academic's way of disguising his anger toward the executive who fires.

Some solutions? First, understand that the manager who fires is usually just playing out the downside of the savior role—saving the jobs of many by keeping the company competitive and therefore alive. Second, develop employee transition programs to assist the employee in his or her retraining for a new career opportunity. Third, develop industry-wide manager transition programs to help these managers feel as valuable to a sick company as surgeons feel to a sick person.

---

* See chapter 6, section titled *Is Unemployment to a Man the Psychological Equivalent of Rape to a Woman?*

TOWARD THE SANITY TRACK

The Warrior of Love Vs. *the Warrior of Money*

Men's immediate path from the Insanity Track to the Sanity Track[33] is in demanding that *both* sexes have the freedom to strike a balance between homeplace and workplace. Men must expect their wives to financially support them to be fathers as much as they now financially support their wives to be mothers. Women must have our approval to marry the warrior of love rather than the warrior of money. This means that men must be strong enough to speak up to women who refer to a man primarily as a financial identity. For example, when a woman says, "I just met this wonderful lawyer . . . ," men must have the guts to ask, "How often have you said 'I just met this wonderful father'?" or "How would you feel if I said 'I just met this wonderful, large-breasted woman'?"

We can also learn a lot from some workplace changes that have evolved since women's participation increased. For example, when psychologists and psychiatrists were mostly males, five to twelve years of postgraduate work were required. When more women entered therapy professions, two to three years of training became acceptable for MSWs and MFCCs. Within a decade, insurance companies loosened their restrictions and were covering MSWs with only a two-year degree and a year of training. If the reverse had been the case, we would have heard of "the sudden loosening of restrictions when men entered the field—typical of a male-dominated system."

Female participation, though, has made both therapy and other fields more flexible. As women entered medicine, states began placing limits on the numbers of hours doctors could work for the first time. In the therapeutic community, therapists can now work as few as five hours a week. Fields that male therapists would not permit for themselves were quickly allowed once women entered— massage therapy, sex therapy, addiction therapy, feminist therapy. Both clients and therapists benefited from the choices. When it was predominantly a male profession, psychiatrists' suicide rate was high, and even 46 percent of the less pressured clinical psychologists acknowledged by the 1970s that if they had to live their lives over again, they would choose different careers.[34] The entrance of females, flexible work hours, and less training made "career track" compatible with "sanity track."

As females enter the workplace, will our tendency to protect women create rules that will also protect men? Yes and no. Yes, when, for example, the new concern for doctors working fewer than eighty hours per week also affects men. No, when working-class jobs get divided into the males taking the hazardous jobs at inconvenient times in locations like Alaska and women taking safer jobs at convenient times in locations like Santa Fe and Santa Barbara. And in professional careers, if males take irregular hours and specialties such as surgery, while females take regular hours and specialties like psychiatry, then we will only reinforce the female-protected class and the male-disposable class.

CHAPTER 9

Violence against Whom?

ITEM. For every woman who is murdered, three men are murdered.[1]

ITEM. With the exception of rape, the more violent the crime, the more likely the victim is a man.[2]

ITEM. Males are the primary victims of all violent crimes except rape. These violent crimes (excluding rape) have increased by 36 percent.[3] Rape, the one violent crime in which females are the primary victims, has *decreased* by 33 percent.[4]

ITEM. Forcible rape constitutes less than 6 percent of all violent crimes; violent crimes of which men are the primary victims constitute the remaining 94 percent.[5]

ITEM. The average American has 1 chance in 153 of being murdered; a black man has 1 chance in 28 of being murdered.[6]

ITEM. When the Department of Justice conducted a nationwide survey, it found that Americans rated a wife stabbing her husband to death as 41 percent less severe than a husband stabbing his wife to death.[7]

ITEM. *Wives* report that they were *more* likely to assault their husbands than their husbands were to assault them. (This according to the National Family Violence Survey's nationwide random sampling of households.[8])

ITEM. Blacks are six times more likely than whites to be victims of homicides.[9] Forty-five percent of black males will become victims of violent crime three or more times.[10]

AREN'T MEN THE PERPETRATORS OF THIS VIOLENCE, AND ISN'T THIS VIOLENCE A REFLECTION OF MALE POWER?

We have no problem seeing this last Item as a reflection of black powerlessness; but we rarely see *men*'s greater likelihood of being victims of violence as a reflection of male powerlessness. When we hear men are the greater victims of crime, we tend to say, "Well, it's men hurting other men." When we hear that blacks are the greater victims, we consider it racist to say, "Well, it's blacks hurting blacks." The victim is a victim no matter who the perpetrator was.

But why do men commit most of the violent crime? Is it a reflection of male power? Hardly. Blacks do not commit proportionately more crimes than whites because blacks have more power. Flint, Michigan, gives us a clue.

In the mid-1980s, Flint was faced with the closing of a number of General Motors plants, forcing 30,000 auto workers to leave the area and leaving numerous others unemployed.[11] By 1985, a town formerly low in its crime rate reported huge increases not only in suicides and alcoholism, but in spouse abuse, rape, and murder. Flint soon had a higher rate of violent crime than New York City. And it reported 285 rapes in 1985, a staggering figure for a city of 150,000.

What does this tell us? It gives us a hint that murder, rape, and spouse abuse, like suicide and alcoholism, are but a minute's worth of superficial power to compensate for years of underlying powerlessness. They are manifestations of hopelessness committed by the powerless, which is why they are acts committed disproportionately by blacks and by men.

Crime, especially crime involving money, reflects the gap between the *expectation* to provide and the *ability* to provide.[12] Thus women who work and earn enough to meet their expectations rarely commit crimes. But women who are working and not meeting expectations do commit more crime.

If we really want men to commit crime as infrequently as

women, we can start by not expecting men to provide for women more than we expect women to provide for men.

OUR MOST INVISIBLE DOMESTIC VIOLENCE

ITEM. A man entered a classroom at the University of Montreal and killed female students. The incident made headlines throughout the world as an example of woman-hating. The Canadian government spent millions reeducating men in their attitudes toward women. At about the same time, a Chicago woman (Laurie Dann) shot five elementary school boys, poisoned food at two fraternities, burned down the Young Men's Jewish Council, burned two other boys in their basement,[13] *shot her own son*, and justified her murder of an 8-year-old boy by claiming he was a rapist. Not a single headline or article summary in the index to the Chicago *Tribune* pointed out that every person killed or wounded by the Chicago woman was a boy.[14] No government spent millions reeducating women on their attitudes toward men.

ITEM. In the riots resulting after the Rodney King verdict, police officers killed ten people. All ten were men.[15] Had all ten been blacks or Hispanics or women, would it have gone unnoticed?

Why was the man as victim invisible? In part because the social expectation that the man—not the woman—loots the store is also invisible. Did fewer women steal because women are more moral? Not quite. First, thousands of women also looted—but none were killed by police. Second, few men bring home a stolen TV if they know their wife won't watch it. Third, when blacks and Hispanics looted after the Rodney King verdict, both political parties sensed it was at least in part because the poor felt less hope and had less power. But the fact that *men* did most of the looting led no one to conclude that men felt less hope and had less power.

Choking the Teacher

A 17-year-old Michigan high school student attempted to choke a male teacher.[16] Afterward, teachers got no additional protection.

Two months later, a 14-year-old attempted to choke a female teacher—in the same school. The school immediately withdrew all female teachers from the school, reducing the staff from twenty-one to nine. Now here's the rub. The male teachers were still expected to remain but now they had to handle classes that were *more than twice the size*. The larger the class size, the greater the chance of violence. **Protecting every woman put every man in jeopardy—without the men's consent.**

Corporal Punishment as Boy Punishment

Corporal punishment in schools is still legal in twenty-nine states.[17] But in most school districts practicing corporal punishment, a teacher who slaps a *girl* with a ruler fears a parent will slap the teacher with a lawsuit. And a male teacher who spanks a girl with his hand can forget about tenure or retirement pay. **In practice, corporal punishment is boy punishment.** Many schools protest the propensity to hit black boys more than white boys, but no schools protest the propensity to hit exclusively boys. We don't protest violence against boys because it is invisible.

The Invisible Sexual Abuse

When we think of sexual abuse of children, most of us think of girl children as the victim about nine out of ten times. In reality, it is one boy to 1.7 girls.[18] We usually think of the sexual abuser as a man. In reality, girls' abusers are usually men, boys' abusers are usually women—mothers, older sisters, female babysitters, and older female relatives.[19] We cannot discover this by polling child-abuse centers. Polling child-abuse centers will always uncover more girls because, when girls are abused, we offer them help. It is only when we poll both sexes equally as adults and ask them parallel questions about their childhood that the abuse against both sexes becomes visible.

Why do we overlook men who need help—be they the victims of sexual abuse, spouse abuse, PTSD, or prostate cancer, or the 85 percent male homeless? **Historically, woman-as-victim attracts men; man-as-victim repulses women.** Even today, when a woman's tire goes flat, she will suddenly allow a strange man off the highway an opportunity to help her. If his tire goes flat, she rarely

Calvin and Hobbes   by Bill Watterson

CALVIN AND HOBBES 1986 copyright Watterson. Dist. by UNIVERSAL PRESS SYNDICATE.
Reprinted with permission. All rights reserved.

stops to help a man, despite the opportunity she's had to look him over first.

Men will make progress to the degree society understands that the attraction to woman-as-victim is a reflection of male low self-concept: a feeling that a man is worthy of a woman only if he can do something for her—that he is *conditionally visible*.

The "War against Women"?

. . . attitudes toward women help breed violent crimes against them and can rob them of full equality in American life. . . . It is unthinkable that my granddaughters not have the same opportunity as my grandsons. . . . This war against women must stop.

—PRESIDENT BUSH, June 26, 1989,
to the American Association of
University Women[20]

The headlines after President Bush's speech read "The War on Women Must Stop."[21]

Imagine President Clinton delivering the following speech to an American Association of University *Men* (which, of course, would no longer be allowed to exist):

My fellow Americans . . .

. . . attitudes toward boys help breed violent boys who become violent dads and husbands. So Hillary and I are asking, "Why do we cheer for our sons to be violent and then put them in jail when they grow up to be violent?"

It is immoral to use our education dollars to train our sons to play "smash face," er, pardon me, football, in junior high school.[22] To tell boys this age we will applaud for you if you mutilate yourselves is not education, it is child abuse. And to give that message only to boys is sexism that deprives our sons of the right to choose. When Hillary and I see how our cheers encourage boys to swallow their fears and repress their tears, we realize it is time to repress our cheers so our boys can express their fears.

Football scholarships are mutilation scholarships. If cheerleaders were as likely as football players to have herniated disks and dislocated shoulders, fractured vertebrae and damaged knees that haunted them into old age, would we be using taxpayer money to support cheerleading? Even Hillary doesn't think so.

We feel it is immoral to teach our sons to increase their sex appeal by increasing their risk of concussions. Would we encourage girls to increase their sex appeal by using their bodies—by having sex on the fifty-yard line with boys from another school? Which of us would yell, "First of ten, do it again"? Oh, my . . . Our men will become gentler when cheerleaders are shouting, "First and ten, be *gentle* again."

Hillary and I realize football is only a metaphor for preparing our sons to be sixteen times as likely as our daughters to die at work; for preparing only your 18-year-old son to register for the draft. We realize we can no longer claim to favor equality between the sexes and then make your sons the disposable sex.

So I am introducing today the ELA: the Equal Life Amendment. None of us can tolerate being part of a country that robs men of an equal life.

This war against our sons must stop. It is America's longest war. And it is preparation for nuclear war. It is our most unrecognized domestic violence. And it is preparation for future domestic violence.

> —PRESIDENT CLINTON, June 26, the
> future American Association of
> University *Men* convention

WHEN VIOLENCE AGAINST MEN DOES BECOME VISIBLE, DO WE STILL IGNORE IT?

ITEM. When a female jogger in Central Park in 1989 was raped and brutalized,[23] "Take Back the Night" demonstrations were nationwide. The solution? A headline in an Ellen Goodman column read "Safety for Women? Try Removing Men."[24]

ITEM. When a male jogger in Central Park in 1989 was hospitalized after being brutally beaten on the head with a club, he reported the incident to the police.[25] Coincidentally, he had witnessed two similar incidents of men being kicked, punched, or beaten in Central Park within the previous month. He had also reported both of those incidents to the police. He later called the police to see how many such attacks had occurred in the previous two months. He was told there had been none at all.

Our anger toward men as victimizers blinds us to men as victims. The attacks the male jogger reported—all attacks on men— were never acknowledged as even having occurred. If a woman had reported three separate rapes to the police and not a single one was even acknowledged as having been reported—much less investigated—it would be hard to imagine the degree of outrage. When crimes against women are more readily recorded, crimes against women become more readily visible.

Violent crimes against innocent women create distrust toward innocent men. Every man who invites a woman back to his home has to risk rejection not only because he is expected to do the asking but because the rape she just read about or heard about adds to her likelihood of rejecting him. He is tainted with suspicion even if he himself has also been victimized by other men or been injured while protecting women.

WHAT DO WE CALL VIOLENCE AGAINST AN INFANT BOY?

I saw them strap my son spread-eagle and put this steel thing on his penis. As soon as I heard my boy scream, I knew it was very wrong. I've never heard a kid cry like that before. I'll never forget it.[26]

When we commit violence against an infant girl, we call it child abuse; when we commit violence against an infant boy, we call it circumcision. Circumcision is America's most common surgical procedure.[27] The need to remove the foreskin on an infant boy's penis has been rejected by almost all other medically advanced countries: Norway, France, Sweden, England, Denmark, Japan, and Finland. The circumcision rate in Britain has plummeted from 50 percent in 1950 to less than 0.5 percent today.[28]

Circumcision in the United States is routinely performed without anesthesia.[29] Yet, as the *New England Journal of Medicine* reports, when newborns receive anesthesia to protect them from pain during surgery, it dramatically improves their chances of surviving.[30] The anesthesia reduces the infant's stress and prevents infection and blood clots.

Do babies who are being circumcised actually feel the pain? According to the *Journal of the American Medical Association*, babies being circumcised cry vigorously and experience "dramatic changes in heart and respiratory rates, and in transcutaneous oxygen and plasma cortisol levels."[31]

If babies make it through this initial period of trauma, what is the long-term impact? *Unstudied.* We also don't have clear enough data on the conditions under which circumcision might help prevent or cause cancer, and prevent or cause infection. As a result, we have to rely on indirect data, such as our knowledge that other newborn traumas, such as incubator isolation, do seem to affect later development and behavior.[32] Or the fact that the lack of circumcision has not seemed to lead to infection, hygiene problems, or cancer in Canadian and Australian men.[33] But the lack of information leaves us less than certain, and this ignorance persists despite the fact that a nationwide study on the long-term impact of male circumcision could be conducted for less than it cost us to conduct any *two minutes* of the Persian Gulf War.[34]

Perhaps the biggest setback to the questioning of circumcision occurred when a study found that wives of uncircumcised men had more cervical cancer than wives of circumcised men.[35] This study received enormous publicity.[36] When two follow-up studies refuted the female-as-victim perspective, both received almost no publicity.[37]

The most frequent reason given for circumcision relates to health and sanitation. It is definitely true that circumcision reduces the necessity for cleaning; an intact penis will have more smegma appearing on the outside of the penis, requiring a gentle soap and water washing. But the smegma is a natural lubricant, like body and hair oils. In countries where an intact penis is the norm, a boy learns to clean his penis just like he learns to wash his hair, take a bath, or clean under his fingernails. No one suggests removing the fingernails so cleaning will not have to be done.

Edward Wallerstein, probably the country's most knowledgeable urologist on circumcision issues, explains that almost every reason used for circumcision could also be used to justify removing a girl's clitoral hood.[38] Females produce smegma identical to males' under their clitoral hood, the female equivalent of the tip of the penis. As a result, dirt and germs, as well as odor and infection, can occur if it is not cleaned. But we do not circumcise the female's clitoral hood to prevent smegma secretion.

When circumcision of the clitoral hood is done in some African tribes, we see it as a barbaric example of our disregard for women. Yet in the United States, when the same surgery is performed on boy infants, we call it healthy. Rabbis often justify continuing the tradition of circumcision on the eighth day for health reasons. But if a boy dies before the eighth day, circumcision is performed before he is buried—after he is dead. Obviously it is not for health reasons. Something else is going on.

Were we to still be circumcising the hood of the female clitoris, we would not have difficulty considering this a continuation of our tradition to keep girls sexually repressed. America's reflexive continuation of circumcision-without-research reflects the continuation of our tradition to desensitize boys to feelings of pain, to prepare them to question the disposability of their bodies no more than they would question the disposability of their foreskins.

VIOLENCE AGAINST MALE ADULTS BY ANY OTHER NAME IS . . .

ITEM. A Coke ad shows a man willing to "go for the Coke" at the risk of a shark's fin slicing through his testicles as it simulates a buzz saw.

Coca-Cola knew that only a man's life was worth, well, a little bit less than a Coke!

The average American child watches more than 40,000 people killed on TV prior to high school graduation—before the age of consent.[39] Of those killed on TV entertainment programs, about 97 percent are men.[40] Yet the feminist slogan is "There is *never* an excuse for violence against *women*."

Why does the percentage of men killed seem a little exaggerated? In part, because when almost 100 percent men are killed in westerns and war movies, we don't call westerns "violence against men"—we call them "entertainment." And in part because entire programs often focus on a woman's life being in *jeopardy*, leaving us with the emotional impression of violence against her.

When a woman is so much as wounded, as in the 1992 western *Unforgiven*, the entire film focuses on punishing those who hurt her. About a dozen men are killed in the process of teaching two men that a woman had better not be hurt. (Notice I said "*about* a dozen"—the men who died were less visible than the one woman hurt.) **In woman-in-jeopardy films, the woman is typically saved while many men die saving her.** A man who puts a woman in jeopardy is *Unforgiven*. Because a woman in jeopardy is unforgotten. The men dead from attempting to save her are forgotten. So the 97 percent of men killed are invisible.

Do American Films Exploit Violence against Women?

It is tempting to answer, "No, American films exploit violence against *both* sexes," but that's not quite fair. What is fair is that while our attention has been called to violence against women in film, approximately 95 percent of those killed in movies are men.[41] As with TV, not only are the westerns and war movies virtually orgies of men killing other men, but so are murder mysteries and women-in-jeopardy films. And think of who gets killed in *Goodfellas*, *West Side Story*, *Boyz 'n the Hood*, *Hoffa*, or in any film on the mob or on gangs. All six of these film types persist because we repeatedly pay to watch men murder men—and even boys murder boys.

In contrast, the unwritten, unconscious rule of thumb in the movie industry is that "*Innocent women* don't get killed after their third appearance." Here's how the rule works. (But beware; once you read this, you will be able to predict the outcome of almost any fictional woman-in-jeopardy movie.)

As a rule, a woman will not be killed unless:

- It is a horror movie (killing a man is not horrible enough to make it a horror movie).
- She is shown to not be a "real woman," thereby undoing her special right as a woman to protection. That is, she is an alien (e.g., *Aliens*, *Bladerunner*); she has all the negative characteristics of a man (*Aliens*); or she is an out-and-out protagonist who is clearly crazy *and* a murderer (e.g., *Misery*, *Fatal Attraction*).
- She threatens the life of an innocent woman (*Shining Through*, *Fatal Attraction*, and *Total Recall*).

- She has been seen in no more than *three* scenes (we have not gotten to know her—she is not a "real woman" to us).
- The rest of the movie is focused on avenging her death (*Death Wish*), making it, in essence, a morality film showing us that a woman killed leads to a man killed.

In contrast, in the woman-in-jeopardy movie, it is not just the life of the man who puts the woman in jeopardy that is expendable, it is also the lives of innocent men. For example, in *Silence of the Lambs*, the fact that a man *had* killed women *off* screen and there was the *possibility* of a woman being killed *on* screen created the excuse to have us watch on screen the murder of many *innocent* men (the prison guards), but no women.

The innocent prison guards were not just mutilated heartlessly and thoroughly, they were murdered incidentally. Their mutilation was a plot additive—as invisible as salt, serving only as spice for the main dish of concern for Jodie Foster. Were innocent women prison guards murdered, it would never have been as a plot additive. Only the murder of men can be as invisible as salt. Had this unspoken rule been broken and innocent women been killed as an additive, we can predict that the outrage would have made the film so politically incorrect as to prevent it from making a sweep of the Academy Awards.

Overall, then, women-in-jeopardy movies are often an excuse for kill-the-man movies.

What happens if a *novel* violates the "innocent women don't get killed after their third appearance" rule of thumb? We can predict two things: (1) the novel will not be made into a film and (2) if any violence is protested, only the violence against women will be protested. For example, the novel *American Psycho* involved the graphic murder of men, women, and a boy (it featured the deaths of eight men and a little boy, including the actual murder of three of those men and the little boy).[42] Hundreds of nationwide protests and articles focused only on its violence against women. We can predict the novel will not be made into a major American film, much less be eligible for Academy Awards.

Women-in-jeopardy movies are, in essence, the updated versions of men dying to save the princess from the dragon to earn her love. They are modern-day training films for teaching women to select the best protectors while weeding out the rest. And then we call the woman "victim" and the man "powerful."

Violence against Men As Women's Liberation

Thelma and Louise was widely touted as a film of women's liberation. (It was, for example, the only film celebrated by the National Organization for Women at its twenty-fifth convention.) Never in American history have two men been celebrated as heroes of men's liberation after they deserted their wives, met one female jerk after another, and then killed one woman and left another woman stuffed in a trunk in 120-degree desert heat. *Male serial killers are condemned—not celebrated—at men's liberation conventions.* The moment a men's movement calls it a sign of empowerment or brotherhood when men kill women is the moment I will protest it as fascism.

When men protested, the common reaction was, "Isn't it interesting that when men kill, no one protests, but now that women kill, there's a protest?" Which, of course, missed the point of the protest. Men kill *men* in gang movies, cop movies, mob films, westerns, murder mysteries, and war movies; if a man kills a woman, he is killed by other men. Men frequently die protecting women; women almost never die to protect a man. In contrast, *Thelma and Louise* did not show any women trying to apprehend the two women who killed the men; it did not show any women trying to kill any other women; it did not show any woman dying to protect a man.

The "Shoot a Man, Find a Human" School of Film

In the 1990s, the killing of men in films reached a new level: it is not called violence against men, it is called male self-help.

In *Regarding Henry*, brain damage from bullet wounds "kills" an arrogant attorney and transforms him into a caring attorney; in *Doctor*, cancer "kills" the arrogant doctor and transforms him into a caring doctor; in *Doc Hollywood*, a car accident "kills" Doc Hollywood and transforms him into Doc Sensitive; in *Defending Your Life* and *Switch*, it took death itself to transform insensitive executive-type men into caring executive types; in *Robin Hood*, it takes war and a mutilated dad hanging from a rope to "kill" Robin's spoiled-nobleman past and transform him into a hero of the poor.

Taken together, two doctors, a lawyer, an executive, and a nobleman symbolize the feeling that the only man worth preserving is the man who emerges as he is dying. If a spate of films suggested that when a black, a woman, or a Jew is dying, something worth preserving finally emerges . . .

DEATH AT THE TOP; THE ONE-SHOT PLEBESCITE

In real life, unlike in the movies, the *more* a man is a hero, the *more* likely he is to die or be killed. A quarter of American presidents have died in office, many by assassination. Almost every liberal, charismatic male leader of the 1960s through the '80s was assassinated or mysteriously killed. Not just the Kennedys, King, and Malcolm X of the United States, but Salvador Allende of Chile, Patrice Lumumba of the Belgian Congo, Olaf Palme of Sweden, Anwar Sadat of Egypt, and Dag Hammarskjold of the United Nations. They were all "done away with" when someone perceived that the role they were playing was no longer protecting their interests. Assassination, the modern-day equivalent of regicide, has left many male leaders giving their lives for their country in politics just as men do in the military. Thus today the male leaders are buried, their wives are alive.

With the exception of Indira Gandhi, female leaders have not been assassinated in recent history. It is much more common for a woman to come to power after her husband's assassination than to herself be assassinated. Corazon Aquino became president of the Philippines after her husband was assassinated; Violeta Chamorro was elected president of Nicaragua after her husband was similarly slain; and Benazir Bhutto was elected prime minister of Pakistan after the assassination of her *father* (only a slightly different twist).

WHAT ARE WE DOING TO STOP THIS VIOLENCE AGAINST MEN?

The sexist perception that violence by anyone against only women is antiwoman while violence by a woman against only men is just generic violence creates a political demand for laws that are even more protective of women. For example, when we publicized studies of battered women but ignored a dozen studies pointing to equal numbers of battered men,[43] we felt justified in legislating a "battered woman syndrome," but didn't even think of a "battered man syndrome." Soon, the battered woman syndrome became but one of twelve defenses potentially available for a woman who killed, but not available for a man who killed. Now, if the media even *simulates* violence against women, we might call it a civil rights violation while *real-life* violence against men in football and wrestling is called education.

Although men are more likely than women to be victims of all violent crime except rape, the U.S. Senate is sponsoring a Violence Against *Women* Act—an act which makes violence against women a hate crime and a violation of women's civil rights, but not violence against men a hate crime and an act against men's civil rights. In brief, it legislates sexual *in*equality. The only way such an act could be constitutional is if women were subject to much more violence than men. Because it is men who are subject to much more violence, not only is a Violence against Women Act unconstitutional, but a Violence against Men Act might well be constitutional.

The Violence against Women Act provides $300 million for the protection of women against violent crimes, but nothing to protect men; $75 million for women's shelters, but none for men's shelters. Its subtitles tell the story: Safe Streets *for Women*, Safe Homes *for Women* (emphasis supplied) . . .

By law, all governmental acts are molded and modified based on testimony before the relevant congressional committee. The testimony is supposed to reflect all sides of an issue. But in this case, only women testified—fifteen women and no men—before the Committee on the Judiciary.[44] No man who requested permission to testify was permitted.

What can we do to stop violence against both sexes? We can start by decreasing the expectation on men to be our killers and protectors—from our personal bodyguards to our nation's bodyguards. And we can stop electing legislators who feel they must protect women and forget men. The process starts with remembering that legislators cannot hear what we do not say.

CHAPTER 10

If We Cared As Much about Saving Males As Saving Whales, Then . . .

In the preceding chapters, we saw how survival historically depended on a woman choosing a man who would die to protect her. We also saw why choosing male killers to protect us now threatens survival. But what are some of the most important gut-level internal responses we must confront if we are to stop dividing the sexes into the disposable sex vs. the protected sex? And how is our tendency to do that already affecting our ecology and preparing us for two legal systems—one to prosecute the "perpetrator" sex and one to protect the "victim" sex? The best confrontation starts with self, so I'll start by confronting myself.

A few years ago, I was walking in the woods with a womanfriend when a man jumped out in front of us. Within a second, my womanfriend had jumped back and I had jumped forward. Whether we did it because of differences in our size or differences in our socialization made little difference. Like most men, I unconsciously bring to my relationships with a woman an unspoken understanding: "My body, *not* my choice."

I wish this happened only in the woods. But when I have been with a woman in my home and a suspicious noise scared us, it took a long time before I no longer felt guilty asking her to accompany me as *we* checked it out. (The first time a woman *volunteered* to go with me, my respect for her increased enormously.)

Most men are not only women's unpaid bodyguards, they *actually pay* to be a woman's bodyguard: when they pay for the date, pay for the weekend, and therefore pay for the walk, they are really *paying to be* her bodyguard. It is one of many male forms of indirect nurturance. By calling it "power," we have made the nurturance invisible.

Don't many women today protect themselves, and protect children too? Yes, and yes. Women often protect themselves and risk their lives to protect children, but a woman will rarely risk her life to protect an *adult* man. We have all read of a mother lifting a car to save a child, but not to save an adult man.

In Stage II societies, confronting the desire to save the female first starts with the propensity to save girls first.

SAVE-A-GIRL FUND

ITEM. When Children International seeks sponsors for children, seventeen out of eighteen of the children it shows are female.[1] The viewer is told, "When you adopt a child, *she* will write, she will have food, she . . ."

In other ads, poverty itself is defined as "hunger and a little *girl* . . ."

Why this focus on the suffering *girl*? The organizations are trying to raise money. Their experience has taught them that we care more about saving girls.

HOW IGNORING MALE ECOLOGY DESTROYS GLOBAL ECOLOGY

At Three Mile Island, where 80 percent of the workers were men,[2] sleep loss and exhaustion led to a failure to recognize the loss of coolant water.[3] By morning, the lack of coolant water caused the near meltdown of the reactor. Workers' sleep loss was also found to be the common denominator for the explosion of the space shuttle *Challenger* and the catastrophe at Chernobyl.[4] And as we saw above, when the *Exxon Valdez* spilled oil, although the captain was blamed, investigators later conceded that the underlying culprit was the decision to send the exhausted crew back to sea after skipping their scheduled day's rest.[5]

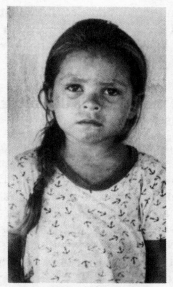

Had workers been rested, some of the worst ecological disasters in our history might have been prevented. In a karmic sense, our world's ecology was being punished for not caring about male ecology.

SHOULDN'T A FUTURE MOTHER BE MORE PROTECTED THAN A FUTURE FATHER?

Our desire to give special protection to working women who are of childbearing years seems especially understandable. Geneticists are now finding, though, that exposing men of child-creating years to chemical toxins might hurt the children just as much. Why? All the eggs a woman has are present and whole before birth. But to create sperm, cells have to *divide*.[6] And it is when the cells are dividing and their borders are newly forming that they are especially vulnerable to toxins and therefore to genetic damage. A safe sperm gathers no defects.

The causes of 60 to 80 percent of birth defects are still not known; scientists have discovered approximately 30 of an estimated 900 chemicals that are toxic to human development. When we consider that it is men who are primarily exposed to toxic chemicals, we get a sense of the degree to which caring for our children's safety also means caring for men's safety. Elmo Zumwalt, Jr., was just the tip of the iceberg.

THE FALLACY OF THE WORKPLACE AS A SOURCE OF FULFILLMENT

One of the biggest fallacies of the women's movement was expecting work to mean "power" and "self-fulfillment." Employers wouldn't have to pay people if they were giving away power and self-fulfillment. For those employees able to feel freedom and fulfillment on the job—well, "more power to 'em." But the average man knows the employer is paying to use his body during work in exchange for freeing his body *after* work. Additional benefits *from* the employer come from creating additional benefits *for* the employer. They are not expected, they are earned. At least that's the way the average man sees it.

But how does understanding this translate into the way we interact with men every day?

DOES AN AWARENESS OF MEN'S PROBLEMS MAKE ANY DIFFERENCE IN OUR EVERYDAY EXPERIENCE OF MEN?

While on a flight to Houston recently, I met an aerospace worker employed at Boeing. My old tendency would have been to ask him—maybe debate with him—about the Stealth bomber that Boeing helps produce; but instead I asked him about his working conditions. I discovered that he was working with chemicals which could cause memory loss, fatigue, and possibly hepatitis. He told me that he couldn't be specific about the names of those chemicals—they were confidential. When I asked him why he didn't see a doctor, he told me the chemicals were so confidential that they couldn't be disclosed to a doctor. When I pressed, "Isn't your life more important than confidentiality?" he answered, "It's not just my life. . . . If I lose my job, it's my wife and my two kids who suffer." With a tad of encouragement, he then showed me a picture of his wife and two children in front of their Christmas tree.

WHY DON'T MEN SEEM TO BE THAT CONCERNED ABOUT WOMEN AS PROSTITUTES?

I am often asked why men don't get as worked up as they might about women—particularly poor women—having to use their bodies as prostitutes. Because most men unconsciously experience themselves as prostitutes every day—the miner, the firefighter, the construction worker, the logger, the soldier, the meatpacker—these men are prostitutes in the direct sense: they sacrifice their bodies for money and for their families.

The middle-class man is a prostitute of a different sort: he recalls that when his children were born, he gave up his dreams of becoming a novelist and began the nightmare of writing ad copy for a product he didn't believe in—something he would have to do every workday for the rest of his life. The poorer the man, the more he feels this. To men, prostitution is not a female-only occupation.

Most men barely allow themselves even to think about the freedom to look within until after their families are as economically secure as they desire. But many a man finds that just as his goal is within reach, his family is wishing for a nicer home, a better car, a private college. If he is one of the rare men able to satisfy his family enough to look within, he fears discovering the prostitute he has become in the process of providing for others. This is men's version of subservience—of "wife and children first, husband last."

HOW CONSERVATIVES AND LIBERALS BOTH REINFORCE MALE DISPOSABILITY

Both conservatives and liberals reinforce the protection of women and the disposability of men. Conservatives justify it—they call it sex roles. **Liberals call it sexism if it hurts women, but blame men if it hurts men.** For example, male-only clubs hurt women and therefore liberals call it sexism; male-only draft registration hurts men so liberals blame men for causing the wars they've just required only men to fight. Both parties rationalize biology as destiny if it helps women or hurts only men. Similarly, almost all protective legislation is supported by liberals *if* it protects women.* When it comes to protecting women and disposing of men, both parties are conservative—both are Stage I parties. The underlying justification is the unquestioned assumption of woman as victim.

Female Victim Power, AKA Gulf of Tonkin Power

Victim Power is to relationships what Gulf of Tonkin Power is to warfare. Lyndon Johnson could get away with falsely accusing the Communists of attacking an American ship in the Gulf of Tonkin because he knew the assumption of Americans as innocents and Communists as perpetrators would make Congress afraid to question the accuracy of his accusation. **In America today, women have Gulf of Tonkin power: the assumption of their innocence gives them the power to make an accusation without being cross-examined in the same way a man would be.** The degree to which the government has substituted protecting women for questioning women creates the most shocking part of this book: Government as Substitute Husband.

---

* Liberal support for legislation making violence against women (but not violence against men) a "hate crime"; support for protection of mostly women from sexual harassment hazards, but not protection of mostly men from death profession hazards; support for easing requirements for aid to mothers with dependent children, but not to fathers; and support for nearly all of the female-only legal protections (the focus of Part III).

PART III

GOVERNMENT AS SUBSTITUTE HUSBAND

An Overview

When only one sex wins, both sexes lose.

—WARREN FARRELL

When a woman committed a crime in the United States in the 1800s, it was her *husband* who served time.[1] Similarly, under English law, when a family went into debt, it was the husband who went to debtor's prison. When it comes to male-female issues, men's unconscious lawmaking was programmed to protect women. Laws were almost always made *by* men, but not *for* men.

The discoveries of this chapter are that in an era of alleged female independence, one law after another came to be made with such attention to protecting women that if a man's constitutional rights conflict with a woman's protection, most of his rights disintegrate before most of her protection disintegrates.

That is what is happening legally. But what is happening legally almost always reflects what is happening on a deeper level psychologically. We will see that when divorces left women without husband-as-savior, many women looked for substitute saviors; and when divorces left men without a source of love, men competed to obtain women's love by finding new ways of saving women.

The search for saviors and the competition to save appeared in various garbs. New Age women went from father to husband to guru; men competed to be their guru. Traditional women went from father to husband to "God the Father"; men competed to be their "fathers" (priests, ministers, and rabbis). Feminist women went from father to husband to options: the option to save themselves or to turn to the biggest savior of all—government as substitute husband; men competed to turn the government into a substitute husband.

Divorces led to bodies of men (called legislatures) protecting women collectively as other men (called husbands) failed to protect women individually. This meant raising taxes mostly on other men to provide money mostly for women. When divorces deprive women of husbands to protect them, then, our collective unconscious still wants to protect women.

And women's collective unconscious still wants the protection. For example, a San Diego police officer is now serving a fifty-six-year sentence for raping women on local beaches; his wife is suing the police department for the income that he cannot now provide her . . . she expects the government to be her substitute husband. She is also suing the department for having hired him to begin with . . . she expects the government to be a better judge of her husband's character than she was able to be.[2] The more things change . . .

Do these man-made laws reflect male values? In part. Part of men's values is to protect women even more than themselves. Are these laws made in men's self-interest? Sort of. Men who want female love learn to look out for women's interests more than their own.

Doesn't the fact that almost all legislators are men prove that men are in charge and can choose when to and when not to look out for women's interests? Theoretically, yes. But practically speaking, the American legal system cannot be separated from the voter. And in the 1992 presidential election, 54 percent of the voters were female, 46 percent male.[3] (Women's votes outnumber men's by more than 7 million.)

Overall, a legislator is to the voter what a chauffeur is to the employer—both look like they're in charge but both can be fired if they don't go where they're told. When legislators do not appear to be protecting women, it is almost always because women differ on what constitutes protection. (For example, women voted almost equally for Republicans and Democrats during the combination of the four presidential elections prior to Clinton.)

We will see how the legal bias for special protection for women has begun to wreak havoc with the Constitution's guarantee of equal protection. How the 1980s, for example, witnessed two definitions of self-defense: one for men and one for women; and two definitions of first-degree murder—depending on your sex. We will see how, by the '90s, there were twelve defenses that were potentially available for a woman who killed but not for a man who killed. How, at many colleges, a woman could have a man kicked out of school for date rape—even after she had chosen to drink and chosen to say "yes" while drinking.

These chapters will give us a view of why sexual harassment and date rape legislation are now occurring; the dilemmas they will create for business, government, the law, and ultimately women themselves in the twenty-first century; and the steps we can take before we paint ourselves into a corner.

We will look at how the original feminist stance against legal discrimination based on biological differences has changed to one of favoring the use of biological differences if they expand women's rights—such as the right both to bear a child despite the father's objection and then to sue the father for eighteen years of support.

We will look at the dilemma for employers of granting women special rights while being required to treat women with equal respect. For example, feminist support for a pregnant woman's special rights to disability pay soon made pregnancy the only work-place "disability" that did not occur in the workplace, and the only disability that the employee purposely created.

These "protect women" laws have already been put into place in what has been, perhaps, the quietest legal revolution in history. In 1970, feminist legal scholarship was virtually unheard of. Today, most of the books and articles in a recent seventy-one-page bibliography on women and legal scholarship are written by feminist legal scholars.[4] No scholar of prominence has criticized feminism in the law journals. When asked why, Yale Law School professor Geoffrey Hazard explained that in the "politically correct" atmosphere of the universities, any dissent would leave a scholar labeled as antiwoman.[5]

But we still haven't *proven* that the system does protect women. Or that there really are two laws—a male law and a female law.

CHAPTER 11

How the System Protects Women, Or . . . Two Different Laws We Live In

UNEQUAL TIME FOR EQUAL CRIME

ITEM. A man convicted of murder is twenty times more likely than a woman convicted of murder to receive the death penalty.[1]

ITEM. No woman who has killed only men has been executed in the United States since 1954.[2]

ITEM. Since the 1976 reinstatement of the death penalty, 120 men—and only 1 woman—have actually been executed.[3] The woman, from North Carolina, said she preferred to be executed.

ITEM. In North Carolina, a man who commits second-degree murder receives a sentence an average of 12.6 years longer than a woman who commits second-degree murder.[4]

ITEM. The U.S. Department of Justice records the following sentence differences nationwide:

Number of Months to Which Females vs. Males Were Sentenced for the Same Offense[5]

Offense	Female	Male	Percent of Added Time Males Serve
Rape	117	159	74
Aggravated assault	49	83	59
Burglary	46	66	70
Larceny	36	48	75

ITEM. Being male contributes to a longer sentence more than race or any other factor—legal or extralegal.[6] Yet sentencing guidelines were introduced largely to end racial discrimination.

Do sentencing guidelines reduce discrimination against men? Sort of. . . .

ITEM. The sentencing guidelines of the state of Washington are among the strictest. Overall sentences of men, however, are still 23 percent longer than those of women.[7] Even when offense histories are the same and the seriousness of crime is the same, women are 57 percent more likely to receive treatment sentences than prison sentences.[8] Women are also more likely to be made eligible for early departure from prison; and once made eligible, are another 59 percent more likely to actually be released early. Here are some examples from 1991:

Percentage of First-time Offenders Eligible for Early Departure Who Were in Fact Released Early, by Sex[9]

	Female	Male
Residential burglary	63	35
Assault 3	20	13
Burglary 2	40	32
Theft 2	38	25

Percentage of First-time Offenders Eligible for Early Departure Who Were in Fact Released Early, by Sex[9] (*continued*)

	Female	*Male*
Theft 1	17	9
Forgery	48	35
Bail jump/Class B or C	36	15

ITEM. Prosecutors consistently note that women almost always receive lower bail for equal crimes.[10]

In essence, there are two bails: the male bail and the female bail. Women are also more likely to be released on their own recognizance. But the real sexism begins before the bail. . . .

PARTNERS IN CRIME, NOT IN DOING TIME

Plea Bargain as Female Bargain

In plea bargaining with a married couple, often we say, "Well, let's get the man." We're satisfied with getting the husband to plead guilty and dropping the charges against the woman. Of course, then he has a criminal record, she doesn't. If they both repeat the crime, he can "legitimately" receive a longer sentence.

—Assistant Prosecutor J. DENNIS
KOHLER[11]

ITEM. A husband and wife run an illegal drug business out of their home—both of them packaging drugs on their kitchen table. After their trial, the husband is labeled the "kingpin" and put in prison. The wife goes free on probation. A defense lawyer for drug dealers calls this double standard the "drug dealer pattern."[12]

The drug dealer pattern and the plea bargain as female bargain violate the Fourteenth Amendment's guarantee against discrimination according to sex. If prosecutors systematically told only the white man that charges would be dropped against him if he testified against the black man, we would have a racial crisis.

In the case of a man and a woman, *both* will often agree to the *man* taking the rap—despite the man being more likely to receive a longer sentence and more likely to be raped in prison. If blacks were agreeing to do that for whites, the black community would be smart enough to call that "learned subservience."

When Men Are in Charge, Men Do More Time; When Women Are in Charge, Men Do More Time . . . How's That?

When a man and woman jointly commit a crime, but the man is "in charge," the woman gets a much shorter sentence or no sentence because she is said to be brainwashed, powerless, and an unwilling follower. When a *woman* is in charge and a *man* works for *her*, does his claim to be brainwashed carry any weight? In the McMartin Preschool case, Peggy McMartin was the school's director and had hired her 19-year-old grandson—a college dropout.[13] After working for five years under his grandmother's direction, he and his grandmother were *both* indicted on fifty-two counts of child molestation. His grandmother's bail was one third of his[14] and *he* spent nearly five years in jail *before* the jury finally ruled that the two were *not* guilty. She—the director—spent less than two years in jail.

Had a male school director hired his 19-year-old granddaughter, would the granddaughter have been put in jail for five years prior to the verdict? Would we have tolerated the longest trial in U.S. criminal history while a girl found not guilty nevertheless spent half her twenties in prison for allegedly touching children?

CAPITAL PUNISHMENT: THE MALE-ONLY DEATH PENALTY

[The executioner] found it difficult to reconcile himself to the task of destroying the life of a member of the sex which his whole upbringing had taught him was deserving of respect and tenderness as the giver of life.[15]

ITEM. Twenty-three Americans have been executed and later found innocent. All twenty-three were men.[16]

ITEM. Approximately 1,900 women commit homicide in the United States *each year*.[17]

ITEM. When women commit homicide, almost 90 percent of their victims are men.[18]

Since 1954, then, approximately 70,000 women have murdered; their victims include about 60,000 men, but, as we saw in the second Item of this chapter, **not one woman has been executed after killing only a man.**[19]

For nearly four decades now, we have become *in*creasingly protective of women and *de*creasingly protective of men—even if that man is a boy and a legal minor, as was Heath Wilkins. Here's how this happens.

ITEM. Marjorie Filipiak and 16-year-old Heath Wilkins both pled guilty to being coconspirators in a murder. Neither was a hardened criminal. Heath Wilkins got the death sentence; Marjorie Filipiak went free.[20]

ITEM. When Heath Wilkins was found to have been a victim of child sexual abuse, it did not deter the judge from giving him the death sentence.[21] When Josephine Mesa was found to have been the victim of child abuse, the jury freed her.[22] Josephine Mesa had killed her 23-month-old son with a toilet plunger.

INSIDE PRISON, USA

Women felons go to a former school a few miles east of the state capitol. The men's institutions are prisons, plain and hard. They offer cells, guards, cell block gangs. . . . The women's institution feels like the school it was built to be, and its staff encourages reform and rehabilitation.

—Attorney DAVID D. BUTLER,[23]
describing differences in Iowa

ITEM. Any given man in prison is still 1,000 percent as likely as any given woman to die via suicide, homicide, or execution.[24]

Although women's prisons are safer than men's prisons and designed more for rehabilitation, virtually all the recent press coverage has focused on the plight of the female prisoner—as if that plight were unique to the female prisoner. The result? States such as California are now financing the study of *only* female prisoner health issues.[25] And states like Wisconsin are spending $2,000 per month for female prisoners as against $1,000 per month for male prisoners.[26]

Women's prisons, as a rule, do suffer one area of discrimination—job training. Men are more likely to be trained in skills for higher-paying jobs such as welder or mechanic while many women's facilities focus more on skills for lower-paying jobs such as beautician or launderer.[27] This needs to be changed.

Nevertheless, now that the female prison population has increased so that 6 percent of the country's inmates are female,[28] many states are developing programs that offer women special privileges. Mothers in Lancaster, Massachusetts, have special facilities in which to see their children; fathers do not.[29] In New York's Bedford Hills Corrections Facility, mothers have a live-in nursery; fathers do not. In Minnesota, women's prisons are built in residential communities alongside schools; hard-core female prisoners are placed in battered women's shelters to do community service. No equivalent exists for men.

Once in prison, women tend to be "dependent" prisoners: they lean more heavily than their male counterparts on the prison staff, on drug rehabilitation programs, and on counselors.[30] They also tend to make more use of the prison medical facilities for headaches, upset stomachs, and other complaints.

How the Inequality Is Rationalized

Sentence Compounding

When the state gives the female the first option to plea-bargain and receives extra evidence about a man in exchange for repressing evidence about a woman, this leads the press to report the evidence against the man, which leads the public to reinforce its stereotype of man-as-criminal, woman-as-innocent. Thus the initial belief that women are more innocent becomes a self-fulfilling prophecy which becomes the rationalization for continuing to allow the woman the first option to plea-bargain.

Should they both commit a second crime, not only is the man the only one with a prison record, which justifies his getting a longer sentence, but his longer time in prison is also more likely to harden him, something a jury will pick up on and something that contributes to his higher recidivism rate. In these respects, men's criminal records are multiplied, women's minimized. And so, discrimination begets discrimination begets discrimination.

How the Commissions on Gender Bias Rationalize Gender Bias

Recently, state commissions on gender bias have reported that it is women who are victims of discrimination. For example:

> ITEM. When women go free on probation while men get prison sentences, the state commissions on gender bias say women are victims of discrimination because women receive longer periods of *probation!*[31]

The commissions also mention that women are discriminated against because there are fewer women's institutions, forcing relatives to go farther to visit them. Not mentioned is the reason: There is rarely any need for more than one women's prison near a city because of all the discrimination in *favor* of women. Were women to receive equal charges, equal bail, and equal sentencing, there would be more women's prisons.

For women to have the privilege of avoiding prison by going free on probation, doing less time when sentenced, or receiving treatment sentences rather than prison sentences—and then to complain about there being fewer prisons, well . . . there could hardly be a better example of chutzpa. Yet *The New York Times* reports these conclusions without questioning them.[32]

Why wouldn't a government commission on gender bias see through this gender bias? Because these "government" commissions are not really government commissions—they are feminist commissions. That is, the government relies upon recommendations of organizations such as the feminist National Organization for Women and the mostly feminist National Association of Women Judges in choosing which issues to research and which to ignore.[33]

They are government commissions only in the sense that they are *paid for* by the government—meaning us. Even the key staff members are more likely to be women than men—frequently feminist activists, almost never a men's movement activist.[34]

Thus the commissions were able to see the overcrowding in women's prisons while ignoring the more intense overcrowding in men's prisons; they were able to see how women's prisons need to pay attention to problems unique to women, but not how men's prisons also need to pay more attention to problems more common among men, such as male-to-male rape.

A feminist government commission on gender bias is the equivalent of a Republican government commission on political party bias. Imagine having a government commission on political party bias sponsored by one political party, staffed by the same party, systematically having the other party excluded, its findings unquestioned in *The New York Times*, and having your taxes increased to pay the bill. If a political party did this, we'd call it a scandal; when feminists do this, it's called official. **Feminism has become gender politics' one-party system.**

Is It Just the Feminists Who Rationalize Sex Bias?

While it is understandable how a feminist-sponsored commission *on* sex bias would be a commission *with* sex bias, similar bias is also common in reports from male-dominated government agencies such as the U.S. Department of Justice. For example:

The U.S. Department of Justice reports that men have longer sentences than women.[35] They rationalize the longer sentences by pointing out that men are more likely to be sent to prison than women and prison sentences tend to be longer.[36] (Jail is for shorter sentences, so naturally the sex with the longer sentences would go to prison.) Here's the sexism: Why are men more likely to be given longer sentences for the same crime and equivalent criminal histories to begin with?

Imagine reading a government report saying a sister and brother stole bubble gum, and the boy was sent to prison while the girl was confined to her room. If it then explained that the boy was kept in prison longer simply because prison sentences tend to be longer than room confinement, wouldn't we be asking, "Wait, that misses the point: Why was the boy put in prison and the girl put in her room for the same crime to begin with?"

The need to deny sexism when it cuts against men then, runs much deeper than feminism: it is part of our collective unconscious process of using government-as-protector to substitute for male-as-protector.

The Chivalry Factor[37]

White middle-class people in the criminal justice system basically look at women as incapable of committing some of the crimes they are charged with. They therefore try to find rationales as to why the woman wasn't really involved. But the women who are being dealt with sympathetically are the white, middle-class women, not the poor and minorities.

—BARBARA SWARTZ, Director,
Women's Prison Project[38]

The Chivalry Factor works this way. The courts are designed to give equal protection. The more a judge (or jury) sees women as the weaker sex, the more the judge reasons (usually unconsciously) that the court needs to give a woman *extra* protection (to compensate for her being the weaker sex) in order for the result to be equal protection. This is the reasoning process of the judges we call chauvinistic, chivalrous, or patriarchal. It is also the reasoning process of the adolescent feminist. The chauvinist and feminist are both *female* protective. Many female judges, though, are less female protective than either chauvinists or feminists. As one attorney put it, "If there were more women judges, more women would go to jail."[39]

Chivalry's Integrated Circuit: Judge, Jury, Lawyers, and Female Client

I tell women what to wear, how to dress, how to make up their hair. They must have a great deal of sex appeal to the men on the jury—and to the judge, too. But at the same time she can't antagonize the women on the jury by being too flashy-looking. If she cries softly while the case is going on, that's wonderful.

—Attorney FRANK P. LUCIANNA[40]

"It's difficult for a prosecutor to harshly cross-examine a woman, or he'll alienate the jury. He has to walk on eggshells," New Jersey lawyer Michael Breslin explains.[41] He finds the protective instinct operates for everyone but is especially prevalent among older jurors. So if he is defending a woman, he tries to select older jurors. A criminal attorney specializing in civil rights put it bluntly: "I always prefer to represent a female client; the system is clearly biased in her favor."[42]

Judge, jury, lawyers, female clients, and police, then, all contribute to chivalry's integrated circuit. Lawyers in many cities report that a jury is so unlikely to convict a woman of drunk driving that police do not even bother to arrest her.[43] It's true that "it's a male system with male chauvinist judges"—and it's unfair. The men who receive longer sentences find it quite unfair.

This protect-the-woman instinct penetrates not only criminal law but family law. It is fairly obvious in the area of fathers versus mothers: **we tell women they have the right to children but tell men they have to fight for children.** It is less obvious in the double standard of community property. Remember Jim and Tammy Faye Bakker? . . .

THE DOUBLE STANDARD OF COMMUNITY PROPERTY: HER RIGHTS, HIS RESPONSIBILITY

When Tammy Faye Bakker divorced Jim, community property laws guaranteed Tammy Faye rights to half of the profits of their ministry. Why? Marriage makes a couple legal equals. How a couple divides roles is private business, but community property laws were supposed to make equal rights and responsibilities for the couple's profits or debts public business. But do they?

Although Jim and Tammy Faye had equal rights to profits no matter what role she played, when the business got into trouble, Jim got forty years in prison and Tammy Faye got none. Tammy Faye did not have to even appear in court.

On the surface, this appears justifiable *if* she didn't know what was going on. But if equality means a woman shares legal rights to the *profits* of a marriage *no matter what role she plays* or how illegally those profits were accrued, then equality also means a woman shares legal responsibility for any illegalities in creating those profits—no matter what role she plays. **If community property is "couple profit" regardless of role, it must become "couple responsibility" regardless of role.**

But shouldn't we hold a man more responsible if the financial operations for which he was assigned role responsibility get into legal trouble? Sure, if he systematically falsifies information despite his wife's questioning. But **if the married man is held more responsible for finances that go legally awry, then the married woman should be held more responsible for children who go awry.** No one even suggests we make *only the mother* financially responsible for damage caused by the minor "since the father was unaware of what was going on." We would say his lack of awareness was part of what *created* the delinquency. An unaware father is considered negligent, not innocent.

When a child goes awry, not only are both parents equally responsible but, practically speaking, the man usually earns the additional money required to pay damages. No one tells the mother, "You yelled at your husband for criticizing your mothering, so he backed off—so now you are responsible for the half million dollars of liability incurred from your son driving without insurance. You, mother, can either pay or spend forty years in prison." So *the man* pays when there's a mess up in the male role *or* in the female role.

Community property without community responsibility reinforces traditional sex roles: it encourages women to assign their husbands all the financial risks. By saying *"You* sign that legal document" or *"You* sign the check," she can avoid the downside of prison but receive the upside of profits. If he makes a fortune through tax evasion, inside trading, drug dealing, or a Ponzi scheme and gets away with it, she shares the profits. If he gets caught, only he goes to prison. In its present version, community property is equal rights without equal responsibilities. Which is not equality.

When a woman senses her financial innocence will allow her to share a profit margin but not a prison cell, she is usually unaware how her innocence makes him more likely to become guilty than he would had she been involved in the finances. The greater her financial innocence, the more the financial burden falls on him and the more likely he is to handle that burden by flirting with the boundaries of the law. Just as, if he never paid any attention to the children, his "innocence" would make her feel more overburdened and abusive to the children. Few judges have looked at this connection between her financial innocence and his financial guilt.

When a wife's financial innocence is accompanied by financial pressure, a husband is an accident waiting to happen. As he feels the psychological pressure for a larger home, he first tries something *marginally* legal. If it works, expectations rise and he soon feels a new pressure (to send the kids to a better college), so he tries something *il*legal. If he gets caught, he doesn't tell the court: "I felt this psychological pressure from my wife, Your Honor. I had this feeling of 'learned helplessness.' " If he did, he would be laughed out of court.

Both sexes sharing community property but with male-only responsibility returns us to an era of woman-as-child. It makes family teamwork dependent on female innocence rather than female equality. It returns us to the Stage I family in which the division of labor led to a division of interests. When both sexes share property and share responsibility, we have an integration of labor and an integration of interests—a Stage II family with Stage II teamwork. A Stage II family unit. And a Stage II united family.

How Community Property without Community Responsibility Hurts Women

Community property without community responsibility ultimately boomerangs against women. When ignorance allows her to share a fortune but not share a jail cell, then ignorance pays in the short run. But in the long run, it creates the most ubiquitous form of female "learned helplessness"—financial learned helplessness. Thus if she has doubts about her marriage and knows her financial ignorance is not her best postdivorce survival tool, she fears expressing her feelings and begins to feel like a marital prostitute.

The feeling of being a marital prostitute is part of the female morality dilemma. We cannot really consider ourselves moral until we know what compromises we are willing to make to provide financially for our family. But being financially ignorant allows many women the luxury of focusing on spirituality or on the family rather than having to "dirty their hands" with finances. It teaches a woman who ignores the moral responsibilities of financial responsibility to consider herself morally superior. Yet exactly as she is feeling this moral superiority, she is also feeling like a marital prostitute. Thus creating the female morality dilemma.

The collective unconscious that supports shared community property with male-only financial responsibility is the same collective unconscious that retains its need to see woman as child. In a Stage I world, this division was understandable. But by the year 2020, it is likely that a woman will become president of the United States (probably one who is first elected vice president). To see this woman as a child is to predict that a child will soon run the country. Is that an exaggeration? Well, think of how we treated Geraldine Ferraro as a child: When her husband's money financed her run for Congress, we thought of it as "family money"—at least half hers; yet as soon as the money was thought to have been produced illegally, only her husband risked a possible prison sentence, and her husband was seen as having "dragged Geraldine Ferraro down." We did not treat Ms. Ferraro as if she were equally responsible. Did we unconsciously think of her as a child? Let's look.

Had a househusband run for office on money produced by his wife, we would have thought he was "using" her. We would have questioned whether a man who could not financially support his family could financially lead a country. And if his wife earned the money illegally, we would say, "If he can't keep corruption out of his home, how can he keep it out of government? . . . If he can't share responsibility for corruption with the one person he loves, how can he share it with the thousand strangers he appoints?"

Yet when a feminist who was a potential U.S. president used money produced by her husband, no one questioned it. Nor did we question her right to share the money while avoiding responsibility for illegalities incurred in its creation. No one asked, "If they were a team 'for better,' why weren't they a team 'for worse'?" **We saw the attack on him as sexism against her, rather than as sexism against him.** (When a man is a candidate and a woman a spouse, the man gets investigated; when the reverse is true, the man still gets investigated. That's sexism against men.)

Encouraging women to run for high political office cannot be separated from simultaneously treating women like full adults—

not as adults when it comes to rights and children when it comes to responsibilities. The alternative? Having a country run by a child. The solution? Sharing community property and sharing community responsibility—creating a Stage II family for a Stage II country.

Women Who Kill Too Much and the Courts That Free Them: The Twelve "Female-Only" Defenses

Neither men nor women are exempt from killing loved ones. The difference is in what happens to them when they do. Twelve distinct female-only defenses allow a woman who commits a premeditated murder to have the charges dropped or significantly reduced. No man has successfully used any of these defenses in similar circumstances. Nor do men have any equivalent "male-only" defenses. *Each* of these defenses therefore violates the Fourteenth Amendment's guarantee of equal protection to both sexes under the law. And all twelve defenses combined create overwhelming evidence of a double standard of self-defense that will be wreaking havoc in the legal system for decades and be affecting for a lifetime our children's decisions as to whether to marry.

I. THE "INNOCENT WOMAN" DEFENSE

I am starting with the "Innocent Woman Defense" because it underlies all twelve defenses. At first I had called this the "Female

Credibility Principle" because of the tendency to see women as more credible than men because of being thought more innocent. However, even when women admitted making false allegations that they were raped or that their husbands abused them, for example, their admission that they lied was often *not* believed. Therefore the belief in the innocent woman ran even deeper than the tendency to believe women. Bessie Reese, for example. . . .

Bessie Reese's husband went on a trip and decided not to return to Bessie. Since her husband had gone with James Richardson, Bessie decided to retaliate by poisoning the lunches of the seven Richardson children. All seven children died.[1]

Bessie Reese never became a suspect. She was never given a polygraph test. Was she deserving of such credibility? Not exactly. She had gone to trial for the poisoning of her first husband. (She was set free.[2]) And she was found guilty of shooting her second husband. (She did a short stint in jail.)

James Richardson got the death sentence. Yet James and his wife were eight miles away working in a citrus grove in Arcadia, Florida, when Bessie was serving the children lunch. Richardson was falsely accused of failing a polygraph test—yet the prosecutor who handled the Richardson appeal acknowledges that no one during the original trial ever saw the test.[3]

James Richardson literally watched his own coffin being built. But . . . the death sentence was temporarily commuted in 1972. And then, after James spent two decades in prison, Bessie Reese finally confessed to poisoning the children. But the belief in "the innocent woman" and "the guilty man" was strong enough that even a second signed affidavit by Bessie did not lead to a new trial for James. **Which illustrates the basis of the "Innocent Woman Defense"—the "Innocent Woman Principle": women are believed when they say they are innocent of violence and most easily doubted when they say they are guilty of violence.**

It took political protests over the racism (James was black; Bessie was white) to lead to a new trial and Richardson's release (after twenty-one years in prison).

I asked the new prosecutor why Bessie Reese had never been a suspect. He couldn't give an official answer, only that "several of the townsfolk had seen the sheriff stop by Bessie Reese's home at all times of night and day" for months.[4] He could only say, "The rumor was they were having an affair."

The Visibility of Racism versus the Invisibility of Sexism

This case became known only as an example of racism. But were it only racism, then Mrs. Richardson, who is black, would also have been investigated. Although Mrs. Richardson was at the same place as her husband when the poisonings occurred, neither she nor Bessie ever became a serious suspect. In essence, *neither* woman became a serious suspect—only the man.

Sexism permeated the Bessie Reese case. It was inherent in the entire community's unwillingness to create the political pressure necessary for Bessie to become a suspect despite her history of husband killing and the rumors of her affair. And perhaps the most dominant sexism was how Bessie's sexual power led to the sheriff protecting Bessie at the cost of transforming himself from a stopper of crime to a criminal.

The cost of protecting women who kill is the same as the cost of protecting men who kill: the killer continues to kill—not just disposable men but precious children.

To this day, Bessie Reese has not been charged with the murders to which she confessed.[5]

What It Takes to Doubt a Woman's Innocence

Tawana Brawley

ITEM. Black 15-year-old Tawana Brawley claimed she'd been gang-raped by white racists, stuffed into a plastic garbage bag, and covered with excrement.[6] But a doctor testified that there was no evidence of either rape or assault. And a woman testified that she had seen Tawana climb into the plastic garbage bag of her own accord. Then cotton wads were found in Tawana's nose so she wouldn't have to smell the excrement. Nevertheless, Governor Mario Cuomo of New York said, "You can't tell me she did it to herself unless you give me some motive."

In fact, Governor Cuomo was given a motive: Tawana and her mother were trying to provide an excuse to the mother's live-in companion for Tawana's failure to return home. But perhaps the governor's need to see a woman as innocent and his fear of being called racist and sexist did not allow him even to acknowledge hearing what turned out to be the motive.

The country recognized only the racism behind Tawana Brawley's hoax, not the sexism of two women conspiring to concoct a story of multiple male perpetrators/single female victim. No one confronted her for perpetrating the stereotype of male as rapist. Or men as gang rapists. Or of playing into females' fears of men; or of forcing every man to have to prove himself even more before he becomes worthy of a female's trust. The racism was visible; the sexism, invisible.

The *Arsenic and Old Lace* Case

When Blanche Taylor Moore and her husband went on a honeymoon and he suddenly had to be taken to the hospital, the doctor discovered he had been poisoned by arsenic. The dose wasn't enough to kill him, so Blanche gave him a couple of extra poisoned milk shakes. When the story got out, some people recalled that Blanche's first husband had died from arsenic poisoning. Others remembered a boyfriend had "died of a heart attack." But now the police became suspicious. They dug up her boyfriend's body and discovered his corpse retained a toxic dose of arsenic. Her father's body was then exhumed; it also contained arsenic.[7]

As Blanche's activities became public, people began calling the police saying they had reason to believe that Blanche had killed their relatives as well. Blanche had remained innocent for a quarter century. To my knowledge, no man in American history has ever been assumed innocent while his mother, first wife, and a womanfriend died of poisoning and a second wife almost died of poisoning. Especially when all this happened in one community, as it did with Blanche.

Is it possible that by not subjecting Blanche to the type of investigation to which a man would have been subjected she was able to kill people for a quarter of a century?

The Excedrin Poisonings: "Take Two and I'll Bury You in the Morning"

For five years Stella Nickell studied library books on how to poison, and even experimented on her husband, Bruce.[8] Finally she got it right: she laced Excedrin with cyanide and waited for Bruce to get his final headache. The coroner's report did not detect the cyanide and therefore recorded Bruce as dying from pulmonary emphysema. But this angered Stella. She wanted the cyanide to be discovered so the death could be listed as accidental and blamed on the altered Excedrin. Why? If he died of an accident, she would collect $176,000 in insurance money (versus $71,000 if he died of a heart attack). So to prove it was an accident, she put cyanide in the Excedrin in local supermarkets. A beautiful woman named Sue Snow bought some Excedrin and was killed.[9] Immediately eighty-five FBI agents and police officers got into the act. Ultimately Stella was convicted. But only Stella's greed led to Stella's conviction.

As with Blanche Taylor Moore, when we work from the unconscious assumption "she's a woman, she's innocent, don't investigate" we risk the lives of other innocent women and men. The release of Willy Horton was enough to ruin a presidential candidate, but the initial refusal even to investigate Stella and Blanche left us with female Willy Hortons roaming free—free to mother, collect insurance, remarry—but instead of being called a criminal on probation, they were called a mother who was widowed. In this sheepskin their serial killing female style snatched yet another body.

What It Takes to Believe a Man

When Delissa Carter stabbed her mother to death, she said her husband, Nathaniel, had done it—that she *saw* him do it.[10] Two witnesses testified to Nathaniel's presence in Peekskill, New York, at the time of the slaying (a considerable distance from the murder scene). Although Delissa was at the scene of the crime, the New York State Supreme Court took her word over a man's and two witnesses. Nathaniel was sentenced to twenty-five years to life in prison. Had three unusual events not occurred, Nathaniel would never have been found innocent.[11] By that time, though, Nathaniel had already served more than a year in prison.

When a woman and man are each trying to persuade a judge and jury to believe them—when their credibility is pitted against each other—she is unconsciously assumed innocent unless proven guilty; he is presumed guilty unless proven innocent. The Innocent Woman Principle underlies not only the Innocent Woman Defense, but almost all the others as well.

II. THE PMS DEFENSE ("MY BODY, NO CHOICE")

In 1970, when Dr. Edgar Berman said women's hormones during menstruation and menopause could have a detrimental influence on women's decision making, feminists were outraged. He was soon served up as the quintessential example of medical male chauvinism.[12]

But by the 1980s, some feminists were saying that PMS was the reason a woman who deliberately killed a man should go free. In England, the PMS defense freed Christine English after she confessed to killing her boyfriend by *deliberately* ramming him into a utility pole with her car; and, after killing a coworker, Sandie Smith was put on probation—with one condition: she must report monthly for injections of progesterone to control symptoms of PMS.[13]

By the 1990s, the PMS defense paved the way for other hormonal defenses. Sheryl Lynn Massip could place her 6-month-old son under a car, run over him repeatedly, and then, uncertain he was dead, do it again, then claim postpartum depression and be given *out*patient medical help.[14] No feminist protested.

In the 1970s, then, feminists were saying, "My body, *my* choice." By the '80s and '90s, they were saying, " 'My body, my choice' if that increases my freedom to kill," and " 'My body, *no* choice' if *that* increases my freedom to kill."

Ms. magazine justified these contradictions with, "Well, each woman is different."[15] True. But PMS as a legal defense for murder is sexism against women waiting to happen. Why? If a woman could murder while under the influence of PMS, couldn't she be a reckless driver while under the influence . . . and if she doesn't know *when* she is under the influence, doesn't this become a reason not to let women drive? We are back to women as children.

The "hormones affect some women more than others" excuse allows one woman to apply for an executive position and say, "Hire me—PMS doesn't affect me," while another murders and says, "Free me—PMS affects me." It also allows a woman to get a job as an executive, murder later, and say, *with legal clout*, "Free me—PMS just started affecting me." If raging hormones continue to be a *legal* defense for females who murder, it will soon be a legitimate question for female employment. Discrimination for women begets discrimination against women.

The PMS Defense also paves the way for the TP Defense—the Testosterone Poisoning Defense. If women can murder and claim PMS, why can't men rape and claim testosterone poisoning? The solution? Punish the crime—with female or male hormones as only a minor mitigating factor.

III. THE HUSBAND DEFENSE

The film *I Love You to Death* was based on the *true* story of a woman who tried to kill her husband when she discovered he had been unfaithful. She and her mom tried to poison him, then hired muggers to beat him and shoot him through the head. A fluke led to their being caught and sent to jail. Miraculously, the husband survived.

The husband's first response? Soon after he recovered, he informed authorities that he would not press charges. His second response? He defended his wife's attempts to kill him. He felt so guilty being sexually "unfaithful" that he *thanked* his wife! He then reproposed to her. She verbally abused him, then accepted.

I Love You to Death was a true story produced as a comedy. Imagine the protests if a *true* story of a husband attempting to murder his wife was produced as a comedy.

Is this Husband Defense an isolated example? No. You won't believe this one. . . . The headline summarizes it: "Woman Who Shot Mate 5 Times Gets Probation."[16]

When Jennifer Eidenschink and her husband, Steven, separated, Jennifer bought a gun. She invited Steven over to remove a deer head from the wall, and then, while his hands were occupied, she unloaded all eight shots from her .22-caliber semiautomatic pistol.[17] Five shots entered him—three in the abdomen.

Steven, an athlete, suffered irreparable nerve damage and a permanent limp that would prevent him from playing the sports that meant so much to him. Jennifer said he had abused her. But because Steven survived, he was able to present evidence that made her acknowledge she was lying.[18] The Dane County Court of Wisconsin did not sentence her to a single day in jail or prison . . . just counseling and two and one half weeks of voluntary service. For attempted murder. The judge was influenced by two things: the children's needs for their mother, and Steven's testimony *on his wife's behalf*.[19] But that's only the beginning. . . .

When Steven recovered, *he moved back in* with his wife—just like in the movie! Oh yes, the state did order Jennifer to pay $22,000 for her husband's medical bills. But Jennifer was not working. *Guess who paid his wife's bill for shooting him?*

It's easy to think, "Oh, my God, they deserve each other!" But something else is going on here. I call this the Husband Defense because I have yet to hear of a wife providing the legal defense for a husband who premeditated her murder.

The Husband Defense is quintessential learned helplessness. When women display even a fraction of this learned helplessness, we recognize it not only as a disease but as a disease that overpowers her to such a degree that it can now be used as a defense to kill a man and go free. When a man experiences this learned helplessness, he can never use it to get away with trying to kill her, only to defend her for trying to kill him. It works like this . . .

IV. THE "BATTERED WOMAN SYNDROME" DEFENSE, AKA LEARNED HELPLESSNESS

ITEM. December 1990. The governor of Ohio releases from prison twenty-five women who had been convicted of killing or assaulting their husbands or companions.[20] Each woman claimed the man had abused her. Within months, other governors had followed suit.[21]

Until 1982, anyone who called a *premeditated* murder self-defense would have been laughed out of court. But in 1982, Lenore Walker won the first legal victory for her women-only theory of learned helplessness, which suggests that a woman whose husband or boyfriend batters her becomes fearful for her life and helpless to leave him so if she kills him, it is really self-defense—even if she had premeditated his murder.[22]

The woman is said to be a victim of the Battered Woman Syndrome. Is it possible a woman could kill, let's say, for insurance money? Lenore Walker says no: she claims, *"Women* don't kill men unless they've been pushed to a point of desperation."[23] Ironically, feminists had often said, "There's never an excuse for violence against a woman." Now they were saying, "But there's *always* an excuse for violence against a man . . . if a woman does it." That sexism is now called the law in fifteen states.

By the 1990s, states such as California and Ohio allowed a woman to kill her sleeping husband and claim self-defense because she *"felt* helpless."[24] Allowing a woman to claim self-defense after killing a man who was asleep gave these states a female-only definition of self-defense. For the first time in American history, premeditated murder, normally called first-degree murder (the worst kind), was called self-defense—but only if a woman was accused; and only if a man was murdered. Which leaves us with a Battered Woman Syndrome but no Battered Man Syndrome—as if women were the only victims of learned helplessness.

Do *both* sexes suffer from feelings of learned helplessness? Yes. For example. . . .

What Happens When a Man Has "Battered Man Syndrome"?

Tom Hayhurst grew up watching his mother throw phones and dishes at his dad. His dad *never returned the beatings*[25] and was too emotionally dependent to leave. Finally, his dad fatally shot himself in the head.

Tom's mom abused each of the children as well. The children eventually moved away, except for Tom's sister, who was developmentally disabled. But then Tom's mother was seriously injured in a car accident. She asked Tom to return home to help her and his disabled sister. Tom left his job in Arizona and took care of his mom without pay. This left him with too little money to afford an apartment. Because he knew he couldn't handle living with his mother, he lived in a van in the driveway. However, as the court report reads, "She began verbal and physical abuse of him, brandishing a knife, and throwing objects at him."[26] "Finally," Tom explains, "I just blew it. I grabbed a crowbar and hit her." The blow from the crowbar killed her.

Tom, a slight-built man, was evaluated by the psychologist as "driven by a sense of duty and altruism . . . passive and nonaggressive . . . one who appreciates life's aesthetics." Tom was given fifteen years to life in prison—meaning he would be subjected to convicts who typically seek slight-built men to rape. Unlike mothers who kill husbands and are freed on probation to care for their children, Tom was not freed to continue the care he had been giving his disabled sister.

Few humans could claim a more impeccable history of learned helplessness than a son who watched his dad kill himself rather than walk away or fight back. Few humans could feel more trapped than a son who was living in poverty so he could help a disabled mom and sister. And few people who kill can say that every family member was so severely abused prior to one defending himself.

What type of sentence would have been given had Tom been a Theresa—a daughter quitting her job to respond to the desperate call of an abusive dad and disabled brother? If Theresa's dad had continued abusing her and she finally responded by hitting him and accidentally killing him, would she have gotten any sentence? Or been put on probation, given counseling, become a feminist hero, and had a TV movie made about her "devotion in the face of abuse"—a movie ending happily with her "fighting back and breaking the cycle of dependence," with her freeing herself to take care of her developmentally disabled brother without the abusive dad around?

The Burning Bed *Murders*

In 1984, Farrah Fawcett starred in an NBC-TV movie called *The Burning Bed*, based on a true incident in which an abused wife murdered her husband by burning him to death while he slept. The courts freed her because she had been abused.[27] The TV movie's Nielsen rating exceeded that of the World Series, making it "one of the highest-rated TV movies of all time"[28] In *Why Men Are the Way They Are*, I expressed fear that the movie's popularity reflected a willingness to hear the message that if a woman feels she is abused, she can choose to kill her husband rather than leave him. Ultimately, this had to lead either to a sex-biased system of self-defense or to also allowing men who are abused by women to kill women rather than leave women.

Since the mid-eighties, *Burning Bed* murders have abounded. Judy Norman of North Carolina murdered her husband by shooting him in the head while he slept. She claimed self-defense because she had been abused. The state supreme court held that self-defense was applicable only to cases in which one is in imminent danger of being killed, and that, although she had been abused, she could have walked out while he was sleeping. When the supreme court failed to rescue her, the governor stepped in. He commuted her sentence. Judy served only two months, during which she worked on her high school diploma.[29]

By 1990, Ohio became the fifteenth state[30] to allow women to murder their sleeping husbands and possibly get away with the murder by *claiming* past abuse (their husbands were not in a position to argue the claim). They were not required to prove they were in imminent danger of being killed without any possible *physical* escape. On this basis, the governor of Ohio released from prison "The Ohio Twenty-five."[31]

What Are the Rationales behind Freeing These Women?

RATIONALE #1: When a woman is repeatedly physically abused, the emotional consequences are with her for years, making the attack on her abuser a form of emotional self-defense.

Fact. The emotional consequences of physical abuse *are* with many women for years. And the emotional consequences are also with men who have been battered for many years. **The only *two*-sex studies that have ever been done (more than a dozen) find women and men to be *equally* as likely to initiate domestic violence at *every level of severity*.**[32]* The emotional consequences of being stabbed or having one's face cut with a frying pan are severe enough to men that they are ashamed to even report it.

Similarly, veterans of every war suffer Battered Man Syndrome in the form of posttraumatic stress disorder. The emotional consequences are also with them for years. But if a sufferer killed Admiral Zumwalt for ordering the spraying of Agent Orange, he would be convicted for murder. Men who suffer Battered Man Syndrome are not allowed to attack their abuser and call it self-defense. They cannot do that even though the law required them to subject themselves to battering and gave them no way to escape.

---

* The fourteen studies are described in my forthcoming book. A couple of these are in the endnotes.

RATIONALE #2: It's physical self-defense.

Fact. Of women imprisoned for murdering their husbands, almost one third murdered men who were incapacitated (e.g., asleep, in wheelchairs, drunk to the point of incapacitation). Approximately 60 percent premeditated the murder.[33] Yet, more than half of the women who battered even the incapacitated men later claimed self-defense (as in *immediate* danger).[34]

RATIONALE #3: "Women don't kill men unless they've been abused and pushed to the point of desperation."

Fact. Thirty percent of women in prison for killing men had histories of violent offenses.[35]

Fact. Some women in prison for killing their husbands have been abused by them. However, when Dr. Coramae Richey Mann did a study of hundreds of women imprisoned in six major cities for murdering their husbands or lovers, *not one woman was found to have been battered by a man.*[36] Some women, then, do kill without first being abused.

Fact. When a woman kills a man, it is most frequently a man whose insurance policy exceeds his immediate ability to provide for her.[37] (She seldom kills her source of income.)

RATIONALE #4: Women are more afraid than men to report their abusers to the authorities.

Fact. Despite fourteen separate two-sex studies finding that women and men are *equally* as likely to batter,[38] more than 90 percent of police reports are made by women about men, and more than 90 percent of temporary restraining orders in the United States are initiated by women against men.[39] Women, then, are about nine times as likely as men to report their abusers to authorities. Male socialization to "take it like a man" makes men the sex more fearful of reporting their abusers.

RATIONALE #5: The woman says she has nowhere to turn for help.

Fact. Ironically, during the 1980s, women's paths for escaping their husbands became perfected via hotlines, shelters, and women's centers. TV ads give women the numbers to call. Almost every community has shelters for battered women but no shelters for battered men; most communities have women's centers; their only "men's centers" are prisons. A woman has much more closely developed networks of womenfriends who are likely to be sympathetic to her being abused than a man does of men friends who are likely to be sympathetic to his being abused. Only abused women have government-subsidized paths of escape from their abusers, yet only abused women are freed when they kill their abusers.

RATIONALE #6: No matter how hard a woman tries to escape, the man can still track her down and "get her" (as in the film *Sleeping with the Enemy*).

Fact. Both sexes have this problem. Kevin Svoboda's wife had been put in jail for hiring a "hit man." Nevertheless, this did not prevent her from trying again. While awaiting sentencing, she again hired hit men to murder Kevin.[40] She was caught only because one of her hit men turned out to be an undercover police officer. Kevin has concluded, "I will never feel safe." He feels she might have wanted him dead to collect his $130,000 life insurance policy. Should we allow Kevin to kill his wife in "self-defense"?

Similarly, Daniel Broderick tried to escape the abuse of his ex-wife, Elizabeth Broderick. Even after Elizabeth had driven a truck through the front door of their home, burglarized his home in defiance of a restraining order, destroyed valuable artwork, and left repeated messages threatening to kill him, Dan Broderick knew that, despite being one of San Diego's best attorneys, there was no way he could kill her first without being convicted of first-degree murder. No Battered Man Syndrome would lighten his sentence. Was he, though, really in danger? Well, Elizabeth bought a gun, walked into the bedroom where Dan and his new wife, Linda, were sleeping, and emptied her gun into both of them. Both are dead.

RATIONALE #7: The police will not take a woman seriously for complaining about abuse, so reporting it to the police is useless.

Fact. When a woman complains in any of twelve states and many cities in America, **the police now have a mandatory policy of arresting a man, even when there is no evidence of abuse, and even when the woman refuses to press charges.**[41] Which means that the woman is taken extremely seriously when she complains; she is ignored only when she refuses to press charges. It is part of the Innocent Woman Principle.

Although many mandatory arrest laws are written in gender-neutral language, in practice they are not used to protect a man against a woman or to protect a gay man against his possible abuser. When gay men who are battered call the police, a common practice is to arrest both parties.[42]

In communities without mandatory arrest policies, only the woman is encouraged to press charges immediately, while she is angry, even if the police see no evidence of abuse; she is generally not told that if she later drops those charges, the man can be put on trial anyway; that is, *he can be put on trial against her will*—by the government. Again, she is treated overly seriously when she complains, but like a child when she says, "Let *me* take responsibility." **The belief in her innocence outweighs the belief in her.**

How the Battered Woman Syndrome Works in Real Life

Marlene Wagshall waited until her husband, Joshua, was asleep. She then stood beside their bed, assumed a crouched, combat position that she had trained for, pointed a .357 Magnum at his chest, and squeezed the trigger.[43] Their daughter watched, terror stricken, as her dad struggled to close the door so she would not see him die. That was the last time she saw her dad.

After eighteen hours on the operating table and the removal of his spleen, parts of his liver, his pancreas, and upper intestine, Joshua survived, in part. His children, though, were gone—Marlene had kidnapped them.

The grand jury found Marlene indictable not only for attempted murder but for numerous other counts. However, feminist District Attorney Elizabeth Holtzman reduced the attempted murder charge to second-degree assault and accepted a plea for Marlene to spend *one day in jail*. After one day, Marlene could be free on five years' probation.[44]

Why? Marlene claimed she was a victim of the Battered Wife Syndrome. However, there was no corroborative evidence—no children as witnesses, no hospital records, no accounts of neighbors. Newspaper accounts suggested she had found photographs of her husband with a nude woman and that she took her gun to him in a rage. Josh testified, however, that the confrontation was systematic and methodical.

Think about it. If every wife has permission to kill a husband who has an extramarital sexual relationship, and we use the Fourteenth Amendment to protect men equally, we would have to give husbands permission to kill each wife who has an extramarital relationship. The result of this equality? We'd all be investing in funeral parlors.

Does freedom for women who shoot men have the potential for becoming even more commonplace? Elizabeth Holtzman, the district attorney who plea-bargained murder and kidnapping down to one day in jail, is now, as comptroller of the city of New York, one of the country's highest female officials—a potential future candidate for president of the United States or a Supreme Court appointment.

Is the Battered Woman Syndrome Defense Really a Political Defense?

Delia Alaniz paid a destitute young man $200 to kill her husband. But when she was caught and found guilty, Hispanic and feminist groups inundated the governor's office with telephone calls; they staged vigils and organized marches. They wanted her claim of having been abused to be enough to release her from prison.[45] The pressure on the governor increased when *60 Minutes* responded with a piece that neglected the perspective of the dead husband (or his family and friends) but was sympathetic only to *her* plight.[46] (Only at the end of "60 Minutes" did Harry Reasoner mention as an aside that *the woman had a lover at the time of her hiring the hit man*.)

Governor Gardner of Washington felt the pressure.[47] He freed Alaniz after a year and ten months. The young man she hired—

from a disadvantaged background—is still serving a thirty-year prison term.[48] (No one asks if he is also a victim of abuse, as was Alaniz. And if he was, could he also kill his abusive parents and then receive a governor's pardon?)

When Governor Gardner freed Delia Alaniz, he explained, "Violence against women and children is all too common in our society."[49] Now notice this: She kills him, and violence against women is the only problem. She exploits a disadvantaged youth, and violence against women is still the only issue. . . . When a woman kills a man, the only thing we know is that the woman is violent and the man is dead. **The message the Learned Helplessness Defense and the Battered Woman Syndrome sends to women is: A dead husband is better than a live witness. The best defense is a dead offense.**

Do feminists express the same concern when a wife has repeatedly abused her husband? Betty King of Florida had thrown acid on her husband, Eddie, slashed his face with a carpet knife, left him in a parking lot with a knife in his back, and shot him with a gun—all on separate occasions. Eddie King reported none of these incidents. The only two for which Betty was reported and arrested were those seen by witnesses in public (one of the stabbings took place in a bar).[50]

Finally, during a shouting match at a friend's house, Betty King once again reached into her purse to shoot Eddie. Fearing for his life, he pulled out a gun and shot her first. An investigation confirmed his life was, in fact, *imminently* threatened. Yet feminists and the media led an outcry of *opposition* to the verdict of self-defense for Eddie—an abused *husband*.

How the Learned Helplessness Defense
Perpetuates the Abuse of Women

The Learned Helplessness Defense wreaks the most havoc when it is applied to mothers. Studies find that mothers who murder bring up children who murder.[51] Mothers who kill are characterized by their "simmering resentment of others for the wrongs they have suffered, the belief they are the only ones who are so afflicted and that the world is conspiring against them."[52] Obviously the children pick up this attitude. Especially the girl children whose role models are their mothers. *Do we want these mothers, then, to bring up another generation of children?*

Ideological feminists also often see the world as a conspiracy. Even Gloria Steinem still speaks in terms of "us" versus "the enemy."[53] They see *others* as being responsible for the wrongs they have suffered. **These characteristics are almost identical to those found by Kirkpatrick and Humphrey[54] in their studies of women who murder. The Learned Helplessness Defense turns a dangerous personality problem into a legal defense.** It reinforces some women's beliefs that they can solve a problem by murdering the problem.

To free this woman to be a mother is to transfer the psychology of helplessness to the next generation of children. When mothers who kill are returned to their daughters, we are training daughters who will kill. Which is why fathers who are murderers are not set free to bring up their children. And it is why creating the new "any mother can kill and go free" legal defenses wreaks havoc on the children these mothers raise.

V. "THE DEPRESSED MOTHER" DEFENSE: BABY BLUES AND TERRIBLE TWOS

The Baby Blues

Remember Sheryl Lynn Massip, a mother in her mid-twenties who murdered her 6-month-old son by crushing its head under the wheel of the family car? Massip systematically covered up the murder until she was discovered. Then she testified that she suffered from postpartum depression—or "baby blues." Her sentence? Treatment.[55]

Do Dads Get the Baby Blues?

Mothers do, of course, get the baby blues. As do dads. A dad often feels like the mother has left him for "another lover." Husbands often say, "It's she and the baby cuddling on the couch and me looking on," or, "Now I know the meaning of 'two's company, three's a crowd,' " or, "My wife and I used to spend lots of time together but now we don't"; or, "We've barely made love for two years—since the baby was born." Were the husband to kill his baby, as Sheryl Lynn did, it is unlikely we would just treat him for baby blues or Save the Marriage Syndrome. Why does her version of baby blues allow her to receive *treatment* for child murder while he would receive *life in prison* for child murder with or without baby blues?

The Terrible Twos

Josephine Mesa beat her 2-year-old son to death with the wooden handle of a toilet plunger.[56] She then buried the battered baby in a trash bin. When scavengers found the baby outside her Oceanside, California, apartment, she denied she knew him. When the evidence became overwhelming, she confessed. The excuse? She was depressed. The child was going through the terrible twos. The punishment? Counseling, probation, and antidepressants. *She never spent a day behind bars.*[57] (Even her own probation officer had recommended at least thirty days in jail after Mesa had repeatedly been delinquent in showing up for appointments.)

Los Angeles Times

Woman Who Killed Child Remains Free

Judge Says He Hopes Treatment Will Improve Her Mental Health

By TOM GORMAN, *Times Staff Writer*

VI. THE "MOTHERS DON'T KILL" DEFENSE

ITEM. Illinois. Paula Sims reported that her first daughter, Loralei, was abducted by a masked gunman. In fact, she murdered Loralei. But she got away with it.[58] So when her next daughter, Heather Lee, disappointed her, she suffocated her, threw her in the trash barrel, and said another masked gunman had abducted her daughter. It wasn't until the second "masked man" abduction that a serious search was conducted. Only the serious search led to evidence.

Might Heather Lee be alive today if mothers did not have special immunity from serious investigation?

VII. THE "CHILDREN NEED THEIR MOTHER" DEFENSE

ITEM. Colorado. Lory Foster's husband had returned from Vietnam and was going through mood swings both from post-traumatic stress syndrome and from diabetes.[59] They had gotten into a fight and he had abused her. So she killed him. Yet, even the prosecutor did not ask for a jail term. Why not? So Lory could care for the children. . . .

Lory was given counseling and vocational training at state expense. In essence, then, the state paid for her to get the help she needed after she broke the law but didn't pay to give him the help he needed after he obeyed the law.

What's Really Going On Here?

Josephine Mesa, Paula Sims, and Lory Foster were all mothers who killed and who were freed. The most frequent justification for freeing mothers who kill children is that their children need them. But Josephine Mesa was freed even though she killed her only son. And when Paula Sims killed her first child, her freedom allowed her to kill her next child. Moreover, if mothers were freed because "children are the first priority," then fathers would be freed just as often. But they are not. Even when no mother is available. Is the Children Need Their Mother Defense a rationalization to free women, not a prioritization to love children?

Should a Man Be Allowed to Kill an Abusive Wife and Be Freed Because He's a Dad?

To my knowledge, no man has ever gone free after the premeditated murder of his wife because the "children need their father." Even if he had proof she intended to kill him. Remember Dan Broderick (above), who had plenty of evidence that his ex-wife, Elizabeth, intended to kill him but could do nothing legal to stop her (although he was one of San Diego's best attorneys)? Even after Elizabeth drove a pickup truck through the front of his house and endangered both his own life and his children's lives (Dan had sole custody of the children), Dan could not use a "Father Defense" to kill Elizabeth. Nor could he use self-defense. Why not? Because when courts consider the application of self-defense *for a man*, they require that he be responding to an *immediate* and *imminent* danger to his life with *no method* of escape,[60] and Dan couldn't prove his life was in *immediate* physical danger until he was dead.

Should Dan Broderick have been allowed to legally kill Elizabeth based on her threats to both his and the children's lives? No. The law can only encourage people like Dan to prosecute for breaking and entering, child endangerment, and attempted murder. Similarly, it must encourage a woman who is abused to report the abuse. Neither sex should be allowed to kill first and report later.

VIII. THE "BLAME-THE-FATHER, UNDERSTAND-THE-MOTHER" DEFENSE

ITEM. Ramiro Rodriguez was driving back from the supermarket. His daughter was sitting on his wife's lap.[61] As Ramiro made a left turn, a van crashed into the car and his daughter was killed. Ramiro was charged with homicide. The reason? His daughter was not placed in a safety seat.

Ramiro explained that his daughter was sick and wanted to be held so *his wife decided* to hold her. Yet only Ramiro was charged.

Although it was the *mother's* decision to hold Veronica (rather than put her in a safety seat), *only* the father was charged with homicide. The mother was charged with nothing. Ramiro was eventually acquitted after protests over the racism.[62] No one saw the sexism.

The larger picture? *Both* parents made a decision to have the mother do the holding and father do the driving. Either both should be charged with vehicular homicide—or neither. Ramiro and his wife shared parenting, but only Ramiro was accused of homicide. How can Ramiro be accused of homicide when Sheryl Lynn Massip deliberately crushed her baby's head with her car and is freed?

IX. THE "MY CHILD, MY RIGHT TO ABUSE IT" DEFENSE

ITEM. Kimberly Hardy used crack cocaine just *hours* before her son was born. When the son was born crack addicted, she was convicted (of delivering cocaine to her son through the umbilical cord). This decision was *reversed* by the Michigan Supreme Court.[63]

ITEM. A million crack-addicted children have been born since 1987, but only sixty of the mothers have faced criminal charges. One was convicted.[64]

ITEM. In the United States, 11 percent of all babies are born to drug-abusing mothers.[65] This happens predominantly in mother-only homes[66] (although only 21 percent of children live in mother-only homes[67]). ("Mother's Day," in drug dealer terminology, is the day mothers get welfare checks and line up at crack houses.[68])

When a mother aborts a fetus, it is debatable whether that fetus was a human life. But when a mother feeds crack to a fetus hours before it's born and it is born as a crack-addicted child, it is clearly an abused *child*. If the child dies immediately, it is manslaughter. Does the right to choose mean the right to abuse?

What is really going on here? Is the issue whether or not the fetus has legal rights? No. We already know the answer to that. For example, if a crack-addicted mother got into a car accident and she killed the fetus of another woman, the crack-addicted mother would be held legally responsible. **A woman does not have the right to abuse the fetus of another mother, she has the right to abuse just her own.** Which is why this defense is called the *My* Child, My Right to Abuse It Defense. What is really going on here is not fetal rights, not children's rights, but mothers' rights. In the case of the 3 percent of Washington, D.C., *infants* who *die* from cocaine addiction while *no* mothers go to prison, the right to choose means the right to kill—not a fetus but a child.

If we hold a drunk driver responsible for injury, why shouldn't we hold a crack-addicted mother responsible for injury? In reality, the drunk driver injures a human being only occasionally; the crack-addicted mother injures a human being almost 100 percent of the time. Should the mother who addicts her child to crack have any more rights than another child abuser or drug dealer? How can we give a normal drug dealer a life sentence but claim that a mother who deals drugs to her own child should not so much as stand trial? If we feel compassion for the circumstances that drove her to drugs, where is our compassion for the circumstances that drove the drug dealer to drugs, the child abuser to abuse, the murderer . . .

The mother who addicts her child to crack cocaine is not just a drug dealer and child abuser. In 1991 the first large wave of children prenatally exposed to crack entered the nation's schools. Some of these children are prone to mental retardation, mild speech impairment, and cerebral palsy. Others acquire language slowly, offer a jumble of markings as their names, do not understand numbers, or find it impossible just to line up quietly.[69] These children are driving the best teachers to quit, therefore these mothers are not just abusers of their own child, they are abusers of their community's children.

When the crack children are separated out into special classrooms, the yearly cost of educating them averages $15,000 per year, versus the normal $3,500 per year.[70] It is one of the reasons public schools cost so much more than private schools. In this respect, average taxpayers are paying to have their own children's education undermined; they are subsidizing their own children's abuse.

X. THE PLEA BARGAIN DEFENSE

Once a woman is seen as more innocent, her testimony is more valued, which leads to prosecutors offering the woman the plea bargain in crimes committed jointly by a woman and a man. And if a district attorney is up for reelection, the Chivalry Factor allows him to look like a hero when his office prosecutes a man, or a bully if he should put a woman behind bars. Moreover, he soon discovers it is easy to portray the man as the mastermind, whereas if he prosecutes the woman, her attorney can use the Svengali Defense. . . .

XI. THE SVENGALI DEFENSE

ITEM. A beautiful woman—dubbed "The Miss America Bandit—conducted an armed robbery of a bank. Federal sentencing guidelines called for a minimum of four and a half to five years in federal prison. The federal judge gave her two years because she told the judge she was in love with her hairdresser and he had wanted her to rob the bank. The judge concluded, "Men have always exercised malevolent influence over women, and women seem to be soft touches for it, particularly if sex is involved. . . . It seems to me the Svengali-Trilby relationship is the motivating force behind this lady*. . . the main thing is sex."[71]

Imagine a judge reducing a man's sentence because he was in love and "women have always exercised malevolent influence over men"? If justice is not the issue, what is? The "Miss America Bandit" was beautiful. And judges, like most men, instinctively protect beautiful women. If such an "angel" breaks the law, the judge must do a devil hunt. (And the devil, of course, is a male.) For exactly this reason, it was important that *The Burning Bed* be played by the woman considered the most beautiful at the time: Farrah Fawcett.

Which sex is best able to persuade a sexual partner to do something immoral? Let's look.

XII. THE CONTRACT KILLING DEFENSE . . . DEFEND SELF BY HIRING SOMEONE ELSE

Is Contract Killing the Female Method of Choice?

When I did the first review of my files in preparation for this section on contract killing, I was struck by some fascinating patterns. First, all of these women hired boys or men. Second, their targets were usually husbands, ex-husbands, or fathers—men they

---

* Svengali is a fictional character said to have hypnotic qualities of persuasion over the innocent Trilby. (Guess which is the woman!)

once loved. Third, the targeted man usually had an insurance policy significantly larger than the man's next few years' income.[72] Fourth, the women often were never serious suspects until some coincidence exposed their plot. Fifth, the woman usually chose one of three methods by which to kill: she (1) persuaded her boyfriend to do the killing (in reverse Svengali style); (2) hired some young boys from a disadvantaged background to do it for a small amount of money; or (3) hired a professional killer, thus usually using the money her husband had earned to kill her husband.

ITEM. Dixie Dyson tucked in her husband for his last night's sleep. She had arranged to have a lifelong friend and a boyfriend pretend to "break and enter," then "rape" her, kill her husband, then "escape." She would collect the insurance money.[73]

At the last moment, the lifelong friend backed out, but the boyfriend and Dixie managed to kill Dixie's husband after twenty-seven stabbings. They were caught. Dixie "cut a deal" to reduce her sentence by reporting the boyfriend and his friend. The friend *who backed out* got twenty-five years to life for *conspiracy.*[74]

ITEM. Deborah Ann Werner was due one third of her dad's estate. She asked her daughter *to find some boys* to murder him by plunging a knife through his neck.[75]

ITEM. Diana Bogdanoff arranged to be with her husband at a secluded portion of a nudist beach. Her husband didn't mind, but then again, Diana hadn't mentioned that she had hired two young men to kill him while she watched. After he was shot through the head, she reported the killers[76] but produced no motive for the murder—no money was stolen and she was not sexually molested.[77]

Diana did not become a suspect until an anonymous caller contacted a nationwide crime hotline. The caller coincidentally heard about the murder on the radio and remembered a friend describing just such a murder he had refused to do . . . on an isolated nude beach while a woman named Diana watched. Without this tip, Diana would never have become even a suspect.[78]

ITEM. Roberta Pearce, a teacher's aide, offered two of her 15-year-old students $50,000 each, sex, and a car if they would do just one thing—kill her husband.[79] Roberta would get the home she and her husband were fighting over and $200,000 in life insurance money.

ITEM. Mary Kay Cassidy and her teenage lover killed Mary Kay's husband.[80] Although the husband had told friends that he feared his wife might be trying to kill him, his wife never became more than a routine suspect. She and her teenage lover "mourned" the husband's death and continued to be lovers for months as they received sympathy from the townsfolk of Monongahela, Pennsylvania.

By coincidence, the husband's relatives were cleaning out the house and discovered a wiretap apparatus with a tape of a conversation between Mary Kay and her teenage lover as they plotted to kill her husband. The husband had apparently begun tapping his phone just hours before he was killed. He had never heard the tape himself. Only when confronted with the tape did Mary Kay confess.

ITEM. Pamela Smart, a New Hampshire schoolteacher, convinced her teenage boyfriend to kill her husband.[81] Pamela and her boyfriend tried to get a teenage girl involved in the murder. When the teenage girl gave the police a taped conversation of Pamela Smart planning the murder, Pamela allegedly hired a hit man to kill her.[82] Pamela never accused her husband of abusing her. Her motive? Her husband was an insurance salesman. Yet not one of 500 newspaper articles acknowledged the possible motive of insurance money.[83]

The reaction? She is supported by a worldwide fan club called Friends of Pamela Smart. When they held a vigil outside her prison, prison officials allowed her to address a crowd of over 400 via a telephone hook-up over stereo speakers.[84]

I know of no example of a fan club for a man killing a woman— especially a woman who had never abused him.

• • •

Perhaps the most appalling dimension of the nonprofessional contract killings is the use by many of these women of teenage boys to conduct the murder—usually boys from disadvantaged backgrounds. These women have committed both murder *and the psychological rape of a boy*. Any adult man hiring a 15-year-old girl to kill his wife would be on death row. Especially if he had had sex with the girl.

When professionals are hired to do contract killing, the ability to pay the money to hire a professional implies a middle-class background. **Women who hire professionals are often middle-class women who kill their husbands with money that their husbands earned.** Thus Constantina Branco took money out of her husband's bank account to hire a man to kill her husband.[85]

What does the poor woman have in common with the middle-class woman? Neither is likely to kill a man whose salary is currently protecting her unless his potential insurance money exceeds his next few years' salary.[86] In essence, these women do not kill their source of income, but they do kill to create income.

Contract killing offers potential for insight into the difference between the female and male style of murdering the people they had once loved. The man does the killing himself. The woman hires another man. Generally, when a man kills a woman, he does it in a fit of rage. He is "out of control." Contract killing is premeditated. When a man does premeditate a murder, he often kills his wife, his children, and *then himself*. The woman rarely kills herself.

Do men sometimes contract-kill women? Some men do hire contract killers to kill women, but something happens on the way to the killing. The hit man can't stomach killing a woman; he turns the man who hired him in to the police![87] (Even a hired killer has a protective instinct when it comes to killing a woman.) So it is not that men are completely exempt from using the contract-killing method, but that when they do, it almost invariably, shall we say, backfires.

IF THERE WERE MALE-ONLY DEFENSES, WHAT WOULD THEY BE?

There is no male-only defense for killing a woman. Nor should there be. But if there were, the male equivalent of the female PMS

Defense would be the Testosterone Defense; the equivalent of the Innocent Woman Defense would be the Rational Man Defense—the equally sexist assumption that a man would not commit a crime unless he had a rational reason to do it; there would be Father Defenses, Battered Man Syndromes, and special defenses tailored for the burdens of the male role . . . such as a Bodyguard Defense.

The Bodyguard Defense

Remember when Marlon Brando's son Christian was so furious that his half-sister Cheyenne had been "slapped around" by her boyfriend that he pulled a gun on him and then, in a struggle, shot him?[88] He said it was by mistake.

Should Brando have claimed the Bodyguard Defense? The rationale? If a woman can kill a man who abuses her and then go free, why can't another man also kill a man who is abusing a woman and also go free?

HOW INDIVIDUAL WOMEN ARE GIVEN MORE POWER TO KILL THAN THE ENTIRE U.S. GOVERNMENT

Taken together, the twelve female-only defenses allow almost any woman to take it upon herself to "exercise the death penalty." Ironically, we now consider it liberal to *favor* a *woman* exercising the death penalty and to *oppose* the *government* exercising the death penalty. The government is not allowed to kill someone first and declare him or her an abuser later—only a woman can do that to a man. But perhaps most amazing is that denial of due process is called "liberal" if a woman denies it to a man; "totalitarian" if anyone denies due process to a woman.

DO MEN KILL WOMEN MORE THAN WOMEN KILL MEN?: THE SIX BLINDERS

The Department of Justice tells us that men kill women *twice* as often as women kill men.[89] But let's look more closely. Certainly men *are* more likely to be serial killers of women. Almost always these killings follow a pattern and the man is found. Therefore the Justice Department statistics can reflect this reality. Other killings by men of women also provide easy evidence—the man spontaneously shoots his wife or woman friend and then takes a gun to his own head. The evidence is lying on the floor.

Six blinders, though, prevent us from seeing the female methods of killing. First, a woman is more likely to poison a man than shoot him, and poisoning is often recorded as a heart attack or accident. Thus Blanche Taylor Moore (the *Arsenic and Old Lace* case) murdered men for a quarter century before she was discovered. And Stella Nickell's Excedrin murders were blamed on vandals.

Contract killing is also less detectable because it is premeditated and often hired out to a professional. When it is discovered, the Department of Justice registers it as a "multiple offender killing"—*it never gets recorded as a woman killing a man.*[90] This creates a second blinder.

While men who murder women generally come from lower socioeconomic backgrounds, women who murder husbands or boyfriends are more likely to come from middle-class backgrounds. Thus the third blinder: the money factor. For example, Jean Harris (who killed the author of *The Scarsdale Diet*) was at one time a private school headmistress[91]; Elizabeth Broderick had gone from elementary schoolteacher to high society wife; Pamela Smart was a schoolteacher in New Hampshire.[92] The money allows the best lawyers, more acquittals, and therefore fewer female murderers to become Justice Department statistics.

Probably the most important blinders are the Chivalry Factor and the Innocent Woman factor, which prevent many women from becoming serious suspects to begin with. In addition, the Plea Bargain Defense sometimes leads to the dismissal of charges. When, for example, a woman hires a boy who is a minor or a man who is a boyfriend or professional.

When the Six Blinders—the poisoning disguise, contract killings disguised as accidents and registered as multiple-offender killings, the money factor, the Chivalry Factor, the Innocent Woman factor, and the Plea Bargain Defense—are combined, we can see how we have consciously and unconsciously kept ourselves blind to seeing women who murder men.

A distortion of statistics is created by the Six Blinders. But a distortion of perception is created by the media's tendency to make it international news when men murder women (the University of

Montreal murderer, the Hillside and Boston stranglers) and, unless the man is famous, to make it local news when a woman murders only a man.

In brief, it is impossible to know the degree to which the sexes kill each other. The only thing we know for certain is that both sexes kill men more than they kill women.

TOWARD A SOLUTION

No One Makes a Commitment to a Disadvantage

Laws that make one sex more powerful than the other boomerang against both sexes—no one makes a commitment to a disadvantage. And when one sex doesn't commit, both sexes lose love. We can see this happening in Australia, for example, where domestic violence is now defined to include a man raising his voice to his wife—"the domestic decibel rule." However, the opposite, a woman raising her voice to her husband, is considered an understandable defense to male dominance.[93] These double standards have made men in Australia very fearful of getting married. However, Australian feminists are pressing for legislation to make all laws that apply to marriage also apply to couples living together. Laws like these have the effect of separating the sexes.

How Can We Decrease Abuse and Murder in the Future?

If a woman murders her husband because she feels helpless, then perhaps the man also batters his wife because he too feels helpless. For *both* sexes, abuse derives not from power but powerlessness. Abuse is a temporary display of power that usually emerges from feelings of powerlessness and defeat.

The solution to abuse, then, does not come with creating artificial divisions between physical and emotional abuse. It comes with resocializing both sexes to listen in new ways—ways most of our parents never had the luxury to learn; it comes with resocializing both sexes to select partners who are secure enough to listen before they attack, and secure enough to leave if repeatedly attacked—either verbally or physically.

There are no guarantees of safety to one's life, but the solution has more to do with avoiding the dangerous parts of town than selecting the dangerous parts of town and shooting the people who make us fear for our life.

The solution comes with requiring communication in school, not excusing murder in marriage. It comes with becoming as sensitive to the 20:1 ratio at which schoolgirls hit schoolboys as we are to the 1:20 times in which schoolboys hit schoolgirls.[94] In brief, solutions to abuse start with counseling, not killing; with both sexes knowing how to protect themselves rather than permitting only one sex to use the government as a protector.

CHAPTER 13

The Politics of Sex

WHY SEXUAL HARASSMENT IS SUCH A BIG ISSUE FOR WOMEN

If a woman at work caressed a man on his rear, he'd thank her, not sue her. So how can a man understand why sexual harassment is such a big issue for women?

Men, imagine growing up always receiving compliments from women on your mechanical abilities (as many women receive from men on their bodies). But suddenly a social worker is responsible for evaluating you *as a dad*, and if she doesn't take you seriously, you risk losing your child. Imagine that as you're changing diapers, the social worker tells you how the traces of grease under your fingernails are a real turn-on. You observe that she's not focused on your parenting skills. Does it feel you're being told that "a man's place is under the car"? If the stakes were that your child might be taken from you if you are not taken seriously (just as a female junior executive might lose her job if she is not taken seriously), might you find yourself feeling ambivalent about what would, in another context, feel like a compliment?

Now suppose the social worker's compliments about mechanical abilities were directed at the *other* men, not you. Would you be relieved? On one level, yes. But if you found out she got these other men to give her free car repairs and afterward evaluated these men as the best *dads* (!), might you become hypersensitive to compliments given to *other* men about their mechanical abilities? Especially if only one dad could get the child (just as sometimes only one woman can get the promotion)?

It's hard for men to "get" this because most boys got their adolescent attention from performing and pursuing, and the workplace is just an *extension* of performing and pursuing. And in the workplace, performing and pursuing mean pay and promotions. But the adolescent girls who got the most attention got it from physical attractiveness. For an engineer, though, physical attractiveness is not supposed to lead to pay and promotions. So **the workplace feels more alien to many women—the workplace is not an easy extension of female adolescence.**

How can a man understand this on a *gut* level? Think of every woman as in a beauty contest every day of her life. (Whether attractive or unattractive, she is evaluated by parents, relatives, boys, and other women.) In my workshops—especially corporate workshops—I ask men to actually experience the "Female Beauty Contest of Everyday Life." As he's being evaluated for his body, I ask him to pretend the judges are mostly female executives who must decide whether to promote him to the executive level. The men chosen as finalists are feeling complimented but frustrated that maybe they're being appreciated for the wrong reasons. They experience the love/hate relationship that so many women feel toward their bodies. On the other hand, the men not chosen as finalists feel rejected. In different ways, each of the men feels like he is in a hostile work environment. I have seen some men walk away in tears. These men have "walked a mile in women's moccasins."

Why Do Some Women Get So Upset about Pinups at Work?

A pinup at work symbolizes to many women that the man cares more about a woman's body than about a woman's work. The woman who is serious about work feels she has to deal with a man who wants to combine the two—without regard for her desire. Combining the two doesn't seem any more appropriate to her than it would seem appropriate to a man to take a woman to her bedroom and see a bowl of hundred-dollar bills on her night table.

Many women respond to pinups of women by bringing in pinups of men: "This'll show 'em." But it has the opposite effect. It signals to men that the woman is so interested in men's bodies and sex that she can't stop thinking of it while she's working. Which is fine with him.

How can a woman get a man to understand how she might feel about pinups? I ask women to bring in pictures of men who are "success objects"—especially men who become successful in their field at a young age. If she's into computers, she might frame a picture of Steven Jobs; or a picture of the owner of the company she works for; or of her manager's boss; if she's in college, of Bon Jovi or Axl Rose . . . Or just frame a list of "*Forbes'* Wealthiest One Hundred." Why? This helps men feel the inadequacy many women feel looking at a pinup. Both types of pinups make our colleagues feel inadequate—like a second choice. This feeling of rejection in the very area for which one is usually the most valued contributes to a hostile environment.

WHY SEXUAL HARASSMENT LEGISLATION FEELS UNFAIR TO MEN

ITEM. 1991. The University of Toronto finds a chemical engineering professor guilty of sexual harassment for "prolonged" staring at a female student at the university swimming pool.[1] He was guilty of creating a hostile environment for her.

ITEM. 1991–92. Graffiti in a high school men's room which the school neglected to remove resulted in the school being accused of sexual harassment and paying $15,000 for "mental anguish" to the girl mentioned in the graffiti.[2]

ITEM. 1992. Six-year-old Cheltzie claimed the boys on her bus used nasty language and teased her. So her mom filed a sexual harassment lawsuit on Cheltzie's behalf. The school superintendent responded, "In the future, we're going to have to consider language 'sexual harassment' rather than a cause for discipline."[3]

In the 1960s, the term "sexual harassment" was unheard of. As women who were divorced in the '60s and '70s began to receive income from the workplace, they began to demand the protection from the workplace that they once had in the homeplace. Almost overnight, workplace rules changed.

Previously, few men even thought of using a lawsuit to protect themselves from an offensive joke. A Polish man who heard a Polish joke was expected to laugh, not sue. But men did have ways of defending themselves. If a colleague was offensive, they avoided him. If he couldn't be trusted, they gave him a bad reputation. If a boss was authoritarian or overloaded them with work, some became passive-aggressive—saying "yes, sir" and doing half the job; others worked overtime; others took the boss aside and talked with him; others complained in a written evaluation. And if nothing worked, they applied for a transfer or got another job.

Men never thought of suing the mouth that fed them. Why not? The mouth that fed them also fed their families. The fights that men fought almost all helped them better feed their families—either via higher salaries and workers' compensation when they were alive or via insurance or widows' benefits when they were dead. In essence, he fought for what protected his family more than for what protected him.

In the early 1970s, we began to hear of sexual harassment, but it most often meant a woman being told that if she didn't have sex with the boss, she'd lose her job. Most everyone agreed that was harassment. Harassment soon came to include a boss promising a quicker-than-earned promotion in exchange for sex. Almost all men were *opposed to* this because it was mostly men who lost the work favor and whose sexual favors were worth nothing. But because most men felt it was in the *company's* interest to *fire* a boss who exploited the company for personal pleasure, they didn't feel the necessity for government interference.

While men went about their business, so to speak, the federal government expanded the legal definition of sexual harassment to anything *a woman defined* as a "hostile work environment."[4] Men were oblivious until the Clarence Thomas hearings pulled their heads out of the sand: they saw that the definition of harassment had expanded to include *discussing* pornography, telling a dirty joke, calling an employee "honey," or taking a longer look at a shorter skirt.

Does the federal government actually make a dirty joke potentially illegal? Yes.[5] And a look? Yes. And calling an employee "honey"? Yes. *All* these things are illegal *if* a *woman* decides she doesn't like it, and if a man committed the "offense."

Aren't these guidelines gender neutral? Sometimes, yes; often, no. For example, the sexual harassment guidelines mandate employers to consider it their "affirmative duty" to *"eliminate"* behavior that *women* consider "hostile" or "intimidating"—behavior such as "unwanted sexual advances"[6] or dirty jokes. The Department of Labor's guidelines are explained in a publication entitled "A Working *Woman*'s Guide to Her Job Rights" (emphasis added) not "A Worker's Guide to Job Rights."[7] Practically speaking, any man who sued a woman for discussing pornography or for asking him out (à la Hill–Thomas) would be laughed out of the company before the ink on the lawsuit dried.

Who defines "hostile environment"? The woman. *Not even the man's intent makes a legal difference.* In all other criminal behavior, intent makes all the difference. Even in homicide. **Sexual harassment legislation in its present form makes all men unequal to all women.** It is in blatant violation of the Fourteenth Amendment's guarantee of equal protection *without* regard of sex. Thus the political will to protect only women prevails over the constitutional mandate to protect both sexes equally.

Suppose it is her word against his? When the guidelines of the Equal Employment Opportunity Commission (EEOC) were first formed, a "bare assertion" of sexual harassment—a woman's word against a man's—could not lead to conviction without factual support. Ironically, when Clarence Thomas was chairman of that commission, he was responsible for *reversing* that decision—**now, if it's her word against his, a "bare assertion" of sexual harassment can stand without factual support!**[8] Clarence Thomas now knows why it is important for lawmakers to have to live by the laws they create.

But it's worse than that: a woman doesn't even have to tell the man that he's bothering her. She can now complain *to a girlfriend at work.* The EEOC's decision number 84-1 allows complaining to a girlfriend at work to be "sufficient to support a finding of harassment."[9] That used to be called gossip. Now it's called evidence.

All this led to the filing of 50,000 sexual harassment lawsuits between 1980 and 1990 alone,[10] scaring about three quarters of America's major companies into developing programs designed to fulfill the EEOC guidelines. **In one decade, women had gotten more protection against offensive jokes in the workplace than men had gotten in centuries against being killed in the work-**

place. As women entered the workplace and government became a substitute husband, many men felt it was becoming more profitable to be a victim than an entrepreneur; that this was creating a shift in the nation's work ethic: from a nation of entrepreneurs to a nation of victims.

"Your Lips Tell Me 'No, No,' but There's 'Yes, Yes' in Your Eyes": The Politics of Indirect Initiatives

Believe it or not, this is still not the core of what bothers most men. What is? First, men still see women playing *their* old sexual games. And second, men do not see sexual harassment legislation requiring women to take responsibility for their games. For example, the magazine read by the largest number of single working women—*Cosmopolitan*—instructs women on how to take indirect initiatives *at work* to which men *unconsciously* respond.[11] What if the wrong man responds? Other articles tell her how to file a sexual harassment lawsuit should these indirect initiatives elicit direct initiatives from the wrong man![12]

Here are a few indirect initiatives *Cosmopolitan* tells women to take *in the workplace*:[13]

- "As you pass his desk, drop a pile of papers or a purse, then stoop down to gather them up. He'll help. Lean close to him, put your hand on his shoulder to steady your balance. . . ."
- "If you have good legs, wear a very tight, short skirt and very high heels. Bend over with your back to a man (to pick something up or look in a file drawer, etc.). . . ."
- "Brush up against somebody in the elevator. . . ."
- "Say something slightly inappropriate during a business lunch or dinner, such as, 'You look great in blue.' This should be done while you are talking about something else—for example, 'I was working on the Apex campaign, and did you know you look great in blue?' "

The power of the woman's indirect initiative is that it puts neither her ego nor her career on the line. For example, *Cosmopolitan* advises "*immediately* after you meet him—within seconds—touch him in some way, even if it's just to pick off imaginary lint."[14]

Now, if he responds by asking her out but later calls off the relationship, *he's* subject to a harassment suit. (He "initiated.") Once in court, few men would feel comfortable telling a judge, "Your Honor, I asked her out because of the way she picked imaginary lint off my jacket."

What happens if he misses the lint hint? *Cosmopolitan* advises: "Look down at his crotch . . . with a playful look or smile."[15] And if he misses the crotch cue? She can "wear gorgeous red underwear, and show it 'accidentally'—your blouse is open a bit, so a man gets a peek of red lace bra. . . . You cross your legs and your skirt rides up. . . ."

It doesn't stop with *Cosmopolitan*. As women's workforce participation increased, Harlequin Romances discovered a formula that appealed to the working woman. It involves a successful man pursuing a working woman, the working woman resisting, *the man overcoming her resistance*, and her being "swept away." It was the age-old formula—he: pursue, persist; she: attract, resist. But now it was also the definition of sexual harassment.

Were women buying this formula less? Hardly. *The average woman who reads romance novels now reads twenty books per month*, about twice as many as in 1983.[16] And the Harlequin Romance working-woman formula transformed Harlequin from a company on the verge of bankruptcy in the early 1970s to a company that now accounts for 80 percent of the romance market.[17] And the romance market itself has soared—now accounting for 46 percent of all United States mass market paperback sales.[18]

Being "swept away" is her fantasy, not his. He is as much victim as perpetrator. A feeling reinforced when he sees a woman reading books called *Love at Work: Using Your Job to Find a Mate*,[19] with the author's list of the top ten high-powered professions among men and, under each profession, the ten best jobs a woman can get to "target your man."[20]

What's the Big Deal with a Miniskirt?

Many women ask, "What's the big deal with a miniskirt, perfume, and a little flirting in the workplace?" It would not be a big deal for most men if no one were making a big deal of the man's response.

It is a big deal, though, for the woman—if her goal is to be treated seriously at work. Here's why. Her *in*direct initiatives signal to the man her tendency to avoid direct responsibility. *In*direct initiatives signal to him that he is dealing with a woman who is traditional. And traditionally, **indirect initiatives were designed to lead to marriage and the end of her involvement in the workplace. So the miniskirt, perfume, and flirting unconsciously tell the man that this woman wants an end to her involvement in the workplace**—or, at least, an end to her involvement by obligation. If you were a boss who had to choose between promoting someone who had the option to work versus someone with the obligation to work (e.g., to support a spouse and three children), whom would you take more seriously?

None of this female behavior is any more inherently wrong than the male form of direct initiative taking. In almost all cultures throughout human history, women's *in*direct initiatives were their way of signaling their desire for men to take *direct* initiatives. A flirtation was an invitation. In some cultures, lipstick was a woman's way of signaling her willingness to perform fellatio. In the South Sea islands, a fresh flower in a woman's hair signaled availability. The purpose of the flower, lipstick, or the miniskirt is to put the signal out strongly enough to stimulate *every* man's interest. It is only when she has every man's interest that she has real choice—the choice of the "best" men.

What has been the historical importance of her barriers—her "no, noes"? It was her way of selecting a man who could handle life's rejections and survive, who cared enough for her to take risks, and who would assume total responsibility should anything go awry. In a sense, **sexual harassment lawsuits are just the latest version of the female selection process**—allowing her to select for men who care enough for her to put their career at risk; who have enough finesse to initiate without becoming a jerk and enough guts to initiate despite a potential lawsuit. During this process, she gets a sense of his trustworthiness, his commitment, his ability to overcome barriers, the way he handles rejection. It allows her to select for men who will perform, who will assume total responsibility. The more things change . . .

In the past, though, the process of his overcoming her barriers was called "courtship." Now it is called *either* "courtship" *or* "sexual harassment." Here's how gray the boundary is. . . .

When It Works, It's Called Courtship; When It Doesn't, It's Called Harassment

When I ask women in my audiences who had entered the workplace when single and later gotten married to "raise your hand if you married a man you met at work (or through a workplace contact—a client, or someone to whom you were a client)," almost two thirds raised their hands.[21] Another 15 percent of these women lived with or had a long relationship with a man they met while on the job, but never married him. Now here's the dilemma.

The majority of the men these working women married were above them at work; additionally, almost all of these men took the

"Ms. Chase: Being of good intentions and protected by counsel, I hereby respectfully invite you to dinner this evening, an overture you may freely decline if it in any way suggests sexual harassment to you."

first initiative. **Sexual initiatives by men toward women below them at work is the most frequent definition of sexual harassment. When it works, it's called courtship. When it doesn't work, it's called harassment.**

Isn't it harassment only when he persists? Not legally. For some women, any initiative—even one—could make her feel uncomfortable and therefore create a hostile environment. And that is all she needs to have her lawsuit upheld.

Many women acknowledge being married to men to whom they had at first said "no." By today's standards, they are married to sexual harassers; but some of these women are glad these men pursued.

SHOULD COWORKERS BE LOVERS?

Women especially say it is important to get to know someone before having sex with them. The workplace gives a woman the opportunity to observe a man—how he handles people above him and below him, his competence, his temper, his ethics, values, habits. For most women, it works a lot better than bars. Overall, 35 million Americans report some kind of "social-sexual" experience on their jobs *each week*.[22] More than 80 percent of all workers say they've had such an experience on their job.[23] When it works, we call it a wedding and the woman's picture is in the paper; when it doesn't, we call it a lawsuit and the man's picture is in the paper.

WHY DO MEN TELL DIRTY JOKES?

First, both sexes tell dirty jokes. Even as the mostly male Congress had passed legislation to allow dirty jokes to constitute a "hostile environment," female members of Congress were circulating male-bashing humor.[24] Example? "What's the difference between government bonds and men?" "Bonds mature." This was permitted. But had the men asked, "What's the difference between government bonds and women?" and answered, "Bonds are worth more when they mature," they could be sued. Similarly, the women were joking, "Why is it a good thing there are female astronauts?" and answering, "So someone will ask directions if the crew gets lost in space." Apparently the male congressmen were afraid to ask, "Who answered when the female astronaut asked for directions?"

Although both sexes have their own styles of humor, we often heard during the Thomas–Hill confrontation that dirty jokes were the way male bosses exert their power over women. Hardly. Men share dirty jokes with peers, buddies, and *with anyone with whom they feel comfortable*. A dirty joke is often a male boss's unconscious way of getting his staff to not take him so seriously and therefore *not* be intimidated; his way of creating an atmosphere of *easier* feedback, of getting his staff to bond. Men get confused when women say they feel left out when they're not included, then sue when they are included!

Ironically, at the same time millions of dollars are being spent learning about the health benefits of humor, we are spending millions of dollars to censor a form of humor.[25] Like "clean" jokes, dirty jokes that produce laughter stimulate our system with oxygen. "Dirty" jokes are really no dirtier than clean jokes—they just play to our hypocrisy: the hypocrisy that makes us call sex "dirty" and then go out and have sex with someone we love.

When a man is attracted to a woman, being expected to take the sexual initiative does not increase his power, it increases his paralysis. The possibility of a lawsuit just intensifies the paralysis. Ironically, the more dangerous the waters, the more joking serves as a way of testing the waters: if she laughs, maybe she's interested; if she looks disgusted, maybe she's not. He would feel much more powerful if *she* took responsibility for testing the waters.

Sexual-harassment consultants are now encouraging women to keep private journal notes about hostile-environment behavior such as dirty jokes. Most bosses don't think their employees are intimidated by dirty jokes, but if they are, would like to be told privately rather than discover a woman has kept journal notes and complained to girlfriends on office time, and is now suing them. If a woman is offended, he would like her to tell him, not sue him.

WHAT WOMEN SEE AS HARASSMENT, MEN SEE AS HAZING

A female navy psychologist tells her female plebes that the question "Why did you come to the U.S. Naval Academy?" is a classic example of sexual harassment *when a man asks it.*[26] *Psychology Today* applauded this approach.[27] Yet one has to ask whether this level of sensitivity contributes to the 50 percent higher attrition rate among women in the services.[28] Why? It didn't help the new women plebes understand that *every* male and female plebe would be hazed for some reason—the form of woman's hazing took might be called "sexism," but a short man would be subject to "shortism" ("Which is higher, your IQ or your size?"); a stutterer, to guys imitating his stutter; a man from the rural South to "ruralism" (guys imitating his accent); a Jewish plebe might be called "Captain Hooknose"; a plebe who got the praise of superiors, "ass kisser." . . .

The underlying assumption behind hazing is that everyone has an area of vulnerability. The function of hazing is to train the novice (or the plebe) to survive attacks to vulnerable areas, to subordinate self to the team. The plebe learns to laugh and toss off criticism, to use criticism as grist for improvement, not to cave in. **If a woman isn't being hazed, she's not being tested; therefore, she is not being trusted.**

Equality includes equal hazing—or equal training in survival skills. Which is why hazing is most severe in professions in which survival is most at stake: firefighting, crime fighting, the military, logging. Ironically, the Naval Academy's course that failed to connect harassment and hazing with survival was called "Survival Skills."[29] Yet, if a job is survival based, someone who is not hazed is not trusted.

Does the navy plebe or corporate rookie learn to "not take the attack personally"? No. The attack often *is* personal. The rookie learns to take it *despite the fact that the criticism might indeed be a personal attack*. The purpose of the personal attack is to *either* make us a stronger link in the chain *or* to get *rid* of us should we choose to remain a weak link. It *is* personal because only a personal attack can answer the key question: "Are you willing to make your personhood subservient to the machine?" Or, "Do you understand that you are a replaceable part?" **Women protest criticism and hazing more because fewer women have been trained to think of themselves as such replaceable parts.**

Is this system of institutionalized harassment, though, a system we want to continue? It has trade-offs. One contribution women will make will be to curb its excesses. Sensitive artists don't kill dragons. But **men's defenses are the armor that allows others not to have to wear armor.** Without men's armor, the United

States would have been helping Hitler stuff Jews into gas chambers. Harassment is not a system that creates male power—it is a system that deflates male power. And then promotes him to the degree he understands the larger picture—that he is irrelevant.

The female navy psychologist, while not understanding how hazing helped develop the characteristics needed to make sacrifices, expected only men to make all these sacrifices. Perhaps the saddest commentary is that *Psychology Today* applauded her view of hazing as sexism as if hazing were a plot against women[30] rather than understanding that **hazing was actually a plot against men that was finally being protested because it was hurting women.**

CAN SEXUAL HARASSMENT LEGISLATION HURT WOMEN WHO WANT REAL EQUALITY?

Sexual harassment legislation increases the price of hiring women and therefore gives employers a legitimate reason to discriminate against women. A friend of mine who ran one of the largest research firms in California let go a woman who was unable to get along with most of the employees. A few weeks later, she sued him for sexual harassment. He had no interest in her, had never had a complaint against him for such behavior, nor had anyone in his company ever had a complaint against him for sexual harassment. Well, there was one exception: The woman who filed the complaint had herself been the subject of complaints that *she* had sexually harassed two different men and discriminated against them when they were unresponsive. Nevertheless, the legal hassle that resulted diverted the firm from its function and catalyzed a decline that eventually led (in conjunction with the recession) to the company's extinction.

My friend felt as though he had been raped. At first he tried talking about it with friends, but he could see them looking at him suspiciously. So now he keeps quiet. But at a price. The same price women paid when they felt they had been raped but got only looks of suspicion from friends, family, and police.

The more men a company employs, the more each woman hired forces the company to protect itself from potential lawsuits against these men. It leaves almost every male executive vulnerable to having his career ruined and almost every company with male executives vulnerable to having a finely honed management team broken up, its morale destroyed, and the remaining executives walking on eggshells. All this is an invitation to executive hypocrisy—in which all the rules of affirmative action are followed but everyone shuts his mouth when a woman comes into the room, thus creating genuine discrimination and a thick-glassed ceiling.

The woman who wants real equality pays a big price. **Sexual harassment legislation often creates a hostile environment: an environment of female-as-child**, one that makes even female employers more desirous of hiring men. As the men walk on eggshells, a formerly fluid work environment becomes a paralyzed environment.

In a global sense, if the government forces companies to protect women more and promote women equally regardless of whether they perform equally, it damages the ability of the nation's industries to compete globally, thus reducing both the jobs and promotions available to American women.

Some companies found it ironic that just as the Soviet Union was disowning Big Brother, the United States was adopting Big Brother. (And, even more ironically, it was feminists demanding Big Brother!)

The solution? Find out how to protect people without paralyzing the workplace—find out who is really being hurt. This becomes clearer when we see that there are really *seven* different sexual interactions occurring in the workplace.

THE SEVEN HIDDEN LEVELS OF ON-THE-JOB SEX

· **Sexual blackmail.** A boss threatens to *fire* an employee unless she or he is sexual.

If, for example, a male vice-president threatens to fire a female secretary unless she has sex with him, it is in the *company's* best interest to get rid of him. Why? If a vice-president is willing to get rid of someone who is helping the company make a profit, he's betraying the company for sex. Almost every vice-president knows she or he would be fired if even the slightest evidence of sexual blackmail were proven. Which is why sexual blackmail so rarely happens in major companies.

· **Sexual bribery.** An executive promises a *promotion* in exchange for sex. This can be explicit or implicit.

The company stands to lose a fortune if less competent employees are promoted by an executive in exchange for sex. It is, therefore, in the company's self-interest to fire that executive. The employee who accepts sex in exchange for a promotion, though, should not be allowed to sue if things don't turn out well later. Rather, she or he might be sued by the person losing the promotion.

· **Workplace prostitution.** An employee is sexual in exchange for a promotion; a salesperson is sexual to win a sale. The sex can be given or just promised.

For example, if a female employee promises sex to get a promotion and a man accepts, *both* might legitimately be subject to class-action suits from all employees—male and female—for discrimination against *them*: they lost equal opportunity to get the promotion through legitimate means.

Similarly, if a woman promises sex to win a sale from a potential customer and succeeds, then, first, the *customer's* employer should *fire* him—especially if, just to enhance his sex life, he bought a product he would not otherwise have bought. Second, the woman should be sued. By whom? By the companies competing against her. They were competing against the illegal sale of a female body—not exactly fair competition.

· **Workplace incest.** Consensual sex among employees. The workplace, like the family, has lines of authority which sexual bonding tends to blur. Workplace incest occurs in two basic forms:

· *Employer-employee sex.* When it is consensual, **employer-employee sex has one of the same problems of parent-child incest: it undermines the ability of the employer to establish boundaries because the employer often feels needy of the employee.** It is this same problem that is at the core of parent-child incest: parental authority becomes undermined because the child senses it has leverage over the parent. When only one employee has this leverage, it is also a setup for workplace jealousy and resentment.

· *Peer sex.* Peer sex is to the workplace family what sibling incest is to the homeplace family.

The sexual bond often leaves other employees feeling excluded. If the sexual relationship is kept secret, it can be crazy making. It is best revealed, with the feelings it creates discussed openly.

Workplace incest makes the company and other employees vulnerable.

• **Sexual harassment.** Repeated sexual advances at work after an employee has said "no."

For legal action to be successful, the "no" would probably need to be in writing, otherwise it cannot be distinguished from the courtship-in-the-workplace process participated in by almost all single male and female employees (and many who are less than single!). Why this distinction between a verbal "no" and a written "no"? This is explained below.*

• **Workplace flirtation.** Suggestive dress, flirtatious eye contact, a combination of touching and eye signals . . . the types of indirect initiatives *Cosmopolitan* encourages working women to take at work. A workplace flirtation is a workplace invitation to think of or do something other than work.

Flirtation can be to the workplace what a virus is to a computer: both screw up the intended program. It leads to less than honest feedback for fear of undermining a potential romance. It leads many male executives to hire for reasons that undermine the company's goals.

• **Workplace porn.** Pinups, lewd jokes, and sexual innuendos made in groups (without flirtatious eye contact directed at a particular person).

Workplace porn—such as lewd, sexist jokes and pinups—is largely a male style of testing the waters, and also part of what the EEOC has defined as sexual harassment. It can cost a man career advancement. Workplace flirtation—more a female style of indirect initiative-taking (see *Cosmopolitan* examples)—has been to-

---

* See chapter 14, "The Politics of Rape."

tally ignored by the EEOC and, therefore, can be done by women, free of risk. Here's the twisted result. . . .

Guy wrote to me that he had taken a picture of a woman at work who was sitting seductively in a miniskirt with her blouse unbuttoned enough to expose her bra (and some breast). He pinned the picture up on a file cabinet. The woman's face was turned away so she wasn't immediately recognizable.

Guy's boss immediately called him in to his office and ordered him to "remove the pornography from the file cabinet." When Guy explained, tongue-in-cheek, that it was "just a real-life picture of our work environment," the boss caught the joke and laughed, but still ordered him to remove the picture. **The woman, however, whose picture was the "pornography," was not asked to dress in a less pornographic manner.** The workplace reality created by some females is, when photographed, the workplace pornography protested by other females.

Months later, Guy was called in to the office again. His boss told him he was being fired from work because of complaints that he was "too interested in men's issues." None of these complaints documented any interference with his otherwise exemplary work history. And Guy worked in a "male-dominated" profession under a male boss.

Guy's workplace porn was not expected to get the woman sexually turned on, yet Guy was fired despite the fact that a purpose of female flirtatious dress is to sexually activate men like Guy. Workplace porn (the male style that bothers only some females) is condemned while flirtatious dress (the female style that actively disturbs the great majority of the males) is protected.

EDUCATOR SEX: THE "OPPRESSOR PROFESSOR" VERSUS THE "PRUDENT STUDENT"

ITEM. While I was working on *Why Men Are the Way They Are* at a University of California library in San Diego, I heard some panting from a nearby office. Of course, I refrained from looking (!), but it "just so happened" that the curtain was left slightly open (ah, for the slippage of spontaneity), exposing a professor and a student who were . . . well . . .

Had I reported them, who should have been punished? (You can check more than one.)

_____ 1. No one—they were two consenting adults.

_____ 2. If she was 17, the professor—for statutory rape.

_____ 3. If she was 18, the professor—for sexual harassment.

_____ 4. Because of their roles, both—for a type of incest ("educator incest," which gives her potential academic advantage over other students).

_____ 5. The female student should at least be tried for the possibilities of sexual bribery, student prostitution, and educator incest.

All these are possible approaches to educator sex. But as of now, whether she or I report the incident, she is helped and he is ruined.

Educator sex does create some of the same problems as workplace sex. But lawsuits are not the solution. The legal system is adversarial; sex between men and women can be consensual. The law sees mostly black and white; males and females see nuance—and they don't just see: they smell, hear, feel, and change their mind.

Now here's the deeper dilemma. A professor told me of a female student who was failing and came to him near semester's end, all upset and down on herself. They went to the campus pub to talk. Crying, she confessed to feeling stupid. He took her hand for a minute as he tried to reassure her she was bright and could "make it."

At semester's end, though, she didn't make it. Shortly after, she sued him for harassment with the testimony of a student who had seen them in the pub when the professor was "holding her hand and she didn't appear too happy about it"! First thing next semester, he was tried and convicted in the campus headlines.

Three quarters of Harvard women prefer faculty who "get to know me personally."[31] Which inevitably leads to a breakdown in objectivity. Are the women asking professors to give them academic favors while the university protects them from "sexual favors"?

Part of the contribution of a university is the training to understand problems beyond the "good guy"/"bad guy" level or, in the case of "Educator Sex," beyond the false dichotomy of "oppressor professor"/"prudent student."

WHAT WOMEN SEE AS "BLAMING THE VICTIM," MEN SEE AS "TAKING RESPONSIBILITY"

If a man touches a cocktail waitress on the rear, he can expect a lawsuit—even though she's making tips from getting him drunk. But had fans touched Elvis Presley on the rear while he was walking down the street at night in his stage outfit and Elvis had sued the fans, he would have been told to take responsibility for provoking it (because of what he was wearing). Some might even have accused him of "using" his position to "lure" young girls. When a female genetic celebrity uses her position, we protect her; when a male celebrity uses his, we protect her. The sex that is responsible is reversed, but the sex we blame is the same.

We apply a similar double standard to educator sex. When a police officer stops a driver, the driver feels vulnerable. When a professor tests a student, the student feels vulnerable. But if the driver flashes a hundred-dollar bill, she or he can get charged with bribery. When a female student flashes a "come hither" look to a professor, is that sexual bribery? If she then turns around and sues the professor for responding to her "come hither" look, is that sexual entrapment?

Sexual flirtation and come hither looks are the equivalent of flashing hundred-dollar bills to a police officer. Perhaps even a woman "charming her way" into permission to turn in an exam late (the "charm" being a hint of sex) is as much a form of sexual bribery as is a "prolonged" look from the professor a form of sexual harassment. If *both* the police officer and the driver are held responsible for a monetary exchange, shouldn't both the professor and student be held responsible for a mutual sexual exchange? Otherwise sexual harassment legislation is a male-only chastity belt. With women holding the key.

SEXUAL HARASSMENT'S POTENTIAL FOR ABUSE

One woman's accusation of sexual harassment can stop the government in its tracks (à la Anita Hill), can ruin a corporation (my friend's research firm), or ruin a man's career (Senator Brock Adams). Women can use sexual harassment against the government, corporations, or men. But the government and corporations can also use it against men. A government that can label sexual language it considers incorrect as sexual harassment has more potential for abuse than a government that can label political language it considers incorrect as a threat to national security. And a corporation that can do the same has the potential to turn every American male employee into "the new 'yes-man.' "

ITEM. Gordon Hamel was a respected employee with a virtually impeccable record. When he saw his company doing something dishonest, he became a whistle-blower. The company felt powerless to retaliate until it remembered it could charge him with sexual harassment. Since sexual harassment could be defined as something as minimal as a leer or a dirty joke—anything that created a "hostile atmosphere" for a woman—the company could virtually ruin him. Gordon Hamel lost his home defending himself and acknowledges that if he had known what would happen, he would never have been honest.[32]

Two of the most famous cases of sexual harassment in the early 1990s were those made by Dr. Frances Conley against Stanford University and by Anita Hill against Clarence Thomas. No one knows where the truth starts and ends. But we do know the American people were left with an image of an all-male Senate committee judging a woman and an all-male medical community harassing a doctor. We were left with images of Dianas versus Goliaths.

When Frances Conley announced her resignation from the medical school, she said she did so because she was tired of enduring twenty-five years of "gender insensitivity." She immediately made the prime-time news and the front covers of *People*, *The New York Times*, *Time*, *Newsweek*, and *Glamour*. For months, not a single article offered the position of her accused male colleagues. The media made almost no effort to interview them. And the men, fearful of a shouting match, volunteered little.

By the time a single major news account of Fran Conley's resignation included the following information, impressions had been made, bronzed, and framed. Here are the perspectives we didn't hear.

Frances Conley's colleagues report that it was "standard Fran" for her to joke about the evils of male testosterone and to threaten to castrate the men—to "cut off" their "left one."[33] That she would refer to her male patients as "Mr. This" and "Mr. That." When she instructed a male resident to start surgery on a man, she'd yell, "Roto-Rooter—your standard plumbing job." She would tell male residents she was supervising they had gained weight; if they dared protest, she'd respond, "Well, maybe your fat was redistributed between your ears."[34]

Frances said the men were constantly propositioning her. She later admitted the last proposition was ten years ago. A neurosurgery nurse who worked directly with Fran in the O.R. for fourteen years and reviewed Fran's complaints, commented, "None of this happened. None of it. And I like Fran. She's been a friend, believe me. But I think she's gone off the deep end."[35]

What appeared to be Fran's motivation? Fran's colleagues, mother, and sister all reported that Fran had wanted to be chair of the neurosurgery department and was furious when two outside consultants found Gerald Silverberg to be the strongest candidate.[36] From that point on, she had been threatening to quit.

The day before Fran's resignation became effective—after all the publicity about her being terrorized—Fran called the dean of the medical school. She had changed her mind. She'd stay.[37] What could be more amazing? The department that had been nationally humiliated invited her back.

The broader problem? When an army of reporters and feminists listens only to female perspectives while the frozen tongues of the silent sex sit in deep freeze, the anger toward men hardens. This anger sets the stage for Anita Hill. . . .

The Other Side of Anita Hill

Anita Hill was presented as a politically conservative female testifying against a politically conservative Clarence Thomas to an all-male committee that just didn't "get it." There seemed to be little motivation other than courage. This picture was not balanced by the fact that Anita Hill had been rejected for the position of chief attorney-adviser at the EEOC.[38] Or that many of her colleagues at EEOC considered her the least capable of the many advisers on Clarence Thomas's staff.[39] Phyllis Berry, a colleague of

Anita Hill's, wrote, "I found her to be untrustworthy, selfish, and extremely bitter following a colleague's appointment to head the Office of Legal Counsel at EEOC."[40] From the EEOC, Anita Hill went to teaching at Oral Roberts University and the University of Oklahoma, generally considered a fourth-rate law school.

At Oral Roberts University, students reported some bizarre experiences with Anita Hill. Lawrence Shiles, now a lawyer, filed a sworn affidavit with the Senate Judiciary Committee explaining that when he was a student of Anita Hill's, "I found ten to twelve short, black pubic hairs in the pages of my returned assignment. I glanced over at Jeff Londoff's assignment and saw similar pubic hairs in his work."[41] Mark Stewart, another student, also said he had pubic hairs in his assignment. Rather than file a sexual harassment suit, the guys did what guys do—they turned it into a standing joke, one which many students have confirmed.

At the University of Oklahoma, Anita was known for saying that nothing was lower in evolution than a white male and that "women are always taken advantage of."[42] Male students tried to write in flowery cursive to fool her into thinking the paper was from a woman. One colleague explained, "Her flirtatiousness, her provocative manner of dress, was not sweet or sexy, it's sort of angry, almost a weapon."[43]

What about Anita Hill's history prior to the EEOC? She worked at the law firm of Wald, Harkrader, and Ross. She was caught falsifying time cards used in billing hours to clients[44]; her overall performance level was so low that John Burke, a partner, gave her notice.[45] She immediately leveled an accusation of sexual harassment there which the office staff felt was also designed to distract from her poor performance.[46]

Few Americans were aware that Anita Hill did have a supervisor at the Equal Employment Opportunity Commission who had a collection of pornographic material and spoke about it explicitly, but it wasn't Justice Thomas.[47] Or of the four witnesses who testified in support of Anita Hill, the only one to say her harasser was Justice Thomas referred to a time period before Anita Hill had even gone to work for Justice Thomas.

Again, I do not know where the truth starts and ends. I know only that what became part of the public consciousness was the image of a conservative woman with no motivation, not of a more complex woman with, perhaps, more complex motivations. To make judgments about men as sexual harassers without knowing that the women making the accusations were possibly bitter about promotions they were denied is like making judgments about women as mothers without knowing that the men making the accusations were probably bitter about custody they had been denied. When the media makes women innocent victims and men evil perpetrators *before* it investigates, it censors women's shadow side and men's light side and creates the very hatred it later condemns.

SOME SOLUTIONS?

If a woman feels sexually harassed, encourage her to tell the man *directly*. How do I know this will work? Well, when two feminists compiled the sexual harassment stories of 100 women, **every single man who was told by a woman directly that she felt his behavior was harassing her stopped immediately.**[48] All of the men apologized, some brought in flowers. When women do not understand men's vulnerability, they miss the degree to which men want to please women, not anger women. Thus the authors who compiled these hundred stories never noticed how each of the men who was informed immediately stopped!

Second, give both sexes an understanding of the other sex's best intent. How, for example, both sexes are doing what we are doing because that was functional for millions of years (men: pursue, persist; women: attract, resist), but how it is no longer functional in an age of equality.

Third, socialize both sexes to share responsibility for taking sexual initiatives. Without shared responsibility, sexual harassment legislation will be just another hoop through which men at work must jump to prove themselves worthy of loving women at work.

Fourth, the adult feminist—as opposed to the adolescent feminist—will encourage women to share the expectation of risking the first kiss on the lips, the first caress on the genitals. Only the adolescent feminist fails to place as much emphasis on resocializing women to take direct initiatives and resorts instead to encouraging women to sue the men who do it badly and marry the men who do it right (*if* they are the right men initiating it at the right moment). The adult feminist is willing to exchange the power of *in*direct initiative taking for the responsibility of direct initiative taking. She is willing to exchange victim power for adulthood.

Fifth, instead of articulating sexual harassment via the perspectives of the women's movement, raise the level of discussion to sexual *contact* via the perspective of a gender transition movement.

All forms of sexual contact at work and at school are best dealt with by the institution's improving communication rather than the government's mandating legislation. The potential damage to the institution gives the institution an incentive to correct it. This is not a perfect solution. It is only more perfect than having government legislation of sexual nuance with its potential for annihilating anyone we dislike via a false accusation.

CONCLUSION

Sexual harassment is a perfect metaphor for some of the most important challenges of the twenty-first century: the challenge to our genetic heritage of protecting women; the challenge to the stereotype of innocent woman/guilty man; the challenge to keep our workplace flexible and fluid rather than petrified and paralyzed; the challenge to respond to sexual nuance more with communication and less with legislation—understanding that communication at least responds to nuance with nuance, while legislation responds to nuance with rigidity. When we respond to the nuance of the male-female dance with the rigidity of Stage I regulations, we are going backward, not forward.

If we desire to protect *people* from being hurt, we also have to make laws against love. And against marriage. And automobiles. And gossip. If we desire to protect men from hurt, we would have to outlaw women's sexual rejection of men. Most of us, though, would rather live in a country in which we are free to make our mistakes rather than in one in which we are subject to litigation for each mistake we make.

Early feminists sensed this: they were strong *opponents* of protective legislation. They knew that as long as the princess was protected from the pea, women would be deprived of equality. The modern-day woman's "pea under the mattress" is the rough spots in the workplace. When today's feminists are proponents of protective legislation, they oppose equality.

Sexual harassment legislation is sexist because it makes only the man responsible for the male role in the sexual dance. It protects the woman who is sexual without protecting coworkers from a woman who would use her sexuality for unearned advancement; nor does it protect the company from this woman. Ultimately, it ignores women's role and therefore ignores women. Except as victim.

CHAPTER 14

The Politics of Rape

All men are rapists and that's all they are.

—MARILYN FRENCH, author of *The Women's Room*[1]

Men who are unjustly accused of rape can sometimes gain from the experience.

—Vassar College Assistant Dean of Students[2]

Imagine your son dating a woman from Vassar who feels that a man could gain from being falsely accused of rape. When he comes home for the holidays and tells you he might be spending next semester in prison—where he will be considered "fresh meat" by the prisoners—do you tell him that "men who are unjustly accused of rape can sometimes gain from the experience"? Do you feel good about paying taxpayer dollars to support colleges that are that callous toward your son because he was born male? If your son entered the armed services rather than college, how would you feel about the U.S. Air Force study that is being kept quiet because it discovered that 60 percent of the rape accusations turned out to be false—not unfounded, but false?[3]*

On the other hand, imagine your daughter. You know that date rape *is* a legitimate issue. You want your daughter to experience

---

* See below for details.

dating in a way that contributes to love, not hate. You also sense that if your daughter is raped by a man she is dating, her ability to trust will also be raped. So the big question is: How do we make dating the most positive experience possible for both our daughters and our sons? Do we do that by not interfering? By criminalization (e.g., putting all men in jail who pursue a woman after she says "no")? By resocialization? And if it's by resocialization, does that mean teaching children what we learned or what they should learn? And exactly what should they learn?

So far in the 1980s and '90s, we've focused on criminalization. And the criminalization has been focused on criminalizing only the male role. I believe we need resocialization more than criminalization; and that both roles need revamping, not just the male role. We need to make a transition from Stage I dating to Stage II dating—together. We can start by clearing up the false assumptions that have led to our current focus on criminalization.

IS RAPE AN OUTGROWTH OF MALE POWER?

Myth. Rape is a manifestation of male political and economic power.

Fact. Any given black man is three times as likely to be reported a rapist as a white man.[4]

Do blacks suddenly have more political and economic power? Maybe rape does not derive from power, but rather from powerlessness. More on that below.

IS RAPE AN OUTGROWTH OF MALE VIOLENCE?

Myth. Rape has nothing to do with sexual attraction—it is just an act of violence.[5] This is "proven" by the fact that women of every age are raped.

Fact. **Being at the age of greatest sexual attraction makes the chances of being raped at least 8,400 percent greater than being over age 50.[6]**

When a woman is between the ages 16 and 19, her chances of being raped are 84 in 20,000; when she is between 50 and 64, her chances are less than one in 20,000.[7] Sexual attraction, then, *does* have something to do with who is raped.

If rape were just an act of violence, then it should not be distinguished from any other violent crime. Other violent crimes are not distinguished by the body parts involved. And if they were, the vulnerability of the testicles would make "assault to the testicles" an especially violent crime; and the importance of the head would make "assault to the head" a crime deserving of extreme punishment. **Unless feminists are saying that a woman's vagina is more important than a woman's head, rape must be acknowledged as something more than violence toward a body part in order to give it its special treatment.**

What are we really doing when we ignore the role of sexual attraction? We are ignoring our responsibility as a culture for reinforcing men's addiction to female sexual beauty and then depriving men of what we've helped addict them to. We will not be willing to stop reinforcing men's addiction to beautiful women until we are willing to stop the benefits that beautiful women receive when men's addiction gets men to perform for women, pay for women, and pursue women.

Is Date Rape a Crime or a Misunderstanding?

PREVAILING PERSPECTIVE. Date rape is a crime, not a misunderstanding.

ANOTHER PERSPECTIVE. Anyone who works with both sexes knows it is possible for a man to feel he's just made love and for a woman to feel she's been raped. It's also possible for a woman to feel she's made love in the evening when she's high, and feel raped in the morning when she's sober—without the man being a rapist. Or for a woman to feel she's been made love to one evening if the man said, "I love you," but feel raped the next evening if he hasn't called back. But again, that doesn't mean the man raped her.

It is also possible for a woman to go back to a man's room, tell him she doesn't want to have intercourse, mean it, start kissing, have intercourse, and then wish she hadn't in the morning. How? Kissing is like eating potato chips. Before we know it, we've gone further than we said we would.

The woman who says "I just want to talk" when she goes to the room but is then responsive to a shoulder rub, a caressed hand, and a first kiss has not *verbally* said, "I've changed my mind," but she has said it *non*verbally. Therefore her last *words* were "no" to anything physical. If *he* is asked to take responsibility because *her* last *words* were "no," we are then making him more responsible for her than she is for herself. To make him into a criminal for not taking responsibility for her is to make him into a criminal for not being her parent. Which is not equality, but woman-as-child.

All of this together leaves some men uncertain whether "read my lips" means reading what her lips are saying or reading what her lips are doing.

The problem with every judgment of sexual behavior is that it is made by people who aren't being stimulated as they are making the judgment. A jury that sees a woman in a sterile courtroom, asks her what she wanted, and then assumes that anything else she did was the responsibility of the man is insulting not only the woman but the power of sex. A man being sued after a woman has more sex than intended is like Lay's being sued after someone has more potato chips than intended. In brief, date rape can be a crime, a misunderstanding, or buyer's remorse.

ISN'T IT THE MALE ROLE THAT NEEDS CHANGING BECAUSE IT IS MEN WHO RAPE?

PREVAILING PERSPECTIVE. The problem in dating is the male role because it is men who rape, not women.

MY PERSPECTIVE. The problem is both sexes' roles: Both sexes' roles lead to both sexes' problems—the problem for women of date rape; and problems for men such as date robbery, unequal date rejection, unequal date responsibility, date fraud, and date lying.

Date Rape

Here is how the male-female roles combine with thousands of years of sexual selection to lead to the problem of date rape for women. The social role:[8]

- Reinforces boys' addiction to sex with girls even as it warns girls against sex with boys. It tells everyone sex is dirty and dangerous (herpes, AIDS) and then . . .
- It tells boys, "You take responsibility to get all this 'dirty' stuff," which leads to boys being mistrusted and rejected.
- Rather than take rejections personally, a young man learns to turn a woman into a sex object—it hurts him less to be rejected by an object.
- Being objectified makes her feel alienated and being rejected makes him feel hurt, angry, and powerless. When rejection and sexual identity go hand in hand, we sow the seeds of violence—especially among boys who have *no* source of power. His violence and objectifying reinforce the starting assumptions: Sex is dirty and dangerous, and men can't be trusted.

All this leads to the Male Sexual Catch-22: A man is sexually rejected until he proves himself worthy of trust by "not going after sex," but sexually ignored until he "goes after sex."

Note that this is a two-sex process, not a one-sex process. If we want to stop date rape by men, we have to also stop "date passivity" by women. Thus far, women *retain* the old option to be passive and take indirect initiatives, yet *gain* the new option to take direct initiatives. Women, though, are not *expected* to initiate. Nor are they told there is something wrong with them if they don't. So women gain new options without new expectations. Men retain old expectations without new options. Except the option of prison if they do their old role badly.

While the label "date rape" has helped women articulate the most traumatic aspect of dating from women's perspective, men have no labels to help them articulate the most traumatic aspects of dating from their perspective. Now, of course, the most traumatic aspect is the possibility of being accused of date rape by a woman to whom he thought he was making love. If men did label the worst aspects of the traditional male role, though, they might label them "date robbery," "date rejection," "date responsibility," "date fraud," and "date lying."

Date Robbery, Date Rejection, and Date Responsibility

The worst aspect of dating from the perspective of many men is how dating can feel to a man like robbery by social custom—the social custom of him taking money out of his pocket, giving it to her, and calling it a date. **To a young man, the worst dates feel like being robbed and rejected.** Boys risk death to avoid rejection (e.g., by joining the army). Evenings of paying to be rejected can feel like the male version of date rape.

Many men are beginning to object to the unquestioned dating expectation on men to assume unequal date responsibility and receive unequal date rejection. They still find that when the check appears on the table women disappear to the ladies' room. Men have not explained to the world how the expectation to pay pressures him to take jobs he likes less only because they pay more; how this leads to stress, heart attacks, and suicides that are the male version of "my body, *not* my choice." They know only that women have the option to ask and the option to pay, that men are still expected to ask and expected to pay.

Date Fraud and Date Lying

If a man ignoring a woman's verbal "no" is committing date rape, then a woman who says "no" with her verbal language but "yes" with her body language is committing date fraud. And a woman who continues to be sexual even after she says "no" is committing date lying.

Do women still do this? Two feminists found the answer is yes. Nearly 40 percent of college women acknowledged they had said "no" to sex even "when they meant yes."[9] In my own work with over 150,000 women and men—about half of whom are single—the answer is also yes. Almost all single women acknowledge they have agreed to go back to a guy's place "just to talk" but were nevertheless responsive to his first kiss. And almost all acknowledge they've recently said something like, "That's far enough for now," even as her lips are still kissing and her tongue is still touching his.

We have forgotten that before we began calling this date rape and date fraud, we called it exciting. Somehow, women's romance novels are not titled *He Stopped When I Said "No."* They are, though, titled *Sweet Savage Love*,[10] in which the woman rejects the hand of her gentler lover who saves her from the rapist and marries the man who repeatedly and savagely rapes her. It is this "marry the rapist" theme that not only turned *Sweet Savage Love* into a best-seller but also into one of the most enduring of women's romance novels. And it is Rhett Butler, carrying the kicking and screaming Scarlett O'Hara to bed, who is a hero to females—not to males—in *Gone with the Wind* (the best-selling romance novel of all time—*to women*). It is important that a woman's "noes" be respected and that her "yeses" be respected. And it is also important when nonverbal "yeses" (tongues still touching) conflict with those verbal "noes" that the man not be put in jail for choosing the "yes" over the "no." He might just be trying to become her fantasy. The danger is in the fine line between fantasy and nightmare.

The differences in each sex's experiences are so enormous emotionally that I can create understanding only by conducting role-*reversal* dates: having the women ask the men out and discover which of the *men*'s "noes" mean "no" forever, which mean "no" for the rest of the date, which for a few minutes, and which just mean slow down . . . and having the men feel what it's like to have their "noes" ignored.

WHAT'S THE DIFFERENCE BETWEEN STRANGER RAPE, ACQUAINTANCE RAPE, AND DATE RAPE?

We often hear, "Rape is rape, right?" No. A stranger forcing himself on a woman at knife point *is* different from a man and woman having sex while drunk and having regrets in the morning. *What* is different? When a woman agrees to a date, she does not make a choice to be sexual, but she does make a choice to explore sexual *possibilities*. The woman makes no such choice with a stranger or an acquaintance. In this respect, date rape is really quite different from acquaintance rape and the terms should *not* be used interchangeably, as they often are.

Why have all these complications arisen in the last decade or so? Let's look. . . .

THE POLITICS OF MAKING DATE RAPE AN EPIDEMIC AND MAKING ONLY MEN RESPONSIBLE

Almost half of all women are raped or victims of attempted rape at least once in their lives.[11] . . . Under conditions of male dominance, if sex is normally something men do to women, viewing "yes" as a sign of consent is misguided.[12]

—CATHARINE MACKINNON, NBC'S only choice to analyze the entire Clarence Thomas hearings as Tom Brokaw moderated

The country's leading feminist legal expert on date rape, Catharine MacKinnon, says that a woman's "yes" can*not* be considered genuine. Why not? Because she is forced to say "yes" *in order to survive.*[13] If a woman can be considered raped even if she says "yes," it is understandable how MacKinnon concluded that half of all women are subject to rape or attempted rape in their lifetime.

A *Ms.*-sponsored study which the mass media widely quoted[14] as saying that 25 percent of all women were raped *by the time they were in college* used this question to reach the 25 percent figure:[15]

Have you given in to sexual intercourse when you didn't want to because you were overwhelmed by a man's continual arguments and pressure?[16]

Notice that these women did not define themselves as raped, just as "overwhelmed." She might have felt "overwhelmed" exactly because she was afraid of losing the guy if she said "no." So she might have said "yes" to keep him. It is only when we broaden the definition of rape in this way—to include women who might have said "yes"—that we discover an "increase" in rape.

How do I know these women did not necessarily define themselves as raped? *Because 42 percent of these women said they had sex with these men one or more times after this (the mean was 2.02 times).*[17]

None of this, of course, empathizes with The Male Date Rape Catch-22: We are still requiring men to be the sexual salespersons but now defining them as rapists when they do it well.

The truth is that *both* sexes participate in unwanted sexual activity. A feminist who was brave enough to ask these broad-based questions of both sexes astonished herself to discover that *94 percent of the men* (as well as 98 percent of the women) said they had had *un*wanted sexual activity by the time they were in college.[18] But even more surprising was her finding, reported in the *Journal of Sex Research*, that 63 percent of the men and 46 percent of the women said they had experienced *unwanted intercourse*.[19] By feminist definitions of rape as unwanted sex, virtually everyone has been raped. And that's how rape begins to look like an epidemic. It's also how rape gets trivialized.

A woman friend of mine read this and said, "I have difficulty thinking of concrete examples of why a man might not want to have sex with a woman." Why not? A college man sometimes fears intercourse when he feels a woman will read into it more of a commitment than he wants. But he has it anyway because he was the one pressing for it before she made it clear it meant a commitment to her, and in the heat of passion he doesn't know how to say "no" despite the strings that are attached. In fact, it is exactly that scenario—with the man not calling the next day for fear of further misleading her and the woman feeling rejected because he didn't call after sex—that leads to the woman feeling "raped," and sometimes even reporting it as rape.

Men, like women, often don't want to have sex for the first time when they are drunk or exhausted but sometimes do it because they fear rejecting the other one. Men, like women, feel torn between passions of the moment and the desire, the following morning, to have an excuse for not being home when their loved one called for the fourth time at 3 A.M.

Exactly how frequent is rape, then? The best answer comes from the national survey of households in which women are asked *anonymously* whether they've ever been raped and also asked whether or not they had reported it to the police. As it turns out about a third of women did not report completed rapes to the police; about half did not report attempted rapes.[20] When we add these women to the women who did report, we discover that about one in twenty-five women is a victim of a completed rape in a lifetime, about one in twenty-three women is a victim of an attempted rape in a lifetime.[21]

Do the ever-broadening definitions of rape affect the outcome of the more objective government studies? It's possible. For example, *prior* to the William Kennedy Smith and Mike Tyson date rape trials, the Justice Department found that the rate of rapes and attempted rapes *decreased* from 1973 to 1988 by 33 percent (from 1.8 per 1,000 women to 1.2 per 1,000 women).[22] After the trials, when women started considering themselves raped if they *felt* forced, the Justice Department found its first recent increase in rapes and attempted rapes.[23]

Laws against date rape with broad definitions are like fifty-five-mile-per-hour speed limits—by making everyone a violator, they trivialize those who are real violators. But at least the anyone-who-drives-is-a-violator laws for speed limits are applicable to both sexes. Any-man-who-dates-can-be-a-rapist laws are applicable to only one sex. They are sexist laws. **Laws with broad definitions of rape are like laws making fifty-five-mile-per-hour speed limits for men and no speed limits for women.**

Every exaggerated claim of the increase in rapes magnifies every woman's fears as she walks down the street at night. And it magnifies her distrust of men. In brief, exaggerated claims hurt women. *Exaggerated claims of rape rates might be good for politics, but they are bad for women who want to love men.* To exploit women for the sake of politics is not my definition of liberation.

CAN A MAN BE LEGALLY ACCUSED OF RAPE IF HE HAS SEX WITH A WOMAN WHO SAYS "YES"?

ITEM. Wisconsin, 1990. Mark Peterson is found guilty of sexually assaulting a woman who, doctors say, has forty-six personalities.[24] She claimed that one of her personalities, a girl the age of 6, informed her afterward that she had been having sex. She then accused Mark Peterson of having sexually assaulted her. Six of the woman's different personalities were summoned to the witness stand; four were individually sworn in. She acknowledged that the personality that had sex—the "fun-loving" personality—did not object.

To add insult to injury, Mark made the national press as a criminal. He will always be known in his community as a man convicted of rape. His criminal record will surface in any investigation, requiring him to explain himself. Meanwhile, the woman's name did not make the papers. Men in Wisconsin don't know whether the woman they are about to have sex with might be she. Or one like her.

It is one thing to expect men to find out which "no" means "no"; now we're expecting men to know which "yes" means "yes." No, we're not just expecting him to know—we're convicting him as a criminal if he doesn't know.

This story of a woman with the multiple personalities whose "yes" could mean "no" could be an old Indian legend told by an Indian elder to boys coming of age as a metaphor to warn boys of their helplessness before the mixed messages of the female. But instead, it is a 1990s legal case in a state considered legally progressive. Instead it is a present-day metaphor for the degree to which the legal system is willing to protect women and prosecute men. If a woman swears on the Bible in a court of law that she said one thing, then swears she said something else, and we convict him because *he* didn't know more about what she meant than she did, isn't this the perfect metaphor for telling men that women have only rights, that men have only responsibilities?

Is the multiple personality case a metaphor for a new reality? Yes. Across the country, campuses now considered "progressive"—from Berkeley to Harvard and Swarthmore—already allow a woman who is drunk to claim the next morning that she was raped even if she said "yes" the evening before![25] Put simply, your son can be with a woman who has a few drinks, has sex with him all she wants and, in the morning, claims your son raped her because the evening before, she was under the influence of alcohol and it was a different personality that said "yes."

Now MacKinnon, the National Clearinghouse on Marital and Date Rape, and other feminists plan to extend this beyond the campus—to criminal law.[26] Is this possible legally? Yes. Many states already have laws saying a person cannot be considered to have consented to something if they are "under the influence"—if they have diminished mental capacity.

Once a woman can claim her "yes" didn't really mean "yes" because she was "under the influence," this opens the floodgates. We have already seen how Sheryl Lynn Massip's "baby blues" became the legal excuse for her crushing her son's head under her car. So it opens the floodgates for a woman declaring she felt raped because she was under the influence of a traumatic divorce, a child dying, or just extreme stress. Even a man's hint of a long-term relationship the night before can be said to have put her "under the influence." ("When he didn't call the next morning I knew then he was lying—I would never have gone to bed with him if I didn't think he wanted a commitment; I was under the influence of him saying he loved me last night. He lied—he raped me.")

In an era of equality, we are making her not responsible because she is drunk and making him responsible even though he is also drunk. It is ironic that feminism is pioneering this new *in*equality.

Sexually, of course, the sexes aren't equal. It is exactly a woman's greater sexual power that often makes a man so fearful of being rejected by her that he buys himself drinks to reduce his fear. In essence, her sexual power often leads to him drinking; his sexual power rarely leads to her drinking. If anything is evidence of her power over him, it is his being expected to spend his money to buy her drinks without her reciprocating. In brief, **many men feel "under the influence" the moment they see a beautiful woman.**

"Under the influence" legislation—or multiple personality legislation—has enormous potential for backfiring against women. Women buy perfumes that promise to put men under the influence. Women laugh at how a man with a hard penis has a soft brain. We have seen how almost every culture reinforced men's addiction to beautiful and young women exactly so a man would make an irrational decision when he was "under the influence." It is men—far more than women—whose mental capacities are diminished when they are "under the influence" of a beautiful woman.

It is ironic that in an era in which we are increasingly holding people more responsible if they drink and drive, we are holding women less responsible if they drink and have sex. Of course, if she drinks and just has sex, that's her business. But if she drinks and claims the man raped her, she is injuring a man. Sometimes for life. And so she is as responsible for drinking and declaring rape as a driver is for drinking and causing an accident.[27]

The difference between a woman saying "yes" and "no" is all important when it comes to drinking. A man should be held responsible when a woman drinks and still says "no" with both her verbal language and all her body language. If anything, he should be held more responsible if she says "no" after drinking.

As long as society tells men to be the salespersons of sex, it is sexist for society to put only men in jail if they sell well. We don't put other salespersons in jail for buying clients drinks and successfully transforming a "no" into a "maybe" into a "yes." If the client makes a choice to drink too much and the "yes" turns out to be a bad decision, it is the *client* who gets fired, not the salesperson. We expect *adults* to take responsibility.

IS A FALSELY ACCUSED MAN A RAPED MAN?

When a woman says she is raped, it is important to listen, support her, believe her, and help her make a transition back to a life of maximum trust. Every human being, when hurting, needs listening and love more than anything else—including having their problem solved.

When a man says he has been falsely accused of rape, he is also telling us he has been raped. He is being accused of being one of life's most despicable persons. Even if the accusation is made by an adolescent girl who acknowledges she's lying before there's a trial, a man's life can be ruined. As with Grover Gale.

A 13-year-old North Carolina girl accused Grover Gale II of raping her four times.[28] By the time Grover spent thirty-six days in jail, he had lost his construction job, fallen into debt, couldn't pay his rent for his family at home, and was on the verge of divorce. Then the girl, whose name still didn't make the papers, admitted she made the whole thing up, saying she was just trying to get her 17-year-old boyfriend's attention.[29]

But when Grover returned from jail, his own son was afraid to hug him. Wherever he went in town, people pointed to him and called him names like "child molester" and "rapist." At the mall, someone spit on him. Although in debt, the family felt forced to move. They moved out of state to a small town where no one knew him. Two years later, the charges still plague him. He's still $15,000 in debt because of bail fees, trial costs, and back rent he's never been able to catch up on.

Grover doesn't know whether to sue or forget. When he tries to forget, the anger builds up inside. Sometimes he storms out of his apartment, jumps into his car, and tears down a country road, heading for nowhere. He pulls over and kicks the car until he has calmed down. He says, "I've been lost ever since." His wife can't speak about the accusations—or hear him speak about them—without crying.[30]

Grover has lost his life and his wife. He has been raped. Yet he cannot afford counseling and the state won't pay for him to be counseled. The psychologists themselves fear a liability suit: "If you treat him as a nonrapist and he later rapes, you can be sued for not treating him as a rapist—as a psychologist you supposedly should have known."[31]

Once accused, no trial can erase the shadow that follows a man wherever he goes. *Dr.* William Kennedy Smith is still rarely referred to as "doctor." When he was accused of date rape, his residency in internal medicine at the University of New Mexico Hospital was put on hold. Understandable. But after he was found *not* guilty, the university could not decide whether or not it should rescind the offer.[32] The shadow followed him after the trial.

But is Grover Gale an exception? Aren't false accusations of rape rare?

AREN'T FALSE ACCUSATIONS OF RAPE RARE?

To my considerable chagrin, we found that at least 60 percent of all the rape allegations were false.

> —DR. CHARLES P. MCDOWELL,
> Supervisory Special Agent, U.S.
> Air Force, Office of Special
> Investigations[33]

When the U.S. Air Force investigated 556 cases of alleged rape, 27 percent of the women eventually admitted they had lied (either just before they took a lie-detector test or after they failed it).[34] Because other cases were less certain, the air force asked three independent reviewers to review these cases. They used twenty-five criteria that were common to the women who had acknowledged they lied. If *all three* reviewers agreed that the rape allegation was false, it was ranked as false. (There were no convictions of these women—it was just a study.) Their conclusion? A total of 60 percent of the original rape allegations were false.

Dr. McDowell, the supervisory special agent, had already distinguished himself by being among the first to predict that Cathleen Crowell Webb's false accusation of Gary Dotson was, in fact, false. Webb was so impressed with his analysis that she published it as an appendix in her book *Forgive Me*.[35] Dr. McDowell nevertheless feared publishing the air force findings, thinking they might be representative of findings only in military situations and that publishing them might therefore be misleading, so he examined the police files from a major midwestern and a southwestern city. The findings of 60 percent false accusations held, but the cities requested anonymity for fear of political repercussions.

Most counties and cities do not open their files to the public. Those that do usually categorize false reports—in which the woman admits she lied—as "unfounded" (not false), the same as reports in which there is no evidence, or not enough to warrant a trial. When *The Washington Post* got some counties in the Washington area to open their files, two of the largest counties, Prince George in Maryland and Fairfax in Virginia, had recorded 30 and 40 percent false or "unfounded," respectively.[36] (In contrast, false claims of burglaries, robberies, and auto thefts range between 1 and 5 percent.[37])

Aren't these findings in conflict with the FBI's *Uniform Crime Reports* which the media has popularized as saying that only 9 percent of rape accusations are false or unfounded?[38] No. The FBI knows the number of women who reported they were raped, but not whether the rapist was found guilty or innocent. In 47 percent of the cases, the alleged rapist has not even been identified or found, or if he has been found, there was insufficient evidence to arrest him.[39] The remaining 53 percent were arrested, but *the FBI doesn't receive data as to whether they were eventually found guilty or innocent*.[40] In brief, as far as the FBI knows, the percentage of false accusations overall could be anywhere from zero to 100 percent.

While every man who is falsely accused is, in essence, emotionally raped, a false accusation often also creates an economic rape. In 1993, when a woman lied about being raped in Nordstrom's, Nordstrom's had changed their security system in seventy-two stores in ten states prior to laboratory tests uncovering evidence in direct contradiction to the woman's story (which led to the woman acknowledging she lied).[41] The reputation of the victim (Nordstrom's) was damaged for two weeks in the national media while the name of the victimizer was kept confidential. The district attorney's office refused to prosecute the woman. No one compensated Nordstrom's. Nor does anyone compensate everyone who shops at Nordstrom's who is paying for that false accusation.

The only things we know for sure, then, are that false accusations are not a rarity, that they are themselves a form of rape, and that they are a political hot potato. It will doubtless take a female politician of enormous integrity to confront the issue. But the exact percentage of false accusations is of secondary importance. Of primary importance is that the judge and jury realize that either sex could be the victim; that in the case of date rape, there could be, in fact, a misunderstanding; that a woman *can* feel intimidated about making a genuine accusation; and that a man's life can be ruined (losing job, wife, and children) even if he is found *not* guilty; that both parties must therefore receive due process (as opposed to having rape shield laws protecting the female more than the male).

WHY WOULD A WOMAN MAKE A FALSE ACCUSATION OF RAPE?

When I first heard of date rape allegations and the possibility of false accusations, my personal response was, "Lots of guys don't know when to take 'no' for an answer, and besides, what would motivate a woman to make a false accusation if there wasn't at least some truth to it?" But when the governor of New York was fooled by Tawana Brawley's convincing claim of gang rape (which turned out to be a hoax) and the governor of Illinois refused Gary Dotson a retrial years after DNA tests virtually proved him innocent, I felt I had to open my mind. Which led to my wondering what motivated false accusations.

The Washington Post investigation found a wide range of motivations.[42] Anger toward former boyfriends was common. Kathryn Tucci's former boyfriend spent thirteen months in jail before Kathryn acknowledged she lied. (Kathryn's punishment was community service.) Perhaps most common was the need of young girls to give excuses to their parents for arriving home late, staying out all night, or being pregnant.

One woman accused her newspaper delivery man of raping her at gunpoint because she needed an excuse to be late to work. This was her second false report in a year. The first time no charges were brought against her so she thought there would be no consequences the second time. The second time there were consequences: she received counseling.[43]

The air force study has the only systematic reporting of motivations:

Motivations Given by the Women Who Acknowledged They Had Made False Accusations of Rape[44]

Reason	Percent
Spite or revenge	20
To compensate for feelings of guilt or shame	20
Thought she might be pregnant	13
To conceal an affair	12
To test husband's love	9
Mental/emotional disorder	9
To avoid personal responsibility	4
Failure to pay, or extortion	4
Thought she might have caught VD	3
Other	6
TOTAL	100

Dr. McDowell found that most false accusations are "instrumental"—they serve a purpose. If the purpose isn't avoiding guilt or getting revenge, it might be to allow her to tell her parents, "I did not purposely go out and get pregnant—I was raped"; or tell her husband, "I did not have an affair; it was not my fault. . . . I was raped."[45]

When society lays judgments on women who have sex before it thinks they should, it sets women up to make false accusations to avoid those judgments. One of the cases from the air force study illustrates this:

A 22-year-old enlistee attended a party and while there had intercourse with her companion. She admitted to being intoxicated at the time and subsequently began to feel ashamed because others at the party knew what she had done, so she decided to claim that she had been raped.[46]

In the past, the woman would have had to take responsibility for being sexual "too quickly." Now the date rape accusation gives her a way out. She can transfer the burden of guilt and shame to the man. What the society needs to confront is whether it is really necessary to create the guilt and therefore to have to find someone to blame.

There is, though, a time to accept blame—when we break a commitment. When accusing a man of date rape holds so much power that the entire U.S. Navy is intimidated into not investigating whether the woman is using that accusation to avoid blame for a broken commitment, then we are creating an incentive for false accusations to be used by the least responsible women.

Kermit Cain, a friend of mine who had been chosen Sailor of the Year in 1980, found his career a victim of just such a motivation when he and a female service member returned to his place after a date and, Kermit explains . . .

> I told her I was going upstairs to my room. She followed me and as soon as the door closed, she took off most of her clothes and got up onto my bed. The next morning we went back to her place.
>
> Weeks later, I was ordered into my Department Head's office where I was informed I was going to prison, no explanation given as to the charges, only that "anything else you do will only add time to your sentence." After that the command's Internal Affairs officer began questioning every female that I'd come in contact with, stating that I was a rapist and implying they'd be helping to protect women if they gave a statement against me. In two cases, they were able to get further false statements against me by making the women think they were doing the right thing.
>
> No lawyer would take my case. So my dad and I conducted our own research for three years and found that the girl had gone AWOL to avoid a drug test, having already failed a previous test and knowing that a second conviction would give her a Bad Conduct Discharge. When she returned home and her parents asked her why she had left the base, she said she'd been raped. The mother called the congressman who called the Office of Legislative Affairs who called the Commanding Officer who called the Captain. . . .
>
> I discovered part of this when one of the girl's three roommates,

seeing what had happened to me (I had lost 50 pounds and was on the verge of suicide), took pity on me and told me that she had overheard my accuser planning the whole scenario with her roommate—who was also her lover—as an excuse to be off base at the time of the drug test. She reported she heard them laughing and joking about it.

By the time I completed my research, my evidence was so overwhelming that I was able to get an attorney. When we went to the Naval Investigative Service, we found they already had enough statements to prove my innocence—but they would not give them directly to my attorney; we had to discover them on our own. Only after this process was I eventually cleared of all charges and reinstated. But obviously my career as it otherwise would have been was ruined. I don't know that I would be alive today had I not met Susan [the woman he now lives with], or if my accuser's roommate had not overheard the planning, or if my dad had not helped me when I most needed it.[47]

Kermit's experience allowed me to see how one or two women could set into motion the Machinery of Male Protectors who were so fearful of not protecting a woman that they steamrolled over the most basic rights of humans, and in so doing trapped themselves into covering up even more of the woman's lies for fear of looking like fools. Male chauvinism is about protecting women. Male chauvinism and feminism have this in common.

Protecting women from assuming responsibility is not limited to conservatives in the armed services. At universities from Berkeley to Harvard to Swarthmore, a woman can now have sex while drunk on the drinks the men paid for at night and claim in the morning she was raped because she was drunk and therefore she couldn't really consent.[48] The man's social expectation to pay for the drinks is now seen as evidence he was "plying" the woman with drinks and "luring" the woman to bed. Now, especially on liberal campuses, this is viewed as evidence of man as oppressor and woman as innocent.

One would think that the universities with the best and brightest women would pioneer the effort to socialize women to ask men out, take initiatives, pay for men's drinks . . . in preparation for running their own businesses (and their own lives). Instead, they are simultaneously treating these women as children who cannot take responsibility while socializing men to take all the responsibility. These universities then blame businesses for discriminating when these women are less successful in business.

THE SOCIAL INCENTIVES FOR FALSE ACCUSATIONS

We are now making false accusations of rape more than a method by which women can avoid guilt, avoid blame for broken responsibilities, and exact revenge. We are also creating positive, proactive incentives for false accusations. As when women who accuse men of rape are turned into feminist heroines even before there is a trial (as with Tawana Brawley and the accusers of Tyson and Smith).

Three less visible social incentives are now adding even more to the temptation for false accusations: (1) monetary incentives; (2) abortion laws; and (3) TV.

Monetary Incentives

ITEM. Eleven women from the Miss Black America Pageant all claimed Mike Tyson touched them on their rears. So the founder of the pageant filed a $607 million lawsuit against Mike Tyson. Several of the contestants eventually admitted they had lied in the hope of getting publicity and cashing in on the award money.[49]

Think about it. If each woman had the potential for being awarded $20 to $30 million, aren't we really bribing women to make false accusations? And the Miss Black America Pageant itself got more publicity than it had received in its history. The lawsuit made tabloid headlines; the dropping of the lawsuit was buried in the back pages.

When we fail to give as much attention to an accusation being false as to the original accusation, the accused is left with an image problem. When this image problem was added to Tyson's already tarnished image, Tyson was doubtless more likely to be found guilty when one of the Miss Black America contestants (Desiree Washington) accused him of date rape than he would have if tabloid headlines had recently been saying "Black Beauties Bribed by Big Bucks."

We often hear that women are hesitant about bringing up sexual harassment suits and date rape charges because they won't be believed, their personal lives are invaded, their identities known, etc. This is *true*. For *most* women. But it is not true for some women. And from the man's perspective, it takes only a few women to make dating feel like a minefield—not only of rejection but of life-ruining lawsuits. When dating is a minefield for men, both sexes suffer the loneliness.

Abortion Laws

ITEM. In order to get an abortion, Norma McCorvey, the "Jane Roe" of *Roe* v. *Wade*, claimed she was raped. Fourteen years later, she acknowledged she had lied.[50]

If a teenage girl cannot get an abortion unless she says she was raped, she will feel pressure to claim she was raped. The next question is: "Who was the rapist?" Next, there's a lineup of men. Which often pits the future of an unwed teenage girl against "some boy out there." Next, the media has convicted him. If the boy tries to defend himself by suing for libel, he only gives the girl an incentive never to confess that her accusation is false. If he doesn't sue for libel, he's left defenseless. He loses if he defends himself, and loses if he doesn't.

Is it possible to allow the woman just to say, "I need an abortion—I was raped," without trying to find the rapist? No. This is the same as abortion on demand with the downside of making the woman a liar and the rape statistics soar.

When abortion is made "illegal except in the case of *incest*," a woman will feel pressure to report a family member—usually her father, stepfather, uncle, or brother—in order to get an abortion. This does not encourage family unity.

Meanwhile, the falsely accused man loses his job and his reputation—even if the woman later reveals, as did Jane Roe, that she "had to claim rape" just to get an abortion. By accusing a man to free a woman, have we really come any further than when we accused blacks to free whites? What used to make both races paranoid now makes both sexes paranoid. When it happens to blacks, we call it racism; when it happens to men, we call it women's liberation.

Now here's the rub: Every false report makes police and judges doubt women who genuinely have been raped.

TV

ITEM. Florida. A 9-year-old girl said her mom's boyfriend, Ivie Cornell Norris, had raped her. Norris spent 513 days in Pinellas County Jail in Florida and could have been there for life. Why was he released? When the girl turned 11, she convinced enough people that she had lied.[51]

Why did she lie? Her mom and Mr. Norris often argued, and she wanted to get Norris "out of the way." How was she so convincing at age 9? She based her testimony on an episode of the television drama *21 Jump Street* that depicted a rape case.

Similarly, at least one of the false accusations among the air force women was an exact replica of the television rape drama she had seen earlier in the evening.[52] It was only when the inconsistencies of her story were uncovered that the woman volunteered she had patterned her story on the TV rape drama. The woman's motivation? She wanted to get her husband to pay attention to her.

THE POLITICS OF HIS WORD AGAINST HERS

When the name Gary Dotson is mentioned, most of us think of a man falsely accused of rape. Few people realize that although Cathleen Crowell Webb was so easily believed when she accused Gary Dotson, she was not believed when she said Gary Dotson was innocent. Or that it took five amazing coincidences to get Dotson a new trial. Without any one of these coincidences, Gary Dotson today would be serving his twelfth year of a twenty-five to fifty-year sentence.

The first coincidence was that Cathleen Webb found God—and became tormented by her guilt. Only then did she acknowledge she had made up the story to cover up a sexual encounter with her boyfriend.

The second coincidence was the development of DNA tests which proved the semen stains on Webb's underwear were not Dotson's, but did match the semen of Cathy's boyfriend at the time. Then, *although the two circumstances that were enough to convict Dotson—Cathy's say-so and "Dotson's" semen—were re-versed, reversal was not enough to even get Dotson a new trial.* Imagine if we had sent a woman to prison for attempting to murder a man and the man later acknowledged he had falsely accused the woman. Would the woman be denied a new trial?

The third coincidence was the timely emergence of two extraordinary journalists who dedicated part of their lives to uncovering the complete facts in Dotson's case. The fourth involved the availability and willingness of a famous attorney to defend an already-convicted rapist.

The fifth coincidence is the most outrageous. When the original trial judge refused to grant Dotson a new trial, Governor Thompson just happened to be running for reelection. Because Thompson had the unique credentials of being the chairman of the Illinois Prisoner Review Board and a former prosecutor, he had the credibility to conduct an extraordinary public "review" of the case—thereby doing an end run around the judge's refusal to grant a retrial.

The governor's public "trial" became a virtual TV soap opera in Chicago. It was only as the public felt for Cathy's and Gary's pain and the public sentiment shifted that the governor felt he could take political action without committing political suicide. Although Dotson had completed high school and started college while in prison, Thompson felt he still needed to "be tough" and put Dotson on restrictive parole.

I knew that if all this had happened to a woman, she would be seen as a victim of male injustice who had nevertheless overcome the odds and now deserved recognition as a hero. I knew the networks would compete to make TV movies out of her plight, paying her hundreds of thousands of dollars for the story. Although Dotson's case is the most celebrated of its kind and has all the elements of a real-life soap opera, John Hoover, the man who owns the rights to Cathleen's story, has found such in-house resistance to its production by feminist producers that he cannot get a major studio to bid for it.[53] What most amazed him was how many feminist producers could not accept—to this day—that a woman could lie about being raped.

What is most revealing is the ease with which a 16-year-old girl was believed when she claimed rape, but disbelieved when she acknowledged—even at the more mature age of 23—that she had lied. Cathleen Webb expressed amazement at this difference in her book *Forgive Me*.[54]

What was Dotson's attitude toward Cathleen Webb after the twelve-year nightmare finally ended in his release? Dotson said, "I forgave her a long time ago. I've got no animosity." (I'm never sure which is greater—men's ability to forgive, or men's ability to repress emotions.)

On CBS's morning talk show, Phyllis George asked Dotson and Webb to hug. Suppose Dan Rather had asked a woman to hug her rapist?

Has the discovery of false accusations encouraged judges to make jurors aware that a guilty verdict must be based on guilt "beyond a reasonable doubt"? No. California now requires that jurors be explicitly told that *a rape conviction can be based on the accuser's testimony alone, without corroboration*.[55]

THE DOUBLE STANDARD OF RAPE SHIELD LAWS

Rape shield laws shield a woman's sexual past from being used against her in court. They do not shield a man's sexual past from being used against him in court. When first suggested by feminists, the laws were assumed to be a flagrant violation of our constitutional right to due process (because they shielded one party more than the other in the trial and therefore denied one party a fair trial). They were also assumed to violate the equal protection clause of the Fourteenth Amendment because they protected men less than women.

However, as people were increasingly convinced that women had no motivation to lie about rape, the political atmosphere changed. Women who claimed they were raped were virtually assumed to have already been victimized, and therefore dragging out her sexual past in court appeared only to be double victimization. As courts began to buy this assumption, they began to reason that women needed extra protection in order to have equal protection. By the early 1990s, the Supreme Court upheld this as the law of the land.[56]

We have seen, though, that not only are there numerous motivations to lie about rape, there are a half dozen or so social *incentives* to lie about rape. Just as importantly, we have also seen that a false accusation is its own form of rape. Once we know this, we know that it *is* a violation of due process and equal protection to shield a woman's sexual past during a trial more than a man's. **The purpose of a trial is to determine whether or not there has been a rape, not to assume who needs the shielding during the trial.** The job of a lawyer is to convince the judge that the past is relevant; it is not the job of the law to assume the female's sexual past cannot be used against her but the male's can.

Practically speaking, then, when a woman accuses a man of rape, the FBI or police seek out women from the man's sexual past, tell them that he's been accused of rape, ask them if they too had ever felt raped by him, and if they say, "Well perhaps once when . . . ," they are encouraged to testify to "stop this from happening to other women." In contrast, as of the most recent Supreme Court decision, he cannot even present evidence of her having a previous sexual relationship *with him* unless he first notifies the court in time for her to prepare her defense.[57]

And practically speaking, as the trial is occurring, feminists are brought on TV to tell us that rape is the only crime for which the victim is disbelieved. This is an incredible statement because thus far we do not yet know who the victim is. In criminal law, the person *claiming* to be the victim is *always* legally disbelieved and the evidence always cross-examined until the person being accused is proven guilty beyond a reasonable doubt. This is what distinguishes freedom from a dictatorship. When we ignore this constitutional protection of the accused, we have McCarthyism, fascism, and witch-hunts.

Rape shield laws have been declared constitutional because, in our heart of hearts, no one wants to be suspicious of a woman who claims she was raped. And conversely, no one wants to defend a potential rapist unless he's someone we love. The rape of a woman places The Most-Evil Male against The Most-Innocent Woman—in archetypal fashion. *None* of our initial instincts is to defend The Most-Evil Male.

THE UNCONSTITUTIONALITY OF PROTECTING THE IDENTITY OF THE ACCUSER AND EXPLOITING THE IDENTITY OF THE ACCUSED

The day after William Kennedy Smith was accused, he was in every tabloid and on every TV screen; he came into our supermarkets and our bedrooms—most people saw more of him than of their families. But the identity of his accuser was kept so secret that few men would recognize her if they met her in a bar tonight. The assumption is that the victim needs protection. But that's assuming she's the victim before the trial. If we know that, why have a trial? If a man is falsely accused, it is *he* who is victimized. Why are we protecting only her identity if the very purpose of a trial is to *determine* who is victimized, not to *assume* who is victimized?

In no other situation is the accuser's identity protected. If a man accused Jackie Kennedy Onassis of trying to murder him, would his identity be protected? To protect a woman and make millions of dollars of profit exposing the man leaves a man damaged for life even if he is found not guilty. Is this true? Well, *before* the Kennedy Smith trial, how would you have felt if your daughter called you and said she was dating a Kennedy—William Kennedy Smith? How would you feel now?

DOES THE LAW PROTECT THE MAN WHO IS RAPED BY A WOMAN?

ITEM. A female child-care worker acknowledges having a six-month sexual relationship with a 12-year-old boy under her care. She receives no prison term—not a single day. She is allowed to go free on probation, having to pay only $500 for the boy's counseling.[58]

The release of this female statutory rapist caused no uproar. This was in 1992—the same year that Mike Tyson received a six-year prison sentence.

CAN AN ADULT MAN BE RAPED BY A WOMAN?

We have already seen how when we allow men to define rape as unwanted sex—as women are allowed to do—that 94 percent of men said they had had unwanted sexual activity by the time they were in college.[59] But aside from the false accusation, there are other ways adult men can be raped by women.

Technical Rape

We often say a man can't be raped by a woman because a man needs an erection to have intercourse, and "any man who has an erection obviously 'wants it,' therefore that's not rape." The female equivalent of having an erection is being vaginally lubricated, but a man cannot defend against a rape charge by saying, "Yes, Your Honor, she did say 'no,' but she was lubricated, so obviously she wanted it and therefore it isn't rape."

Being erect—or being lubricated—is *often* a sign that a person is sexually excited. But not always. A man can have an erection in the middle of the night but be too exhausted to want sex. Should we allow sex with a baby because he has an erection?

Birth Control Rape

Perhaps the most frequent way men are raped by adult women might be called "birth control rape." If a man is considered a date rapist by a woman who consents at night but feels raped in the morning, then a man can feel raped by a woman who says she is on birth control at night and says she feels pregnant the next week. And if she says, "I'm going to have the child, like it or not," this rape of him imprisons him for a lifetime. The big difference is that the rape of him is sanctioned by law. To pay for the child, he is forced to take a job he likes less, often leading to greater stress and earlier death. A decision by her that involves him also involves his body. If it involves his body, it is also his business. If it violates his body without consent, it is rape.

WHEN MEN RAPE MEN, THERE'S STILL A VICTIM, BUT . . .

Most rapes of men occur in prison. But even outside of prison, about 9 percent of reported rapes are against men (probably mostly by men, but no one knows for sure).[60] Even rape outside of prison, then, is about as significant an issue for men as AIDS is for women—about 10 percent of the people dying of AIDS are women.[61] Do we hear more about men being raped or about women getting AIDS?

The real area of neglect, though, is the rape of men in prison. In part because of the trauma he experiences, and in part because a man raped in prison by another man is more likely to rape a woman when he gets out of prison.[62] The connection is depicted graphically in the film *American Me* (based on a true story). If we care about women being raped, then, we must know what happens to men in prison.

From the moment they are put in jail to await trial, innocent men, considered "fresh meat" by other inmates, are subject to rape. We tend to say to ourselves, "Well, it's *men* doing it to other men and, after all, they *are* in prison." But it doesn't make the man who is a rape victim feel better because he is raped by another man; or feel sexually secure after years of being labeled "gay" or "queer" by the men who raped him. Many of these men become "punks"—prison lingo for a sexual slave who is rented to other prisoners by the first person who raped him in exchange for drugs or other goods; many are gang-raped; and many are raped by a convict's fist or a broom handle being thrust into his anus until his anus is ripped apart.[63]

It appears that as many males might be raped in jails and prisons each year as females who are raped outside of prison.[64] We have not cared enough to study male rape in prison the way we have female rape outside prison, so we can project only from the most recent prison study of male rape—a 1982 study of a California prison. If the 14 percent projection is close to accurate, approximately one million males are raped each year in jails and prisons.[65] In contrast, approximately 120,000 women are subjected to rape or attempted rape outside of prison each year.[66]

If female prisoners were being raped with such frequency by female inmates,[67] we would quickly cite it as a violation of the Eighth Amendment to the Constitution forbidding "cruel and unusual punishment" and of the Thirteenth Amendment forbidding slavery ("punks"). We would demand a separate cell for each inmate, strict punishment for the perpetrators, the hiring of more prison guards, and the firing of prison guards who turned their backs on a raped female. Instead in many states, we spend twice as much on each woman in prison as on each man.[68] As more and more women are being sent to prison, we see more and more TV specials on the plight of women in prison. We do not yet understand that when we neglect men, we rape women.

SPOUSAL RAPE

ITEM. A husband and wife in Australia were making love (or so he thought) and she asked him to stop. The following morning she called the police and reported him as a rapist, claiming it took him thirty seconds to stop. He claims he stopped right away. He received four years in prison.[69]

Australian men responded by a typical burying of feelings (jokes about "the thirty-second rapist"), while Australian women's magazines continued their articles criticizing men for their fear of commitment.

ITEM. In the United States, William Hetherington puts it this way in a flyer appealing for a retrial:[70]

MY NAME IS WILLIAM HETHERINGTON. I am a man falsely accused, convicted, and IMPRISONED FOR 15 TO 30 YEARS for spousal rape. All I ask is a chance to be fairly heard in court. . . .

I WAS FALSELY ACCUSED AND CONVICTED OF RAPING MY WIFE after having normal marital relations. Neither force nor coercion was used or ever proved. Nor did personal injury occur. Her accusation was all that was needed to convict me and send me to prison.

MOTIVATION FOR THE RAPE ACCUSATION was to gain an advantage in a pending divorce action and to gain custody of our three children. They had been in my care for the previous three months as my wife had deserted our family.

This was the fourth time my wife had made this allegation. All other cases were dropped.

I COULD NOT HIRE A LAWYER OR INVESTIGATOR of my choice because my wife obtained an order in the divorce case freezing my assets. The criminal court judge refused to appoint a criminal defense attorney for me, stating I had assets even if I could not use them. I never even had an appeal because I must be found indigent to get a transcript.*

MY LIFE IS A NIGHTMARE. I have served 4 years in jail for the "crime" of having marital relations with my wife of 16 years and afterward accused of rape.

I ask for the right to legal counsel.

I ask for access to my assets to pay for legal fees.

I ask for regular visitation with my children.

---

* A transcript is needed to prove a mishandling of the trial and is thus a prerequisite for the appeal.

What the flyer did not mention was:

- Hetherington's wife made *all four* of the rape charges during times the couple was fighting over child custody.[71]
- The political dynamics: Hetherington's wife wanted to drop the case, but the prosecutor was running for reelection and the ACLU and feminist groups were pressing for conviction.[72]
- Because Hetherington had no prior convictions, state guidelines recommended a sentence of no more than ten years. The judge gave Hetherington fifteen to thirty.[73]

What has allowed spousal rape to become such an issue almost overnight after thousands of years of marriage? Spousal rape accusations are rife in countries in which divorce is rife—countries like Australia and Canada. Spousal rape legislation gives the woman a nuclear bomb. Most husbands realize that their careers could be ruined merely by having the accusation made public and their employer being afraid of headlines saying, "Pleasantville Teacher Accused of Rape."

As we have seen, both sexes have sex when they don't want to—even on the first date. But in a relationship this is especially true: **Both sexes engage in "mercy sex."** And that's the difference between having a relationship and not having a relationship—*all good relationships require "giving in,"* especially when our partner feels strongly. The *Ms.* survey can call it a rape; a relationships counselor will call it a relationship.

Spousal rape legislation is blackmail waiting to happen. If a man feels he needs to file for divorce, his wife can say, "If you do, I'll accuse you of spousal rape." Spousal rape legislation is worse than government-as-substitute-husband; it's government in the bedroom.

What, though, can be done? Should the law have any role?

TOWARD A SOLUTION

Criminalization

Can the Law Prevent Date Rape?

The law *can* prevent some date rapes. If a man can be put in jail for exerting emotional pressure, men will exert less of it; if a woman who is "under the influence" can yell rape the following morning, fewer men will buy women drinks, so there will be less sex, so there will be less unwanted sex. And a strict law will also prevent millions of men from asking women on dates to begin with for fear that a romantic evening might become a ruined life. Which will also prevent date rape: there can be no date rape if there is no date.

The law can prevent most anything—the question is, at what cost?

To go from Stage I's "male pursue/female resist" to the feminist "male pursue/female sue" is not a progression but a regression. Big Sister will leave America as impoverished emotionally as Big Brother left Soviet citizens impoverished economically.

A law can give us security—but the hope of a date is love. Love requires risks. As does the life in which we hope to share that love. A law that prevents risks prevents love.

If we choose to retain laws against date rape, the punishment must be made suitable to the crime, creating degrees for rape as we have for murder. If intercourse with a woman who made a choice to date, made a choice to drink, and made a choice to have oral sex (which both Tyson and Kennedy Smith claimed) is put in the same category as sex at knife point, we both trivialize rape and criminalize only the male portion of the male-female role.

And if we choose to retain laws against date rape, then **a false accusation of rape must subject the accuser to the same imprisonment a convicted rapist would receive.** In China false accusations of any crime are rare—if the accusation proves false, the accuser receives the punishment.

Finally, if we retain laws against date rape, then we must use DNA tests and lie-detector tests whenever possible; they must be monitored by a neutral party and given a second time when in doubt. Lie-detector tests are not perfect, but it usually takes special training to fool them—training few college students and date rape litigants have had. To eliminate them as one admissible piece of evidence is to eliminate the single biggest protection men have against their own lives being raped.

Ultimately, though, criminalization reflects the failure of prevention. So let's look at prevention.

Resocialization

The solution to all this is not criminalization but resocialization. The law cannot compete with nuance. Body language is more powerful than verbal language; and eyes that say "yes" speak louder than words that say "no." If the law tries to legislate our "yeses" and "noes" it will produce "the straitjacket generation"—a generation afraid to flirt, fearful of finding its love notes in a court suit. **Date rape legislation will force suitors and courting to give way to courts and suing.**

The empowerment of women lies not in the protection of females from date rape, but in resocializing both sexes to share date initiative taking and date paying so that both date rape and date fraud are minimized. We cannot end date rape by calling men "wimps" when they don't initiate quickly enough, "rapists" when they do it too quickly, and "jerks" when they do it badly. If we increase the performance pressure only for men, we will reinforce men's need to objectify women—which will lead to more rape. **Men will be our rapists as long as men are our initiators.** Increasing only men's responsibility does not create female equality, it perpetuates female entitlement.

Laws on date rape create a climate of date hate. Only communication will lead to love. So how do we replace criminalization with resocialization and legislation with communication? By teaching a new "relationship language."

FROM RAPE LANGUAGE TO RELATIONSHIP LANGUAGE: STAGE I TO STAGE II

Just as schools introduce students to Stage II technology by teaching computer language, schools must now introduce Stage II communication by teaching relationship language—teaching males and females to take responsibility for their verbal and nonverbal cues (including dress and makeup), what they attract, and how to change these cues to attract a better relationship. Let's look at how this might have prevented the date rape portrayed in the film *Thelma and Louise.*

Thelma wants to connect with a guy. So Stage II Relationship Language Training would have her make a decision about the type of guy she wants and the type of experience she wants to have with him. We find out in the film that while she definitely doesn't want to have her "noes" ignored, she is definitely open to having intercourse. So if she wants a reasonably sensitive but exciting lover, she might start by trying to find him at a supermarket squeezing cantaloupes rather than at a bar squeezing women.

Nevertheless, even in a bar, relationship language training would teach Thelma to look around for a man who was listening to a woman, not ignoring women's "noes." And if she didn't find such a man, to *leave* the bar (or stay, but just drink).

If she spotted such a man, Stage II Relationship Language Training resocializes Thelma to approach the man, start a conversation, and use her body language in such a way as to let him know she wasn't a game player or teaser. How? For example, by buying him a drink and asking him to dance. This communicates to him that *she* makes decisions. If he can't handle it, she weeds him out—why get involved with a man who can't handle a secure woman?

Contrast this to what Thelma actually did. She got drunk and approached no one. Instead she ultimately danced, kissed, and necked with the one man whom she and Louise had rejected about seven times—including Louise blowing smoke in his face and telling him to get lost. **She selected from the worst possible environment the worst possible man—the only man who had proven he couldn't and wouldn't take "no" for an answer.** Then, when she joins him in a dark parking lot and he persists after she says "no" to intercourse, we viewers are left with the image that men—*as a group*—are insensitive rapists. Rather than showing Thelma and Louise use relationship language training to control their own lives, they are portrayed as feminist heroines for their willingness to murder and commit suicide. To me this is both antimale and antifemale. To me it is more empowering to give women the tools to control their own lives rather than applaud them for killing men and committing suicide.

The most important part of Stage II Relationship Language Training is the training to take initiatives and therefore have "original choice power" rather than "veto power"—the more typical female power. But if a woman is still vetoing, she will at least learn to understand the subliminal messages different vetoes send. For example, when a man asks a woman for a drink and she says "no," then he risks rejection a second time and she says "no" again, but the third time she says "yes," **we have the beginning of their relationship language: the message she sends is that he must risk rejection three times before her "no" becomes a "yes."** If this language remains consistent between them, why should it change just prior to intercourse?

Relationship language training must also teach men to understand that (1) women who take initiatives are much less likely to be victims and blamers than women who do not initiate, (2) women who initiate are willing to take responsibility and risk rejection, and (3) these women are therefore the most likely to empathize with men since they share the male experience.

Boys must also be taught their investment in change. Which is considerable: Most guys would *love* a woman to ask him out, caress his body, and pick up the check. Reinforcing men's addiction to women's bodies and then depriving men of what they are addicted to only makes men feel *less than equal* to women. (Could that be why feminists are not suggesting a role reversal?)

Boys must learn that constantly risking rejection forces them to cut off their feelings. Parents must support programs to resocialize our daughters to share that responsibility with our sons. Which means parents must resocialize themselves so their children have good role models.

If we want to reduce rape, our laws need to require high school and college courses in gender transition and understanding the other sex. *Genderwise, the human race is in its adolescence.* It is in an awkward transition between Stage I and Stage II. And as in the normal male-female adolescence, the females have matured and the males still have pimples.

Resocialization requires teacher training to train the more mature female students to ask out the boys via in-class role playing and follow-up discussions. And to train the boys to appreciate what the less attractive girls have to offer, thus reducing boys' addiction to beauty and increasing boys' interest in girls' substance. In brief, we would train teachers to do role-reversal exercises so that even if the old roles remain, at least both sexes have learned to walk a mile in the other sex's moccasins.

If we give driving violators the option of retaking driver training, we can give first-time dating violators the option of taking courses on relationship training—courses they never had. When we resocialize women to share responsibility to risk the entire gamut of 150 risks of rejection (from eye contact to intercourse) *as often as men do*, we will be minimizing the male anger and powerlessness that lead to date rape and the female anger and powerlessness that lead to false accusations; they are the flip sides of the same coin.

Stage II relationship language training must teach both sexes to say "yes" to sex and both sexes to say "no." (Men have less permission to say "no" than women do: we don't question a woman's femininity when she doesn't want to be sexual; we do "wonder" about a man when he doesn't want to be sexual. We don't make her a sexual deviant; we do make him a sexual deviant.) Men will learn the importance of "no" to the degree that women learn to ask men who might not be interested in them.

There are no easy answers, but the answers we do develop cannot emerge from feminism-in-isolation but from both sexes helping each other reweave the tapestry that has been passed from one generation to the next over the centuries for purposes that were functional then but dysfunctional now.

CHAPTER 15

From Husband Sam to Uncle Sam: Government as Substitute Husband

TRUE OR FALSE? Employers are prohibited from practicing sex discrimination in hiring and promoting employees.[1]

ANSWER: False. The U.S. Supreme Court ruled in 1987 that in job areas dominated by men, *less* qualified women could be hired.[2] It did not allow less qualified men to be hired in areas dominated by women (e.g., elementary school teacher, nurse, secretary, cocktail waiting, restaurant host, office reception-ist, flight attendant). The law also *requires* sex discrimination in hiring by requiring quotas, requiring vigorous recruitment of women, and requiring all institutions that receive govern-ment aid to do a certain percentage of their business with female-owned (or minority-owned) businesses.

When an employer hires a woman today, he or she might be required to finance her pregnancy (the Federal Pregnancy Discrimination Act[3]), feel pressured to finance maternity leaves and get into the child-care business (incurring new real estate costs, higher insurance premiums, and the costs of hir-ing teachers and administrators for her children).

The Government as Substitute Husband did for women what labor unions still have not accomplished for men. And men pay dues for labor unions; the taxpayer pays the dues for feminism. Feminism and government soon became taxpayer-supported wom-en's unions.

THE COMPETITION TO SAVE THE WOMAN

Hundreds of federal programs subsidize "female-only clubs": clubs such as the "Women, Infants, and Children Club" (called the WIC program) but no "Men, Infants, and Children Club." Federal and state money subsidizes more than 15,000 women's studies courses versus 91 men's studies courses.[4] Almost every state government uses taxpayer money to form Women's Divisions with no parallel Men's Divisions.[5]

Feminist ideology, initially opposed to male-only clubs in the areas of male dominance, soon supported female-only clubs in areas of female dominance. Money to men was seen as taking money away from women. So while the Office of Family Planning initially provided family planning services for both sexes, by 1982, it provided money *only* for *female* clients.[6] This attitude pushed men out of the family. While male-only clubs in areas of male dominance were being declared illegal, female-only clubs in areas of female dominance were being subsidized.

In Canada, government support for women-only interests (as defined by feminists) is even more extreme: Canada's Department of Education helps fund the Canadian equivalent of the National Organization for Women[7] and every Canadian province has a Women's Directorate (Ontario's has a staff of fifty-one and a budget of $8 million per year).[8]

All this creates a huge taxpayer subsidy to look at virtually every aspect of life from the perspective of women as defined by feminism. Feminist ideology was soon called women's studies and the women's studies graduates called their ideology education. As thousands of women's jobs became dependent on a feminist perspective, feminism bureaucratized. Like communism, feminism went from being revolutionary to dictating politically correct ideology. And, like communism, this political correctness was supported most strongly in the universities.

ARE THE POLITICAL PARTIES KEEPING WOMEN DEPENDENT IN EXCHANGE FOR VOTES?

The political parties have become like two parents in a custody battle, each vying for their daughter's love by promising to do the most for her.

How destructive to women is this? We have restricted humans from giving "free" food to bears and dolphins because we know that such feeding would make them dependent and *lead to their extinction*. But when it comes to our own species, we have difficulty seeing the connection between short-term kindness and long-term cruelty: we give women money to have more children, making them more dependent with each child and discouraging them from developing the tools to fend for themselves. The real discrimination against women, then, is "free feeding."

Ironically, when political parties or parents compete for females' love by competing to give to it, the result is not gratitude but entitlement. And the result should *not* be gratitude, because **the political party, like the needy parent, becomes unconsciously dependent on keeping the female dependent.** Which turns the female into "the other"—the person given to, not the equal participant. In the process, it fails to do what is every parent's and every political party's job—to raise an adult, not maintain a child.

But here's the rub. When the entitled child has the majority of the votes, the issue is no longer whether we have a patriarchy or a matriarchy—we get a victimarchy. And the female-as-child *genuinely* feels like a victim because she never learns how to obtain for herself everything she learns to expect. Well, she learns how to obtain it for herself by saying "it's a woman's right"—but she doesn't feel the mastery that comes with a lifetime of doing it for herself. And even when a quota includes her in the decision-making process, she still feels angry at the "male-dominated government" because she feels both the condescension of being given "equality" and the contradiction of being given equality. She is still "the other." So, with the majority of the votes, she is both controlling the system and angry at the system.

While both parties are needy of the female vote, the Democratic party cannot live without it. So the Democratic party, in particular, keeps its child a child because it fears losing her. And the female in transition who wants the option of independence without losing the option of government as substitute protector keeps voting to keep its protector protecting.

In the meantime, many men's alienation from the Democratic party makes that party even more female dependent. As one voter put it:

My family and I are voters of the "traditional Democratic constituency" who have just become Republicans.

The Democratic party . . . has consistently:

—favored discrimination against men in employment, university admissions, divorce, and child custody.
—supported absurd laws (such as those on "marital rape" and "sexual harassment") which allow the conviction of innocent men on the sole basis of uncorroborated . . . accusations by women. . . .

The Democratic party seems intent on reducing American men to second-class citizens.[9]

—Eric D. Sherman

How the Law Allows Even Poor Women to Be Three-Option Women

We have seen how the income of a *middle-class* man provides a mother with three options (full-time work; full-time children; combination of both). But if the man is poor, it doesn't. So the *government* provides the woman with *more* than what a poor man provides—enough so that she "marries" the government rather than the poor man: the government becomes a substitute husband. The man who is poor becomes disposable.

The problem is not that women and children are fed, but that men are excluded from the lives of women and children. The lack of an MIC program (for *Men*, Infants, and Children) makes WIC a federally financed females-only club. (And every state supplements the federal money with state money.)

At least programs with names such as *Women*, Infants, and Children make the sexism apparent; names like Aid to *Families* with Dependent Children hide the sexism. Yet to receive AFDC—or numerous other awards to "families"—men must meet much more stringent standards than women. For example, the AFDC's "hundred hour rule"[10] allows a mother to work one hundred hours a month and still receive her aid money. But a father who works a hundred hours a month receives *no* aid money.[11] Even if a father is starting a new business and is *losing* money, he still gets no aid. In contrast, *if a mother is doing the same, she gets all her aid*. This obviously violates the Fourteenth Amendment's provision for all citizens to receive equal protection of the law. Yet no one challenges it.

Paying only the woman is the law's way of keeping a man who is without money "in his place"—out on the streets—until he becomes a wallet. If he fails, he remains on the streets; if he succeeds, he gets to compete with other men for a woman's love—and with AFDC and WIC. Of course, he must earn not only what AFDC and WIC pay her, but enough to also support himself.

We often hear that "the amount a woman receives on AFDC is hardly enough to support a family." True. No *one* government program provides the woman with more options than a lower-income male would provide. AFDC provides more than 10 million women with only $10 billion per year.[12] That alone does not provide enough for a family. But that doesn't include food stamps, Medicaid, subsidized housing, school lunch programs, WIC, or any undeclared under-the-table income.

The effect? A new nuclear family: woman, government, and child. The woman legally retains her three options until the child is 6. Then she can have another child and keep these options another six years. For the woman, there is no end. For the dad, there is no beginning.

In the black community especially, this reinforces the stereotype of the black man as one who has sex, deserts his responsibilities, and "returns only for more sex." **Many black men leave their family because they are financially responsible—not because they are emotionally irresponsible.** For many black men, leaving their source of love is painful. It is a sacrifice. Why have we chosen to view it *only* as irresponsibility? Many whites and many black females forget that a black man also yearns for stability and love.

In the meantime, a father's absence in the family is the single biggest predictor of a child's deterioration. Why? A father's absence appears to damage what might be called the child's "social immune system." When the child's social immune system is damaged, it is more vulnerable to drug abuse, delinquency, teen pregnancy, etc. Thus **when a government subsidy deprives the child of its dad and destroys the child's social immune system, the government is really subsidizing child abuse.** Which means *we* are subsidizing child abuse.

Why do we tolerate this? Our instinct to protect women from

immediate harm is stronger than our instinct to provide long-term protection to any given child. This derived from our Stage I survival heritage (if a woman survived, she could always have another child). Our laws evolved from that heritage, but Stage II survival depends on laws which allow children to have dads—and allow dads to have children. Why? The next generations' children will need that sense of stability and internal security to solve the world's problems with love rather than war.

DON'T FEMINISTS SUPPORT GOVERNMENT PROGRAMS BECAUSE THEY PROTECT CHILDREN . . . NOT WOMEN?

ITEM. The child was over three. The judge assessed that good baby-sitters were available, poverty was hurting the child, and the child would benefit if the mother worked.[13] The judge ruled the mother should work.

The feminist response to the judge's decision was that the mother's "right to choose" was being violated, not that the judge had wrongly assessed the best interests of the child. The mother's choice was considered primary; the best interests of the child secondary. Yet one rationale for a woman's "right to choose" in abortion cases has always been the importance of "a child having a decent life."

Since most tax money is paid by men, her "right to choose" is the choice to obligate mostly men to pay for her choice. When he adds this to his obligation to support his own wife and children, he is often forced to take a job he likes less because it pays more—which produces the stress that leads to his earlier death.

In essence, a woman's choice can kill a man. If it were only her body, it would be only her business, but his earlier death means his body is also at stake. And the child's life is at stake if it lives in poverty.

THE PSYCHOLOGY OF THE ENTITLED CHILD

When political parties are dependent on keeping woman-as-child, we encourage women to develop the psychology of the entitled child: an ever-sharper eye for seeing only the discrimination against her, not the discrimination *for* her. For example, feminists claimed that Social Security was discriminating against women because the average woman receives slightly less per month than the average man.[14] They neglected to mention that the average man pays in more per month.

They also neglected to mention the real discrimination: Men as a group pay *twice* what women pay into Social Security[15] but women receive more than 150 percent of what men receive in total retirement benefits from Social Security.[16] Men *as a group* also receive less than women in any given year. But no men's movement suggests that, as a result, men should be charged only about 33 percent of what women are charged for Social Security (because as a group they pay twice as much in and receive a third less).

By looking at everything from only the woman's perspective, here's what happened to pension plans and insurance premiums:

ITEM. Pension plans *used to* use mortality tables to rationalize paying women less money per month—otherwise women collected much more money given a retirement about twice as long as men's. The lower monthly payments were labeled discrimination against women and declared unconstitutional[17]; the higher lifetime payments to women were not labeled discrimination.

ITEM. Insurance companies use the same mortality tables to charge men higher monthly premiums than women because men die sooner and thus make fewer payments during their lifetime. Men's higher monthly payments have *not* been called discrimination against men; nor have they been declared unconstitutional. Men's lower lifetime reimbursements also have not been declared discrimination or unconstitutional.[18]

In brief, when women pay more, it is declared unnconstitutional; when men pay more, it is unnoticed. Sexual politics became constitutional politics.

REAL MEN DON'T SUE . . . THEY SUCCEED

Feminism introduced women not only to succeeding in the workplace but to suing the workplace—and in almost the same breath.

Men who succeeded rarely learned this one-two punch. When Thomas Watson, Sr., was fired from National Cash Register in 1914, he started a little company of his own. He called it IBM. When Henry Ford II fired Lee Iacocca from his job as president of Ford Motor Company, Ford told Iacocca, "I just don't *like* you."[19] Some feminists might have sued. Iacocca succeeded.

People who succeed rarely treat those who fire them as personal enemies. George Steinbrenner fired Billy Martin as manager of the New York Yankees even after Martin had won the pennant. Then he hired him back; then he fired him again; then he hired him back again, then fired him again—despite Martin's having won two pennants and a world championship in seven seasons. Had Martin turned Steinbrenner into an enemy rather than viewing him as playing a role, he would never have been able to be rehired.

This, of course, is not the attitude of all men, or only of men. It is the attitude of *people* who succeed—an attitude that says, "I am responsible for becoming a person who can bring a company profits." Successful employees make it in the company's *self*-interest to take care of them. They make it their responsibility to *take care of the company* so the company will take care of them (so they can take care of their families). They become "company nurturers" (in order to be family nurturers).

People who succeed do not expect every company to reward fairly; they *screen for* companies which will recognize their contribution. And if they aren't being recognized, they change employers, they don't sue employers.

People who succeed monetarily *and spiritually* don't think of men as being the sex that has the power as much as being the sex most willing to pay the price of power. They know there are few privileges without responsibilities and, if a responsibility doesn't give them some leverage for a privilege, they avoid it; they don't take it on and then gripe about it.

By giving women training to sue a company for a "hostile environment" if someone tells a dirty joke, we are training women to run to the Government as Substitute Husband (or Father). This gets companies to fear women, but not to respect women. The best preparation we can give women to succeed in the workplace is the preparation to overcome barriers rather than to sue: successful people don't sue, they succeed.

PART IV

WHERE DO WE GO FROM HERE?

Conclusion

The wound that unifies all men is the wound of their disposability. Their disposability as soldiers, workers, dads. The wound of believing that they are lovable if they kill and die so others might be saved and survive.

Stage II technology has *reversed* what humans need to do to survive. **Stage II societies created the technology for our species to survive without killing but also created the technology to end our species if we do kill.** We have responded by changing only what women do to survive. While we have used birth control, population growth, and technology to free women from female biology as female destiny, we have also used birth control and technology to create *female* biology as *male* destiny: she can choose to abort or to sue for support.

The freedom of women from biology as destiny has not freed men from male biology as male destiny. We have not demanded that both sexes equally share the hazardous jobs and the risks of dying. We are still socializing men to be our killers, and therefore unlovable . . . and therefore disposable.

Changing millions of years of genetic heritage will play many tricks on both sexes. Women will think that being divorced means they are independent even as they seek dependence on the government as substitute husband; men will think that they are helping to make women equal even as they are passing laws to protect women from a dirty joke rather than passing laws to protect themselves from dying on a construction site.

Ideally there should not be a men's movement but a gender transition movement; only the power of the women's movement necessitates the temporary corrective of a men's movement. And this creates a special challenge for men: **There are few political**

movements filled with healthy people, yet few healthy changes have occurred without political movements.

Whether or not a men's movement makes a genuine contribution will depend on its ability to communicate that all the world's evils are not men's responsibility: The origin of war was not men, it was survival. That men have never been their own commanders; the commander of men is the command to protect. That had men not protected, no one would be here asking for more rights. But that in the future, we cannot socialize a sex to be more willing to kill *for* us without producing a sex able to kill us; that we cannot socialize a sex to be more willing to die without producing a sex in denial—in denial of its self-esteem and its feelings. (We reinforce low male self-esteem by telling men they are the oppressors who cause war and therefore they *deserve* to be the only sex sent to war.)

With nuclear technology, the survival of the species is finally compatible with men demanding the socialization to love and be lovable. But men will not demand this until men see how the influences that make them disposable surround them in every direction from the outside and have infiltrated every cell of their insides—and how, by calling that disposability "power," they have accepted bribes to blind themselves to their powerlessness.

THE CLEAREST SIGN OF POWERLESSNESS

Subjection of a group of people to violence based on their membership in that group is a clear indicator of that group's powerlessness, be it Christians to lions or the underclass to war.

In the United States, we subject men to violence via law (the draft), via religion and custom (circumcision), via socialization and incentive (telling men who are best at bashing their heads against eleven other men that they have "scholarship potential"), via approval of beautiful women (cheerleaders cheering for men who play "Smash Face"), via parental approval and love (the parents who attend the Thanksgiving games at which their sons are battering each other), via taxpayer money (high school wrestling and football, ROTC, and the military), and via our entertainment dollar (boxing, football, ice hockey, rodeos, car racing, westerns, war movies . . .). But North Americans do refrain from subjecting men to violence via bullfights—we feel it's cruel to the bull. After we subject only our sons to this violence (before the age of consent), we blame them for growing into the more violent sex.

But here's the rub. When other groups are subjected to violence, we acknowledge their power*less*ness. What are the implications of calling men power*ful* when we subject men to violence? When we acknowledge a group's powerlessness, we acknowledge our obligation to help that group. With men, we blame the victim. **We blame men because we have camouflaged men's victimization by teaching men to also be the victimizer. Men's victimizer status camouflages men's victim status.**

With women, then, we often hear that the 50 percent of the population that is female lives in fear of the other 50 percent that is male because, for example, "We never know which man will be the rapist." We forget that men are statistically in much greater jeopardy of homicide and violence and, therefore, the 50 percent of the population that is male also fears most men because men are equally ignorant of which men will commit that violence.

Our understanding of only women's fears leads to public monies for female-only shelters and female-only psychological support. The higher taxes means that mostly white males take jobs they like less to earn more and die sooner to keep women alive longer.

The practical result is not only that women live longer, but that white women live the longest, black women second, white men third, black men fourth. In the industrialized world, men are the new "niggers"; black men are "niggers' niggers." This result helps us see a different relationship between the civil rights movement and the women's movement. . . .

THE FALSE PARALLEL BETWEEN THE CIVIL RIGHTS MOVEMENT AND THE WOMEN'S MOVEMENT

One of the underlying mistakes of the past quarter century was taking the gains of the civil rights movement and passing them on to women as if women had served as men's slaves and were now entitled to those rights just as blacks had served as whites' slaves and were now entitled to those rights. This both encouraged an ideology of female-as-victim and blinded us to how the underlying issue between men and women was not the *dominance* of *one* sex over the other, but the *subservience* of *both* sexes to the real master—the survival needs of the next generation.

In race relationships, one race's gain was often another's loss. In male-female relationships, when either sex wins, both sexes lose. When an individual woman benefits from affirmative action for a promotion, the wife and children of the man she defeats lose the benefits of that promotion. Which is why one sex having privileged opportunity is an inferior solution to equal opportunity.

The old belief that men have the power and women are powerless leads predictably to a battle between the sexes. How? The perception of women as powerless makes us fear limiting the expansion of women's power. **Fear of limiting the power of the sex with the greater spending power, the greater beauty power, the greater sexual power, the greater net worth among its heads of households, and the greater options in marriage, children, work, and life creates the corruptness of absolute power which will ultimately lead to a much bloodier battle between the sexes.**

In contrast, the new Stage I-II framework leads to understanding between the sexes—to understanding how just as the number of children a mother raised was a sign of the amount of obligation a woman undertook (not the amount of power she had), so the number of dollars a father raised was a sign of the amount of obligation he undertook to feed those children. It leads us to understanding how each sex had more rights and more power in the area in which it had more responsibilities; how each sex dominated in the area in which it was most likely to die; how each sex paid the other for performing its role; *how both sexes paid a price for the price they were paid.*

The Stage I-II framework, by not denying either sex's power or burdens, frees us to move from a battle between the sexes to love between the sexes; from a women's movement to a gender transition movement.

How do we make that transition?

THE STAGE II JOURNEY

We start by questioning even the best of what was functional in Stage I. For example, the hero's journey described so eloquently by Joseph Campbell was, nevertheless, a Stage I journey. And its rituals were Stage I rituals. **Both the journey and the rituals were the Stage I man's boot camp for male disposability.** The label "hero" was the bribe of appreciation given by the protected to get the protector to risk his life. Appreciation kept the slave a slave. Thus, as we saw, the very word *hero* derived from the words *servant, slave,* and *protector.*

In Stage I, we needed rituals of structure to prepare for the rigid roles that were necessary for survival; in Stage II, we need rituals of choice to prepare for changing roles that are now necessary for survival. In Stage I, it was dysfunctional for men to be in touch with their feelings; in Stage II, it is dysfunctional for men to *not* be in touch with their feelings. In Stage I, we claimed that men or women who made their own needs secondary to role expectations had high self-esteem; in Stage II, self-esteem involves knowing how to negotiate a balance between the needs of others and the needs of self. In Stage I, Superman detected the external earthquake and prevented it from destroying the life of the woman he loved; the Stage II superman detects the earthquake inside himself and uses his findings to communicate with the woman (or man) he loves. In Stage I, sacrificing for survival was both a means and an end; in Stage II, sacrificing for survival is a means to a different end—the end that Joseph Campbell called "following one's bliss."

Men have the next layer of work to do because, as we have seen, the process of succeeding enough so a woman had time to make her Stage II journey was exactly the process that kept men Stage I men. His income gave her the luxury to contemplate what she didn't like about herself *and him.* But he felt in a Catch-22: he feared that if he lost the success that freed her, she'd leave him; yet he also feared that if he stayed focused on being successful, she'd leave him.

The implication? Unless both sexes take the Stage II journey simultaneously, we will tend to produce Stage II *individuals* (usually women), but not Stage II *relationships.* We will suffer another lonely "me" generation. A Stage II woman and man, then, must first discover who they want to be, and then negotiate a transition with their family.

A Stage II journey cannot toss out survival skills with the bath water. Instead it gives *both* sexes survival skills *and* self-actualization skills. Is the current men's movement the beginning of men developing both sets of skills, as women have already begun to do?

Is the Mythopoetic Men's Movement Making a Positive Contribution?

The men's movement that has caught the public eye (the mythopoetic movement led by Robert Bly) has helped men enter the Stage II journey by discovering what men never gave themselves permission to have in Stage I: vulnerability, intimacy, self-determination and, therefore, real power. Beginning this exploration with drumming is appropriate because it helps men to emote. Beginning it in the woods is useful because men need to begin by looking within (not blaming) and in isolation from females, children, parents, work—all those to whose expectations men conformed before giving themselves permission to ask whom they really wanted to become and how they wanted to get there.

Men's gatherings are an important conduit into Stage II because **Stage I men never learned to share their fears with those who share their fears.** Which is why men at these gatherings have developed rituals using a Talking Stick—a stick wrapped in a vine similar to the caduceus, the ancient medical symbol—to symbolize healing. Why? Talking about feelings is healing; and feeling heard heals even more.

The Talking Stick symbolizes men's intuitive sense that for a man to ask women and children to listen to his doubts about being their wallets is like IBM expecting its employees to listen lovingly while it decides whether it should continue producing computers. Men are learning that putting all their emotional eggs in the basket of women and children helps neither women nor men.

Many women worry that when men get away for weekends by themselves, the men will gather together and blame women. Not to worry. **Men were socialized to save women, not blame women.** All-male sports did not teach a losing team to blame the other—or even to try to get the other team to change. To men, self-improvement and strength do not imply blaming men *or* women, but especially not blaming women.

The Stage II journey begins for men by appreciating the Stage I hero's journey—how its structure, discipline, and ritual helped the man overcome obstacles, protect women, and sustain survival. Calling the weekends Wild Man and Warrior are part of that acknowledgment.

Why is the acknowledgment necessary? Perhaps it isn't, but

humans tend to start the process of change by acknowledging themselves—thus blacks asserted black pride and black is beautiful; women declared "I am woman, I am strong"; men are saying "I am man, I am okay." After a quarter of a century of male bashing, that's not a bad start.

Why has the male sacrifice been more structured, disciplined, and ritualized? Since a social role is more optional than a biological role, male socialization had to be especially strong to transform a self-centered male infant into a self-sacrificing male adult who would die so others could live. Stage II male socialization therefore requires an especially strong confrontation of men's propensity to protect women—it requires confronting the four incentives to protect women that are used in Stage I societies to get men to call it "glory" to die. The four incentives men must confront are:

1. The social reinforcement to men's addiction to female beauty and sex
2. Deprivation of the beautiful woman and sex with her until the man guarantees economic security in return
3. Status, praise, and other "bribes" in exchange for protecting women, especially if he risks his life or dies doing it, and
4. The combination of ritual and religion (e.g., circumcision) that desensitizes men to pain, and music and religion (e.g., "The Battle Hymn of the Republic") to stimulate men to endure pain

How do we prepare the next generation to negotiate these changes? The top priority is modeling these changes ourselves. But a second priority is working with the school system. . . .

RESOCIALIZING THE STAGE II CHILD

The Male Teacher

The Stage II elementary school needs to have more male teachers than female teachers in districts in which the preschool children are exposed more to mothers than fathers.

The male teachers need to be men who understand the value of risk taking, even if the child fails or gets hurt and humiliated once in a while; who understands the value of a child being held on his lap and is willing to stand up for that value to a community over-anxious to call him a molester; who can take a drug dealer and help him or her understand how to translate the entrepreneurial skills of drug dealing into the entrepreneurial skills needed to run a business; who understands that we protect our children more in life by not overprotecting them in school; who understands that when we protect our children in school we are usually just protecting ourselves from accusations by one or two parents which we fear will threaten our job.

The Journey of the Stage II Adolescent

At all ages, the Stage II journey involves rituals of options.

Imagine a Stage II video game for adolescents called "The First Date." Sometimes an identical choice ("Kiss Her") creates one outcome (passion), sometimes another (rejection). The game allows both sexes to experiment with new roles before they try them out in the real world.

A Stage II school balances messages of sexual caution with messages of sexual joy. It doesn't turn sex into discussions of only safe sex, AIDS, herpes, rubbers, sexual abuse, date rape, stranger rape, harassment, power, and violence and *then tell the boy to take all the initiatives*. Discussion of sex in school has become like buying a cheap hamburger: "Where's the joy?"

Courtship rituals might include an adolescent boy being his girlfriend's servant one weekend and being served by his girlfriend the next; cooking for her the first Saturday of each month, having her cook for him the third; taking her to a restaurant for a candlelit dinner, being taken by her. . . . When they are older, they might choose more traditional roles, but at least it will be out of choice, not out of fear of peer disapproval or not knowing how to cook.

A Stage II school not only requires team sports for both sexes but uses the period after the game to understand the learning experiences of the game ("How does my unwillingness to pass the ball off relate to my larger life?"). Alternative sports like flag football and rotation baseball (each player at a different position each inning) are part of the school curriculum. This does not mean that football, even in its one-sex, smash-face form, cannot be financed *privately;* it does imply not financing it publicly. **Male child abuse might be fun to watch, but taxpayers should not be required to pay for it.**

Stage I sports was designed to build *defenses against* the outside world, so "our team good, their team bad" was understandable. Stage II sports is designed to prepare us for *trade with* the outside world—for a global economy in which we are all part of the same team. Stage II sports help us to rejoice in someone else's special competence rather than be jealous of it.

The Stage II school system will help the student understand why individual sports and team sports lead to different life journeys. If Jane focuses exclusively on gymnastics, she learns little about how to negotiate with her peers. And if Dick focuses only on team sports, he has not necessarily prepared himself to be a good self-starter or a good creative thinker—skills needed to start one's own business, be a writer, artist, or an intellectual who thinks for her- or himself (rather than worrying about being politically correct).

The Stage II male-female journey involves both sexes learning from the male heritage of risk taking and the female heritage of caution; from the male heritage of learning not to limit oneself for fear of a broken bone and the female heritage of not having to prove oneself by breaking one's bones.

The Journey of the Stage II Family

Because Stage II individuals can live without each other, their union is one of choice, not survival. Choice is a more fragile unifier than the need to survive. Yet most everyone wants both choice and stability. So Stage II rituals must celebrate both choice and continuity. For example, as a child moves out of the house, *the family might conduct a remarriage ritual to recognize its new family form, celebrating both the change and the continuity.*

These changes require changes in consciousness, which implies activism and politics.

WILL THE MEN'S MOVEMENT BECOME POLITICAL AND ACTIVIST?

The men's movement is a misnomer. It is neither political like the civil rights movement nor activist like the women's movement.

—*TIME*, JULY 8, 1991[1]

Within the next ten years, *Time* magazine will doubtless eat those words. Why? First, political structures are formed and forming. Second, the political agendas are concrete. Third, men's emotional and economic pain is significant enough to motivate change.

First, the political structures. The National Congress for Men and Children and the National Coalition of Free Men have for years been consciously focusing on issues like fathers having access to their children after divorce and joint custody. The media often portrays these men as focusing on "father's rights," but these dads could just as easily be portrayed as focusing on loving children. The pain among these men emanates from dealing with the law when they want to be dealing with love.

The mythopoetic men's movement is just on the verge of developing political consciousness. Its political consciousness is evolving more unconsciously, from the men's personal discoveries. During the men's weekends, many men explore what might be called "the two Fs"—fathering and feelings. But as men discover they have been deprived *of* their fathers, they start asking if they are also being deprived of *being* fathers. And as men start seeing that *other* men have shared *their* personal experience, they slowly discover that the personal is political. This leads to fathers discovering their first right.

A father's first right—fathering (sharing child care while his wife does her financial share)—requires renegotiating. Renegotiating requires men to speak up. That's where the search for the second F—feelings—comes in.

Until now, men invested all of their emotional eggs in the basket of the women they loved. So they feared speaking up for fear of losing their only source of emotional support. As men's weekends provide an alternate source of emotional support, men gain the courage to say what they feel without fear of emotional isolation. Although some women find this new male courage threatening, others find it appealing. Many couples find it breathes life into a relationship dying of boredom.

But do men really want a change—do they want more time with their children? We have seen that almost 90 percent of men say that *full-time* involvement with their children would be their *preference* for between six months and a year if they knew they wouldn't be hurting their family economically and they knew their wife approved.

What are the implications of men becoming more fully invested in their children? Fathers and children who feel more loved and loving. And this has political implications: fathers will protest when judges assume a child is its mother's first, its father's second. Politically, fathers will seek to remove judges who award more than 60 percent of contested custody cases to either sex.

Once a man allows himself to love a child deeply, he wants the right to love equally. He realizes that **when a woman and he have created a pregnancy, the issue is not the rights of the female versus the fetus, but the rights of the female, the fetus, and the father.** He realizes that a woman who says, "It's my body, it's my business," and then chooses to have a child that she makes him pay for forces him to take a job he might like less just because it pays more; forces him to stress himself out and die early—and forces him to use his body for eighteen years. If it's his body being used for eighteen years, and his body dying sooner, shouldn't it be his business, too? Isn't two decades of a man's life worth nine months of a woman's?

The issues of fathering and feelings are emerging from one portion of the political structure. But nothing affects men's powerlessness more than the issues of disposability. Here is a concrete agenda for dealing with male disposability.

The Ten "Glass Cellars" of Male Disposability

Just as women identified the "glass ceilings" which they believed prevented equality of opportunity, ten "glass cellars" might be thought of as creating men's inequality of disposability. Instead of addressing these issues with the help of an Equal Employment Opportunity Commission (EEOC), men need to be developing an Equal Life Opportunity Commission (ELOC). Men's issues are issues of life and death. The concrete agenda of an ELOC? For starters, to eradicate these ten glass cellars:

Suicide. If a man is ten times as likely to commit suicide after the death of a spouse,[2] then the ELOC has a mission to develop special outreach programs when a man's spouse dies. On a deeper level, if boys commit suicide 25,000 percent more as their sex roles become apparent,[3] maybe we should be changing the male role *before* it becomes apparent.

Prisoners. If an ELOC stops the rapes of men and boys in prison, fewer men will rape when out of prison. If imprisoned mothers are softened by contact with their children, wouldn't imprisoned fathers be?

Homelessness. An ELOC would discover what leads to men becoming about 85 percent of our street homeless,[4] and develop intervention programs before male hopelessness becomes male homelessness.

Death Professions. Socialization for the death professions starts at an early age. An ELOC can provide grants to train mentor teachers to resocialize boys to not have to pay for girls at an early age in preparation for taking hazardous jobs that earn more at a later age.

Disease. The ELOC's mandate would include research and early detection education to prevent men from dying earlier of all fifteen of the major diseases and causes of accidents.

Assassinations and Hostage-taking. An Equal Life Amendment implies foreign policy considerations. How should the United States respond to Saddam Hussein's releasing only women and children? Or to our taxpayer money financing the assassination of foreign leaders? Would we have allowed our government to make repeated attempts to kill Castro were Castro a woman?

Executions. We give women the death penalty but in the final analysis, we execute only men. If we executed only women, would there be a protest?

Draft. An Equal Life Amendment would acknowledge male-only draft registration as slave registration. An Office of Equal Male Life might organize a class-action suit on behalf of men who were drafted and are now psychologically handicapped. It would pressure the government to end the cover-up concerning MIAs and POWs—all members of the disposable sex.

Combat. An ELOC would be certain that both sexes were about equally subjected to direct combat obligations and that failure to be so exposed would result in decreased benefits.

Early Deaths. An ELOC's mandate would also include discovering nondisease factors that lead to men's early death—the pressure to perform, pay, and pursue, the loneliness, risks of rejection, lack of support.

We can think of every boy as being assessed at birth a 10 percent male disposability tax—symbolizing his 10 percent shorter life expectancy. Were men to create the equivalent of an Equal Rights Amendment to symbolically confront their disposability, it might be called an Equal Life Amendment. In reality, it would be nothing more than an Equal Rights *and Responsibilities* Amendment, since if men and women had equal rights and responsibilities, they would approach a much more equal life expectancy.*

THE EQUAL RIGHTS AND RESPONSIBILITIES AMENDMENT

An Equal Rights and Responsibilities Amendment (ERRA) would outlaw male-only responsibility for draft registration; it would prevent men in the armed services from being required to enter combat (if needed) unless women were also required to enter combat (if needed); it would permit community property only in conjunction with community responsibility; it would give incentives to schools to educate females to be equally responsible for taking sexual initiatives and risking sexual rejection rather than lecturing only males on how not to do it wrong; it would replace discussions of sexual harassment in the workplace with discussions of how both sexes make sexual contact in the workplace.

An ERRA would allow affirmative action programs for recruitment and training of the underrepresented sex in a given profession, but not for the hiring of less qualified members of that sex; it would deprive congressional districts of AFDC funding if judges assigned the children to women more than 60 percent of the time in cases of contested custody; it would deprive universities of public monies as long as there were significantly more women's studies courses than men's studies courses; it would deprive TV stations of federal licensing if the FCC found a consistent pattern of male-bashing or consistent attention to women's issues and neglect of men's issues. The ERRA would mean a *new* era—an era of shared rights and shared responsibilities, meaning shared perspectives rather than opposite sexes.

---

* If we adhere to the equal protection clause of the Fourteenth Amendment, then the constitutional equivalent of an Equal Rights Amendment already exists: inequality of rights protects the sexes unequally and is therefore unconstitutional. Although the ERA does have symbolic value, if it is to symbolize genuine equality, it needs to be an Equal Rights *and Responsibilities* Amendment.

But are men (and ideally women) motivated to make this happen?

WHAT EXACTLY DOES IT TAKE TO MAKE A MOVEMENT?

Major movements have two core stimuli: (1) *emotional rejection;* and (2) *economic hurt*. **When a large number of people feel emotionally rejected and economically hurt at the same moment in history, a revolution is in the making.**

For example, when blacks were told to "sit in the back of the bus," they experienced emotional rejection; when they also faced job discrimination, they experienced economic hurt. When it happened to large numbers, it created political possibilities. We then had the bases for the civil rights movement.

Similarly, when millions of *women* simultaneously experienced divorce (emotional rejection) and job discrimination (economic hurt), we had the political, emotional, and economic bases on which to build the women's movement.

Like women, men experience emotional rejection if they divorce; but unlike women, men are much more likely to be involuntarily deprived of their children, thus experiencing a double dose of emotional rejection. Many men feel unloved and unneeded by anyone after divorce, which is why men commit suicide more than women after they divorce. When, on top of this, men are told to pay money for what they're deprived of (children and wife), they simultaneously experience economic hurt.

Fathers today are often being taxed for their children without equal representation in their children's lives. They are experiencing their version of "Taxation Without Representation." It is the *simultaneous* experience of this by millions of fathers that creates the men's movement's political base; it is their emotional rejection that creates its emotional base; their economic hurt that creates its economic base. Which is why the next stage of the men's movement will be both political and activist.

If we ignore these men's activists or dismiss them as crazy, angry, or bitter, we miss the life experience of millions of other fathers who are either too afraid to speak up or so busy producing money to support their "ex" and their children that they don't have time to speak up. If we force these activists to become strident to be heard in the process of achieving equity, many of these men will be wasted, their children damaged, and upcoming generations will be provided with another distorted version of love. If, on the other hand, we hear men, we can minimize gender war and maximize gender love.

If this seems scary, don't worry; it won't happen overnight. We're not talking about just a priority shift but an evolutionary shift.

THE MEN'S MOVEMENT AS EVOLUTIONARY SHIFT

The men's movement will be the longest of all movements because it is not proposing merely to integrate blacks or Hispanics *into* a system that already exists, it is proposing an evolutionary shift in the system itself—an end to "'woman the protected" and "man the protector." This division is rooted in our biology; it exists among animals.

The men's movement will be the most incremental of movements because it is hard to confront the feelings we've learned to repress and hard to confront the women we've learned to protect. And it is especially hard to risk alienating our only source of love.

What will be the men's movement's greatest day-to-day challenge? Getting men to ask for help *for themselves*. Movements make gains by asking for help for themselves. Men were always able to ask for help *on behalf of others*—for a congregation, their wives, children, or a cause—*but not for themselves*. Why not? **For thousands of years, complaining was functional for women—it attracted a protector; complaining was dysfunctional for men —it attracted nobody.** Women avoided men who complained and selected for men who were responsive to *women's* pleas for help. So asking for help for themselves will be the biggest challenge and the catalyst to any evolutionary shift.

Part of the women's movement has already initiated that evolutionary shift—the part that says, "I, woman, must take responsibility for what occurs in my life"; that says, "Don't kill your husband if he's abusing you, walk away"; the part that encourages women, "Pick up his dinner check as often as he picks up yours"; the part that says, "Don't 'marry up,' depend on yourself"; the part that empowers women to the point of being willing to consider a loving man "eligible" even if he expects *her* to financially support *him* while he nurtures her. This part of the women's movement is the Division of *Adult* Feminism.

Another part of the women's movement reinforces age-old patterns—the part that wants combat rights but not combat obligations; that speaks of the "glass ceiling," but not the "glass cellar"; that wants government protection for battered women but denies even the existence of battered men; the part that neglects to encourage women to feel as comfortable "marrying down" and financially supporting a man to be the dad as "marrying up" and having a man support her to be the mom. This part only reinforces women's genetic heritage—find a hero, marry him, depend on him; *or* divorce him and get the government to play substitute husband. It reinforces women discovering a variety of ways to be victim in order to find a variety of ways to be saved. This part of the women's movement is the Division of *Adolescent* Feminism.

For women, complaining and asking to be saved was a necessary part of their Stage I role of protecting children. For men, asking for help is useful only in Stage II. **Complaining and asking for help, then, are not evolutionary shifts for women; complaining and asking for help are evolutionary shifts for men.**

Men will learn to ask for help when we help men understand it is the *in*ability to ask for help that is weakness. Men must gather a new strength—the strength to fight the only world war in which the fodder is feelings, be strong enough to find these feelings and courageous enough to risk the loss of superficial love to create deeper love.

If a men's movement really does create an evolutionary shift, though, it must go beyond being gifted of the mouth and retarded of the ear. We must help both sexes tune each other in as we would the Discovery Channel rather than tune each other out as we would in a "Battle of the Sexes"; to respect that our socialization is as difficult to remove as is syrup from a pancake, and that sometimes the best way we can show our caring is not by solving someone's problem but by acknowledging and sharing.

OUR STAGE II CHALLENGE

The challenge of *The Myth of Male Power*, then, is to care enough about men to spend as much of the next quarter century helping men become Stage II men as we did the last quarter century helping women become Stage II women; to move toward equality of obligation for the death professions and combat roles, not just the "pick-and-choose liberation" of female opportunity when desired; to cease expecting men to earn more money than a woman before they are "eligible" and then calling the expectation "power," "patriarchy," "dominance," or "sexism" rather than "pressure" and "obligation"; to develop affirmative action-type outreach programs for men until men and women have the same life expectancy; to give men special outlets and special incentives to express their feelings and perspectives until men commit suicide no more frequently than women; to confront our monetary incentives to keep men disposable rather than pay, for example, what it would cost to have a house built half by female construction workers; to monitor media sexism that defines relationship issues disproportionately from the female perspective in books, magazines, newspapers, talk shows, and sit-coms; to care as much about battered husbands as battered wives; to acknowledge the working dad as much as we acknowledge the working mom; to give fathers as much right to their children as we do mothers; to not stop merely with caring as much about saving males as saving whales, but to stop only when we care as much about saving males as saving females; to go beyond woman as sex objects and men as success objects to both sexes as objects of love.

Notes

Introduction

1. Phrase credited to attorney Ronald K. Henry.

Chapter 1
Is Male Power Really a Myth? A First Glance

1. Lawrence Diggs, *Transitions*, Nov./Dec. 1990, p. 10.
2. The Battle of the Somme was in 1916. British casualties were 420,000; French were 195,000; German were 650,000. See John Laffin, *Brassey's Battles: 3,500 Years of Conflict, Campaigns, and Wars from A-Z* (London: A. Wheaton & Co., 1986), p. 399.
3. 1920 statistics from the National Center for Health Statistics, *Monthly Vital Statistics Report*, vol. 38, no. 5, supplement, September 26, 1989, p. 4. In 1920, the life expectancy for men was 53.6 years; for women, 54.6 years.
4. Ibid., vol. 39, no. 13, August 28, 1991, p. 17. In 1990, women's average length of life was 78.8 years; men's, 72.0.
5. Ibid., vol. 38, no. 5, op. cit.
6. Ibid. The exact life span difference is 6.9 years between men and women. The life span for white females is 78.9; for black females, 73.6; for white males, 72.2; and for black males, 65.2.
7. U.S. Bureau of Health and Human Services, National Center for Health Statistics (hereinafter USBH&HS/NCHS), *Vital Statistics of the United States* (Washington, D.C.: USGPO, 1991), vol. 2, part A, "Mortality," p. 51, tables 1–9, "Death Rates for 72 Selected Causes by 5-Year Age Groups, Race, and Sex: U.S., 1988." The exact rates are:

Suicide Rates by Age and Sex per 100,000 Population

Age	Male	Female
5–9	0.1	0.0
10–14	2.1	0.8
15–19	18.0	4.4
20–24	25.8	4.1

8. The 25,000 percent figure is derived by comparing the 0.1 suicides per 100,000 boys under the age of nine to the 25.8 suicides per 100,000 boys between ages 20–24 in the table in the endnote above, from ibid.

9. Latest data available as of 1992. From USBH&HS/NCHS, *Vital Statistics of the United States*, vol. 2, "Mortality," part A, 1987.

10. Among those over the age of 65, 2.7 women per 1,000 and 6.2 men per 1,000 are victims of crimes of violence. U.S. Bureau of Justice Statistics, Office of Justice Programs, Bureau of Justice Statistics, *Criminal Victimization in the United States, 1988*, National Crime Survey Report NCJ-122024, December 1990, p. 18, table 5.

11. Ibid., *1987*, publication NCJ-115524, June, 1989, p. 16, table 3, "Personal Crimes, 1987."

12. Ibid.

13. "7 Deadly Days," *Time*, July 17, 1989, p. 31.

14. These are the latest data available (as of 1992). It is from U.S. Department of Commerce, Bureau of the Census, *Statistical Abstracts of the US, 1989*, 109th edition, p. 459, table 747—"Household Net Worth—Median Value of Holdings: 1984." Their source is U.S. Department of Commerce, Bureau of the Census, *Current Population Reports*, ser. P–70, no. 7. Since women's income has *increased* relative to men's since 1985, the gap is likely to be even greater when the next data are released. The Census Bureau defines head of household (or householder) as any person in whose name a home is owned or rented. Prior to 1980, this used to be the husband in married couple households. Now it is either the husband or wife, doubtless more often still the husband in homes where the man is earning *more*.

15. The wealthiest women's net worth averages $1.17 million; the wealthiest men's averages $1.11 million. Based on the latest data available from the Internal Revenue Service as of 1990. See the *Los Angeles Times*, August 23, 1990.

16. Jacque Lynn Foltyn, "Feminine Beauty in American Culture" (Ph.D. diss., University of California at San Diego, 1987). Foltyn measured floor space of departments offering male versus female items in shopping malls and boutiques, on the assumption that if women's departments were not creating enough profit per square foot, they would be forced to give way to men's or general departments. Foltyn found seven times as much floor space was devoted to female personal items as to male personal items. She also found the more valuable floor space was devoted to women's items (e.g., perfume counters immediately as we enter a department store).

17. See Diane Crispell, "The Brave New World," *American Demographic*, January 1992, p. 38. The article concludes that women dominate consumer spending in personal items, cleaning supplies and housewares, and food. In the category of furniture/cars, it is close to even—men have only a technical dominance.

18. A. C. Nielsen ratings, 1984.

19. Harry F. Waters, "Whip Me, Beat Me, and Give Me Great Ratings," *Newsweek*, November 11, 1991.

20. This is based on my own informal discussions with waiters in restaurants around the country in cities where I speak.
21. Also, 86 percent of engineering *graduates* are men; 83 percent of art history graduates are women. Unpublished information, U.S. Department of Education, Office of Educational Research and Improvement, National Center for Education Statistics, "IPEDS Completions Study," 1989, 1990. Interview on June 1, 1992, with Norman Brandt of the U.S. Office of Education.
22. The starting salary for a female engineer exceeds that for a man by $571 per year. See the Engineering Manpower Commission's *Women in Engineering* (Washington, D.C.: American Association of Engineering Society [AAES]), EMC Bulletin no. 99, December 1989, table 5.
23. Sonni Efron, "Honey, I Shrunk the Nest Egg," *Los Angeles Times*, June 20, 1992, front page.
24. In an interview on February 11, 1992, John Oddison of the government's United States Fire Administration reported that *99 percent of volunteer municipal firefighters are men.* Of all municipal firefighters, 964,000 are volunteers and 240,000 are career.
25. F. Thomas Juster and Frank P. Stafford, "The Allocation of Time: Empirical Findings, Behavioral Models, and Problems of Measurement," *Journal of Economic Literature*, vol. 29, June 1991, p. 477. Her average hours both inside and outside the home add up to fifty-six; his, to sixty-one.
26. Martha Hill, *Patterns of Time Use in Time, Goods, and Well-Being* (Ann Arbor: Institute for Social Research, University of Michigan, 1985), ed. F. Thomas Juster and Frank P. Stafford. See also Joseph H. Pleck, *Working Wives/Working Husbands* (Beverly Hills: Sage Publications, 1985), p. 41, table 2.3.
27. Carol J. Castañeda, *San Diego Union*, May 21, 1988.
28. Frederic Hayward, "The Male's Unpaid Role: Bodyguard and Protector," as reprinted in Francis Baumli, Ph.D., *Men Freeing Men* (Jersey City, N.J.: New Atlantis Press, 1985), p. 238.
29. Naomi Weisstein, "Women as Nigger," *Psychology Today*, vol. 3, no. 5, October, 1969, p. 20. This article is considered a classic of feminist literature. See, for example, Wendy Martin, *The American Sisterhood: Writings of the Feminist Movement from Colonial Times to the Present* (New York: Harper & Row, 1972), pp. 292–98.
30. Credit to Lawrence Diggs for some of these ideas related to symbols of deference, contained in his audiotape called "Introduction to Men's Issues" (P.O. Box 41, Roslyn, SD 57261).
31. U.S. Department of Education, National Center for Education Statistics, *Digest of Education Statistics 1991*, p. 167, table 161, "Total Enrollment in Institutions of Higher Education" shows that women are 54 percent of those enrolled in college; p. 234, table 228, "Earned Degrees Conferred by Institutions of Higher Education," shows that women are 55 percent of those receiving bachelors' degrees from college.
32. Women who are heads of households have a net worth 141 percent greater than that of men who are heads of households. This is the latest data available

from the Bureau of the Census as of 1992. See U.S. Department of Commerce, Bureau of the Census, *Statistical Abstracts of the US, 1989*, op. cit.

33. A. C. Nielsen ratings, 1984.

34. Interview, February 18, 1985, with John Markert, independent researcher and contributor to *Romantic Times* and author of "Marketing Love," dissertation in progress.

35. *Forbes* reports that the average romance novel buyer spent $1,200 in 1991. The average romance costs about $5 in 1991, leading to the purchase of approximately 240 books a year, or 20 books per month. For women who also read their friends' books, the number of books they read is more than 20 per month; for women who do not do this but buy some hardcovers, the figure is less than 20 per month. See Dana Wechsler Linden and Matt Rees, "I'm hungry. But not for food," *Forbes*, July 6, 1992, pp. 70–75.

CHAPTER 2
Stage I to Stage II: How Successful Men Freed Women (But Forgot to Free Themselves)

1. Joseph Stein, *Fiddler on the Roof* (New York: Crown, 1964), based on stories by Sholom Aleichem. Musical score by Jerry Bock; lyrics by Sheldon Harnick.

2. Herbert Hildebrandt, Edwin Miller, and Dee Edington, "The Newly Promoted Executive" (monograph, University of Michigan, Graduate School of Business Administration, Ann Arbor, 1987).

3. The Equal Pay Act of 1963 is part of U.S. Code, Title XXIX. Also, Title VII of the Civil Rights Act of 1964 forbids discrimination in employment on the basis of sex.

4. See Jessie Bernard, *The Future of Marriage* (New York: World Publishing, 1972), table 20, "Some Selected Socio-Economic Variables Among Never-Married White Men and Women 45–54 Years of Age." Bernard cites the U.S. Department of Commerce, Bureau of the Census, *1960: Marital Status*, tables 4, 5, and 6.

5. In 1920, life expectancy for women was 54.6 years. In 1990, it was 78.8 years. This is an increase of 44.3 percent. In 1920, the life expectancy for men was 53.6 years. In 1990, the life expectancy for men was 72.0 years. This is an increase of 34.3 percent. The 1920 statistics are from the National Center for Health Statistics, *Monthly Vital Statistics Report*, vol. 38, no. 5, supplement, September 26, 1989, p. 4. The 1990 statistics are from the National Center for Health Statistics, *Monthly Vital Statistics Report*, vol. 39, no. 13, August 28, 1991, p. 17.

6. This view is frequently aired by feminist historians like Bonnie S. Anderson and Judith P. Zinsser in their *A History of Their Own* (New York: Perennial Library, 1989), p. 413, by feminist politicians like Congresswoman Patricia Schroeder, and by feminist leaders like Gloria Steinem.

7. Paul Brodeur, *Zapping of America* (New York: W. W. Norton, 1977), p. 177.

8. Sixty-four percent of working women leave the workforce for six months or longer to take care of the family; 1.5 percent of men do. U.S. Department of

Commerce, Bureau of the Census, *Current Population Reports*, ser. P–23, no. 136, "Life-time Work Experience and Its Effect on Earnings," 1984, p. 6, table A, "Work Interruption History, by Race, Spanish Origin and Selected Characteristics: Males," and p. 7, table B, "Work Interruption History, by Race, Spanish Origin and Selected Characteristics: Females." As of 1992, these are the latest available data on workplace leave. Interview with Jack McNeil, Bureau of the Census, July 22, 1992.

9. I polled a meeting of the American Subcontractors Association in San Diego on May 1, 1992.

10. See table 7.3 of Martha Hill, *Patterns of Time Use in Time, Goods, and Well-Being* (Ann Arbor: University of Michigan, Institute for Social Research, 1985), ed. by F. Thomas Juster and Frank P. Stafford. The University of Michigan's Survey Research Center data incorporated the second job into the "hours worked" statistics and found a more than nine-hour difference. (The Bureau of Labor Statistics data do not incorporate the second job data and come up with a just-over-four-hour difference for the first job.) *Un*married men also work nine hours more in the workplace than unmarried women, but this sample grouped full-time, part-time, and nonworkers together. Interview with Martha Hill, May 13, 1991.

11. I have completed the research on these variables, and they are being prepared for my next book, on women's versus men's desire for equality.

12. F. Thomas Juster and Frank P. Stafford, "The Allocation of Time: Empirical Findings, Behavioral Models, and Problems Measurement," *Journal of Economic Literature*, vol. 29, no. 2, June 1991, p. 477.

13. Ibid.

14. The study was by Lenore J. Weitzman, *The Divorce Revolution* (New York: The Free Press, 1985). Weitzman looked only at the first year after divorce— when women earned less and men earned more—rather than at the second year after divorce and beyond during which the average woman's income is equal to or greater than her income at the time of divorce. See Greg J. Duncan and Saul D. Hoffman, "Economic Consequences of Marital Instability," figure 14.3 and table 14.A.8 in *Horizontal Equity, Uncertainty, and Economic Well-Being* (Chicago: University of Chicago Press, 1985), ed. by Martin David and Timothy Smeeding. See also Susan Faludi, *Backlash: The Undeclared War Against American Woman* (New York: Crown, 1991), pp. 19–25, 26.

15. While this practice was common around the world, it is depicted beautifully in the Irish film *Playboys* (1992).

CHAPTER 3
Are "Power," "Patriarchy," "Dominance," and "Sexism" Actually Code Words for Male Disposability?

1. Lisa Tuttle, *Encyclopedia of Feminism* (New York: Facts on File Publications, 1986), p. 242.

2. See Edith Hamilton, *Mythology* (New York: Little, Brown, 1940), p. 290. These myths grew out of rituals in which males were sacrificed to the moon

goddess; see Robert Graves, *The Greek Myths*, vol. 1 (New York: George Braziller, 1959), p. 285.

3. The sons were Cleobis and Biton.

4. Hera was married to Zeus, the king of the gods. See Thomas Bullfinch, *Bullfinch's Mythology* (New York: Avenal Books, 1978), p. 6; and Edith Hamilton, op. cit., p. 28.

5. Related by Robert Bly during a breakfast discussion on February 16, 1992, in Minneapolis.

6. The root of the word "hero" is *ser-ow*. In Greek, the connotation was "protector." The Latin root word for "protector" is *servare*. From the same root word family comes the word *servire*, meaning "slave," from which we get our word "serve." See Julius Pokorny, *Indogermanisches Etymologisches Wörterbuch* (Bern: Francke, 1959); or, for slightly easier reading, *The American Heritage Dictionary of the English Language* (New York: American Heritage Publishing Co. and Houghton Mifflin, 1969), p. 1538.

7. *Encyclopaedia Britannica*, Macropaedia, vol. 18, 15th ed. (Chicago: Encyclopaedia Britannica, 1980), p. 650.

8. Marjorie Rowling, *Everyday Life in Medieval Times* (New York: Dorsett Press, 1968), p. 186.

9. Daniel Ediger, *The Well of Sacrifice* (Garden City, N.Y.: Doubleday, 1971), p. 22.

10. Joseph R. Conlin, *The American Past* (New York: Harcourt, Brace, Jovanovich, 1984), p. 367.

11. Gold was $20 per ounce in 1860 and approximately $360 per ounce today.

12. Albert Burton Moore, Ph.D., *Conscription and Conflict in the Confederacy* (New York: Hillary House Publishers, 1963).

13. The minimum estimate of the number wounded is 471,427, for a minimum total casualty figure of 1,094,453. See E. B. Long, *The Civil War: Day by Day* (New York: Doubleday, 1971), pp. 710–11.

14. Moore, op. cit., p. 32.

15. Ken Burns, *The Civil War* (Alexandria, Va.: PBS Video, 1990), a video recording produced by Florentine Films. The series aired on PBS in 1990 and 1991.

16. Gloria Steinem's best-selling *Revolution from Within* (New York: Little, Brown, 1991) claims that low self-esteem is much more a woman's problem than a man's.

17. Two such examples in English are Klaus Theweleit, *Male Fantasies* (Minneapolis, Minn.: University of Minnesota Press, 1987), vol. 1; and Barbara Ehrenreich, "Iranscam: The Real Meaning of Oliver North," *Ms.*, May 1987.

18. This is an eastern Cherokee parable. The chief can also be thought of as the center of the pond, worshiped because it provided shelter and a podium for food. Credit to Dr. Glenn Solomon of the University of Oklahoma for telling me of its origin.

19. Study conducted for the National Institute of Mental Health by Dr. Mary P. Koss, University of Arizona. Cited in Gerald Eskenazi, "When Athletic Aggression Turns into Sexual Assault," *The New York Times*, June 3, 1990, p. 30.

20. Colin Turnbull, *Mountain People* (New York: Simon & Schuster, 1972), p. 105.
21. Conlin, op. cit., pp. 244–45.
22. Joseph Campbell, *The Power of Myth* (New York: Doubleday, 1988), p. 8.
23. Rosemary Romberg, *Circumcision: The Painful Dilemma* (South Hadley, Mass.: Bergin & Garvey Publishers, 1985), p. 43.
24. Will Durant, *The Story of Civilization III: Caesar and Christ* (New York: Simon & Schuster, 1939), pp. 385–86.
25. Ibid., p. 381.
26. Ibid., p. 388.
27. See David D. Gilmore, *Manhood in the Making* (New Haven: Yale University Press, 1990), p. 206 (Tahitians) and pp. 209–10 (Semai). Concerning the Minoans on Crete, their peaceful period came during that period in which they were both isolated from attack and politically unified (around 2000 B.C.). In a small geographical area, political unification is necessary for peace, otherwise there is fear of attack from neighboring tribes. "Isolation from attack" can also occur from being able to run fast enough to escape it. For example, forest nomads such as the Akuriyo, discovered in the late 1960s in southeastern Surinam, and the Heta, discovered in the 1950s in southern Brazil, were peaceful. Information concerning the Minoans and the forest nomads comes from an interview on November 10, 1992, with Robert Carneiro, curator of anthropology, American Museum of Natural History.
28. Riane Eisler, *The Chalice and the Blade* (Cambridge, Mass.: Harper & Row, 1987), p. xvi.
29. The Roman king was Prasutagus, whose widow sent the men to their deaths during the first-century Roman invasion of Iceni. See Antonia Fraser, *Boadicea's Chariot: The Warrior Queens* (London: Weidenfeld & Nicolson, 1988). For many additional examples, see Jean Bethke Elshtain, *Women and War* (New York: Basic Books, 1987).
30. If creating and protecting children were so important, why did some societies like the Spartans give children no rights (e.g., leaving the weak on a lonely mountain to perish from exposure) while other societies, such as the Jews, focused almost all their laws and traditions around respect for the child? The Spartans believed that strength required selecting the strong by weeding out the weak, whereas the Jews saw in children "the Messiahs of mankind," the "perennial regenerative force," and an opportunity to make good the mistakes of the past because "in the child, God continually gives mankind a chance to make good its mistakes." Cited in *The Pentateuch and Haftorahs*, 2d ed. (London: Soncino Press, 1979), ed. by Dr. J. H. Hertz, C.H., Late Chief Rabbi of the British Empire, p. 54.
31. J. T. Hooker, *The Ancient Spartans* (London: J. M. Dent, 1980), p. 137; and L. F. Fitzhardinge, *The Spartans* (London: Thames & Hudson, 1980), p. 9 and p. 162. Sparta had "a constitution, a military organization, and a set of social institutions enforced by a system of education which controlled every male from seven to sixty" (Fitzhardinge, p. 9). The rigid system is called "the agoge" (Fitzhardinge, p. 162).
32. The altar was the altar of Artemis Orthia. See Plutarch *Lycurgus* 18 as cited

in Arnold Hugh Martin Jones (L.L.D., D.D.), *Sparta* (Oxford: Blackwell & Mott, 1967), p. 35.

33. James D. DeMeo, Ph.D., "The Geography of Female Genital Mutilations (part 3: Desertification and the Origins of Armoring: The Saharasian Connection)," *Journal of Orgonomy*, vol. 24, no. 2, 1990, pp. 233–39.

34. Anne G. Ward, et al., *The Quest for Theseus* (New York: Praeger, 1970), pp. 7–9.

35. Bullfinch, op. cit., pp. 152–53.

36. Campbell, Joseph, and Bill Moyers, *The Power of Myth* (New York: Doubleday, 1988).

37. Genesis 30:3, *The Holy Bible*, New International Version (Grand Rapids, Mich.: Zondervan Bible Publishers, 1978).

38. Ibid., Genesis 30:28–29.

39. First-cousin incest was not a violation of ancient Jewish law, only of modern law.

40. *The Pentateuch and Haftorahs*, op. cit., p. 5. "This is the first precept (mitzvah) given to man. The duty of building a home and rearing a family figures in the rabbinic Codes as the first of 613 Mitzvoth (Commandments) of the Torah."

41. Ibid.

42. Credit to Lionel Tiger for the thought about genes being nature's marketing tool.

43. Genesis 19:31, *Holy Bible*, op. cit.

44. Ibid., Genesis 19:33.

45. The name Moab "is explained as though it were the equivalent of me-ab, 'from father.' " See *The Pentateuch and Haftorahs*, op. cit., p. 69.

46. Rosalind Miles, *The Women's History of the World* (New York: Perennial Library, 1990), p. 94.

47. Helen E. Fisher, "The Four-Year Itch: Do Divorce Patterns Reflect Our Evolutionary Heritage?" *Natural History*, October 1987, p. 22.

48. See Joan Haslip, *Catherine the Great: A Biography* (New York: Putnam, 1977); and Michael Grant, *Cleopatra* (New York: Simon & Schuster, 1972).

49. David Howarth, *Tahiti* (New York: Viking Press, 1983), pp. 32–33.

50. Ibid.

51. Ian Campbell, *Lost Paradise* (London: Century Hutchinson, 1987), p. 36.

52. "Preserve the Mystery . . . Make Love the Old-Fashioned Way. Make Him Earn It," *Cosmopolitan*, September 1984, front cover.

53. I document this sequence in chapter 8 ("Why Did the Sexual Revolution Come and Go So Quickly?") of *Why Men Are the Way They Are* (New York: Berkley, 1988).

54. Concerning the man going to prison for the woman's crime, see *Calvin Bradley* v. *the State*, 156, Mississippi, 1824, in R. J. Walker, *Reports of Case Adjudged in the Supreme Court of Mississippi* (St. Paul, Minn.: West Publishing, 1910), p. 73, section 157. Concerning the man going to prison for the family's debt, see Nicole Hahn Rafter, *Partial Justice: Women in State Prisons, 1800–1935* (Boston: Northeastern University Press, 1985), p. 10. In 1830, only ninety-seven women were imprisoned for all crimes put together in the seven most populous states of the United States.

55. Bernard Bailyn, *Voyagers to the West: A Passage in the Peopling of America on the Eve of the Revolution* (New York: Knopf, 1986), p. 177. The study was based on the most common group of indentured servants—the English.

56. Rowling, op. cit., p. 33.

57. Tuttle, op. cit., p. 242.

58. Karen L. Michaelson and contributors, *Childbirth in America: Anthropological Perspectives* (South Hadley, Mass.: Bergin & Garvey Publishers, 1988), p. 2.

59. *Encyclopedia Americana* (Danbury, Conn.: Grolier, 1989), vol. 24, p. 146.

60. Sally Smith Booth, *The Witches of Early America* (New York: Hastings House, 1975), pp. 87–107.

61. Ibid.

62. Philip W. Sergeant, *Witches and Warlocks* (London: Hutchinson & Co., 1974), p. 12.

63. Arno Karlen, *Sexuality and Homosexuality* (NY: W. W. Norton, 1971), p. 128.

64. *Oxford English Dictionary* (Oxford: Clarendon Press, 1989), 2d ed., pp. 663–64.

65. Karlen, op. cit., p. 128.

66. See A. L. Rowse, *Homosexuals in History* (New York: Dorset Press, 1983).

67. *The Concise Columbia Dictionary of Quotations* (New York: Columbia University Press, 1987), p. 113.

68. See "bheu-" (root word of "husband")—from Pokorny, op. cit., p. 126. Cited in *The American Heritage Dictionary*, op. cit., p. 643 (word definition) and p. 1509 (root definition).

69. "Husband" derives from ON "bondi," meaning "the male of the pair of lower animals; a male kept for breeding" or "one who tills and cultivates the soil." See *The Compact Edition of the Oxford English Dictionary* (London: Oxford University Press, 1971), p. 1352.

70. Jim Kohl, unpublished manuscript "Human Sexuality: Past, Present, and Future."

71. This understanding is compatible with the modifications of Darwinian theory developed by selection theorists. See discussions of Theodosius Dobzhansky, Ernst Mayr, G. G. Simpson, and G. L. Stebbins in Jacques Ruffie, *The Population Alternative* (New York: Pantheon, 1986).

CHAPTER 4
The Death Professions: "My Body, *Not* My Choice"

1. I think the source here is yours truly. (In the late 1960s, when I began speaking in this area, I used to say this. Although I've checked a dozen books of quotations and I believe I created this, I wouldn't bet my life on it!)

2. Les Krantz, editor, *The Jobs Related Almanac* (New York: Ballantine Books, 1989).

3. U.S. Department of Labor, Bureau of Labor Statistics (hereinafter USBLS), *Employment and Earnings, 1988 Annual Averages*, January 1989, p. 187,

table 22, "Employed Civilians by Detailed Occupation, Sex, Race, and Hispanic Origin."

4. The Vietnam comparison comes from the eight plus years of the Vietnam War divided into the 58,000 deaths, or 7,250 men killed each year, versus 6,600 deaths of men each year in the workplace. Source: U.S. Department of Health and Human Services, The National Institute for Occupational Safety and Health (NIOSH), 1989 data (latest available as of 1992).

5. This figure relates to deaths from job-related injuries, not dying of a disease that may or may not be related to work. Source: U.S. Department of Health and Human Services, NIOSH (Morgantown, West Va.), on-line database titled "Basic Information on Workplace Safety and Health in the U.S.," latest information available as of July 1992.

6. The fatality rate for U.S. workers is .105 per 1,000,000 "man-hours" worked. The equivalent Japanese rate is .030. See *1988 Yearbook of Labour Statistics*, International Labour Office, Geneva, Switzerland.

7. NIOSH estimates the annual U.S. workplace fatality rate at between 7,000 and 11,000 lives lost. The National Safe Workplace Institute estimates that if the U.S. had the same job fatality rate as Japan, it would have lost only 2,565 lives rather than an estimated 9,000. Since 94 percent are men, 6,049 men and 386 women unnecessarily lose their lives each year. The National Safe Workplace Institute data are from *Basic Information on Workplace Safety and Health in the U.S., 1992* (Chicago: National Safe Workplace Institute, 1992), p. 6, table 1–8, "Lives Saved if the U.S. had the Same Occupational Fatality Rate as Other Industrialized Nations."

8. The number of job safety inspectors, both state and federal, is 2,000, according to the Occupation Safety and Hazards Administration (OSHA); the number of fish and wildlife inspectors, both state and federal, is 12,000, according to the Wildlife Management Institute in Washington, D.C. See *Basic Information*, ibid., p. 17, tables 3–5.

  On the federal level, OSHA has only 1,100 inspectors for 6 million work places. See A. V. Westin, executive producer, "Working in America: Hazardous Duty," ABC News, airdate April 20, 1989. (Transcript #Burn 6 from Journal Graphics, 267 Broadway, New York, NY 10007.)

9. See Westin, Ibid.

10. Ibid.

11. USBLS, *Employment and Earnings: January 1991*, p. 185, table 22. Within each of the hazardous occupations the safer, nonproduction jobs have higher percentages of women. The media will sometimes report a higher percentage of women in any given *industry*, but their figures often include secretaries and executives, which would account for the difference.

12. In coal mining, for example, there are 11.6 percent women in the safer, nonproduction jobs (secretaries, executives), but only 2.8 percent women in the less safe, production jobs (like mining itself). See the *Coal Chronicle*, "Coal Miner Statistics," vol. 2, no. 9, January 1992, p. 22.

13. The data on the garbage collectors is from H. G. Reza, "Hidden Dangers Are a Daily Part of Job for Trash Collectors," *Los Angeles Times*, April 3, 1989.

14. Ibid.
15. USBLS, *Employment and Earnings*, p. 187, table 22, "Employed Civilians by Detailed Occupation, Sex, Race, and Hispanic Origin."
16. Ann Landers, *Los Angeles Times*, May 5, 1989.
17. See Bob Sipchen, "Hazardous Duty," *Los Angeles Times*, March 7, 1989.
18. Ibid.
19. May 1987 to May 1988. For the disability, movement, and 40 percent figures, see the Associated Press description of the OSHA suit against John Morrell and Co. as reported in the *San Diego Union*, November 24, 1988. See also U.S. Department of Health, NIOSH, "Hazard Evaluation and Technical Assistance (HETA) Report #88–180," Evaluation of John Morrell and Co., South Dakota (Ohio: NIOSH, April 1989).
20. An interview with Dan Haybes of NIOSH revealed that almost 90 percent of the highest-risk jobs were held by men. In recent studies focusing more on the hazards to women, as in NIOSH's 1991 study of Shop Right Supermarkets (where there were a higher percentage of women), *none* of the jobs was ranked "high risk."
21. In 1991, 14,000 agricultural workers were killed on the job, a rate of 44 per 100,000. Unpublished data, made available in interview with Alan Hoskin, Department of Statistics, National Safety Council, June 26, 1992.
22. Jill A. Swanson, M.D., et al., "Accidental Farm Injuries in Children," *American Journal of Diseases of Children*, December 1987, vol. 141, p. 1277.
23. USBLS, *Employment and Earnings, 1988 Annual Averages*, op. cit. (Derived from percentages of heavy and light truckers.)
24. Maria Cone and Chuck Cook, "Deadly Smoke: A Special Report," *Orange County Register*, December 1983.
25. National Bureau of Health Statistics, "Mortality and Incidence Studies of Firefighters in Los Angeles, Toronto, and Boston," 1983. See also ibid. Interestingly, despite the seriousness of the problem, there has not been a more recent study done (as of 1992).
26. International Association of Fire Fighters, *1987 Death and Injury Survey* (Washington, D.C.: IAFF, 1987).
27. International Association of Fire Fighters, *1990 Death and Injury Survey* (Washington, D.C.: IAFF, 1990), p. 8.
28. Ibid., p. 7.
29. In an interview on February 11, 1992, John Oddison of the United States Fire Administration, a governmental agency, reported 964,000 volunteer municipal firemen; 240,000 career firemen.
30. My friend is Steve Collins, Ph.D., a geologist who also is to be credited for all the examples of the uses of coal and petroleum in everyday life.
31. Interview on June 30, 1992, with Con Dougherty, public information officer, Drug Enforcement Administration, Washington, D.C. Since 1921, thirty-nine agents have been killed—all men. The injury data are available only up to 1989. The distribution of injuries between 1985 and 1989 between women and men in the past five years is as follows:

Year	Men	Women
1985	145	1
1986	184	0
1987	425	8
1988	414	14
1989	193	7

32. Paul Dean, "A Shadow World of Life and Death," *Los Angeles Times*, February 23, 1988.
33. Ibid. In his article, Paul Dean cites Robert Bryden, training director, DEA Academy, Quantico, Virginia, who is quoted in *Insight* magazine, January 1988.
34. Dean, op. cit.
35. See Jacqueline Bernard, "A Meeting of the (Women) Miners," gazette section, *Ms.*, November 1979, p. 33. See also *Ms.*, June 1981, p. 55.
36. *Jobs Related Almanac*, op. cit.
37. Paul Muni's 1932 movie *I Am a Fugitive from a Chain Gang* sparked some of these protests.
38. "All Things Considered," National Public Radio, November 25, 1991.
39. Gordon Terroux, acting area director for OSHA, as quoted in Mike Anton in the *Rocky Mountain News*, September 27, 1987.
40. Bob Baker, "Death on the Job—a Lifework," *Los Angeles Times*, April 28, 1990. The National Safe Workplace Institute is in Chicago.
41. Baker, op. cit. Only recently has Gerard Scannell, a worker safety advocate, taken over the OSHA and begun reinforcing guidelines with fines that do not make it pay to disobey, and instituting changes (such as an Office of Construction) to monitor the building industry.
42. Tamar Lewin, "Pregnancy and Work Risks Posing 'Fuzzy' Legal Arena," *The New York Times*, August 2, 1988.
43. T. M. Schnorr, B. A. Grajewski, R. W. Nornung, M. J. Thun, G. M. Egeland, W. E. Murray, D. L. Conover, and W. E. Halperin, "Video Display Terminals and the Risk of Spontaneous Abortion," *New England Journal of Medicine*, March 14, 1991, pp. 727–33.

CHAPTER 5
War Hero or War Slave?: The Armed Prostitute

1. See U.S. Department of Commerce, Bureau of the Census, *Statistical Abstract of United States: 1991*, 111th ed., p. 348, table 571, "Living Veterans—States and Other Areas: 1980 to 1988"; and p. 342, table 555, "Summary of Active and Reserve Military Personnel and Forces: 1989 to 1991." As of 1991, 27,279,000 American men are veterans. Since the male population of the United States is 92,840,000, more than 29 percent of all men are veterans. There are an *additional* 2,130,000 full-time, active-duty military personnel, 88.3 percent of whom are men (1,880,790 men). Male veterans and active-

duty military personnel total 29,159,790, or 31.4 percent of all American men over 18.

2. The Battle of the Somme River was from June 24 to November 18, 1916. On July 1 alone, Britain suffered 57,450 casualties, including 20,000 dead. Overall, British casualties were 420,000; French were 195,000; German were 650,000. See John Laffin, *Brassey's Battles: 3,500 Years of Conflict, Campaigns, and Wars from A–Z* (London: A. Wheaton & Co., 1986), p. 399.

3. Susan Goldberg and Michael Lewis, "Play Behavior in the Year-Old Infant: Early Sex Differences," *Child Development*, vol. 40, no. 1, March 1969, p. 29.

4. Statement made in 1986 before the Defense Advisory Committee on Women in the Services. Quote was confirmed in an interview May 26, 1992, with Kay Leisz, Weinberger's executive assistant.

5. U.S. Congress, Senate, Committee on the Judiciary United States Senate, *Nomination of Sandra Day O'Connor*, Report no. J-97-51, 97th Cong., 1st sess., 1982, p. 127–28.

6. Scott Harris, "In Service Family, a Woman Dies," *Los Angeles Times*, March 1, 1991. Comments of Adrienne Lynette Mitchell's father, after her death in the Persian Gulf War.

7. Richard Halloran, "Military Women: Increasingly Indispensable," *The New York Times*, March 13, 1988, p. E-5.

8. The army and the navy have divided their combat positions into dangerous versus less dangerous positions, with women eligible only for the less dangerous positions. For example, in the army, P-1 positions are positions requiring offensive attack, the ones most likely to result in death and injury; P-2 positions place people in a generalized combat zone, not the offensive, and therefore leave them much less vulnerable.

   The air force is by far the safest of the services. Virtually all of the air force positions are the equivalent of P-2 in terms of vulnerability and therefore women are allowed in all of the air force combat positions. Information obtained from interviews on July 14 and 17, 1992, with Maggie Waleland, head of the Presidential Commission on the Assignment of Women in the Armed Forces, and Capt. Jeff Smith, a Fellow of the Presidential Commission, considered the expert on these matters.

9. Michael Gordon, "Woman Leads GIs in Combat in Panama, in a 'First' for Army," *The New York Times*, January 4, 1990, front page.

10. Ibid.

11. As chair of the House Armed Services Subcommittee on military installations, Congresswoman Schroeder knew women served in Military Police Units, which meant that women, as a rule, performed support functions (e.g., directing traffic). Although vulnerable to being shot, they were kept away from dangerous areas as much as possible.

    The breakdown of men versus women killed is from Harold Heilsnis, Office of Assistant Secretary of Defense, Public Affairs.

12. Interview July 17, 1992, with Janna Simms, public affairs officer, U.S. Department of Defense, Office of Public Affairs.

13. "Desert Shield/Desert Storm," *Fact Sheet*, Department of Defense, Office of Public Affairs, December 19, 1991. Of the 536 people killed in the Persian

Gulf, 15 were women (4 killed in action, 11 killed in accidents) and 521 were men (142 killed in action, 379 killed in accidents).

14. "Women in the Military," *Fact Sheet*, Department of Defense, Office of Public Affairs, January 30, 1991.

15. "Questions and Answers on Women Supporting Desert Shield," Department of Defense, Office of Public Affairs, January 30, 1991.

16. Bob Secter, "The Draft: If There's a War, There's a Way," *Los Angeles Times*, January 3, 1991, pp. E-1 & E-5.

17. The estimate is that of the deputy director of the Selective Service System's Regional Headquarters in Illinois, U.S. Air Force Lieutenant Colonel Ronald Meilstrup.

18. Secter, op. cit.

19. Credit for "If there's a war, there's a way" to Bob Secter, op. cit.

20. Michael Herr, *Dispatches* (New York: First Vintage International, 1991), p. 134.

21. Bruce Gilkin, "To Hell and (Almost) Back: A Vietnam Veteran's Struggle with Posttraumatic Stress," *Men's Health*, summer 1988, p. 44.

22. Letters to the Editor, *Transitions*, May/June 1991, p. 2. The physician explained in the full letter that he or she needed to withhold his or her name because it was so politically incorrect to discuss these issues.

23. Lieutenant Roberta Spillane, USN, "Women in Ships: Can We Survive?" *Proceedings* (of the U.S. Naval Institute), July 1987, p. 44. The exact quote concerning the *Acadia* is: "One West Coast based tender reported that more than 40 percent of her female nonrated seamen became pregnant *during workup for deployment* [emphasis supplied]—and no replacements were authorized."

24. Account based on story by David Fairbank White , "The Men Who Saved the Stark," *Parade*, February 12, 1989.

25. From a 1978 study, "The Khaki-Collared Women of Company C," by Michael Rustad, Wellesley College Center for Women, unpublished. It concerns problems of sex integration in the U.S. Signal Corps. Cited in Virginia Adams, "Jane Crow in the Army—Obstacles to Sexual Integration," *Psychology Today*, October 1980.

26. "Evaluation of Women in the Army" (1977) is a study done by the Army Administration Center at Fort Benjamin Harrison, Indiana. Army personnel, following a research design by psychologist James Sampson, sent questionnaires to 7,751 soldiers and confirmed the prevalence of negative attitudes. Cited in *Psychology Today*, op. cit.

27. From Rustad, op. cit., as cited in *Psychology Today*, op. cit.

28. *Psychology Today*, op. cit.

29. "Women reported for sick call an average of 6.8 times per female cadet, compared to the male average of 1.7 times." Brian Mitchell, *Weak Link: The Feminization of the American Military* (Washington, D.C.: Regnery Gateway, 1989), p. 69.

30. The marine boot camp was in Parris Island, South Carolina. See Melinda Beck, "Women in the Armed Forces," *Newsweek*, February 18, 1980, p. 36.

31. Stanley K. Ridgley, "The Mythical Military Woman," *The* (Raleigh, N.C.)

News & Observer, July 28, 1991, p. 7-J. Both Stanley Ridgley and his wife served as U.S. Army officers.

32. Ibid.

33. Military Selective Service Act. See "Privacy Act Statement," SSS Form 1, Registration Form, September 1987.

34. Ibid.

35. Massachusetts, Illinois, North Carolina, Florida, Tennessee, Louisiana, Mississippi, and Georgia are among the states to require a man to register for the draft before he can attend a state school. Cited in Jim Schwartz, College Press Service, 1986.

36. The Supreme Court ruled that drafting only men was constitutional as long as only men were being prepared for combat. But it has never been confronted with a challenge as to the constitutionality of giving men combat obligations while women get combat options. Justice William Rehnquist explained for the majority: "The purpose of registration was to prepare for a draft of combat troops. Since women are excluded from combat, Congress concluded that they would not be needed in the event of a draft and, therefore, decided not to register them." The case is *Rostker* v. *Goldberg*, June 25, 1981, *United States Reports*, vol. 453, Henry C. Lind, Reporter of Decisions (Washington, D.C.: USGPO, 1983).

   Statutes prohibit the navy from putting females into direct (as opposed to indirect [P-21]) combat, while service regulations preclude the army and Marine Corps from using them in direct capacity.

37. Julian Isherwood, *Armed Forces Journal*, July 1988.

38. The editors of *The Israel Defense Forces Spokesman* define CHEN (the Hebrew acronym for the Women's Corps of the Israel Defense Forces) to mean "charm." See Adams, op. cit.

39. Marlene Cimons, staff writer, "Women in Combat: Panama Stirs Debate," *Los Angeles Times*, January 11, 1990, front page.

40. Halloran, op. cit.; and Adams, op. cit., p. 50.

41. *Europa World Year Book* (London: Europa Publishers, 1992), vol. 1, p. 1475.

42. Helen Shapin, *Islam: A Country Study* (Washington, D.C.: USGPO, 1990), p. 290.

43. John Keegan, ed., *World Armies* (Detroit: Gale Research Co., 1983), 2d ed., p. 308.

44. Shapin, op. cit.

45. Shapin, op. cit.

46. Shapin, op. cit.

47. Philip Knightley, *The First Casualty* (New York: Harcourt, Brace, Jovanovich, 1975), p. 357.

48. Interview with Iraqi soldier, June 14, 1987. He requested anonymity.

49. Story by Artyom Borovik, a journalist for *Ogonyok* (a popular Russian weekly magazine), as cited in Bill Keller, "Russia's Divisive War—Home from Afghanistan," *The New York Times Magazine*, February 14, 1988.

50. This is based on a classic physics experiment explained to me by Steven Collins, Ph.D.

51. Associated Press, "Doctors Assail Project in Which Cats Are Shot," *Los Angeles Times*, August 19, 1989.
52. Ronald Brownstein, "Americans Back Bush Decision Overwhelmingly," *Los Angeles Times*, January 19, 1991, p. A-1.
53. Bruce Gilkin, Vietnam veteran, "To Hell and (Almost) Back: A Vietnam Veteran's Struggle with Posttraumatic Stress," *Men's Health*, summer 1988, pp. 43–44.
54. Keller, op. cit.
55. Lloyd Shearer, "Short End of the Stick," *Parade*, June 10, 1990, p. 20.
56. As quoted in Admiral Elmo Zumwalt, Jr., and Lieutenant Elmo Zumwalt II, with John Pekkanen, *My Father, My Son* (New York: Macmillan, 1986), p. 162. Reutershan, an ex-helicopter pilot, is founder of Agent Orange Victims International (1978). When he was 28, he learned he had terminal stomach cancer.
57. Joel Osler Brende and Erwin Randolph Parson, *Vietnam Veterans: The Road to Recovery* (New York: Plenum Press, 1985), p. 75.
58. Arthur Egendorf, Charles Kadushin, Robert S. Laufer, Georgie Rothbart, and Lee Sloan, *Legacies of Vietnam: Comparative Readjustment of Veterans and Their Peers* (Washington, D.C.: USGPO, 1981).
59. US 96th Cong., 1st sess., House of Representatives Committee on Veterans Affairs, Presidential Review Memorandum on Vietnam Era Veterans (Washington, D.C.: House Committee Print no. 38, 1979), released October 10, 1978. The report listed 29,000 veterans in state or federal prisons; 37,500 on parole; 250,000 under probation supervision; and 87,000 awaiting trial.
60. Louis Sahagun, "VA Hospital Assailed on Care for Homeless Vets," *Los Angeles Times*, May 26, 1989.
61. Brende and Parson, op. cit., p. xvi.
62. Mike Lafavore, "Soldier's Heart," *Men's Health*, summer 1988, p. 45. Mike Lafavore is the executive editor of *Men's Health*.
63. Gilkin, op. cit.
64. Gilkin, op. cit., p. 45.
65. Credit to Jim Novak.
66. The military historian is S. L. A. Marshall. Cited in Jean Elshtain, *Women and War* (New York: Harper & Row/Basic Books, 1987).
67. John Helmer, *Bringing the War Home: The American Soldier in Vietnam & After* (New York: The Free Press, 1974), pp. 225–26.
68. Brende and Paron, op. cit., p. 75.
69. John E. Helzer, Lee N. Robins, and Larry McEvoy, "Post-Traumatic Stress Disorder in the General Population: Findings of the Epidemiologic Catchment Area Survey," *New England Journal of Medicine*, vol. 317, no. 26, December 24, 1987, p. 1631.
70. Interview with Mike Dister, February 27, 1990, Bronx, New York, who did this research.
71. The statement was made on June 15, 1992, in an interview with NBC News.
72. Barbara Crossette, "Gulag Held MIAs, Yeltsin Suggests," *The New York Times*, June 16, 1992, p. A-1.
73. The report is an Interim Report on the POW/MIA issue by the Republican

staff of the U.S. Senate Committee on Foreign Relations. The Department of Defense, *POW-MIA Fact Book*, July 1991, p. 3, lists 2,273 Americans as missing in action or unaccounted for. The information in the sentence in the text is in Karen Tumulty, "Pentagon Official Resigns, Alleges Cover-up on MIAs," *Los Angeles Times*, May 21, 1991, p. A-1.

74. Martin Hirshfield, *Los Angeles Times*, June 22, 1991.
75. See Jill Stewart, "U.S. Families Claim Some Korea POWs May Be Alive," *Los Angeles Times*, July 8, 1990, p. A-19.
76. Karen Tumulty, "POWs May Still Be Held in Southeast Asia, Ex-Pentagon Official Says," *Los Angeles Times*, May 31, 1991, p. A-8.
77. Karen Tumulty, "Pentagon Official Resigns, Alleges Cover-up on MIAs," *Los Angeles Times*, May 21, 1991, p. A-1.
78. Ibid.
79. Ibid.
80. Nora Zamichow, "News from All Over," *Ms.*, August 1986.
81. Zumwalts, op. cit.
82. Zumwalts, op. cit., p. 162.
83. Zumwalts, op. cit., p. 162.
84. Zumwalts, op. cit.
85. Laura Palmer, "Vets Lose Not Only Lives, but Immortality as Well," *Los Angeles Times*, November 11, 1990.
86. The law is 38 USC 316. See U.S. Representative Montgomery (D-Miss.), Bill Tracking Report HR 556, 102d Cong., 1st sess., "Agent Orange Act of 1991."
87. See U.S. Representative Montgomery (D-Miss.), Bill Tracking Report HR 556, 102d Cong., 1st sess., "Agent Orange Act of 1991."
88. The National Academy of Sciences was directed to conduct comprehensive reviews of any evidence that Agent Orange or other toxic chemicals used in Vietnam caused cancer or other diseases in veterans.
89. Barbara Ehrenreich, "Iranscam: The Real Meaning of Oliver North," *Ms.*, May 1987, p. 26.
90. Zumwalts, op. cit., p. 126–27.
91. "No Peace for a Veteran," Labor section, *Time*, July 3, 1989.
92. Pierre Blais, "Hot Coals," *Colorado Daily*, September 11–13, 1987.
93. "Personality type predicts a death from cancer six times better than smoking does." Ronald Grossarth-Maticek, a Yugoslav psychologist working in Heidelberg, as quoted by Joshua Fischman, senior editor, "The Character of Controversy," *Psychology Today*, December 1988, p. 27.
94. Jonathan Van Meter, "Child of the Movies," *The New York Times Magazine*, January 6, 1991, p. 19.
95. Keller, op. cit.
96. Nora Zamichow, "Trading Places," *Los Angeles Times*, January 13, 1991, p. B-1.
97. Ibid. For example, every man featured in the *Los Angeles Times* article as "Trading Places" was either an attorney or a career officer who was taking on the children in addition to his continuing his career.
98. Ibid.
99. The quote is from "Hancock," a poem by Leroy Quintana in *Interrogations*

(Chevy Chase, Md.: Vietnam Generation, and Burning Cities Press, 1990), p. 95. Quoted with permission of Leroy Quintana.

100. NBC News/*The Wall Street Journal* poll, December 8–11, 1990. Poll of 1,002 voters nationwide.

101. Ibid.

102. Gallup Poll, January 31 and February 1, 1980, as published in "Battle and the Sexes: A *Newsweek* Poll," *Newsweek*, February 18, 1980.

103. Voter Research and Surveys, New York City, provided the information to Rich Morrin at *The Washington Post*, who I interviewed on November 17, 1992.

104. See Bob Greene, *Homecoming: When the Soldiers Return from Vietnam* (New York: Ballantine Books, 1989).

CHAPTER 6
The Suicide Sex: If Men Have the Power, Why Do They Commit Suicide More?

1. Jack C. Smith, James A. Mercy, and Judith M. Conn, "Marital Status and the Risk of Suicide," *American Journal of Public Health*, vol. 78, no. 1, January 1988, p. 79, figure 3.

2. U.S. Department of Health and Human Services, National Institute of Health, Eugene Rogat, et al., *A Mortality Study of 1.3 Million Persons by Demographic, Social & Economic Factors: 1979–1985 Follow-up Survey* (Washington, D.C.: USGPO, 1992), p. 335.

3. U.S. Department of Commerce, Bureau of the Census, *Historical Statistics of the United States: Colonial Times–1970*, Bicentennial Edition, Part 2, ser. A24–25 and H981–982. Women's suicides increased by 2 per 100,000, from 2 to 4; men's increased by 14 per 100,000, from 12 to 26.

4. Between 1950 and 1980, suicide rates for males 15 to 24 increased more than three times as much as the rates for females the same age. The male rate increased 211 percent; the female rate, 65 percent. See Mark L. Rosenberg, Jack C. Smith, Lucy E. Davidson, and Judith M. Conn, "The Emergence of Youth Suicide: An Epidemiologic Analysis and Public Health Perspective," *American Review of Public Health*, 1987, vol. 8, p. 424.

5. U.S. Department of Health and Human Services, National Center for Health Statistics (hereinafter USDH&HS/NCHS), Division of Vital Statistics, unpublished data for 1970, 1980, and 1988. These are the most recent data available:

Suicide Rates per 100,000 Population
(Age 25–34)

Year	Males	Females
1970	19.8	8.6
1988	25.0	5.7

6. For all races, men commit suicide at the rate of 19.9 per 100,000 population; women at 4.8 per 100,000 population. Based on the most recent statistics

available (1989) from the USDH&HS/NCHS, Center for Disease Control, Division of Vital Statistics, Office of Mortality Statistics, *Monthly Vital Statistics Report*, vol. 40, no. 8, supplement 2, January 7, 1992.

7. Prior to the age of 5, boys' suicide rate is slightly less than girls'. The 25,000 percent figure is derived by comparing the 0.1 to the 25.8 in the following chart from the USDH&HS/NCHS, Center for Disease Control, Statistical Resources, *Vital Statistics of the United States* (Washington, D.C.: USGPO, 1991), vol. 2, part A, Mortality, p. 51, tables 1–9, "Death Rates for 72 Selected Causes by 5-Year Age Groups, Race, and Sex: U.S., 1988."

Suicide Rates by Age and Sex per 100,000 Population
(1988—*latest available as of 1991*)

Age	Male	Female
5–9	0.1	0.0
10–14	2.1	0.8
15–19	18.0	4.4
20–24	25.8	4.1

8. Julian Weiss, "Trouble in Paradise," *Psychology Today*, August 1984. The Truks live on approximately 100 tropical islands and atolls in the western Pacific. A study by anthropologists Geoff White and Donald Rubenstein of the East-West Center in Hawaii, and their collaborator, historian Francis Hezel, found that 96 out of 126 suicides could be traced to *amwunumwun*. The Truk males who commit suicide at twenty-five times the rate of the average American males are in the 15- to 24-year age range, the same years for which the comparisons to the Americans are made.

9. USDH&HS/NCHS, Center for Disease Control, Statistical Resources, *Vital Statistics of the United States* (Washington, D.C.: USGPO, 1987), vol. 2, Mortality, part A.

10. Robert Fresco, *New York Newsday*, October 9, 1982.

11. USDH&HS/NCHS, Center for Disease Control, op. cit.

12. Shira Maguen, "Teen Suicide: The Government Coverup and America's Lost Children," *The Advocate*, September 24, 1991, p. 47. Nationally, gay teenage boys commit suicide eight to nine times more than straight teenage boys; gay teenage girls commit suicide two to three times more than straight teenage girls. And as we have seen, straight teenage boys commit suicide much more frequently than straight teenage girls.

13. Joel Brinkley, "Lethal Game of 'Chicken' Emerges for Israeli Boys," *The New York Times*, April 3, 1989.

14. The ad appeared during 1988. It was eventually removed from TV after some, but not a lot of, protest.

15. Carol Gilligan, *In a Different Voice* (Cambridge, Mass.: Harvard University Press, 1982), and Jean Baker Miller, *Toward a New Psychology of Women* (Boston: Beacon Press, 1976), 2d ed., 1986, p. 83. In *Psychology Today*, Phyllis Silverman, the codirector of the Child Bereavement Study at Massachusetts General Hospital, explains that Gilligan's and Miller's work demon-

strates that loss is more pervasive for women. Cited in Diane Cole, "Grief's Lessons: His and Hers," *Psychology Today*, December 1988, p. 60.

16. Jack C. Smith, James A. Mercy, and Judith M. Conn, op. cit.

17. Ibid., p. 78.

18. Pat Kelley, public affairs officer for the Naval Medical Command, Southwest Region, as cited in Ed Jahn, "Marines Investigate Suicides," *San Diego Union*, December 3, 1988.

19. Meyer Moldevan, consultant to the Inspector General's Office at McClellan Air Force Base, estimates there might be as many as 9,000 suicide attempts among active-duty personnel, members of their immediate families, and retired military. Cited in Jahn, ibid.

20. This assessment is that of Pat Kelley, public affairs officer, Naval Medical Command, Southwest Region. Cited in Jahn, ibid. Judgments as to causes are usually based on discussions with friends as to suicide notes or what was getting the man down.

21. Pat Kelley, public affairs officer, Naval Medical Command, Southwest Region. Cited in Jahn, ibid.

22. Ibid.

23. Nationwide, men commit suicide at the rate of 19.9 per 100,000. In 1982, upper-midwestern farmers' rates of suicide went to 58 suicides per 100,000. The 19.9 figure is from the USDH&HS/NCHS, Center for Disease Control, Division of Vital Statistics, Office of Mortality Statistics, *Monthly Vital Statistics Report*, vol. 40, no. 8, supplement 2, January 7, 1992. The 58 per 100,000 figure was reached in 1982 according to a study released October 14, 1991, by the National Farm Medicine Center in Wausau, Wisconsin.

24. USDH&HS/NCHS, Center for Disease Control, Division of Vital Statistics, Office of Mortality Statistics, *Monthly Vital Statistics Report*, vol. 38, no. 5, September 26, 1989, p. 25, table 10, "Deaths from 72 Selected Causes by Race and Sex: United States, 1987."

25. Associated Press, "George Reeves, TV Superman, Commits Suicide at Coast Home," *The New York Times*, June 17, 1959, p. 40.

26. Tom Williamson, "Male Helplessness," as reprinted in Francis Baumli, Ph.D., *Men Freeing Men* (Jersey City, N.J.: New Atlantis Press, 1985), pp. 129–30.

27. Sentiment exemplified on greeting card by Flying Fish, 6547 West Boulevard, Inglewood, CA 90302.

28. USDH&HS/NCHS, Center for Disease Control, Statistical Resources, *Vital Statistics of the United States* (Washington, DC: 1987), vol. 2, Mortality, part A. Here is the breakdown:

Suicide Rates by Age and Sex per 100,000 Population

Age	All Races/Both Sexes	Male	Female
85+	22.1	66.9	4.6

29. States require insurance companies to pay after the first two years that a client has had the policy, but not before the first two years (during which only premiums must be returned to the client). Interview on July 9, 1992, with Tim Kime, manager, Metropolitan Life Insurance.

30. Dr. Richard C. Fowler, Dr. Charles L. Rich, Dr. Deborah Young, "San Diego Suicide Study," *Archives of General Psychiatry*, 1986; 43:962–95. See also related article by Allan Parachini, "Youth, Drugs, Suicide: Statistics Tell a New Story," *Los Angeles Times*, June 1, 1988, part 5.

31. Marilyn K. Potts, et al., "Gender Differences in Depression Detection: A Comparison of Clinical Diagnosis and Standardized Assessment," *Psychological Assessment*, vol. 3, no. 4, December 1991, pp. 609–15.

32. David C. Clark, Ph.D., and Peter B. Zeldow, Ph.D., "Vicissitudes of Depressed Mood During Four Years of Medical School," *Journal of the American Medical Association*, vol. 260, no. 17, November 4, 1988, pp. 2521–28.

33. Murray Straus and Richard Gelles, "Societal Change and Change in Family Violence from 1975 to 1985 as Revealed by Two National Surveys," *Journal of Marriage and the Family*, vol. 48, 1986.

34. Maggie Scarf, "The More-Sorrowful Sex," *Psychology Today*, April 1979, p. 45.

35. Janny Scott, "Studies Find Depression Epidemic in Young Adults," *Los Angeles Times*, October 9, 1988.

36. Ibid.

37. Dan Kiley, *Living Together, Feeling Alone* (New York: Prentice Hall, 1989).

CHAPTER 7
Why Do Women Live Longer?

1. In Bangladesh, 55 percent of men and 50 percent of women live to be 65. In Harlem, 40 percent of men and 65 percent of women reach 65 years of age. See Colin McCord, M.D., and Harold P. Freeman, M.D., "Excess Mortality in Harlem," *New England Journal of Medicine*, volume 322, no. 3, January 18, 1990, pp. 173–77.

2. See the *University of California at Berkeley Wellness Letter*, vol. 8, issue 1, October 1991, p. 1. It is published by the University of California at Berkeley in association with the School of Public Health. The "Fascinating Facts" section reads: "An estimated 409 out of 1,000 white girls born in 1989 can expect to reach age 85, but only half as many white boys—224 per 1,000. For nonwhites, the chances of reaching age 85 are lower: 348 girls and 174 boys per 1,000."

3. Forty percent of girls who are born live to 85; 21 percent of boys who are born live to 85. See ibid.

4. *Almanac of the American People*, Tom and Nancy Biracree, Facts on File, 1988.

5. Ibid.

6. U.S. Department of Health and Human Services, National Center for Health Statistics (hereinafter USDH&HS/NCHS), Centers for Disease Control, *Monthly Vital Statistics Report*, vol. 38, no. 5, supplement, September 26, 1989, "Advance Report of Final Mortality Statistics, 1987," p. 6, table D, "Ratio of Age-Adjusted Death Rates for the 15 Leading Causes of Death by Sex and Race: United States, 1987."

7. See U.S. Department of Commerce, Bureau of the Census, *Statistical Abstract of the United States: 1987*, 107th ed., p. 820, table 1439, "Urban Population, Growth, Birth, and Death Rates and Life Expectancy—Selected Countries"; p. 824, table 1445, "Gross National Product in Current and Constant (1982) Dollars and Per Capita: 1975 to 1983."

8. *United Nations Demographic Yearbook, 1967* (New York: United Nations Publishing Service, 1968), p. 730. As cited in Sheila Ryan Johansson, "Sex and Death in Victorian England: An Examination of Age-Specific Death Rates, 1840–1910," in *A Widening Sphere: Changing Roles of Victorian Women*, ed. Martha Vicinus (Bloomington, Ind.: University of Indiana Press, 1977), pp. 163 and 166.

9. Ibid. In the official document, the technical names are used more than I use them in the text. They are:

   1. Diseases of heart
   2. Malignant neoplasms (including neoplasms of lymphatic and hematopoietic tissues
   3. Cerebrovascular diseases
   4. Accidents and adverse effects
   5. Chronic obstructive pulmonary diseases and allied conditions
   6. Pneumonia and influenza
   7. Diabetes mellitus
   8. Suicide
   9. Chronic liver disease and cirrhosis
   10. Atherosclerosis
   11. Nephritis, nephrotic syndrome, and nephrosis
   12. Homicide and legal intervention
   13. Septicemia
   14. Certain conditions originating in the perinatal period
   15. Human Immunodeficiency Virus infection

10. Robert Kennedy, Jr., "The Social Status of the Sexes and Their Relative Mortality Rates in Ireland," in *Readings in Population*, ed. William Petersen (New York: Macmillan, 1972), pp. 121–35.

11. Johansson, op. cit., pp. 163 and 166.

12. See Thomas A. Welton, Esq., "The Effect of Migrations upon Death Rates," *Journal of the Statistical Society of London*, vol. 38, 1875. (For a summary of the data and their interpretations, see pp. 323–27.)

13. In 1920, life expectancy for women was 54.6 years. In 1990, it was 78.8 years. This is an increase of 44.3 percent. In 1920, the life expectancy for men was 53.6 years. In 1990, the life expectancy for men was 72.0 years. This is an increase of 34.3 percent. 1920 statistics from the USDH&HS/NCHS, *Monthly Vital Statistics Report*, vol. 38, op. cit., p. 4. The 1990 statistics are from the USDH&HS/NCHS, *Monthly Vital Statistics Report*, vol. 39, no. 13, August 28, 1991, p. 17.

14. Laurie B. Lande, "First-Time Mothers Return to the Workforce," *Monthly Labor Review*, vol. 113, no. 10, October 1990, pp. 38–39.

15. Sixty-four percent of working women leave the workforce for six months or longer to take care of the family; 1.5 percent of men do. U.S. Department of Commerce, Bureau of the Census, *Current Population Reports* (Washington, D.C.: USGPO, 1984), ser. P-23, no. 136, "Life-Time Work Experience and Its Effect on Earnings," p. 6, table A, "Work Interruption History, by Race, Spanish Origin and Selected Characteristics: Males"; p. 7, table B, "Work Interruption History, by Race, Spanish Origin and Selected Characteristics: Females." As of 1992, these are the latest available data on workplace leaves of absence. Interview on July 22, 1992, with Jack McNeil, Bureau of the Census, Housing and Household Economic Statistics Division.

16. See Table 7.3 of Martha Hill in *Patterns of Time Use in Time, Goods, and Well-Being* (Ann Arbor: University of Michigan, Institute for Social Research, 1985), ed. F. Thomas Juster and Frank P. Stafford. The University of Michigan's Survey Research Center data incorporated the second job into the "hours worked" statistics and found a more than nine-hour difference. (The Bureau of Labor Statistics data do not incorporate the second job data and come up with a just-over-four-hour difference.) *Un*married men also work nine hours more in the workplace than unmarried women, but this sample grouped full-time, part-time, and non-workers together. Interview with Martha Hill, May 13, 1991.

    Men commute four hours per week to women's two hours per week. See John Robinson, "Americans on the Road," *American Demographics*, September 1989, p. 10.

17. Kenneth Wetcher, Art Barker, and P. Rex McCaughtry, *Save the Males: Why Men Are Mistreated, Misdiagnosed, and Misunderstood* (Summit, N.J.: The Psychiatric Institutes of America Press, 1991).

18. Ibid.

19. Edward Dolnick, "Super Women," *In Health*, July/August 1991, p. 45.

20. Wetcher, Barker, and McCaughtry, op. cit.

21. USDH&HS/NCHS, Public Health Service, *Annual Summary of Births, Marriages, Divorces, and Deaths: 1990*, p. 13, table 4. The male-female ratio is 3.1 to 1.

22. Ibid. Similarly, while boys and girls under age 15 rarely die from heart attacks, they nevertheless die at the same rate. But as soon as adolescence is experienced, boys are twice as likely to die from heart attacks. On this last point, see the USDH&HS/NCHS, *Vital Statistics of the United States* (Washington, D.C.: USGPO, 1991), section 1—"General Mortality," p. 44, tables 1–10, "Death Rates for 72 Selected Causes, by 10-Year Age Groups, Race, and Sex: United States, 1987–Con."

23. Alan Rozanski, M.D., "Mental Stress and the Induction of Silent Ischmia in Patients with Coronary Artery Disease," *New England Journal of Medicine*, vol. 318, no. 16, April 21, 1988, pp. 1005–12.

24. USDH&HS/NCHS, Centers for Disease Control, *Vital Statistics of the United States* (Washington, D.C.: USGPO, 1990), part A, section 1—"General Mortality," p. 44, tables 1–10, "Death Rates for 72 Selected Causes, by 10-Year Age Groups, Race, and Sex: United States, 1987–Con."

25. Robert Suro, "Hearts and Minds," *The New York Times*, December 29, 1991,

section 6, p. 18, col. 1. See also Dr. Dean Ornish, M.D., *Dr. Dean Ornish's Program for Preventing Heart Disease* (New York: Random House, 1990).

26. Unpublished data, USDH&HS/NCHS, Centers for Disease Control, National Hospital Discharge Survey, "Number of All Listed Diagnosis from Short-Stay Hospitals, By Age, and Sex: 1987." Cited by Jill Braden, Survey Branch of the National Center for Health Statistics via telephone interview March 15, 1990.

Inpatients Discharged for Alcohol-Related Syndrome
Total: 842,000

Male	15–44	45–64	65+
631,000	349,000	200,000	79,000
Female	15–44	45–64	65+
211,000	121,000	65,000	23,000

Note that after children are grown and men's money problems are less severe on average—ages 45 and above—male alcoholism decreases, yet still exceeds women's by a ratio of more than 3 to 1.

27. Latest HUD estimate (other estimates on homeless men run as high as 2.4 million), as cited in Don Johnson, "The Loneliness of the Male Body," *American Health*, January/February 1989, pp. 63–64. See also Martha Burt and Barbara Cohen, *America's Homeless: Numbers, Characteristics, and Programs that Serve Them* (Washington, D.C.: Urban Institute Press, 1985).

28. U.S. Department of Commerce, Bureau of the Census, *Statistical Abstracts of the United States: 1991*, 111th ed., p. 83, table 120, "Acquired Immuno-deficiency Syndrome Deaths."

Men	69,929	(90.4%)
Women	7,421	(9.6%)

29. From an interview on February 18, 1992, with Jerry Graf, National Park Service, Department of Veterans Memorials.

30. Interview on January 29, 1992, with Jerry Taylor, Department of Defense.

31. U.S. Department of Justice, Bureau of Justice Statistics, *Midyear Prisoners 1991*, June 30, 1991, p. 6.

32. Marc Lacey, "Solving the Ills of Black Men," *Los Angeles Times*, August 1, 1992, p. A-1.

33. USDH&HS/NCHS, *Monthly Vital Statistics Report*, vol. 38, op. cit., pp. 1–4. The life span for white females is 78.9; for black females, 73.6; for white males, 72.2; and for black males, 65.2.

34. 436,000 black males of all ages are in college; 609,690 young black men (50 percent more) are under the control of the criminal justice system. (White males, on the other hand, are more than four times as likely to be in college as in the criminal justice system.) See Marc Mauer, *Young Black Men in the Criminal Justice System* (Washington, D.C.: The Sentencing Project, 1990), p. 3.

35. Interview on September 10, 1990, with Marc Mauer, author of ibid.

36. Mauer, op. cit.

37. The Office of Research on Women's Health is part of the Department of Health and Human Services' National Institutes of Health in Bethesda, Maryland.

38. The Office of Minority Health is part of the Department of Health and Human Services' National Institutes of Health in Bethesda, Maryland.

39. Lynette Lamb, "Is There a Doctor (of Women's Health) in the House?" *Utne Reader*, no. 5, March/April 1992, pp. 26–28.

40. Marianne J. Legato, M.D., and Carol Colman, *The Female Heart: The Truth About Women and Coronary Artery Disease* (New York: Simon & Schuster, 1991), p. xiii.

41. Interview July 14, 1992, with Vivian W. Pinn, M.D., director of the Office of Research on Women's Health, National Institutes of Health. These figures were being prepared to be sent to Congress in late 1992.

42. The *Index Medicus* search was for 1989. It was a *subject* search, which is important because it is possible, for example, for an article on prostate cancer not to have "men" in the title and therefore not come up in a word search of article titles but nevertheless really be an article on men. The subject search minimizes that possibility for both sexes. See Steven L. Collins, "Proportion of Gender-Specific Scientific Research Relevant to Men and Women," unpublished manuscript, July 21, 1990, p. 4.

43. *Cancer Facts and Figures: 1991* (Atlanta, Ga.: American Cancer Society, 1991). The death rate for males of all ages due to prostate cancer is 24.1/100,000; for females of all ages due to breast cancer it is 27.4/100,000, a difference of 13.7 percent. In absolute numbers, prostate cancer killed about 32,000 men in 1991; and breast cancer killed about 44,500 women. Looked at from this perspective, breast cancer killed 39 percent more women and received 660 percent more funding. I did not use the absolute number comparison because what really counts is how vulnerable any given woman or man is.

44. 1991 funding for breast cancer was $92 million; for prostate cancer, $14 million. Projected 1992 funding for breast cancer is $132 million; for prostate cancer, $20 million. Unpublished data, internal documents of the Reports Analysis and Evaluation Branch of the National Cancer Institute, Financial Division. From a February 25, 1992, interview with budget analyst William DiGioia.

45. In 1986, 27,262 men died of prostate cancer versus 32,000 in 1991, an increase of 17.4 percent. In 1986, 40,539 women died of breast cancer versus 44,500 in 1991, an increase of 9.8 percent. The source for the 1986 data is USDH&HS/NCHS, *Vital Statistics of the United States* (Washington, D.C.: USGPO, 1989), tables titled "Mortality for the Five Leading Cancer Sites for Males by Age Group, United States, 1986" and "Mortality for the Five Leading Cancer Sites for Females by Age Group, United States, 1986." The source for the 1991 figures is *Cancer Facts and Figures: 1991*, op. cit., pp. 8–9.

46. USDH&HS, *Cancer Rates and Risks*, April 1985, p. 110.

47. At some time in their lives, 36 percent of men and 30 percent of women will

be mentally ill. Twenty-two percent of mentally ill women receive treatment, but only 12 percent of mentally ill men do. See Sam Shapiro, et al., "Utilization of Health and Mental Health Services," *Archives of General Psychiatry*, vol. 41, October 1984, p. 954, table 2; p. 976, table 5.

48. As of 1992, the most recent data available are from the USDH&HS/NCHS, *Vital Statistics of the United States* (Washington, D.C.: USGPO, 1991), section 1—"General Mortality," p. 44, tables 1–10, "Death Rates for 72 Selected Causes, by 10-Year Age Groups, Race, and Sex: United States, 1987—Con." The National Center for Health Statistics puts all heart attacks in the category of "Major Cardiovascular Diseases." They are as follows:

Major Cardiovascular Diseases

		Number of Deaths/Year
Ages 25–34	Male	14.4
	Female	7.6
Ages 35–44	Male	81.8
	Female	24.1
Ages 45–54	Male	227.4
	Female	88.0
Ages 55–64	Male	872.9
	Female	303.0
Ages 65–74	Male	1,528.1
	Female	863.4
Ages 75–84	Male	4,084.2
	Female	2,790.1
85 +	Male	10,135.4
	Female	9,153.0

The other major category of heart problems, "Diseases of the Heart," follows the same basic ratios of male-female deaths at various ages.

49. Over the age of 85, men die at a rate of 10,135.4 per 100,000 and women at the rate of 9153.0 per 100,000. See ibid. These are the most recent data available as of 1992.

50. See Lawrence E. Lamb, M.D., "Men, Women, and Heart Attacks: Can Aspirin Prevent Heart Attacks in Women?" *The Health Letter*, vol. 39, no. 1, January 1992, p. 2. Dr. Lamb, medical columnist for North America Syndicate, Inc., is a former professor of medicine at Baylor College of Medicine and chief of the Clinical Sciences at the USAF School of Aerospace Medicine.

51. The average man lives to 72.

52. A study of 22,071 male physicians was published in the *New England Journal of Medicine*, July 28, 1989.

53. The study of 87,678 women who were registered nurses was reported in the *Journal of the American Medical Association*, July 24/31, 1991.

54. The study of the men was five years; the study of the women, six years. The

study of the men included 22,071 men; the study of the women included 87,678 women. See the *New England Journal of Medicine*, op. cit., for the men's study; ibid., for the women's study.

55. The work was done by Dean Ornish at the Pacific Presbyterian Medical Center. See Pamela King, "The Pretended Self," *Psychology Today*, May 1989, p. 60.

56. The hospital death rate for men in a study of New England hospitals was 3.2 percent versus 7.3 percent for women. See the *Journal of the American Medical Association*, August 14, 1991.

57. See Lamb, op. cit.

58. Ibid., p. 3.

59. Dr. Vivek Varma, *Journal of American College of Cardiology*, "Are Women Treated Differently than Men with Acute Myocardial Infarction?" vol. 19, no. 5, April 1992. Interview with Dr. Varma on July 23, 1992, confirms text.

60. The increased risk of death was found in data from New England, Denmark, and Canada. See N. P. Roos, "Mortality and Recuperation after Open and Transurethral Resection of the Prostate for Benign Prostatic Hyperplasia," *New England Journal of Medicine*, vol. 320, no. 17, April 27, 1989, pp. 1120–24.

New surgical and pharmaceutical developments have improved men's potency and life expectancy prognoses. The only advocacy group for men with prostate cancer is Patient Advocates for Advanced Cancer Treatments (PAACT) at 1143 Parmelee NW, Grand Rapids, MI 49504 at 616-453-1477.

61. *American Journal of Epidemiology*, December 1990. Cited in "Vasectomies and Prostate Cancer: A Link?" *The New York Times*, January 1, 1991, p. A-16. Dr. Lynn Rosenberg of the Boston University School of Medicine, along with five colleagues, found that 10 percent of men with prostate cancer had had vasectomies, while only 2.4 percent of men without cancer had had vasectomies.

62. Confirmed August 17, 1992, through the American Cancer Society's Cancer Response System at 800-ACS-2345. See "For Men Only," a publication of the American Cancer Society. Call 800-ACS-2345.

63. The print ad ran in *Time, Newsweek, Fortune, Forbes, Smithsonian, Washington Monthly, Scientific American* and a black version with a black model ran in *Essence, Ebony*, and *Black Enterprise*. A parallel TV ad ran during network news and sports. Note that the target audience is not only women but men and women who are potential investors. The rationale? A company that protects women will do well: Invest in DuPont. The publications in which the ad ran are from an interview on March 18, 1991, with Dick Woodward, Corporate Advertising Division of DuPont.

64. Justice John Paul Stevens discovered it in 1992 during a routine screening test when he was 71; Justice Harry A. Blackmun discovered it in 1987 during a routine screening test when he was 78.

65. Verified in an interview on August 4, 1992, with Enid Galliers of the Oral Contraceptives Division of the Food and Drug Administration.

66. Lawrence Schneiderman, *Journal of the American Medical Association*, vol. 241, May 18, 1979.
67. Interview with Dr. Lawrence Schneiderman, December 9, 1991.
68. Lawrence Schneiderman, *Journal of Family Practice*, vol. 23, no. 1, 1986, pp. 49–53.
69. Women constitute 61 percent of office visits; men constitute 60 percent of hospital admissions. These figures do not include veterans' hospitals, in which, of course, almost 100 percent of patients would be men. See USDH&HS/NCHS, "National Ambulatory Medical Care Survey: 1990 Summary," 1992, p. 1.
70. This was true even in religious publications. For example, see Lori Durso, "Minorities Face Large Health-Care Gap," *Catholic Telegraph*, January 13, 1989, p. 6. Lori Durso is a reporter for Maturity News Service.
71. Approximately 7,200 boys died each year of the eight years of the Vietnam War. In 1991, for example, 32,000 men died of prostate cancer. Since prostate cancer is highly curable with early detection, it is probable that well over 7,200 of their lives would be saved with better education programs.
72. *American Journal of Epidemiology*, op. cit.
73. From the U.S. Department of Justice, Federal Bureau of Investigation, *Uniform Crime Reports for the United States: 1988*.

National Arrests for Driving Under the Influence

Men	Women
1,139,227	154,289
88.1%	11.9%

74. Unpublished data, USDH&HS/NCHS, Centers for Disease Control, National Hospital Discharge Survey, op. cit.

CHAPTER 8
The Insanity Track

1. Joseph Campbell and Bill Moyers, *The Power of Myth* (New York: Doubleday, 1988).
2. Herbert Hildebrandt and Edwin Miller, "The Newly Promoted Executive," monograph, University of Michigan, Graduate School of Business Administration, Ann Arbor, 1984. This is the most recent data I was able to track down on this subject.
3. *American Bar Association Journal*, February 1984, as reported by Paul Ciotti, "Unhappy Lawyers," *Los Angeles Times*, August 25, 1988.
4. "The alcoholism rate among lawyers is an estimated 15%–20%, almost twice as high as the general population." Cited in Ciotti, op. cit.
5. Mary Kay Barbieri, 45, as quoted in "Leaving Behind the Sharks of Seattle, Two Legal Eagles Find Happiness Hiking with Llamas," Starting Over section, *People*, October 31, 1988, p. 111.

6. Lujuana Treadwell, placement director, UC Berkeley Law School's Boalt Hall, as reported by Ciotti, op. cit.

7. The firm was Wald, Harkrader, and Ross. See David Brock, "The Real Anita Hill," *The American Spectator*, March 1992, pp. 21–22. "One Wald attorney . . . says that Hill was caught falsifying times sheets used to bill clients, because she couldn't meet the demands placed on young associates at the firm."

8. James Barron, "Making Sure Doctors Get Enough Sleep," *The New York Times*, May 22, 1988.

9. Ibid.

10. Ibid.

11. Suzanne Daley, "Hospital Interns' Long Hours to Be Reduced in New York," *The New York Times*, June 9, 1988.

12. As adapted from David Clement Scott, *A Cyclopaedic Dictionary of the Mang'anja Language Spoken in British Central Africa* (Edinburgh, 1892), p. 97

13. American Medical Association, Division of Survey and Data Resources, "Federal and Non-Federal Physicians by Specialty and Corresponding Board Certification," *Physician Characteristics and Distribution in the United States*, 1988, tables B-13 and B-14.

14. See Colette Dowling, *The Cinderella Complex* (New York: Pocket Books, 1981), p. 41.

15. Term used by Mike Driver, professor of management and organization at the USC business school, as reported in Ciotti, op. cit.

16. Dr. Kiyoyasu Arikawa found that sudden deaths among top executives skyrocketed from 10 in 1969 to about 150 in 1987, and most recently, the number of such deaths has grown fastest among those in their 40s and 50s—men who could normally live to almost 80. Cited by Elaine Kurtenbach, "Death from Overwork Growing Problem in Japan," *The Sunday Camera*, July 16, 1989.

17. Government-affiliated Leisure Development Center survey, 1987. Cited in Kurtenbach, ibid.

18. Leslie Helm, "The Rule of Work in Japan," *Los Angeles Times*, March 17, 1991, p. A-1.

19. Helm, ibid., p. A-25. The Japanese "hell camp" was also featured on "60 Minutes" in early 1991.

20. Nancy Reagan, with William Novak, *My Turn: The Memoirs of Nancy Reagan* (New York: Random House, 1989), as excerpted in "Close-Up on Ronnie," *Newsweek*, October 23, 1989.

21. Ibid.

22. Leslie Helm, op. cit., p. A-1.

23. *Oxford English Dictionary* (Oxford: Clarendon Press, 1989), 2d ed., pp. 437–39 and 663–64. The definition of "faggot" (pp. 663–64) includes, "with special reference to the practice of burning heretics alive . . . a bundle of sticks, twigs or small branches bound together to be used as fuel." Also the definition of "witch" (pp. 437–39) includes a reference to heretics being burned alive. As Arno Karlen discusses on p. 128 of *Sexuality and Homosexuality* (New York: W. W. Norton, 1971), between one fourth and one fifth of the

records from Plymouth Colony dealing with sexual offense punished homosexuals. In non-Puritan colonies (like New York) there were a number of homosexual punishments, including burning at the stake.

24. Richard H. Ropers, "The Rise of the New Urban Homeless," *Public Affairs Report* (Berkeley: University of California/Berkeley, Institute of Governmental Studies, 1985), October–December 1985, vol. 26, nos. 5 and 6, p. 4, table 1, "Comparisons of Homeless Samples from Select Cities."

25. Ibid.

26. James D. Wright, *Address Unknown: The Homeless in America* (New York: Aldine De Gruyter, 1989), p. 59. Wright explains: "To arrive at these results, I simply dropped from the data base all HCH clients known to be members of homeless family groups, and then calculated the age and sex distributions for those who remained. The sample size for the calculations is 17,633."

27. James Wright conducted a nationwide study of 17,633 homeless. See ibid., p. 57.

28. See Wright, op. cit.

29. See ibid., pp. 58–59. Wright explains: "The adult family members also suffer fewer chronic physical disorders, are more likely to be short-term (or situationally) homeless, and are rated as having better housing and employment prospects than the lone homeless are. In general, their prospects for the future are much brighter."

30. State of California, Department of Housing & Community Development, "A Study of the Issues and Characteristics of the Homeless Population in California," April 1985, p. 7.

31. Associated Press, "Co-Workers Comforted Controller after Her Fatal Error, Paper Says," *The New York Times*, February 11, 1991, p. A-12.

32. Ibid. The air traffic controller's name (Robin Lee Wascher) was eventually leaked.

33. The term "sanity track" was coined by Harvard Business School Professor Leonard Schlesinger. Reported by Carol Hymowitz, "Stepping Off the Fast Track," *The Wall Street Journal*, June 13, 1989, p. B-1.

34. E. Lowell Kelly, Lewis R. Goldberg, Donald W. Fiske, and James M. Kilkowski, survey published in *American Psychologist*, vol. 33, no. 8, as cited in "Do Psychologists Have Less Fun?" *Psychology Today*, November 1978.

CHAPTER 9
Violence Against Whom?

1. The latest data available in 1991 are that 74.6 percent of all murder victims are male (13,632 males versus 4,611 females). U.S. Department of Justice, Federal Bureau of Investigations, *Crime in the United States, 1988*, p. 11, table titled "Age, Sex, and Race of Murder Victims, 1988."

2. U.S. Department of Justice, Office of Justice Programs, Bureau of Justice Statistics, *Criminal Victimization in the United States, 1987*, publication #NCJ-115524, June 1989, table 3, "Personal Crimes, 1987," p. 16. Per 1,000

population, males are 1.7 times more likely than females to be victims of violent crimes. This statistic includes rape, but excludes murder, of which males are 3 times more likely to be victims.

3. U.S. Department of Justice, Federal Bureau of Investigation, Uniform Crime Reports, *Crime in the United States: 1990*, pp. 15 and 51. Excluding forcible rape, the numbers of violent crimes are:

1981	1990
1,267,316	1,718,575

4. The *rape rate decreased from 1.8 per 1,000 in 1973 to 1.2 per 1,000 in 1988.* See the U.S. Bureau of Justice, Bureau of Justice Statistics, National Crime Survey Report, *Criminal Victimization in the United States, Annual (1973–1988)*, p. 15. This figure comes from a national sampling of households. It is considered a more reliable comparison of rates than reports of rapes to the police, since reports of rape to the police have increased as public awareness of rape has increased and as the definition of rape has broadened (e.g., to include ignoring a verbal "no") in the last decade. But even here there has been a 9 percent increase in rapes reported to the police between 1981 and 1990 versus a 36 percent increase in violent crimes of which men are the primary victims that were reported to the police between 1981 and 1990. For the source of the 9 percent increase, see ibid.

5. *Crime in the United States: 1990*, op. cit. The exact figures are 102,555 forcible rapes and 1,757,572 violent crimes (murder, robbery, and aggravated assault, excluding forcible rapes).

6. U.S. Department of Justice, *Crime in the United States, 1981*. As cited in Mark L. Rosenberg, M.D., M.P.P., and James A. Mercy, Ph.D., "Homicide: Epidemiologic Analysis at the National Level," *Bulletin of the New York Academy of Medicine*, 1986, vol. 62, no. 5, p. 389.

7. U.S. Department of Justice, Federal Bureau of Investigation, Bureau of Justice Statistics, *National Survey of Crime Severity* (Washington, D.C.: US-GPO, 1985), #NCJ-96017; conducted by Marvin E. Wolfgang, Robert M. Figlio, Paul E. Tracy, and Simon I. Singer from the Center for Studies in Criminology and Criminal Law, the Wharton School, University of Pennsylvania.

8. Murray A. Straus and Richard J. Gelles, "Societal Change and Change in Family Violence from 1975 to 1985 as Revealed by Two National Surveys," *Journal of Marriage and the Family*, vol. 48, August 1986, pp. 465–79.

9. U.S. Department of Health and Human Services, National Center for Health Statistics, *Monthly Vital Statistics Report*, vol. 38, no. 5, supplement, September 26, 1989, p. 6, table D, "Ratio of Age-Adjusted Death Rates for the 15 Leading Causes of Death by Sex and Race: United States, 1987."

10. *Criminal Victimization in the United States, 1987*, op. cit., p. 1.

11. David Zeman, Knight-Ridder Newspapers, "Father, Martyr, Fraud?" *Detroit Free Press*, May 25, 1990, p. 1-F.

12. Robert Gramling, Craig Forsyth, and Jeff Fewell, University of Southwestern Louisiana, "Crime and Economic Activity: A Research Note," *Sociological Spectrum*, vol. 8, no. 2, 1988, pp. 187–95.

13. Todd Sloane, "Laurie Dann: Anatomy of a Killer," *Winnetka Talk*, May 26, 1988, p. D-2.
14. *Chicago Tribune Annual Index*, 1988, pp. 407–8.
15. Paul Feldman, et al., "Faces of Death: 10 Men Slain by Officers in Riots," *Los Angeles Times*, May 24, 1992, front page.
16. Vivian S. Toy, "Violence by Boys Forces Removal of Women Teachers," *Detroit News*, November 17, 1988.
17. Florida, Illinois, Maryland, Ohio, Pennsylvania, and Texas are just a few of the twenty-nine states still allowing teachers and administrators to employ corporal punishment in disciplining students. From a telephone interview February 28, 1991, with Jordan Riak of Parents and Teachers against Violence in Education, a national organization based in Danville, California.
18. Kathleen Doheny, "Sexual Abuse: When Men Are the Victim," *Los Angeles Times*, January 10, 1989, part V, p. 1. The ratio of 1 boy to 1.7 girls is also based on an increasingly broad definition of sexual abuse. For example, a boy who is touched on the rear is far less likely to mention it to anyone, therefore not becoming part of the 16 percent of boys and 27 percent of girls said to be subject to sexual abuse. The definition of sexual abuse has gotten so broad as to make many teachers fear helping elementary school children on or off with their clothes, cuddling them, or play-wrestling with them.
19. Ibid.
20. Associated Press, "War on Women Must Stop—Bush," *Los Angeles Times*, June 27, 1989.
21. Ibid.
22. 1991–92 *Handbook* of the National Federation of State High School Associations, Kansas City, Missouri.
23. Editorial: "The Jogger and the Wolfpack," *The New York Times*, April 26, 1989.
24. Ellen Goodman, "Safety for Women? Try Removing Men," *Santa Barbara News-Press*, Tuesday, January 9, 1990.
25. Gerald Galison, Letter-to-the-Editor, *The New York Times*, May 7, 1989.
26. *No Circ Newsletter*, vol. 3, no. 1, fall 1988, p. 1.
27. Edward Wallerstein, *Circumcision: An American Health Fallacy* (New York: Springer Publishing Co., 1980). Wallerstein is a New York–based urologist.
28. Ibid.
29. Ibid.
30. Anesthesia reduced stress by reducing the level of stress hormones. It prevented infection indirectly by minimizing the suppression of the immune system. It also made newborns less prone to the acid buildup in muscles. See M. C. Rogers, M.D., "Do the Right Thing—Pain Relief in Infants and Children," *New England Journal of Medicine*, January 2, 1992, p. 55.
31. Howard J. Stang, M. R. Gunnar, L. Snellman, L. M. Condon, and R. Kestenbaum, "Local Anesthesia for Neonatal Circumcision: Effects on Distress and Cortisol Response," *Journal of the American Medical Association*, vol. 259, no. 10, March 1988, pp. 1507–11. Dr. Stang is with the University of Minnesota.

32. Edward Wallerstein, op. cit.
33. Ibid.
34. A nationwide study of circumcision could be conducted for under $1 million. The cost of the Persian Gulf War was half a million dollars a minute. See "The Cost of a Day of War," *Los Angeles Times*, February 9, 1991, p. A-5. The newspaper's sources were the Congressional Budget Office and Forecast International, 1990.
35. E. L. Wynder, et. al., "A Study of Environmental Factors in Carcinoma of the Cervix," *American Journal of Obstetrics and Gynecology*, vol. 68, no. 4, April 1954, p. 96.
36. "Circumcision and Cancer," *Time*, vol. 63, no. 14, April 5, 1954, p. 96.
37. M. Terris, et. al., "Relation of Circumcision to Cancer of the Cervix," *American Journal of Obstetrics and Gynecology*, vol. 177, no. 8, December 15, 1973, pp. 1056–62; and A. Lilienfeld and Saxon Graham, "Validity of Determining Circumcision Status by Questionnaire as Related to Epidemiological Studies of Cancer of the Cervix," *Journal National Cancer Institute*, vol. 21, no. 4, October 1958, pp. 713–20.
38. Edward Wallerstein, op. cit., p. 72.
39. The average child watches 3,024 people killed each year. See Tom and Nancy Biracree, *Almanac of the American People* (New York: Facts on File, 1988), p. 241.
40. From my own calculations based on daytime and prime-time TV monitoring and movie monitoring. Percentages are approximate because in westerns and war movies, all the people killed were men, but it couldn't always be determined how many, and at other times I was just watching the movie (!).
41. This is my own approximate calculation based on watching approximately 1,500 to 2,000 movies (just under two movies per week over the last twenty plus years, the time period during which I have been conscious of these differences in violence). I usually just enjoy the film and do a mental calculation later, so this is not a perfect tabulation.
42. Bret Easton Ellis, *American Psycho* (New York: Vintage Books, 1991). The three men murdered are on pages 131, 165, and 217; the murder of the little boy is on page 298. Credit to Robert Keith Smith for this observation.
43. For example, two nationwide studies of both sexes that are among the 14 two-sex studies are reported in Straus and Gelles, op. cit.
44. U.S. Senate, "Women and Violence Hearing before the Commission on the Judiciary, U.S. Senate," part I, June 20, 1990, and part II, August 29, 1990, and December 11, 1990 (Order #J-101-80). Almost all of the fifteen women were feminist oriented (NOW, etc.). Jon Ryan and other men were refused permission to testify.

CHAPTER 10
If We Cared As Much about Saving Males As Saving Whales, Then . . .

1. Television commercials showing during 1991.
2. The 80 percent figure is the estimate of Ralph DeSantis (717-948-8196), of Pennsylvania's General Public Utilities (which runs Three Mile Island).

3. Merrill M. Mitler, Mary A. Carskadon, Charles A. Czeisler, William C. Dement, David F. Dinges, and R. Curtis Graeber, "Catastrophes, Sleep, and Public Policy: Consensus Report," Association of Professional Sleep Societies, Committee on Catastrophes, Sleep, and Public Policy, *Sleep*, vol. 11, no. 1 (New York: Raven Press, 1988), pp. 100–109.
4. Ibid.
5. Documentation that the crew were exhausted and skipped a day's rest was confirmed in an interview on June 29, 1992, by Leon Katcharian, coauthor of the National Transportation Safety Board's official report. See Leon Katcharian, et al., *Grounding of the U.S. Tankship* Exxon Valdez *on Bligh Reef, Prince Williams Sound, Near Valdez, Alaska, March 24, 1989* (Washington D.C.: NTSB/MAR-90/04), pp. 166–67.
6. Dr. Marvin Legator, genetic toxicologist, University of Texas Health Sciences Center, Galveston. Cited in Sandra Blakeslee, "Research on Birth Defects Turns to Flaws in Sperm," Medical Science section, *The New York Times*, p. A-1

PART III
Government as Substitute Husband:
An Overview

1. *Calvin Bradley* v. *the State*, 156, Mississippi, 1824. See R. J. Walker, *Reports of Case Adjudged in the Supreme Court of Mississippi* (St. Paul, Minn.: West Publishing, 1910), p. 73, section 157.
2. Associated Press, "Wife of Convicted Cop Files Claim against City," *North County Blade-Citizen* (San Diego), October 1, 1992.
3. Voter Research and Surveys, New York City, provided the information to Rich Morrin at *The Washington Post*, whom I interviewed on November 17, 1992.
4. Terry Pristin, "Feminists Make Their Legal Case," *Los Angeles Times*, March 15, 1991, p. A-1.
5. Ibid.

Chapter 11
How the System Protects Women, Or . . . Two Different Laws We Live In

1. National Judicial Reporting Program data indicate that "an estimated 2 percent of men convicted of murder or non-negligent manslaughter received a death sentence compared to one-tenth of 1 percent of women." Quote from U.S. Department of Justice, Bureau of Justice Statistics (hereinafter USBJS), *Profile of Felons convicted in State Courts*, January 1990, publication #NCJ-120021 by Patrick A. Largan, Ph.D., and John M. Dawson (BJS statisticians), p. 9.
2. On January 15, 1954, Dovie Smarr Dean was executed in Ohio for the murder of her husband. In an analysis of executions since 1954 by Victor Streib, the

American considered most knowledgeable about capital punishment, it is apparent no woman who has killed only men has been executed—the few women who have been executed have killed at least one woman. See Professor Victor L. Streib, *American Executions of Female Offenders: A Preliminary Inventory of Names, Dates, and Other Information*, 1988, Cleveland-Marshall College of Law, Cleveland State University, Cleveland, Ohio.

3. "Execution Update" (NAACP Legal Defense and Educational Fund, Inc.), January 18, 1990. NAACP Legal Defense and Educational Fund, 1275 K Street NW, Suite 301, Washington, DC 20005.

4. Matthew Zingraff and Randall Thompson, "Differential Sentencing of Women and Men in the USA," *International Journal of the Sociology of Law*, 1984, no. 12, pp. 401–13. The 12.6-year difference is on p. 408. The journal is published by Academic Press, a subsidiary of Harcourt, Brace, Jovanovich publishers.

5. USBJS, *Sentencing Outcomes in 28 Felony Courts: 1985*, July 1987, publication #NCJ-105743, table 5.5, "Average Prison Term (in Months) Imposed, by Sex of Offender and Conviction Offense, 1985."

6. For the smaller impact of racial differences, see USBJS, *Profile of Felons*, op. cit., p. 1, col. 2. For the smaller impact of other differences, see Zingraff and Thompson, op. cit.

7. State of Washington, Sentencing Guidelines Commission, *Sentencing Practices Under the Sentencing Reform Act: Fiscal Year 1987* by Dr. David L. Fallen, research director, p. 72, table 37, "Average Sentence Length by Gender." Women's average sentence length was 3.5 months; men's was 8.3 months.

8. From Dr. David L. Fallen, research director, state of Washington, "Sentencing Practices under the Sentencing Reform Act: Fiscal Year 1991," in unpublished written correspondence to author, March 15, 1992.

9. Washington, *Sentencing Practices . . . 1987*, op. cit., p. 74, table 39. Nineteen percent of women versus 14 percent of men were eligible for early departure.

10. See Howie Kurtz, "Courts Easier on Women," *The Sunday Record* (Bergen County, N.J.), October 5, 1975.

11. Ibid.

12. Attorney David D. Butler, "Males Get Longer Sentences," *Transitions*, vol. 10, no. 1, January/February 1990, front page.

13. Seth Mydans, "With One Trial Just Ended, McMartin Figures Face 2d," *The New York Times*, March 5, 1990, p. A-11.

14. Ann Hagedorn, "Child Molestation Trial Ends in Acquittals," *The Wall Street Journal*, January 19, 1990, p. B-8.

15. Justin Atholl, *The Reluctant Hangman: The Story of James Berry, Executioner, 1884–1892* (New York: J. Long, 1956). This characterization is of James Berry, executioner in London, England, from 1884 to 1892.

16. Hugo Adam Bedau and Michael L. Radelet, "Miscarriages of Justice in Potentially Capital Cases," *Stanford Law Review*, vol. 40, no. 1, November 1987, pp. 21–179. This study covered 350 cases from 1900 to 1984 in which defendants convicted of capital or potentially capital crimes were later found

to be innocent. Twenty-three defendants (all men) executed were later found innocent and eight (all men) died while serving their sentences.

17. USBJS, *Sourcebook of Criminal Justice Statistics*, 1991, p. 442, table 4.7.
18. John T. Kirkpatrick and John A. Humphrey, "Stress in the Lives of Female Criminal Homicide Offenders in North Carolina," *Human Stress: Current Selected Research*, vol. 3, ed. James H. Humphrey (New York: AMS Press, 1989).
19. Streib, *American Executions*, op. cit. See previous citation for detailed explanation.
20. Ron Rosenbaum, "Too Young to Die?" *The New York Times Magazine*, March 12, 1989.
21. Ibid.
22. Tom Gorman, "Woman Who Kills Child Remains Free," *Los Angeles Times*, April 26, 1989.
23. Butler, op. cit.
24. Figures for 1987 (the latest figures available) show that 96 male inmates committed suicide and 91 died by execution or at the hands of another—187 total. With 555,371 men in prison, these deaths amount to 33.67 men per 100,000 men in prison. This compares to 1 woman out of 29,064 women in prison in 1987, or 3.44 per 100,000 women in prison. When the 33.67 is divided by 3.44 and multiplied by 100 (for the percent), the difference is 978.8 percent. Suicide, execution, and homicide data for 1987 are from USBJS, *Correctional Populations in the United States*, publication #NCJ-118762, December 1989, p. 105, table 5.17, "Deaths among Sentenced Prisoners Under State or Federal Jurisdiction, by Sex and Cause of Death, 1987." Prison statistics for 1987 are from the U.S. Department of Commerce, Bureau of the Census, *Statistical Abstracts of the United States: 1991*, 111th ed., p. 195, table 338, which sources the annual reports of the USBJS, *Prisoners in 1987*.
25. The California State task force mandate to study only female prisoner health issues was established in 1992 by Assembly Bill 900, sponsored by Assemblywoman Lucille Roybal-Allard (D), Los Angeles.
26. The average monthly cost per capita from 1988–89 for male prisoners in Wisconsin was $1,120; for female prisoners, $2,100. See the *Summary of Distribution Per Capita Costs for the Year Ended June 30, 1989: Section E*, published by the Madison, Wisconsin, Department of Health and Social Services, Division of Corrections, Office of Policy, Planning and Budget. (Contributed by Jim Novak.)
27. George J. Church, "The View from behind Bars," *Time*, special fall issue 1990, p. 20.
28. USBJS, *Midyear Prisoners 1991*, June 30, 1991, p. 6. The most recent figures available are: 758,294 men; 46,230 women.
29. Fred Strasser and Mary C. Hickey, "Running Out of Room for Women in Prison," Updates section, *Governing*, October 1989, p. 70. (Other examples of special privileges for women are also from above source.)
30. Ibid.
31. Allan R. Gold, "Sex Bias Is Found Pervading Courts," *The New York Times*, July 2, 1989.

32. Ibid.
33. Speech by Norma Juliet Wikler, founding director of the National Judicial Education Project, on its origination in 1979 and its decision to be sponsored by the NOW Legal Defense and Education Fund and the National Association of Women Judges. See Wikler, "Water on Stone: A Perspective of the Movement to Eliminate Gender Bias in the Courts," keynote address, National Conference on Gender Bias in the Courts, Williamsburg, Virginia, May 18, 1989.
34. Most have a ratio of about three or four women to one man. They usually include no men's activists and approximately half women's activists. See, for example, Bruce Hight, "Male Group Says Too Many Women on Panel," *Austin American-Statesman*, January 31, 1992.
35. USBJS, *Profile of Felons*, op. cit., p. 5, table 3.
36. Ibid., p. 5.
37. Howie Kurtz, op. cit. Ms. Barbara Swartz is credited with this term.
38. Ibid. The Women's Prison Project is a New York–based program to teach law to female inmates.
39. Ibid. Article quotes Bergen County (N.J.) Assistant Prosecutor Ronald Schwartz.
40. Ibid.
41. Ibid.
42. Interview with Alex Landon, San Diego, July 16, 1991.
43. Attorney David D. Butler, op. cit.

CHAPTER 12
Women Who Kill Too Much and the Courts That Free Them: The Twelve "Female-Only" Defenses

1. Associated Press, "After 21 Years, Man Is Freed in Poison Case," *The New York Times*, April 27, 1989. See also Mark Lane, *Arcadia* (New York: Holt, Rinehart, Winston, 1970).
2. Ibid. (both)
3. Interview on May 15, 1990, with Don Horn, the prosecutor who handled the Richardson appeal.
4. Ibid. The sheriff's name is Klein; the nurse to whom Bessie Reese confessed is Belinda Frazier.
5. Times Wire Services, "Father in Prison for Poisonings Is Freed," *Los Angeles Times*, April 26, 1989. While Bessie Reese's confession is inadmissible due to "mental incompetence," the state could still bring charges against her on independent evidence collected and most likely used to release Richardson. This the state has not done, leading one to wonder whether categorizing her as "mentally incompetent" was a method the state used to avoid the expense and complications of trying her.
6. See Robert D. McFadden, Ralph Blumenthal, M. A. Farber, E. R. Shipp, Charles Strum, and Craig Wolff, *Outrage: The Story behind the Tawana Brawley Hoax* (New York: Bantam Books, 1990).

7. Eloise Salholz with Andrew Murr, "Arsenic and Old Lace," *Newsweek*, August 14, 1989.

8. Joyce Wadler, "Killing Her Husband Wasn't Enough for Stella Nickell; To Make Her Point, She Poisoned a Stranger," *People*, vol. 30, no. 1, July 4, 1988, pp. 87–92.

9. Donald Dale Jackson, "Who Killed Sue Snow?" *Reader's Digest*, vol. 138, no. 826, February 1991, pp. 149–54.

10. Associated Press, "Wife Admits 1981 Slaying; Husband Freed," *Daily Camera* (Boulder, Colo.), January 1984; and Edward Frost, "Ex-Wife's Confession Frees Convicted Killer," *Reporter Dispatch* (N.Y.), January 18, 1984, p. A-1.

11. First, Nathaniel's attorneys pursued the case on their own even after Nathaniel's conviction. Second, they turned up enough new evidence to get a new trial. Third, when detectives located Delissa to tell her of the new hearing, she thought they were there to arrest her and she spontaneously decided to confess.

12. Mary Brown Parlee, "New Findings: Menstrual Cycles and Behavior," *Ms.*, September 1982, p. 126.

13. Ibid.

14. Andrea Ford, "Woman Who Killed Infant Son Allowed to Get Mental Help on Outpatient Basis," *Los Angeles Times*, March 11, 1989.

15. Parlee, op. cit.

16. Marv Balousek, "Woman Who Shot Mate 5 Times Gets Probation," *Wisconsin State Journal*, August 19, 1988, p. 1-B.

17. Ibid.

18. Interview April 19, 1990, with Assistant District Attorney Judy Schwaemle of Dane County, Wisconsin, who handled the case.

19. Ibid.

20. Isabel Wilkerson, "Clemency Granted to 25 Women Convicted for Assault or Murder," *The New York Times*, December 22, 1990, p. A-1.

21. For example, Governor Schaeffer of Maryland and Governor Gardner of Washington.

22. Nancy Ray, "Judge Allows 'Battered Woman' Defense," *Los Angeles Times*, September 21, 1982.

23. Wilkerson, op. cit.

24. See, e.g., California Assembly Bill 785 by Assemblyman Gerald R. Eaves, D-Rialto, which took effect on January 1, 1992.

25. Tom Gorman, "Court Told How Son Was Driven to Kill Spiteful Mother," *Los Angeles Times*, December 19, 1989, p. B-1.

26. Ibid.

27. The story was based on Francine Hughes. See Susan Paterno, "A Legacy of Violence," *Los Angeles Times*, April 14, 1991, pp. E-1 and E-14.

28. Leonard Maltin, *TV Movies and Video Guide: 1991 Edition* (New York: Signet/Penguin, 1990).

29. The sentence was commuted by Governor James G. Martin of North Carolina. Jane Ruffin, "Battered Wife Released from Prison," *The News and Observer* (Raleigh, N.C.), July 8, 1989, front page.

30. Howard Schneider, "Meeting Battered Women Face to Face," *The Washington Post*, January 15, 1991, p. B-7.
31. Wilkerson, op. cit.
32. For example, two nationwide studies of both sexes that are among the 14 two-sex studies are reported in Murray A. Straus and Richard J. Gelles, "Societal Change and Change in Family Violence from 1975 to 1985 as Revealed by Two National Surveys," *Journal of Marriage and the Family*, vol. 48, August 1986, pp. 465–79.
33. Coramae Richey Mann, "Getting Even? Women Who Kill in Domestic Encounters," *Justice Quarterly* (Academy of Criminal Justice Sciences: 1988), vol. 5, no. 1, March 1988, p. 49.
34. Ibid.
35. Ibid.
36. Ibid., pp. 33–51. I couldn't quite believe this, so I telephoned Coramae Richey Mann at the Department of Criminal Justice at Indiana University on April 23, 1990. She verified the findings. I asked how she obtained the information. She explained that no woman's files included a single indication of the woman having been abused by the husband or lover she killed. It was obvious to her that many women are battered, and some who are battered kill their batterers, but apparently either their prison terms are short enough that at the point in time she did her study none of the battered women were in prison or, on the other hand, some never went to prison to begin with. This study was done years after 1982 (when the battered woman syndrome was first used as a legal defense). The value of her findings is that, contrary to Rationale #3, some women do kill without first being abused. Additionally, 41 percent of the women did not even claim self-defense as a motive, and of the 59 percent who did, Dr. Mann could not find any whose definition of self-defense matched the legal definition of "imminent physical threat to one's life with no means of escape."
37. Ibid., p. 49, footnote 10—interview of Lieutenant Harvey Wyche of the New York City Police Department. See also Mike Clary, "Fast-Lane Saga Over: Widow Guilty in Murder of Husband," *Los Angeles Times*, November 17, 1989.
38. Straus and Gelles, op. cit.
39. Fred Hayward, *Westworld*, September 5, 1989, concerning restraining orders.
40. Kevin Svoboda lives about forty miles from the Lancaster County jail where his wife was imprisoned. See Wire Dispatches and Staff Reports, "Jailed Wife Plots to Kill Husband," *Washington Times*, January 23, 1992, and Chicago Tribune Wires, "Wife Sentenced in Plot to Kill Spouse," *Chicago Tribune*, February 12, 1992.
41. The states are: Delaware, Maine, Minnesota, Nevada, Oregon, Utah, Connecticut, Virginia, Washington, New Jersey, Wisconsin, Rhode Island. Among the cities are: Washington, D.C., and Los Angeles. From Karyl Spriggs at the National Coalition against Domestic Violence (NCADV), 1991.
42. Craig Anderson, a gay counselor at Family and Children Services in Minneapolis, quoted in Julio Ojeda-Zapata, *St. Paul Pioneer Press*, October 21, 1990, p. 1-B.

43. Steve Metzger, "The Shooting of Josh Wagshall," *Transitions*, vol. 8, no. 2, March/April 1988, p. 2.

44. Verified in telephone interview with Nancy Young of Elizabeth Holtzman's press office, February 7, 1991.

45. "Battered Woman Is Freed in Slaying of Husband," *The New York Times*, October 29, 1989.

46. The *60 Minutes* story aired in October 1989.

47. The governor was Booth Gardner.

48. "Battered Woman is Freed," *The New York Times*, op. cit.

49. Ibid.

50. Paul Dean, "Husbands Too Ashamed to Admit Abuse by Wives," *New York Newsday*, January 20, 1981.

51. John T. Kirkpatrick and John A. Humphrey studied seventy-six female murderers at the North Carolina Correctional Center in Raleigh. See John T. Kirkpatrick and John A. Humphrey, "Stress in the Lives of Female Criminal Homicide Offenders in North Carolina," *Human Stress: Current Selected Research*, vol. 3, ed. James H. Humphrey (New York: AMS Press, 1989), pp. 109–20.

52. John T. Kirkpatrick as cited by Glen Collins, *The New York Times* News Service, July 18, 1986.

53. Nancy Gibbs and Jeanne McDowell, "How to Revive a Revolution," *Time*, March 4, 1992, p. 57.

54. Kirkpatrick and Humphrey, op. cit.

55. Ford, op. cit.

56. Tom Gorman, "Woman Who Killed Child Remains Free," *Los Angeles Times*, April 26, 1989.

57. While free on probation, Mesa hid another pregnancy from her probation officer and repeatedly missed appointments. Even her own probation officer recommended a thirty-day sentence. Once again, she was let go. Was it because she needed to take care of the new baby? No. The new baby was put in the custody of the father.

58. "Illinois—Two Times, Too Much," American Notes section, *Time*, July 24, 1989, p. 25; and Associated Press, "Mother Found Guilty in Death of 'Stolen' Baby," *Los Angeles Times*, January 31, 1990.

59. Bruce Langer, "Ward Woman Gets Probation for Killing Abusive Husband," *Daily Camera* (Boulder, Colo.), December 15, 1989.

60. As taken from U.S. Department of Justice, Federal Bureau of Investigation, *Report to the Nation on Crime and Justice*, publication #NCJ-105506, 2d ed., March 1988, p. 31:

> In all States, citizens may use deadly force if they reasonably believe their life is in danger. However, the danger must be imminent and immediate. For example, if an intruder in a dwelling pulls a gun, a confronted person has reason to assume he or she is in imminent and immediate danger of losing his or her life. If the same person encounters the intruder peacefully, several hours after leaving home, no imminent and immediate danger would exist, so deadly force at that time would not

be justified. In most States, if the assailant is provoked, the use of deadly force is not justified.

61. David Margolick, "A Father Is Charged in Crash after Unbelted Daughter Dies," *The New York Times*, December 29, 1990, front page.
62. Ibid.
63. Isabel Wilkerson, "Court Backs Woman in Pregnancy Drug Case," *The New York Times*, April 3, 1991, p. A-13.
64. Ibid.
65. Dianne Klein, "A Coroner's-Eye View of Drug Babies," *Los Angeles Times*, March 3, 1991. The 11 percent figure was confirmed in an interview on April 30, 1992, with Mona Brown of the National Institute for Drug Abuse at the U.S. Department of Health and Human Services.
66. Judith A. Stein, et al., "An 8-Year Study of Multiple Influences on Drug Use and Drug Use Consequences," *Journal of Personality and Social Psychology*, vol. 53, no. 6, December 1987, pp. 1094–1105.
67. U.S. Department of Commerce, Bureau of the Census, *Statistical Abstract of the United States, 1990*, p. 53, table 69, "Children Under 18 Years Old by Presence of Parents 1970–1988."
68. *Newsweek*, September 18, 1989, "Overheard" section, which highlighted the quote from *The New York Times*.
69. Suzanne Daley, "Born on Crack, and Coping with Kindergarten," *The New York Times*, February 7, 1991, pp. A-1 and A-16.
70. *The New York Times*, May 25, 1990. Based on costs incurred in the Los Angeles school system.
71. The federal judge was U.S. District Judge A. Andrew Hauk, one of the federal bench's most senior members. See Gale Holland, *San Diego Union*, May 10, 1989.
72. Interview of Lieutenant Harvey Wyche of the New York City Police Department, in Coramae Richey Mann, op. cit. See also Mike Clary, op. cit.
73. See Jerry Hicks, "Jury Will Decide If Suspect Was Killer for Hire," *Los Angeles Times*, October 11, 1989. Details confirmed in an interview on May 15, 1990, with Sergeant Peterson, Huntington Beach (Calif.) Police Department.
74. Greg Zoroya, "Murder-Conspiracy Convict Gets Maximum Term Despite Jury Pleas," *Orange County Register*, June 6, 1990.
75. Steve Emmons, "Daughter, 3 Others Held in Killing of Man," *Los Angeles Times*, April 23, 1989, p. 18.
76. Miles Corwin, "Murder of Beach-Goer Shocks Santa Barbara," *Los Angeles Times*, September 23, 1989, p. I-25.
77. "Woman Is Charged in Death of Husband on Nudist Beach," *The New York Times*, October 11, 1989, p. A-27 (no author cited).
78. I. P. Weston, "Money, Revenge Motives Claimed in Beach Slaying," *Santa Barbara News Press*, January 3, 1990.
79. Eric Bailey, "Teen Sentenced for Helping Kill Wayne Pearce," *Los Angeles Times*, May 25, 1989; and Rocky Rushing, "Pearce Admits Having Sex with

High Schooler," *North County Blade-Citizen* (Oceanside/San Diego, Calif.), March 2, 1990, p. A-1.

80. CBS, "Hard Copy," March 1991; Associated Press, "Dead Spouse's Recording Trips Up Wife, Teen Lover," *Chicago Tribune*, March 26, 1991.

81. Bob Hohler, "Further Smart Charges Dropped," *The Boston Globe*, April 2, 1991.

82. Ibid.

83. *Newsweek*, vol. 117, no. 13, April 1, 1991, p. 26.

84. Barbara Carton, "Pamela Smart's Booster Club," *The Boston Globe*, June 29, 1992.

85. Branco took $1,000 out of the bank account of her millionaire husband, George Archer Mueller, to give to Ronald Tellez to kill George. See Matt O'Connor, "Ex-Blue Island Cop Convicted in Murder of Indian Bar Owner," *Chicago Tribune*, April 29, 1992.

86. Interview of Lieutenant Harvey Wyche of the New York Police Department, in Coramae Richey Mann, op. cit. See also Mike Clary, op. cit.

87. David Brown hired a hit man to kill his wife, in part to gain $835,000 from her insurance policies, including several that he took out on her life just before her murder. The hit man turned Brown in. He cooperated with police to obtain a tape-recorded conversation in which Brown stated he would pay $21,700 to have his wife killed. The hit man also testified against Brown in court. Unlike Pamela Smart, Brown has no fan club. He is more often described as despicable. See Eric Lightblau, "Prosecutor Portrays the Husband of a Slain Woman as a Despicable Manipulator who Designed His Wife's Death," *Los Angeles Times*, June 13, 1990.

88. Eric Malnic and Scott Harris, "Marlon Brando's Son Held in Fatal Shooting," *Los Angeles Times*, May 18, 1990, p. A-1.

89. From 1985 through 1988, 4,986 men were killed by women; 10,190 women were killed by men. This is from the U.S. Department of Justice, Federal Bureau of Investigation, *Crime in the United States* for the years 1985, 1986, 1987, and 1988 (four different editions), table titled "Victim Offender Relationship by Race and Sex."

90. U.S. Department of Justice, Federal Bureau of Investigations, *Crime in the United States* (Washington, D.C.: USGPO, 1990), p. 11, table titled "Victim Offender Relationship by Race and Sex." The notes adjoining the tables state that "Multiple Offender" killings are not broken down into gender categories. Only "Single Victim & Single Offender" crimes are broken down into gender categories.

91. Wendy Cole, People section, *Time*, May 20, 1991.

92. Lucy Howard and Gregory Cerio with bureau reports, "Reversal of Fortune?" Justice section, *Newsweek*, June 10, 1991.

93. April 11, 1990, interview with Frank Brennan, Australian psychologist, author, and university professor. Brennan can be reached for comment at 95 Clydesdale Street, Como, Perth, Western Australia 6152.

94. Based on a three-year observation (1989–92) of high school students by Elizabeth Brookins, chair of the Department of Mathematics, El Camino High School, Oceanside, California.

CHAPTER 13
The Politics of Sex

1. John Leo, "A Milestone in Sexual Harassment," *US News & World Report*, January 27, 1992. The chemical engineering professor's name is Richard Hummel; the student is Beverly Torfason.

2. Jane Gross, "Schools Are Newest Arenas for Sex-Harassment Issues," *The New York Times*, Education section, March 11, 1992, p. B-8. The high school was Duluth Central High School in Minnesota.

3. Scripps-Howard News Service, "Second-Grader Files Sex Harass Lawsuit," *North County Blade-Citizen* (San Diego), September 30, 1992.

4. Gretchen Morgenson, "Watch That Leer, Stifle That Joke," *Forbes*, May 15, 1989, pp. 69–72.

5. U.S. Department of Labor, "A Working Woman's Guide to Her Job Rights," leaflet no. 55, June 1988.

6. Ibid.

7. Ibid.

8. Clarence Thomas gave his signed approval to these modifications on October 25, 1988. The modifications are explained in a footnote on page 12 of the sexual harassment guidelines of 1988. Cited in Richard Pollak, "Presumed Innocent?" *The Nation*, vol. 253, no. 16, November 11, 1991, pp. 573 and 593. In an interview on April 6, 1992, the EEOC verified that what I said in the text is still accurate under the guidelines as revised in 1990.

9. Pollak, ibid., p. 593.

10. Morgenson, op. cit.

11. "How to Make an Impact on a Man," featured in special section "How to Attract Men Like Crazy," *Cosmopolitan*, February 1989, p. 177. See discussion of women's magazines in *Why Men Are the Way They Are* (New York: Berkley, 1988), pp. 18–23.

12. Ronnie Snadroff, "Sexual Harassment in the Fortune 500," *Working Woman*, December 1988.

13. *Cosmopolitan*, op. cit.

14. Ibid.

15. Ibid.

16. *Forbes* reports that the romance novel buyer spent an average of $1,200 in 1991. Since the price of the average romance novel was about $5 in 1991, an average of approximately 240 books a year, or 20 books per month, were purchased. For women who also read their friends' books, the number of books they read is more than 20 per month; for women who do not do this but buy some hardcovers, the figure is less than 20 per month. See Dana Wechsler Linden and Matt Rees, "I'm hungry. But not for food," *Forbes*, July 6, 1992, pp. 70–75. The 1983 figure comes from an interview on February 18, 1985, with John Markert, independent researcher and author of "Romancing the Reader: A Demographic Profile," *Romantic Times*, no. 18, September 1984 (based on his doctoral dissertation).

17. Ibid.

18. Ibid.

19. There are chapters called "Using Your Job to Meet Men," but no chapters called "Using Your Job to Meet Women." See Margaret Kent and Robert Feinschreiber, *Love at Work: Using Your Job to Find a Mate* (New York: Warner Books, 1988).

20. Ibid., p. 54.

21. I asked this of about 2,000 U.S. and Canadian women between the ages of 25 and 80, from all walks of life, from 1989 to 1992.

22. See James Martin and Sheila Murphy. "The Romantically Charged '80s Office," *Los Angeles Times*, September 11, 1988.

23. Barbara A. Gutek, *Sex and the Workplace* (San Francisco: Jossey-Bass, 1985), p. ix.

24. "Just Desserts," Periscope section, *Newsweek*, August 10, 1992, p. 4.

25. Sexual harassment legislation does much more than censor a form of humor, but it is also doing that.

26. Virginia Adams, "Psychic Combat at Annapolis," *Psychology Today*, October 1980, pp. 56–57.

27. Ibid.

28. From Richard Halloran, "Military Academies Are Becoming Even Tougher on Body and Mind," *The New York Times*, May 22, 1988. "In the eight classes with women who have graduated from the Naval Academy, for instance, 35 percent of the women left before graduation, compared with 23 percent of the men."

29. Adams, op. cit.

30. Ibid.

31. The study, directed by Professor Richard J. Light of the Graduate School of Education and the Kennedy School of Government at Harvard University, is "The Harvard Assessment Seminars: Explorations with Students and Faculty about Teaching, Learning, and Student Life." The first summary was made public on March 4, 1990. As reported in Edward B. Fiske, "Of Learning and College: How Small Groups Thrive," *The New York Times*, March 5, 1990.

32. See Jack Anderson and Dale Van Atta, "White House Board under Scrutiny," *The Washington Post*, March 18, 1991, p. B-8; and Bill McAllister, "Presidential Commission on Carpet," *The Washington Post*, December 11, 1990, p. A-21. Also see "Hard Copy," January 23, 1991.

33. Martha Sherrill, "The Brain Surgeon Who Hit a Nerve: Insensitivity Cuts Both Ways in Stanford's Operating Room," *The Washington Post*, November 6, 1991, p. B-1.

34. Ibid.

35. Ibid.

36. Ibid.

37. Ibid.

38. David Brock, "The Real Anita Hill," *The American Spectator*, March 1992, p. 26.

39. Ibid.

40. Ibid.

41. Ibid., p. 27.

42. Ibid., p. 26.
43. Ibid.
44. Ibid., pp. 21–22. "One Wald attorney . . . says that Hill was caught falsifying time sheets used to bill clients, because she couldn't meet the demands placed on young associates at the firm."
45. Ibid., p. 21. In an affidavit by John Burke, Jr., " . . . her work was not at the level we would expect. . . . I suggested to Anita Hill that it would be in her interest to consider seeking employment elsewhere . . . her prospects at the firm were limited."
46. Ibid.
47. Ibid., p. 25. "Then–Education Secretary Terrel Bell received several allegations of sexual harassment from Anita Hill during the time she worked at the department. . . . The charges were directed at Education officials other than Clarence Thomas. . . . Bell had the charges checked out, but nothing came of them."
48. Amber Coverdale Sumrall and Dena Taylor, *Sexual Harassment: Women Speak Out* (Freedom, Calif.: The Crossing Press, 1992).

CHAPTER 14
The Politics of Rape

1. Gail Jennes, "Out of the Pages," *People*, February 20, 1983.
2. Attributed to Vassar College Assistant Dean of Student Life Catherine Comins, in Nancy Gibbs, "When Is It Rape?" *Time*, June 3, 1991, p. 52. I called Catherine Comins and then faxed a letter to her at Vassar to be certain she was not misquoted. She did not respond.
3. Written correspondence to me from Charles P. McDowell, Ph.D., M.P.A., M.L.S., supervisory special agent of the U.S. Air Force Office of Special Investigations, March 20, 1992. This is based on an air force study of 556 rape allegations, the methodology and details of which are explained just below in this chapter.
4. Thirty-two percent of the alleged rapists were perceived by the victim as being black males; approximately 10 percent of the male population is black. See U.S. Department of Justice, Bureau of Justice Statistics (hereinafter USBJS), *Criminal Victimization in the United States: 1987*, publication #NCJ115524, June 1989, p. 47, table 41, "Percent Distribution of Single Offender Victimizations by Type of Crime and Perceived Race of Offender."
5. This myth was popularized by Susan Brownmiller in *Against Our Will: Men, Women, and Rape* (New York: Bantam, 1976).
6. USBJS, *Criminal Victimization in the United States: 1987*, op. cit., pp. 18–19, table 5.
7. Ibid.
8. For a more detailed explanation of how the male socialization process leads predictably to rape, see Warren Farrell, *Why Men Are the Way They Are* (New York: Berkley, 1986), pp. 242–52; pp. 110–38, and pp. 57–66 (in that order).

9. Charlene L. Muehlenhard and Lisa C. Hollabaugh, "Do Women Sometimes Say No When They Mean Yes? The Prevalence and Correlates of Women's Token Resistance to Sex," *Journal of Personality and Social Psychology*, 1988, vol. 54, no. 5, p. 874.

10. Rosemary Rogers, *Sweet Savage Love* (New York: Avon Books, 1974).

11. Catharine MacKinnon, *Toward a Feminist Theory of the State* (Cambridge, Mass.: Harvard University Press, 1989), p. 176.

12. See Neil Gilbert, "The Phantom Epidemic of Sexual Assault," *The Public Interest*, no. 103, spring 1991, p. 61. In her own words, MacKinnon puts it this way: "Under conditions of male dominance . . . if sex is something men normally do to women, the issue is less whether there was force than whether consent is a meaningful concept." See ibid., pp. 177–78. MacKinnon also credits Carol Pateman with this idea. Pateman says: "Consent as ideology cannot be distinguished from habitual acquiescence, assent, silent dissent, submission, or even enforced submission. Unless refusal or consent or withdrawal of consent are real possibilities, we can no longer speak of 'consent' in any genuine sense." See Carol Pateman, "Women and Consent," *Political Theory*, vol. 8, May 1980, pp. 149–68.

13. MacKinnon's exact words are, "Women, as a survival strategy, must ignore or devalue or mute desires, particularly lack of them, to convey the impression that the man will get what he wants regardless of what they want. In this context, to measure the genuineness of consent from the individual assailant's point of view is to adopt as law the point of view which creates the problem." See MacKinnon, op. cit., p. 181.

14. The study is by Mary Koss, Christine A. Gidycz, and Nadine Wisniewski, "The Scope of Rape: Incidence and Prevalence of Sexual Aggression and Victimization in a National Sample of Higher Education Students," *Journal of Consulting and Clinical Psychology*, vol. 55, no. 2, 1987, pp. 162–70. Among its publicity outlets were *The New York Times*, April 21, 1987, and Peter Jennings's ABC special "Rape Forum," following the documentary "Men, Sex, and Rape," May 5, 1992.

15. Koss et al., ibid., p. 167.

16. Ibid., p. 167, table 3.

17. See Robin Warshaw, *I Never Called It Rape: The Ms. Report on Recognizing, Fighting, and Surviving Date and Acquaintance Rape* (New York: Harper & Row, 1988), p. 63. This book is based on Mary Koss's survey.

18. Charlene L. Muehlenhard and Stephen W. Cook, "Men's Self Reports of Unwanted Sexual Activity," *Journal of Sex Research*, 1988, vol. 24, pp. 58–72.

19. Ibid.

20. Of the 62,830 women who were victims of completed rapes, 37 percent said they had not reported it to the police; of the 67,430 women who were victims of attempted rape, 54 percent had not reported it to the police. See USBJS, *Criminal Victimization in the United States* (Washington, D.C.: USGPO, 1991), p. 102, table 101, "Percent Distribution of Victimizations by Type of Crime and Whether or Not Reported to Police."

21. The rape rate is 1.2 per 1,000 per year based on the most recent year of the

National Crime Survey Report. See USBJS, National Crime Survey Report, *Criminal Victimization in the United States, Annual (1973–1988)*, p. 15. This means women have more than 80 chances in 1,000 of being raped in a lifetime—or about 1 in 12. Since 62,830 women per year are victims of completed rapes versus 67,430 per year who are victims of attempted rapes, about 1 in 25 are victims of completed rapes in a lifetime, about 1 in 23 are victims of attempted rapes in a lifetime. For the breakdown between completed and attempted rapes, see *Criminal Victimization . . . : 1990*, ibid.

22. *The rape rate decreased from 1.8 per 1,000 in 1973 to 1.2 per 1,000 in 1988.* USBJS, *Criminal Victimization . . . (1973–1988)*, ibid. This figure comes from a national sampling of households. It is considered a more reliable comparison of rates than reports of rapes to the police, since reports of rape to the police have increased as public awareness of rape has increased in the last decade. But even here there has been a 9 percent increase in rapes reported to the police between 1981 and 1990 versus a 36 percent increase in those violent crimes of which men are the primary victims that were reported to the police between 1981 and 1990. For the 9 percent increase, see U.S. Department of Justice, Federal Bureau of Investigations, Uniform Crime Reports, *Crime in the United States* (Washington, D.C.: USGPO, 1991), pp. 15 and 51.

23. USBJS, *Bureau of Justice Statistics Bulletin*, "Crime Victimization, 1991," forthcoming, spring 1993. This survey was taken during and after the Mike Tyson and William Kennedy Smith rape trials. Although it is based on such a small sample of women who were victims of rape or attempted rape and therefore within the sample's margin of error, it is nevertheless statistically significant and represents a 59 percent increase in rapes and attempted rapes among women, as well as an increase in the rate among both sexes combined (from 0.6 per 1,000 in 1990 to a 1991 rate of 1.0 per 1,000).

24. Associated Press, "Man Guilty in Sex Assault on Woman with 46 Identities," *Los Angeles Times*, November 9, 1990, p. A-20.

25. For example, see Ira Michael Heyman, Office of the Chancellor, University of California at Berkeley, "Acquaintance Rape," January 20, 1987. He explains it is campus policy that "rape occurs when . . . the victim is prevented from resisting by the use of alcohol or drugs." In an interview on May 18, 1992, Jessica White at Berkeley's Rape Prevention Education Program directly verified that her program interprets date rape as defined in the text. Concerning Swarthmore, see John Wiener, "Rape by Innuendo at Swarthmore, Date Rape," *The Nation*, vol. 254, no. 2, January 20, 1992, p. 54. Concerning Harvard, the *Washington Post* reported that Harvard's date rape task force recommended that the university policy define rape to include a woman who was impaired by "intake of alcohol or drugs." See Cathy Young, "What Rape Is and Isn't," *The Washington Post* (national weekly ed.), June 29–July 5, 1992, p. 25.

26. National Clearinghouse on Marital and Date Rape is in Berkeley, California.

27. If we pass laws allowing women who are drinking to injure men, then we have to make women as guilty for having sex when drinking as we make drivers guilty for driving when drinking.

28. Charles Salter, Jr., "A Lasting Shadow," *The News & Observer* (Raleigh, N.C.), February 17, 1992, p. 1-C.
29. Ibid.
30. Ibid., p. 2-C.
31. Interview on May 13, 1992, with psychologist Michael Teague, North Carolina State Department of Crime Control and Public Safety.
32. Salter, op. cit., p. 1-C. The University of New Mexico hospital did eventually reinstate his job offer.
33. Written correspondence to me from Charles P. McDowell, Ph.D., M.P.A., M.L.S., supervisory special agent of the U.S. Air Force Office of Special Investigations, March 20, 1992.
34. Charles P. McDowell, Ph.D., M.P.A., M.L.S., "False Allegations," *Forensic Science Digest*, vol. 11, no. 4, December 1985, p. 64. The *Digest* is a publication of the U.S. Air Force Office of Special Investigations, Washington, D.C.
35. Cathleen Crowell Webb and Marie Chapian, *Forgive Me* (Old Tappan, N.J.: Fleming H. Revell Co., 1985), appendix B.
36. Stephen Buckley, "Unfounded Rape Reports Baffle Investigators," *The Washington Post*, June 27, 1992, pp. B-1 and B-7.
37. Ibid.
38. The 9 percent are part of the 47 percent (as described in the text), but as is pointed out, they are not necessarily false allegations—they are merely "unfounded." This "unfounded" category probably has the highest percentage of false accusations, but as far as the FBI knows, the percentage of false accusations overall could be anywhere from zero to 100 percent. The "unfounded" category consists of 8.6 percent or 8,818 out of 102,655 reported or alleged offenses. This is from U.S. Department of Justice, Federal Bureau of Investigations, Uniform Crime Reports Section, *Crime in the United States* (Washington, DC: USGPO, 1990), p. 16. Confirmed in telephone interview on April 29 and May 11, 1992, with Harper Wilson, chief of Uniform Crime Reporting, FBI.
39. Ibid.
40. This 53 percent is categorized as "cleared by arrest or exceptional means." The alleged rapist was arrested, but the FBI has no information as to whether he was found guilty or innocent. Ibid (both sources).
41. Associated Press, "San Diego Police: Woman Lied About Nordstrom Rape," *Blade-Citizen*, January 16, 1993, p. A-10.
42. Buckley, op. cit.
43. Ibid.
44. Charles P. McDowell, Ph.D., M.P.A., M.L.S., "The False Rape Allegation in the Military Community," unpublished paper, Washington, D.C.: US Air Force Office of Special Investigations, March 1983. A total of seventy-five women who acknowledged they had made false accusations also volunteered their motivations.
45. McDowell, "False Allegations," op. cit., pp. 68–71.
46. McDowell, "The False Rape Allegation in the Military Community," op. cit.

47. From Kermit Cain's written correspondence to me, September 1991, and interviews with Kermit in June and July 1991, and June 1992.
48. For example, see Heyman, "Acquaintance Rape," op. cit.; Wiener, " . . . Swarthmore . . . ," op. cit.; and Young, op. cit.
49. "Beauty Pageant Official Drops Tyson Lawsuit," Newswire section, *Los Angeles Times*, December 2, 1991.
50. Kenneth B. Noble, "Key Abortion Plaintiff Now Denies She Was Raped," *The New York Times*, September 9, 1987, p. A-23.
51. Associated Press, "Girl Admits Rape Lie; Man Free After 513 Days," *Dayton Daily News*, January 18, 1990, p. 2-A.
52. McDowell, "The False Rape Allegation in the Military Community," op. cit.
53. In-person interview with John Hoover on July 17, 1992.
54. Webb and Chapian, op. cit.
55. Associated Press, "Ruling Favors Victim's Word in Rape Cases," *San Diego Union-Tribune*, May 8, 1992.
56. See *Michigan* v. *Lucas*, 111 S. Ct. 1743, May 1991. The Supreme Court ruled that a woman might be shielded from having her sexual past used against her—the "rape shield" law.
57. Ibid. The Supreme Court ruled that an accused rapist cannot present evidence of the "victim" having a previous sexual relationship even *with him* unless he notifies the court ahead of time.
58. Associated Press, "Pedophile Fined, Given Probation," *Blade-Citizen* (San Diego), March 3, 1992. The woman, Pam Mouer, was forty-five. Note that although she committed statutory rape, she is not called a rapist—only a pedophile. Note that the headline says "Pedophile Fined, Given Probation," not "Woman Rapes Boy." The headline ignores the fact that a woman committed a sexual crime.
59. Muehlenhard and Cook, op. cit.
60. USBJS, *Criminal Victimization . . . (1973–1988)*, op. cit.
61. U.S. Department of Commerce, Bureau of the Census, *Statistical Abstracts of the United States: 1991*, 111th ed., p. 83, table 120, "Acquired Immunodeficiency Syndrome Deaths."

Men	69,929	(90.4%)
Women	7,421	(9.6%)

62. Deryck Calderwood, Ph.D., "The Male Rape Victim," *Medical Aspects of Human Sexuality*, May 1987, pp. 53–55.
63. Ibid.
64. This issue has received little coverage in the mainstream press, with the exception of "Overflowing Problems in U.S. Prisons," *Christian Science Monitor*, August 21, 1990, p. 20, which stated that "more men are raped in America's prisons than women anywhere in the country." This type of statement is a guesstimate and projection. See Wayne S. Wooden and Jay Parker, *Men behind Bars* (New York: Plenum Press, 1982). The penal institution studied was located in California, with a prison population of more than 2,500

men. Eighty percent of the population was heterosexual, 10 percent bisexual, and 10 percent homosexual. Fourteen percent of the prison population had been pressured to have sex against their will—they had either been raped or sexually assaulted. Since every prison has its anomalies, no reliable projection can be made until a sampling of prisons nationwide—especially including maximum security institutions (which this was not)—is made.

65. The figure of one million or more males being raped or sexually assaulted in jails and prisons comes from the fact that 8,643,525 males pass through a combination of state and federal prisons and local jails each year (see *Sourcebook of Criminal Justice Statistics,* 1990, table 6.33 for 1987–88 data on jails; the same *Sourcebook,* table 6.63 for 1985 data on state prisons; and the same *Sourcebook,* tables 6.89 and 6.90 for the numbers in federal prisons [calculated from figures for 1988 and 1990]). Fourteen percent saying they had been raped or sexually assaulted at any given moment in time leads to a total of 1,210,094. However, dozens of factors make this figure little more than guesswork.

66. The 120,000 figure (119,780) is higher than the reported number because it includes the 55 percent of rapes that the Justice Department found were not reported when it asked women nationwide who had been raped whether or not they had originally reported it. See USBJS, Office of Justice Programs, National Crime Survey Report, *Criminal Victimization in the United States: 1973–88 Trends,* July 1991, publication #NCJ 129392, p. 15, table 6, "Rape: Victimization Levels and Rates." For the 55 percent figure, see USBJS, Office of Justice Programs, National Crime Survey Report, *Criminal Victimization in the United States, 1989,* June 1991, publication #NCJ129391, p. 89, table 103, "Personal Crimes, 1989: Percent of Victimizations Reported to Police, by Type of Crime, Victim-Offender Relationship, and Sex of Victim."

67. In a July 1992 nationwide computer search on Lexis/Nexis of more than 700 different newspapers, magazines, and journals during the 1980s until June 1992, there were no stories of women being raped (e.g., via broomsticks, fists, or forced oral sex) by women inmates. There were, however, forty-one stories of various types of sexual encounters between guards and prisoners, some of which clearly appeared to be rape, others of which appeared to be the woman being sexual with the guard in exchange for cigarettes, drugs, privileges, etc.

68. For example, the Department of Corrections in the state of Washington shows that the average daily cost per male prisoner is $37.62; per female prisoner, $80.62. In Wisconsin, the average monthly cost per capita, 1988–89, for male prisoners was $1,120; for female prisoners, $2,100. See "Summary of Distribution Per Capita Costs for the Year Ended June 30, 1989: Section E," Department of Health and Social Services, Division of Corrections, Office of Policy, Planning, and Budget, Madison, Wisconsin.

69. April 11, 1990, interview with Frank Brennan, Australian psychologist, author, and university professor. Brennan can be reached for comment at 95 Clydesdale Street, Como, Perth, Western Australia 6152.

70. From a flyer prepared by the National Coalition of Free Men for the William Hetherington Defense Fund, c/o William Lasley Law Offices, P.A., 215 North

Olice Avenue, #130, West Palm Beach, FL 33401. In an interview on May 1, 1992, William Lasley explained that Hetherington's assets were frozen in his civil case, thus preventing him from using them for his criminal defense or from being declared indigent so he could get a public defender.

71. David Zeman, Knight-Ridder Newspapers, "Father, Martyr, Fraud?" *Detroit Free Press*, May 25, 1990.

72. Interview, October 26, 1990, with Fran Hovey, Ohio reporter covering the case.

73. Zeman, op. cit. An interview with Hetherington's attorney, David Wright, on March 17, 1992, verified that the judge did give Hetherington fifteen to thirty years and that this did exceed the sentencing guidelines for the case.

CHAPTER 15
From Husband Sam to Uncle Sam: Government as Substitute Husband

1. Credit to Fred Hayward for the question and portions of the answer.

2. *Johnson* v. *Transportation Agency of Santa Clara County*, 480 US 616 (1987).

3. Tamar Lewin, "Pregnancy and Work Risks Posing 'Fuzzy' Legal Arena," *The New York Times*, August 2, 1988.

4. Michael Levin's *Feminism and Freedom* (New Brunswick, N.J.: Transaction Books, 1988), p. 175, discusses the 15,000 to 20,000 women's studies courses. The "Directory of Men's Studies Courses Taught in the U.S. and Canada," compiled by Sam Femiano of the American Psychological Association, lists the 91 men's studies courses.

5. For example, Maryland budgets $200,000 each year for the Maryland Commission on Women, and the city of Baltimore contributes $175,000 for its Women's Panel. See Jack Kammer, "A Matter of Men and Children," *The Sun* (Baltimore), March 26, 1992.

6. Congress originally authorized the Office of Family Planning to "provide family planning services for *persons* in need." In 1982, the federal office sent a directive to its local centers telling them they would receive money only for female clients. See Douglas Beckstein and Kevin McNally, "Federal Office of Family Planning Discriminates Against Men," *Men's Reproductive Health*, fall 1987, p. 1.

7. The Canadian equivalent to the National Organization for Women is the National Action Committee, which receives a half million dollars yearly from the Department of Education. There is also a Canadian Cabinet Ministry on the Status of Women. See Betty Steele, *The Feminist Takeover: Patriarchy to Matriarchy in Two Decades* (Gaithersburg, Md.: Human Life International, 1990), pp. 9–10 and p. 68.

8. Ibid., p. 69.

9. Eric D. Sherman, in letter appearing in *Gender Issues* newsletter, June 1988, p. 2, slightly condensed.

10. The Family Support Act of 1988, which became effective in January 1990, gives a parent—in essence, the mother (for the reasons described)—the right

to be involved with the child either full time or part time until the child is 6 and, if she desires to work or go to school, to have transportation, child care, and food provided for the child.

11. "The hundred-hour rule" is only one of a number of direct and indirect discriminations against the male in the workfare and welfare programs. Other provisions (such as the "lump-sum award") make it much more difficult for the family to get aid with the man present than with the man absent. These provisions were explained to me by Colleen Fahey Fearn of the Legal Aid Society of San Diego, Inc.

12. U.S. Department of Commerce, Bureau of the Census, *Statistical Abstract of the United States: 1991*, 111th ed., p. 358, table 584.

13. See Lorie Hearn, "A Woman's Work," *California Lawyer*, February 1989, p. 26. Judge Murphy of San Diego ruled that it was in the best interests of the child for certain mothers to work if the child is over 3, could have a responsible sitter, and so on. This mother nevertheless won the case. See Hearn article for a discussion of state and federal welfare laws exempting mothers with children under 6 from work requirements.

14. Men's average benefit per year is $8150.40; women's is $6223.20. See U.S. Department of Health and Human Services, Social Security Administration, *Social Security Bulletin Annual Statistical Supplement* (Washington, D.C.: USGPO, 1991), p. 149, table 5.A1, "Number and Average Monthly Benefit by Race, Age, and Sex at the End of 1990."

15. Men contribute $75 billion versus women's $38 billion. These figures are from the U.S. Department of Health and Human Services, Social Security Administration, Office of Research and Statistics, *Earnings and Employment Data for Wage and Salary Workers Covered Under Social Security by State and County, 1985*, compiled by Lilian A. Fribush, publication no. 13–11784, October 1988, p. 1, table 1, "Number of Wage and Salary Workers, Taxable Wages, FICA Contributions, and Age Worker Attained in 1985, by State, Sex, and Race, 1985."

16. If the average man and woman retire at age 65 to collect full Social Security benefits and live out their average life span, he will live another seven years, receiving $8150.40 per year for a total of $57,052.80; she will live another fourteen years, receiving $6223.20 per year for a total of $87,124.80—approximately 153 percent of what the man will receive. See *Social Security Bulletin*, op. cit.

17. *LA Department of Water and Power* v. *Marie Manhart*, 435 US 702, (1978).

18. Interview on August 10, 1992, with Metropolitan Life Insurance branch manager Tim Kime.

19. Kerry Pechter, "6 Who Were Sacked," *Men's Health*, summer 1988, p. 22.

Conclusion

1. Richard Stengel, review of *Fire in the Belly* by Sam Keen, "Bang the Drum Quickly," *Time*, July 8, 1991, p. 58.

2. For documentation, see the *AJPH*, January 1988 endnote in chapter 6, "The Suicide Sex."
3. For documentation, see the National Center for Health Statistics, *Vital Statistics: 1988*, endnote in chapter 1, "Is Male Power Really a Myth?"
4. For documentation, see the *Public Affairs Report*, October–December 1985, cited in chapter 10, " . . . Saving Males as Saving Whales . . . "

Bibliography

Allen, Marvin. *In the Company of Men* (New York: Random House, 1993).

Amneus, Daniel. *The Garbage Generation* (Alhambra, Calif.: Primrose Press, 1990).

August, Eugene R. *The New Men's Studies: A Selected and Annotated Bibliography* (Englewood, Colo.: Libraries Unlimited, 1993).

Baber, Asa. *Naked at Gender Gap* (New York: Carol Publishing Group, 1992).

Berkowitz, Robert. *What Men Won't Tell You But Women Need to Know* (New York: Morrow 1990).

Bloom, Allan. *The Closing of the American Mind* (New York: Simon & Schuster, 1988).

Bloomfield, Harold. *Making Peace with Your Parents* (New York: Random House, 1983).

Bly, Robert. *Iron John* (New York: Addison-Wesley, 1990).

Branden, Nathaniel. *The Six Pillars of Self-Esteem* (New York: Bantam, 1994).

Cassell, Carol. *The Tender Bargaining* (Los Angeles: Lowell, 1993).

Davidson, Nicholas. *The Failure of Feminism* (Buffalo: Prometheus, 1988).

DeAngelis, Barbara. *Are You the One For Me?* (New York: Delacorte, 1992).

Diamond, Jed. *Inside Out* (San Raphael, Calif.: Fifth Wave Press, 1983).

Dowling, Colette. *Cinderella Complex* (New York: Pocket Books, 1981).

Ellis, Albert. *Sex and the Liberated Man* (Secaucus, N.J.: Lyle Stuart, 1976).

Farrell, Warren. *The Liberated Man* (New York: Random House, 1974; New York: Berkley Books, revised 1993).

———. *Why Men Are the Way They Are* (New York: Berkley Books, 1988).

Fisher, Helen. *The Anatomy of Love* (New York: W. W. Norton, 1992).

Friday, Nancy. *Men in Love* (New York: Delacorte, 1980).

Friedan, Betty. *The Second State* (New York: Summit Books, 1981).

Fumento, Michael. *The Myth of Heterosexual AIDS* (New York: Basic Books, 1990).

Gerzon, Mark. *A Choice of Heroes* (Boston: Houghton Mifflin, revised 1992).

Gilder, George. *Men and Marriage* (Gretna, La.: Pelican, 1987).

Gilmore, David D. *Manhood in the Making* (New Haven: Yale University Press, 1990).

Goldberg, Herb. *The Hazards of Being Male* (New York: Signet, 1977).

Gordon, John. *The Myth of the Monstrous Male* (New York: Playboy Press, 1982).

Gurian, Michael. *The Prince and the King* (Los Angeles: Tarcher, 1992).

Halpern, Howard. *Finally Getting It Right* (New York: Bantam, 1994).

Harding, Christopher. *Wingspan* (New York: St. Martin's, 1992).

Kauth, Bill. *A Circle of Men* (New York: St. Martin's, 1992).

Keen, Sam. *Fire in the Belly* (New York: Bantam, 1991).

Kiley, Dan. *Living Together/Feeling Alone* (New York: Prentice Hall, 1989).

Kinder, Melvyn. *Going Nowhere Fast* (New York: Prentice Hall, 1991).

Kipnis, Aaron R. *Knights without Armor* (Los Angeles: Tarcher, 1991).

Leonard, George. *The Ultimate Athlete* (Berkeley, Calif.: North Atlantic Books, 1990).

Levin, Michael. *Feminism & Freedom* (New Brunswick, N.J.: Transaction, 1988).

Mitchell, Brian. *Weak Link* (Washington, D.C.: Regnery Gateway, 1989).

Money, John. *Gay, Straight, and In Between* (New York: Oxford University Press, 1988).

Paglia, Camille. *Sexual Personae* (New York: Vintage Books, 1991).

Pleck, Joseph H. *The Myth of Masculinity* (Cambridge, Mass.: The MIT Press, 1981).

Pruett, Kyle. *The Nurturing Father* (New York: Warner Books, 1987).

Remoff, Heather Trexler. *Sexual Choice* (New York: Dutton, 1984).

Robbins, Anthony. *The Giant Within* (New York: Simon & Schuster, 1992).

Osherson, Samuel. *Finding Our Fathers* (New York: The Free Press, 1986).

Schenk, Roy. *The Other Side of the Coin* (Madison, Wisc.: Bioenergetics Press, 1982).

Steele, Betty. *The Feminist Takeover* (Gaithersburg, Md.: Human Life International, 1990).

Sykes, Charles J. *A Nation of Victims* (New York: St. Martin's Press, 1992).

Symons, Donald. *The Evolution of Human Sexuality* (New York: Oxford University Press, 1981).

Tiger, Lionel. *The Pursuit of Pleasure* (New York: Little, Brown, 1992).

Wetcher, Ken; Art Barker; and Rex McCaughtry. *Save the Males* (Washington, D.C.: PIA, 1991).

AUDIOTAPES

Diggs, Lawrence. *Introduction to Men's Issues* (P.O. Box 41, Roslyn, S.D. 57261).

Farrell, Warren. *The Myth of Male Power* (New York: Simon & Schuster, 1993).

———. *Understanding Each Other* (Boulder, Colo.: Sounds True, 1992).

———. *Why Men Are the Way They Are*, abridged (Auburn, Calif.: Audio Partners, 1993).

———. *Why Men Are the Way They Are*, unabridged (Costa Mesa, Calif.: Books-on-Tape, 1988).

SELECTED MEN'S PUBLICATIONS

The Liberator
Richard Doyle/612-464-7887

MAN!
Lyman Grant/512-452-8833

Men's Advocate
Eugene Hopp/206-644-7870

Men's Health Magazine
Michael Lafavore/215-967-5171

Men's Studies Review
Jim Doyle/615-369-3442

Men Talk
Randy Genrich/612-822-5892

The M.E.R.G.E. Journal
Ferrel Christensen/403-488-4593

Seattle M.E.N.
James Smethurst/206-285-4356

Transitions
Tom Williamson/516-482-6378

Wingspan
Dick Halloran/313-273-4330

SELECTED ORGANIZATIONS

American Men's Studies Association
Sam Femiano/413-586-0515

Center for Men's Studies
Sam Julty/510-549-0537

Children's Rights Council
David Levy/202-547-6227

Fathers for Equal Rights
Alan Z. LeBow/313-354-3080

Fathers for Equal Rights/Iowa
Dick Woods/515-277-8789

The Joint Custody Association
James Cook/310-475-5352

The Men's Health Network
Ron Henry/Box 770,
    Washington, D.C. 20044

Men's Rights, Inc.
Fred Hayward/916-484-7333

Menswork Center
James Sniechowski/213-479-2749

National Center for Men
Mel Feit/718-845-2010

National Coalition for Free Men
Tom Williamson/516-482-6378

National Congress for Men and Children
Travis Ballard/202-FATHERS

National Men's Resource Center
Gordon Clay/415-453-2839

South Florida Men's Center
Howard W. Green/305-789-6757

Texas Men's Institute
Marvin Allen/512-608-9201

Index